# ILLUSTRATED ATLAS
## Native *of* American History

# ILLUSTRATED ATLAS
## Native *of* American History

CHARTWELL
BOOKS, INC.

*Page 2:* A 1675 "Mapp of New England," by John Seller.

Published by
CHARTWELL BOOKS, INC.
A division of BOOK SALES, INC.
114 Northfield Avenue
Edison, New Jersey 08837

Produced by
Saraband Inc., PO Box 0032,
Rowayton, CT 06853-0032

Copyright © 1999 Saraband Inc.

Design © Ziga Design

ISBN 0-7858-1118-4

Printed in China

10 9 8 7 6 5 4 3 2 1

**Project Editor:** Sara Hunt
**Associate Editors:** John B. Letterman, Robin Langley Sommer
**Production Editor:** Nicola J. Gillies
**Art Director:** Charles J. Ziga
**Graphic Designer:** Wendy Ciaccia Eurell
**Cartographic Artist:** Christopher Berlingo

**CONTRIBUTING EDITORS:**

**Lorraine B. Myers** (author of the introduction and the Southwest sections of chapters 3, 4, 5, and 6). With a BA in Anthropology from the University of Utah and an MA and ABD in Anthropology from the New School for Social Research, she is an independent researcher into the Native American cultures and archaeology of the Southwest.

**Richard Carlson** (contributing editor for chapter 6). A professor of Native American history who has taught at Yale University and the University of Vermont, he was formerly the editor of the New England Native American magazine *The Eagle*.

**John S. Bowman**

**RESEARCH CONSULTANT AND CARTOGRAPHER:**

**Glenn O. Myers:** A lifelong avocational student of Native American history and archaeology, he is a consultant in international telecommunications engineering who has participated in mapping projects on four continents and under three oceans plus several seas.

**GENERAL EDITOR:**

**Samuel Willard Crompton** is a professor of American history and Western Civilization. He has twice served as a Writing Fellow for Oxford University Press in its production of the 24-volume *American National Biography*, published in 1999. He is also the author of eleven books on American history.

**CONTRIBUTORS**

**John S. Bowman**, Ph.D., a Massachusetts resident, is a well-known writer, editor, and scholar with many publications to his credit. His editorial projects include the *World Almanac of the American West*, the *Almanac of American History*, *Facts About the American Wars*, and the *Cambridge Dictionary of American Biography*.

**Barry Pritzker** is the author of *Native America Today: A Guide to Community Politics and Culture* (1999), and *Native America: An Encyclopedia of History, Culture and Peoples* (two volumes, 1998), both published by ABC-CLIO. In addition to other works about the continent's native peoples, he has written and edited books and CD-ROMs about the American West and is a professor of history and writing.

**Louise Minks**, a historian and artist, is the author of two books for young adults: *The French and Indian War* and *Traditional Africa*. She has been the recipient of a Wurlitzer Foundation painting fellowship to create an exhibition of artwork documenting New Mexico's Pueblo Revolt of 1680.

**Robin Varnum**, a professor of writing, is the author of *Fencing with Words* (1996) and has published articles based upon her research into the pre-Columbian Maya. She grew up in Winslow, Arizona, near the Navajo and Hopi reservations.

**Rosamund Dauer**, the author of six books for children, has also published poetry in major periodicals. A graduate of Middlebury College and Columbia University, she has been a professor at Colby-Sawyer College, curator of education at the Staten Island Institute of Arts and Sciences, and an editor for the *Encyclopedia Americana*.

**Anne Eliot Crompton** is the author of more than a dozen novels. She grew up in a college town in western Massachusetts and became interested in Native American culture at an early age. Among her books, the *Sorcerer*, *The Ice Trail*, and *The Winter Wife* all focus on Native American themes.

**Winslow Eliot**, a former editor in a New York publishing house, is a writer of both fiction and nonfiction, with a special interest in Native American history.

Ho Tak-Wiasee — "For all our relations"

# Contents

# Foreword

O f necessity, many sources and disciplines have entered into the preparation of this atlas, which attempts to trace the movement of North America's indigenous peoples from prehistory to the present day. Oral and written history, anthropology, archaeology, ethnology, and linguistics have all explored the possible origins and migrations of the continent's first people, and new information—which can often be interpreted in widely different ways—becomes available from day to day. While there is sometimes a lack of consensus on how these many pieces fit together into an overall picture, it is surprising how often oral tradition corroborates the findings of non-native researchers working generations after the events in question. For example, the American explorer Charles F. Hall, who reached what is now called Frobisher Bay in 1861, believed himself to be the first white man to visit this Arctic region until he heard an Inuit story of long-ago visits by other *kodlunas*. Following up this testimony, Hall explored what the Inuit called Kodlunarn (White Man's Island), where he found evidence of three successive voyages made by the English explorer Martin Frobisher during the 1570s. The number of ships involved in each voyage tallied with the account preserved in Inuit oral tradition for more than nine generations.

Thus the demographic history of Native America continues to unfold, amplified and amended over time. Although this history may never be completed, we believe that the story presented here will provide a useful reference within the framework of contemporary scholarship.

—SAMUEL WILLARD CROMPTON

## LEGEND

*The maps commissioned for this book use the images below to illustrate the approximate location of various Native American resources, lifeways, and culture centers over the time period covered. The incursions initiated by European explorers are identified by nationality at the far right.*

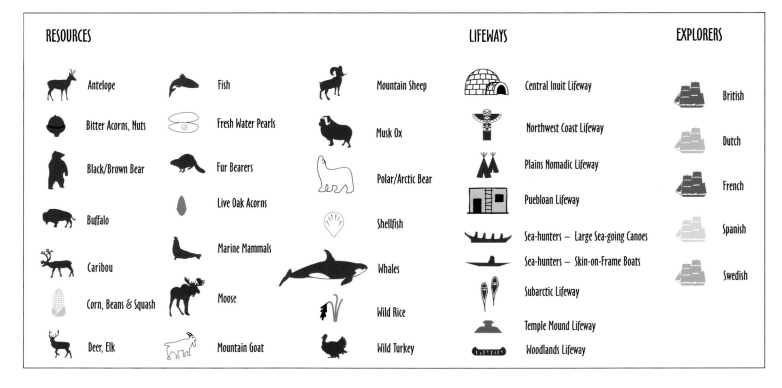

| RESOURCES | | | LIFEWAYS | EXPLORERS |
|---|---|---|---|---|
| Antelope | Fish | Mountain Sheep | Central Inuit Lifeway | British |
| Bitter Acorns, Nuts | Fresh Water Pearls | Musk Ox | Northwest Coast Lifeway | Dutch |
| Black/Brown Bear | Fur Bearers | Polar/Arctic Bear | Plains Nomadic Lifeway | French |
| Buffalo | Live Oak Acorns | Shellfish | Puebloan Lifeway | Spanish |
| Caribou | Marine Mammals | Whales | Sea-hunters – Large Sea-going Canoes | Swedish |
| Corn, Beans & Squash | Moose | Wild Rice | Sea-hunters – Skin-on-Frame Boats | |
| Deer, Elk | Mountain Goat | Wild Turkey | Subarctic Lifeway | |
| | | | Temple Mound Lifeway | |
| | | | Woodlands Lifeway | |

# Introduction

No episode in history can make a greater claim to being the fulfillment of the prophecy of the Apocalypse than the effects of European contact on Native Americans in the centuries following the arrival of Columbus. More rapid than War, Pestilence and Famine galloped with Death down the well-worn paths of centuries-old native trade routes, perhaps hundreds of miles and decades ahead of direct European contact. By the time War reached them, it had little to do but administer the *coup de grace* to already decimated populations, killing some, enslaving more, and submerging the remainder in the general population.

Lacking contemporary written accounts of most of these events, scholars have been forced to deduce the extent of this cataclysm using such information as was available. A number of modern estimates, using interdisciplinary approaches, put Native American population decline during the half century following European contact above 80 percent.

While such a high estimate almost begs skepticism, there exists substantiation for losses of this magnitude in at least one area: what is now the American Southwest. Careful analysis and comparison of the detailed census reports compiled by several sixteenth-century Spanish chroniclers proves a native mortality rate well in excess of 85 percent.

In a larger sense, having no continuous eyewitness accounts of events and circumstances in most of North America for almost all of the first three centuries after the arrival of Columbus makes reconstruction of the native history of that period an extremely complex and difficult task. For this reason, discussion of this subject—particularly for the general reader—has usually been limited to Native American interactions with Europeans and Euroamericans for which records exist, while the effects of those interactions upon and the historic dynamics within Native American societies, being considerably more difficult to research, were largely ignored.

This book attempts to present a more balanced view by recognizing not only that much of native history indeed resulted, directly or indirectly, from the actions and policies of the colonial powers and their independent successors, but that as much or more took place within and among native nations with neither the direct involvement nor the contemporary awareness of Europeans.

To develop a comprehensible picture of events in the latter category, an interdisciplinary approach was again necessary, relying upon the labors of researchers in fields as diverse as archaeology, cultural anthropology, linguistics, zoology, epidemiology, forensic science, and more. Numerous point-in-time and timeframe maps have been provided, which will help the general reader unfamiliar with the finer details of North American geography to more readily understand the general dynamics of native demography and migrations.

Preparing a native geographical history for the general reader also presents both the challenge of and the opportunity to clarify certain commonly held misconceptions concerning Native American cultures. Foremost among these is that, rather than having a single language, religion, political system, etc., precontact North America was far more culturally diverse than Europe in the fifteenth century.

Some linguists, for example, put the number of known separate languages (not counting dialects) in use in North America in AD 1500 at well over 200 and the number of language *families* above seventy-five. The actual numbers were probably higher, as languages that died out before they could be studied are not counted. Further, native languages employ many sounds that do not exist in any European language and cannot be exactly represented using only the Latin alphabet, making their transcription difficult.

To communicate with those natives whom they met during their explorations, Europeans and, later, Euroamericans, were usually forced to use one or even a series of interpreters whose fluency was always problematic. The earliest Europeans in North America could reasonably be compared with a modern tourist who travels to a foreign country with no prior knowledge of the local language, culture, history, geography, or politics, and engages the first person he meets there to be his guide and interpreter. The most meticulous journal of the trip kept by such a person would have to be regarded with skepticism unless and until it could be verified against reliable independent sources. For the purposes of this book, such sources would include a combination of verifiable native oral history, the related archaeological record, and data provided by linguistics patterns, forensic science, and other sources.

Discovering such inaccuracies in many early reports is not difficult. When, for example, an early missionary asked his Ojibwa interpreter the name of a hitherto unknown group of natives they had met, the interpreter gave a long name which eventually became shortened to "Scioux" or "Sioux." That the original word was Ojibwa and essentially meant "enemy" did not become known until long after "Sioux" had become the common name for what is actually a group of nations. The "Sioux" first encountered might have named themselves "Dakota," "Lakota," or "Nakota," depending upon which of the three main dialects of "Sioux" they spoke.

Likewise, the Cheyenne (self name: Tsistsistas) received their common name based upon a Sioux word for them which means "those who speak an incomprehensible language," or more simply, "foreigners."

The Inuit were long known as "Eskimos," from an Algonquian name meaning "eaters of raw meat."

The Etchareottine were named "Slaves" by a Cree interpreter who boasted that his nation often raided the Etchareottine for captives. Reality, however, was somewhat different: the Etchareottine were widely feared warriors. Nevertheless, the lake near which they live is still called Great Slave Lake.

In other cases, descriptive names such as Gros Ventre (French for "Big Bellies") and Nez Perce (French for "Pierced Noses") became current.

Recently, many nations have made an effort to get the public to replace these common names with their own names for themselves. The Gros Ventre wish to be called "Atsina," the Navajo, "Diné," and the Pima, "Akimel O'odham," among others. Respecting such wishes, many current writers use these "new" names exclusively, leaving it to the reader to relate such works to the body of earlier literature. In this book, the currently most widely recognized group names are generally used with the intent of aiding those with limited prior knowledge of this subject to learn more about native peoples using other works, old and new.

Early historical records contain other types of errors as well. Europeans expected the New World to be organized in the same manner as the Old: Native "nations," they believed, must be governed by established (probably hereditary) hierarchies having absolute authority in their domains, which would lie within specific, permanent boundaries. Only after many misunderstandings had resulted from these preconceptions did it become obvious that neither of these concepts was universally—or even generally—true.

Native groups seem to have disbanded and associated fairly readily. Groups contacted once apparently disappear from the historical record while others abruptly appear in the same areas. The later groups might have been the former groups under a new name, newly formed groups that included individuals from the seemingly vanished groups, or entirely different peoples. In other cases, bands of the same group are reported to have been simultaneously encountered at separate locations hundreds of miles apart.

Records of contacts with native groups by early explorers are also of limited value because they rarely indicate if those groups were in their home territory or on a long-range hunting expedition into the territory of some other group. Taken together, these reports seem to suggest that native hunting and even war parties often traversed the nominal territories of others without hostilities ensuing. This may have been due to the low population density, which permitted the intruders to evade the "owners," or, alternatively, the "owners" may have chosen to ignore rather than fight the interlopers—as long as they kept moving.

In other cases, one area may have been customarily used by different groups during different seasons, or temporarily used by several groups at the same time. Confusing their European contemporaries as well as modern students of history, the various native groups who used an area jointly or seasonally would each have considered it part of their territory. For this reason, among others, there are very few areas of North America where tribal boundaries (as a modern person would expect them to be defined) could be validly mapped, even for a very specific point in time. Consequently, this was not attempted in this book.

Precision navigation and cartography did not become practical until the 1730s when both a reliable chronometer and the sextant were invented. Lacking the instruments necessary to fix one's position on the globe with any accuracy, most early explorers were forced to record their routes in terms of estimated distances, approximate directions, and landmarks, as the natives did, and rarely had more than a general idea of their location. If the early maps reproduced here seem hopelessly inaccurate to us today, it is because they were based upon descriptions or sketches that were at best schematic in nature. Even so, they can be valuable historical resources if used with careful consideration and compared with other sources.

A number of tribal amalgamations, separations, and migrations are known or suspected to have occurred after 1492. The Seminole, for example, formed from remnants of the Creek Confederacy and other nations only about 1770. The little-known Chiwere are believed to have migrated southwestward from Wisconsin in the seventeenth century, leaving the Winnebago behind and dispersing into the better-known Iowa, Oto, and Missouri.

There were only two basic causes for native migrations: the desire to maintain life and the desire to improve life. Several nations have oral traditions of migrating away from another nation of which they had formerly been part. Reportedly, ownership disputes over trivial articles—for example, an antelope udder, a buffalo skull—produced schisms that could only be resolved by the opposing parties moving away from each other. Presumably, each group felt that fratricidal violence would be avoided and, by the same expedient, their lives would be better if they ceased to have contact with each other.

Native oral histories have long been eagerly collected by historians and anthropologists, and many have been proven quite accurate. In other cases, those who related, translated, or recorded them were not always willing or able to do so with accuracy. Again, it is necessary to compare such material with archaeological and linguistic information as well as other historical sources to achieve a more reliable understanding of actual events.

An illuminating example was the supposed Lenape (Delaware) oral tradition that recounted their ancient migration in company with the Iroquois from the Rocky Mountains to the Delaware River. Reverend Heckewelder, an eighteenth-century missionary among the Lenape, recorded this tradition many years after his mission had ended, and it was published by the respected American Philosophical Society in 1819. Thereafter, noted scholars treated the tradition as historical fact until, with the development of scientific archaeology, it became apparent that it was highly unlikely that the story could be true. The Iroquois culture had demonstrably arisen in the same area where Europeans found it and the Algonquian culture (of which the Delaware were a part) had originally developed in eastern Canada.

Not all controversies over interpretations of historic records have been resolved, however. Based upon information collected by Champlain from an Ottawa informant concerning "The People of the Fire," many scholars have concluded that this group included the Sauk, Fox (self name: Mesquakie), and Potowatomi, and that their homeland was in lower Michigan. This was in spite of the fact that the first European reports of contact with all these groups were along the shores of Green Bay, on the opposite side of Lake Michigan. The presently understood archaeological record for lower Michigan reveals no evidence for any presence of the Sauk or Fox there in the sixteenth century. Further, recent reanalysis of the historical record and its subsequent interpretations has also brought this assertion into question.

Unfortunately, the scholars who deny that the Sauk and Fox were in Michigan are not yet able to propose an alternative homeland for them. It is for this reason that these groups have been mapped in lower Michigan in the sixteenth century here, but with question marks to indicate this uncertainty.

In light of the various complications described above, it was decided to present in this work only that information which can reasonably be directly obtained or inferred from the sum of the recent works of numerous respected scholars. Nation names are generally mapped into the approximate areas they are known or believed by a consensus of scholars to have been using at the time or during the timeframe of each map. It is hoped that this approach will aid the reader to gain a more realistic appreciation for the dynamics of Native American populations across the period.

Being a review of history, each chapter of this book covers a specific period, but chapters are subdivided into discussions of each of the ten "culture areas" into which anthropologists customarily divide Native North America. In essence, culture areas are distinguished from each other by their unique combinations of climate, terrain, and food resources. These factors tend to cause people who live in the same culture area to develop generally similar cultures, assuming they possess like technologies.

This arrangement of the material offers the reader the options either to learn of the native history of the whole continent in chronological order or to concentrate on the historical development of each culture area by reading only the pertinent sections in sequence.

In conclusion, the total scope of Native American history and population dynamics is not known with precision now, nor is it ever likely to be. Future discoveries in archaeology and linguistics may reveal or clarify more, as may new technologies and fields of study, but so much was lost so soon after European contact, and so much of what remained left unrecorded, that Native American history will probably remain forever incomplete. Yet, if all we can see of our past is a mere shadow, we are wise to study it carefully: It may be a shadow of our future as well.

—LORRAINE B. MYERS

# Native American Origins

## 20,000 BC–AD 1492

*At first there was nothing but sea and sky.*
*Then a woman floated down from the sky.*
*As she touched down, a point of land rose out of the water and became a little island.*
*Here the woman became First Mother and gave birth to three beings: Bear, Wolf, and*
*Deer. The First Mother then ascended into the sky. The little island spread and stretched*
*itself into a mainland, and Bear, Wolf, and Deer became the ancestors of all life.*

— MOHEGAN CREATION STORY

The story of the initial peopling of the Americas is both one of the great epics of history and one of the great challenges to historians. To the descendants of the first people, however, there is no mystery. There is a widespread belief among Native Americans that they have inhabited this territory from time immemorial: they are aboriginals, not immigrants. Their traditional stories, which later people label myths, include creation tales that have the original ancestors coming into existence in this land, either by evolving from animals or by being created whole by the gods.

Native Americans' creation stories from across the continent of North America trace the descent of their respective nations from origins as diverse as a turtle, a watery underworld, the skies, and a kind of primeval mud, to name but a few. Other possibilities have been presented. The far northern Red Paint People hold that their ancestors navigated around the North Pole during the period when it was covered with open water, or traversed the region when it was forested land. For them, this explains the use of red ocher paint used in ancient burials, the tribal worship of bears, and other ritual practices common to the circum-polar regions.

There is nothing unusual about the making of creation tales; every people on earth tells its own. Contemporary science agrees with at least one crucial element in many Native American creation tales: Humankind evolved from animals many millions of years ago. But modern scientists proceed with what they regard as verifiable facts to explain the evolution of *Homo sapiens*, the species name for all living human beings. Most scientists propose that the direct ancestors of *Homo sapiens* first evolved in Africa between about 250,000 and 125,000 years ago. By about 100,000 BC, the first modern *Homo sapiens* had begun their migration from Africa, moving into the Middle East, across into Central, South and East Asia, and eventually (by about 50,000 BC) up into Europe. At first, these human beings made little impact on the balance of the natural world, but over time, as human ingenuity, technology, and ambitions developed, they would alter their environment increasingly. They learned how to overcome creatures that had been unassailable; they sometimes over-killed; and then they moved on. There was always a new, unexploited world ahead.

*Opposite: The earliest Americans are widely believed to have migrated across "Beringia"—land exposed by the drop in sea level during the last Ice Age—and moved gradually to settle the continent.*

## THE FIRST INHABITANTS
## OF THE AMERICAS

When, according to modern scientific theory, did these humans arrive in the Western Hemisphere, what we call the Americas? This is a question that has intrigued people ever since Europeans arrived in the New World at the end of the 1400s. (Although Norsemen had reached Newfoundland about the year AD 1000, they stayed only briefly, and their account of this episode did not come to the attention of other Europeans until many centuries later.) There have long been many claims and theories. Some people at the time of Columbus believed that the New World was the original Garden of Eden and that the so-called Indians were direct descendants of Adam and Eve. Later, others would claim that the Indians were descendants of one of the purported Lost Tribes of ancient Israel, or of the far-wandering Phoenicians, or even of Celtic peoples such as the Welsh. These and similar theories have remained outside the mainstream of academic acceptance.

One theory that does retain support from some serious modern scientists is that small numbers of people from Asia (at different times, Japanese, Chinese, and southeast Asians) made their way across the Pacific on several occasions (between about 3000 BC and AD 700). However, this theory does not claim these Asians to be the ancestors of the American Indians, but merely claims that some Asians introduced certain elements of their culture into South America and Middle America.

It should also be recognized that there are a small number of scientists who claim to find traces of human beings in the Americas dating to considerably earlier than the years accepted by most scholars. Finds made near Los Angeles and San Diego, California, are alleged to have been stone tools and dated by some to as early as 200,000 BC. Other finds from Santa Rosa Island, off the coast of southern California,

*Right: A Haida serving plate bearing stylized animal images from the Pacific Northwestern culture area: Abstracted human/animal faces and forms were also embodied in the region's clan totem poles and other artefacts.*

and China Lake, in south-central California, are dated by some to between 50,000 and 30,000 BC; most students of the subject do not regard these finds as proof of human presence. A Brazilian rock shelter known as Pedro Furada has cave paintings made by humans; associated finds (tools and hearths) are dated to about 33,000 BC, but most archaeologists remain skeptical that the paintings date back so far. Meanwhile, at the Meadowcroft rock shelter, not far from Pittsburgh, Pennsylvania, human artefacts are dated by some to as early as 14,000 BC. Although a number of respected scientists do contend that the first human beings arrived in the Americas at least by 35,000 BC, this remains a minority view.

Most modern scientists, historians, and anthropologists agree on the basic explanation of how human beings first arrived in North America. They believe that the ancestors of modern Native Americans had been living in northeast Asia at least briefly before they made their way across the region we know as the Bering Strait and into the territory we know as Alaska. Exactly when and how these ancestors came, however, does remain in some dispute. But the basic explanation is sometimes called the Beringian Theory because it rests so importantly on the condition of the Bering Strait, at present a narrow body of water between eastern Asian mainland and Alaska. In fact, Alaska's Seward Peninsula and Russia's Chukchi Peninsula are separated by only about 56 miles of water.

The Bering Sea is only 180 feet deep at its deepest point, and during the Ice Age that persisted between about 60,000 and 12,000 BC, a great volume of water became locked up in massive polar ice caps and glaciers, and the world's sea level dropped by as much as 300 feet. During this period the region between Asia and Alaska was left as an extensive land bridge for several periods, often lasting for thousands of years. In particular, the land bridge—often more like a continental mass—known as Beringia existed between about 23,000 and 12,000 BC, and it is during this period, most experts believe, that the first people from eastern Asia made their way across to the hitherto uninhabited continent of North America.

Beringia itself at that time would have been a cold but relatively fertile grassland, teeming with game. Mammoth and mastodon grazed there, alongside horses, camels, musk ox, caribou, and bison. Although wary of bears and saber-toothed cats, these animals knew nothing of the danger of human hunters, who had never before reached their area or threatened their existence. Most likely the first Asians to move onto the land known as Beringia stayed there for many generations, hunting the plentiful game. But when the ocean water began to rise and the climate changed and the plant and animal life that provided their food became more scarce, at least some of these people chose to move on to the east.

They carried with them their spears and spear-throwers (atlatl). Behind the mature males stalked the young men, also bearing spears. Behind them, the women carried infants and led toddlers; older children walked alongside with the dogs. All eyes were trained on the far horizon, where dark, lumbering shapes of edible prey might loom into view. And one day, about 14,000 years ago (although perhaps several thousand years earlier) human hunters first left their skin-boot prints in the snow or grass of present-day Alaska.

If one such band made their way across to this new world, then presumably others must have followed during the next few thousand years. As the glaciers melted, the rising Bering Sea moved in on Beringia, sundering North America and Asia—although during the winters, people could actually make their way across the frozen ice. Moreover, some archaeologists believe that even the earliest arrivals came by small boats and made their way south along the coast of North America and possibly even eastward over a chain of inland waterways.

In any case, these newcomers evidently began moving south and eastward relatively rapidly, exploring their new environment,

seeking new food sources. The earliest human remains in the Western Hemisphere—at least the earliest accepted by most scientists—are from sites in Alaska and are dated to around 12,000 BC. What supports this theory of rapid dispersal, though, and what distinguishes it from those based on isolated sites claimed to be so much earlier, is the fact that a whole series of finds and sites dating from shortly thereafter are known. These are not only from northern Canada, but much farther south. Indeed, during the 1990s excavators of a site located near Monte Verde, Chile, claimed that the site was inhabited by Clovis-type humans as early as 12,500 BC.

But if claims for a few of these early sites remain questionable, there is almost universal agreement that a whole series of finds and sites from the Yukon down to the Andes in South America, from coastal California across to the Appalachians in the east, and most especially in the American Southwest, can be dated to about 11,200 BC and the several centuries following. Because the initial find of the stone tools associated with this people was made at Clovis, in east-central New Mexico, they and their culture are commonly known as Clovis people. The distinctive Clovis point was a sharp, fluted projectile, usually made of obsidian or chalcedony; whether used as a spearhead or as a hand-held knife, it must have been not only an effective weapon for hunting game, but it also indicates both the skill and care employed by its makers. In 1925, at Folsom, in northeastern New Mexico, finds of somewhat similar pointed spearheads were dated to a slightly later timeframe—about 8500 BC; thus the Folsom people would be successors to the Clovis people.

It is now generally accepted that human beings were living throughout many parts of the Americas between about 12,000 and 8500 BC. It has been calculated that merely by advancing one mile per month from the time they crossed into Alaska, they would have reached the southern tip of South America within the first 1,000 years. During that same period, even if only 100 individuals had crossed into Alaska about 12,000 BC, if the population increased

*Left: The turtle features in the creation stories of numerous Native American peoples: Many believed the Earth was the back of a giant turtle.*

**Right:** *Reconstructed stone arrows and spears of the kind widely used to hunt larger game animals, bound using sinews or rawhide with hide glue to the wooden handles.*

**Right:** *A Caddoan mask with antlers carved in wood about* AD *1200.*

at the modest rate of 1 or 2 percent per year, they could have attained a population during that same 1,000 years that was adequate to spread throughout much of the Americas.

The exact sequence of events during the first few thousand years does remain open for debate among the experts. So, too, do the exact relationships of all these people, now divided into so many distinctive "nations" or tribes. But almost all experts agree that the ancestors of the Native Americans are the Asians traditionally classified as Mongoloids. On the one hand, all peoples living on the earth today, including the American Indians and the Mongoloid people of Asia, share the majority of their genetic makeup. But the Indians of North America and various people living in east Asia (including Mongols, northern Chinese, Japanese, and the eastern Siberians) share enough of more specific genetic markers and physical features, such as blood types and teeth forms, to establish their common origins.

Contemporary students of languages also have something to say about these first humans to populate the Americas. There is by no means total agreement among linguists, but one theory is that the first migrants shared a common language or at least a few closely related lan-

guages; in this theory, almost all of the many hundreds of languages spoken across North and Middle and South America evolved from this original language. According to this same theory, a second major group of migrants from northeast Asia settled first in the interior of Alaska and parts of British Columbia; many thousands of years later, descendants of these Indians moved down to become the Navajo and Apache; the language spoken by many of these peoples is known as Athabaskan and it belongs to the Na-Dene group of languages, shared by all of this second wave of migrants. Finally, this theory postulates that the third major group of migrants were those who became the Inuit-Aleut people of the Arctic regions. Again, not all linguists accept this theory. Some, for instance, see the language families as linked to geographic zones as they existed when the migrants first arrived: Thus the Algonquian family includes those languages spoken in a wide band across North America from the northern Plains to the east coast. Meanwhile, other linguists resist such attempts at grouping the many hundreds of American Indian languages; they claim that there simply isn't enough evidence to support these links; the best they are willing to do is

assign the 1,500 or so distinct languages that have been identified as spoken in the Americas to about 155 families of languages that are known to have common origins.

For the first few thousand years at least, these people sustained themselves largely by hunting a variety of land animals, supplemented by gathering wild berries, nuts, and other naturally occurring vegetation as well as by taking some food from the abundant seas and fresh waters. Because they are regarded as sharing a more or less common culture, not yet distinguished by the different lifestyles that would develop in later millennia, they are known as Paleo-Indians ("old" Indians). They and their children are, in fact, the first Native Americans.

*Above: Glaciated peaks rising from Hector Lake, Alberta.*

*Below: Landscape Arch: It took thousands of years for Paleo-Indians to migrate as far as the present-day Southwest.*

## EARLY LIFEWAYS OF THE PALEO-INDIANS

In the early period of human habitation of the Americas, mammoth and mastodon roamed the entire continent of North America. Sheer size, tough skins, and long tusks kept them safe from four-legged predators, but humans learned how to deal with them. They could drive them off high cliffs or into bogs. Then they could surround and spear them, or simply wait for them to die. Two species of bison wandered both the Great Plains and the Northeast. While mammoth and mastodon moved in small, vulnerable family groups, bison roamed in large herds. Again, the determined hunters chased them over cliffs, perhaps with the help of fire. They ate what they wanted on the spot, feasting at times for a week, and left the remains for scavengers. They may have dried some of the meat, but they could carry little for any distance. Men armed with spears and atlatls hunted all of these animals on foot. The atlatl was a throwing stick—a long handle attached to a spear that greatly increased its range and force. (The bow and arrow were first used in the Americas less than two thousand years ago.)

But across North America there were many other animals to be hunted, including moose, deer, coyote, bear, rabbits, giant beavers, muskrats, and several species of turtle. In addition there were birds including turkeys, ducks, and geese. In South America lived tapirs, peccaries, and slow, defenseless ground sloths the size of cattle. Along the coasts and rivers and lakes, too, humans could live well on fish and shellfish, salmon, and marine mammals including seal and whale.

About the time of the appearance of these new predators in North America, some species of megafauna animals appear to have become extinct. The mastodon and mammoths, wild horses, camels, the Shasta ground sloth, and Harrington's mountain goat were among the first to vanish. Some scientists trace their relatively sudden extinction to the new hunters who had appeared on the scene; certainly there have been discoveries of skeletons of mammoths with Clovis spearheads still lodged in their ribs. Other scientists, however, stress the climate change at the end of the Ice Age. In any case, some species may have been in decline before the migrants appeared.

The Paleo-Indians lived in family groups gathered into bands of perhaps fifty individuals. They made spear points, knives, scrapers, and drills of stone, and awls and beads of bone. These bands probably met with other groups at certain times of year, and it may have been during these meetings that the Paleo-Indians began to develop two features of Native American culture: the ritual dance and feather ornamentation—the display of feathers indicating the wearer's personal history and status. (These features are also seen in other indigenous cultures around the world.) Most likely, too, it was on such occasions that certain individuals began to recount the stories that would become the traditional lore of these people and provide the myths that explained their pasts and their lifeways.

For the first few thousand years, then, the inhabitants of the Americas, no matter exactly where they lived, shared a relatively similar way of life. But gradually these people began to develop different cultures in response to the changing environments in which they lived. By the time the Europeans encountered the American Indians, these cultures had quite distinctive and local characteristics, but for many thousands of years it was more a question of broad regional differences.

*Right:* Stone carving of a bear, an animal sacred to the Inuit tribes of the Far North, whose ancestors came from Siberia.

*Below:* An artist's impression of the mastodon, sketched for Records of the Past, *August 1903.*

*Left: A small number of the Central Inuit still construct their traditional igloos, the dome-shaped shelters made of hard-packed blocks of snow and ice.*

## PEOPLE OF THE ARCTIC

One particular exception to the universality of the early culture of the first Native Americans is provided by the people commonly known as Eskimos. In fact, this name is rejected by these people themselves. They prefer to be known as Inuit or Y'uit, words meaning "people." It is believed that the ancestors of the Inuit lived in Beringia for some thousands of years before making their way over into Alaska, probably about 9000 BC; in any case, the Inuit to this day have certain biological traits that link them more closely to people of Siberia than to other American Indians. From Alaska, these people spread across the northernmost shores and islands of Arctic Canada and over into Greenland and northern Labrador. The exact date of their migration eastward is not known for sure, but it is generally agreed that there were two major phases of early Inuit culture. The first emerged about 4000 BC but died out after some 5,000 years. It is possible that a new wave of migrants appeared or that there was simply a resurgence of energy and innovation, but in any case, about AD 800 a new cultural tradition emerged. It is this latter culture that is maintained by many of the Inuit of today.

Using the few raw materials at hand—snow and ice, animal hides and bones, sinew and antlers, rocks and driftwood—the Inuit created a viable material culture that persists in places to this day. The people lived in homes built of ice, snow, driftwood, stone, or sod, and in summer often took shelter beneath tents of animal hide. Some drove dog-sleds in search of bear, seal, walrus, and caribou, knowing no law but that of necessity and custom. The Arctic peoples praised in song "the great light that fills the world" during the endless days of summer. In the dark days of winter, they drummed, danced, told stories, and gambled.

A group closely related to the Inuit are known as Aleut; again, they are more correctly called the Unangan. They inhabit the Aleutian Islands off the southwest coast of Alaska and the extreme west of the Alaska Peninsula. The Aleut fished and hunted whales, sea lions, and seals. They lived in pit-houses and navigated in skin-covered boats. The Aleut developed a more rigidly structured society than the Inuit had.

*Left: Thick native furs and cured hide provided the warm clothing needed to survive in the Arctic.*

*Above: Hunter-gatherers learned to make use of every edible plant in their domains. During seasonal migrations, they harvested tubers, roots, nuts, and berries, as depicted here in a 1908 photograph by Edward S. Curtis.*

## NORTH AMERICA

The first archaeological record of native habitation along the Northwest Coast is around 8000 BC. Between then and the stabilization of the sea levels, around 3000 BC, the natives harvested fish and hunted both land and sea mammals. After 3000 BC, permanent winter villages were built, and dried salmon became the winter staple. By 1000 BC, the Northwest Coast culture patterns were emerging, and by AD 500, much of the future distinctive material culture was present. When these people were discovered by European explorers during the eighteenth century, the various regional tribes had been occupying their territories for about 2,000 years.

In the cold Subarctic region across North America, the great herds of migrating caribou sustained small groups of nomadic hunters.

These early ancestors of the Athabaskan and Algonquian language groups lived in wigwams and wore hide clothing. They traveled on snowshoes and in birch bark canoes in search of caribou, moose, fish, and bear. They were probably guided to their prey by the dreams and visions of highly respected shamans. Their ways are revealed in the Algonquian legend of Glooskap, the hero-god, who boasted to a woman that he could conquer anyone and everyone. She suggested that he try to take maple sugar from a baby sitting nearby. With all his threats and enticements and magic chants, the great Glooskap could not take the baby's maple sugar.

In the Northeast but well south of the Inuit lands, in what would become New England, humans lived in easily dismantled tentlike shelters—wigwams covered with bark. Probably small bands of people wandered from one area to another, according to the season and to harvest the nuts, game, and marine life that provided most of their food. Their tool kit was composed largely of the basic stone tools that humans had been making for many thousands of years—projectile points, scrapers, and such. Most likely their only social organization was that of small bands, but there must have been some interaction among bands as well as some ritual-religious life.

On the Great Plains, the early peoples built earth lodges and hunted bison on foot with spears and atlatls. Neither the horse nor the bow and arrow had yet been introduced, nor would they be until relatively recent times. Later, they lived in transportable tipis and followed the game. During the summer months, the people followed the bison across the great grasslands, raising hide tents where they paused. Dogs carried their bundles and dragged travois on tent poles. The bison provided meat; hides for shelter, clothing, and rope; sinew for thread; bone for awls and other tools; and bladder jugs. Even their dung was valuable as fuel, for wood was scarce on the Great Plains.

Across large parts of the continent, hunting and gathering provided sustenance. Women gathered all the edible seeds, tubers, nuts, fruits, and herbs that they could find. In the East, they gathered berries, chestnuts, butternuts, walnuts, hickory nuts, cranberries, and acorns. They stored much of this bounty in pits to be visited on a return journey, or in a lean season. (Storage pits up to 3,000 years old have been discovered.) In the West, they sought acorns, sunflowers, marsh elder, goosefoot, berries, maygrass, and wild rice.

In addition to gathering food, women also learned and practiced herbal medicine. They began to save seeds and plant them in likely spots. Some two thousand years ago, they began to tend small gardens of sunflowers, marsh elder, and goosefoot, which they valued for their oils. But there was little time to tend these gardens carefully. People were always on the move from hunting camp to fishing camp to berry camp.

Many changes had taken place in the first few thousand years following the Bering Strait crossings. Human settlement of the Americas had become more established, with each tribe more or less staking out its own territory (although these territories were far from static). By about AD 750 the bow and arrow would replace the atlatl in most of North America and would revolutionize hunting and warfare. The crafts of basketry, pottery, and sewing evolved to a sophisticated level. Some wild plants had been domesticated. Trade was brisk up and down both coasts and across the continent. At the same time, violent encounters and even small wars, which earlier had been rare occurrences, were becoming more common.

*Left:* Animal hides have provided clothing for countless generations of North America's first peoples since Paleo-Indian times.

*Right:* *This prehistoric female figure, known as a "Colima flat," may have been used in fertility rituals to ensure the continued supply of corn.*

## MESOAMERICA

But the most important change of all was the discovery, development, and slow spread of a wild seed-bearing grass. This grass, called *teosinte*, would have a truly revolutionary impact upon Native American life and culture. Archaeologists have discovered the earliest maize—Indian corn, or cultivated *teosinte*—in caves near Teotihuacan, Mexico, and they have determined that these tiny ears of corn are around seven thousand years old. Varieties of maize were gradually developed that grew taller, had enlarged kernels, and could be more efficiently propagated. Kernels of early varieties of wild maize were blown to a distance from the plant, thereby spreading themselves about. But the heavy, kernel-laden ears of later maize varieties fell in a heap right below the plant, and thus had no space in which to grow unless they were distributed and sown by human hands. The early farmers surely played an important role in the selection and creation of the many modern varieties of maize.

By 1500 BC small, permanent agricultural towns had spread across Mexico. The people of these settlements lived on maize, beans, chili peppers, squash, and avocados. Maize had become a major source of food in Mesoamerica by the fifth century BC.

The cultivation of maize gave rise to the Olmec culture (1500–750 BC) in Mexico. Judging by the art they have left us, the Olmec began as a peaceful people whose culture center (now San Lorenzo) was near the Gulf Coast. With the cultivation of a stable food source, permanent settlements became possible. And with the growth of villages and towns came new structures of business, law, and taxation, and the development of a caste system. To protect itself from threats to its new prosperity, Olmec society became

*Below:* *The ruins of a Mayan temple at Tulum, Mexico.*

militarized. Olmec religion gradually became more rigid and formal.

The Olmec built large ceremonial and commercial centers over which priests and bureaucrats ruled, while the merchants and craftsmen conducted their business. The Olmec traded widely in goods including basalt, jade, serpentine, and magnetite for artistic use. They developed glyph writing, pyramids, and perhaps calendar systems. The largest of their pyramids, La Venta, was used for religious ceremonies from around 800 to 400 BC. Many of these sites were the scene of ritual human sacrifice.

All of this, the basis of future Mexican civilization that also deeply influenced that of the American Southwest, rested on the shoulders of farmers living in thatched huts clustered around the ceremonial centers. Eventually, however, the Olmec faded from view and were succeeded by the Maya, who built their culture in present-day Mexico and Guatemala.

"Wa" is the Maya word not only for food, but also for maize, the people's principal crop and staple food. They also grew squash, beans, and tobacco. The Maya are the first Indians known to have kept written historical records. They inscribed these on pottery, jade, and bone, and on stone monuments and walls. They devised seven calendar systems, and their art and architecture were highly developed. Their thirsty gods—the maize god always important among them—demanded human sacrifice. They established dozens of city-states. From AD 200 to 900, the Mayan population probably reached two million, with perhaps fifty thousand concentrated in one of their chief cities, Tikal, in present-day Guatemala.

The Maya civilization went into fairly rapid decline and was replaced if not conquered by the Toltec, who originally came as nomads from north of central Mexico. From the tenth through the twelfth centuries AD, they dominated the territory of present-day Mexico from their capital city of Tula. Their trade routes extended from Costa Rica to the American Southwest. Master builders, they created frescoed and colonnaded palaces, tall pyramids, and masonry ball-courts.

Tradition tells that their last king, Topiltzin-Quetzalcóatl, tried to ban human sacrifice. This led to civil war and Tula was destroyed in 1160. Drought and pressures from displaced

migrant peoples may well have contributed to the decline of the Toltec. Whatever the cause, or combination of causes, the Toltec were eventually replaced as the dominant people of Mexico by the Aztec. As the Aztec were the people encountered by the first Europeans in Mexico, they enter history in its recorded phase.

*Above:* Ritual human sacrifice was a hallmark of Mexico's powerful Aztec Empire, which offered human hearts to the god Huitzilopochtli upon massive stepped-pyramid temples.

*Left:* Early maize cultivation against a backdrop of structures and symbols common to the Meso-American culture area.

*Above:* Toltec ruins at Teotihuacan: the Street of the Dead, the remarkably straight, level road at right; and the Pyramid of the Sun.

*Below:* The ruins of a six-story complex built at Pueblo Bonito in western New Mexico around AD 900.

## THE SOUTHWEST

While those events were occurring in Middle America, other American Indians were active to the north. The Mogollon culture began to develop around 1000 BC in the Southwest—in what is today east-central Arizona and west-central New Mexico. These hunter-gatherers stored their goods in caves when they traveled in pursuit of game. Archaeologists have found remnants of these goods, including many baskets. They also stored bags, sandals, and yucca-fiber nets. They buried some of their dead in graves scraped into the floors of these caves. The Mogollon hunted deer with spears and atlatls. They built pit-houses, raising log frames over pits.

Around 3500 BC, maize reached the American Southwest, where ancient kernels dating from 1000 BC have been discovered, mixed with the seeds of such other plants as sunflower and goosefoot. Though not native to the dry Southwest, maize had become common in the mostly wild gardens of women, who must have passed seeds from one to another all the way from Mexico to the region north of the Rio Grande.

Between 700 and 400 BC, the Mogollon increasingly cultivated maize and beans. The stable food supply that this ensured made it possible for them to cease wandering after game and to settle down in large multi-roomed structures known as pueblos. Another dazzling Mogollon breakthrough was use of the bow and arrow, which revolutionized the hunt.

Overlapping the Mogollon people in time were the Hohokam ("those who are gone"), who are thought to have been immigrants from northwestern Mexico. They settled near present-day Phoenix, Arizona, around 300 BC. By AD 800 Hohokam culture shows Mexican influence in its platform mounds, arenas, copper bells, and, remarkably, in its tame macaws. These exotic birds were probably raised for their feathers, which Native Americans always prized highly. The first serious, full-time farmers in America, the Hohokam lived in permanent agricultural villages and cultivated maize. Until their settlement, farming had been women's work. Now men contributed their strength to divert the Gila and Salt Rivers for irrigation. Men may also have actually worked the crops. Abundant harvests made large permanent settlements possible.

The Hohokam villages had been abandoned by AD 1450. This may have been caused by drought, or perhaps by war. The cultivation of maize supported larger populations, which may have created pressures and conflicts that led to escalating violence. Or these new farmers may simply have overexploited the natural resources of their regions, as humans have so often done throughout history. The cultivation of maize exhausts the soil, and people dependent upon it often had to abandon old fields and till new ones. Drought would have compounded problems of soil exhaustion: Throughout Mexico and the Southwest, recurring drought often displaced farmers.

The Anasazi, Navajo for "ancient ones" (AD 700–1500), were descendants of the earlier Desert Culture phase. They spread out over a large area of the Southwest covering present-day northern New Mexico and Arizona and southern Colorado and Utah. Anasazi civilization was based on full-time farming that was carried out by men. The Anasazi dug ditches and pools to catch rainwater, and cultivated maize, beans, and squash. They also raised dogs for meat and domesticated wild turkeys for meat and feathers.

The Anasazi built their villages wherever they found water. Originally, they built pit-houses. Later they constructed stone pueblos of up to fifty rooms atop mesas. By the twelfth century AD, their pueblos housed hundreds of apartment dwellers. The kivas found below the pueblos were vestiges of ancient pit-houses. These underground structures served as men's workshops and places of worship, where they spun cotton and wove blankets, rested, and held ceremonies. In the floors of many kivas were holes, called sipapus, that served as gateways to the spirit world.

*Below:* *The cultivation of maize, sometimes called Indian corn, was endemic to the Southwest when Europeans arrived. Many native peoples considered it the staff of life and used it in every possible form.*

*Right: Monument Valley, although dry, was cultivated by early peoples who dug ditches to collect water.*

*Below: "Long House," extensive three-story cliff-dwellings once inhabited by the Anasazi in the canyon-and-mesa wilderness of present-day Bandelier National Monument, New Mexico.*

Chaco Canyon in northern New Mexico is the largest Anasazi ruin. Here there are Great Kivas in addition to small private ones. Mexican influence is evident in the later buildings, which feature colonnades, round towers, and rubble-core walls of cut stone. Around AD 1150 the Anasazi began to leave their mesas and crowd into cavernous cliff dwellings that were accessible by ladders or climbing with the aid of finger and toe grips.

Shortly after 1300 the Anasazi had mysteriously disappeared from these dwellings. War, soil exhaustion, depletion of woodlands and game in their territories, and crop failures due to drought may have compelled these people to move away. No record or legend remains to explain the abandonment of their dwellings. As for the Anasazi people themselves, they moved elsewhere in New Mexico and Arizona, either merging with the Hopi or settling into the towns where the Spaniards later found them and called them Pueblo Indians.

## THE SOUTHEAST AND MIDWEST

Simultaneous with several of these various American Indian societies was the one that emerged in the Southeast and Midwest of North America. Its most distinctive feature was hundreds of artificial mounds, the oldest of which were built around four thousand years ago. Found from Florida up into South Carolina, they are formed of rings of piled shells. One of the largest, on Sapelo Island in Georgia, is more than three hundred feet across and seven feet high. These shell mounds contain the oldest pottery found on the continent. Some of this pottery is decorated with geometric designs. Interestingly, this same combination of shell mounds and pottery is also found on the Caribbean coast of Colombia in constructions that date from about 2400 BC. This suggests that trade may have existed four thousand years ago between the areas of present-day Georgia and Colombia.

Mounds dating from 1000 BC contain tombs with grave offerings of pottery, art objects, jewelry, and stone pipes. There is also evidence of human sacrifice at these sites. Strangely, there is no evidence of agriculture, to which the practice of human sacrifice is often related. The earliest North American mound builders probably practiced such sacrifice to ensure that chieftains who had passed onto the next world would be properly attended and guarded there.

Around 300 BC, the Adena culture (named for its type site in Ohio) raised burial mounds in Ohio, Illinois, and New York that have been found to contain goods including stone, copper, pearl, and bone carvings with the human remains. These burial mounds were ceremonial and social centers for their communities. The Adena culture was truly indigenous—not subject to Mexican influence as were later mound-building cultures.

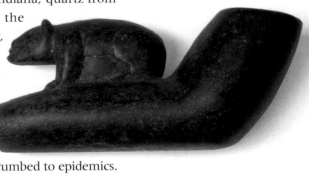

The Adena people began practicing agriculture after 300 BC. By about AD 200, they were cultivating maize as well as pumpkins and squash. They were displaced by the Hopewell people, who covered a much greater area that extended far to the south and west, but shared many practices with the Adena. Their larger burial mounds contained richer grave goods, including obsidian from Wyoming, conch shells from the Gulf of Mexico, copper from the Great Lakes, flints from North Dakota and Indiana, quartz from Arkansas, pearls from the Mississippi River valley, and Canadian silver. The Adena-Hopewell sites in Ohio were abandoned by AD 500. Perhaps these people had exhausted the soil in cultivating tobacco and maize, or succumbed to epidemics.

By AD 700 a powerful, Mexican-influenced culture, the Mississippian, was raising pyramidal mounds along the Mississippi. A thousand years later, the first Europeans to see these mounds could not believe that native peoples had built them, suggesting that they must have been the ruins of structures built by the Spanish, the Canaanites, or the ten lost tribes of Israel. Temples and the homes of chieftains and priests were erected on flat mounds. Other mounds were used for burials. Many remains of human sacrifices have been found in these mounds. As in early Egypt and Mesopotamia, wives and servants were often sacrificed to serve their masters in the next world. Archaeologists discovered fifty-three women in a single mass grave.

The Mississippian mounds were surrounded by populous villages of hunters, farmers, traders, and craftsmen. The traders traveled across the entire continent. Much of this trade must have gone up and down the Mississippi River in an intense traffic of freighted rafts and canoes.

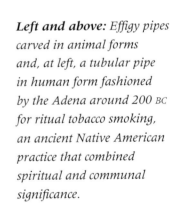

*Left and above:* Effigy pipes carved in animal forms and, at left, a tubular pipe in human form fashioned by the Adena around 200 BC for ritual tobacco smoking, an ancient Native American practice that combined spiritual and communal significance.

*Above: A view from the east of "Monk's Mound," the largest Mississippian mound-building complex, at Cahokia, near present-day St. Louis.*

The largest and best-known Mississippian complex is Cahokia, near present-day St. Louis at the confluence of the Illinois, Missouri, and Mississippi Rivers. The "Monk's Mound" is 100 feet high and covers fourteen acres. It has graded sides, a log stairway, and several terraces. Smaller mounds are concentrated in the surrounding area. From the great Monk's Mound, one can see a nearby mound used for funeral rites and the burial mound that rises beside it. All these earthworks were built between AD 900 and 1100 without the aid of wheels or pack animals, probably by men and women carrying baskets of soil.

The Cahokian complex also includes a "Woodhenge"—forty-eight tall cedar posts set in a large circle like the standing stones at Stonehenge, England. Both "henges" were probably used as calendars to show the exact occurrence of the winter and summer solstices.

Like many other maize-growing cultures, Cahokia apparently failed due to soil exhaustion, drought, and general overexploitation of resources. For many miles around the settlement, no wood remained for building or for fuel. People simply came down from their mounds, packed up their villages, and left.

The Mississippian culture gave rise to the Chickasaw, the Creek, and the Natchez tribes. The Natchez were still living on their mounds in historic times. From what we know of the

Natchez, we can deduce much about the older societies, which were probably very similar in many respects.

**THE NORTHEAST**

According to an Iroquois legend, a thousand years ago an Eastern Woodlands boy went forth to become a man. In a ritual procedure common to many tribes, the boy entered the woods alone, without provisions of any kind. He built himself a modest shelter of branches and bark and lit a small fire outside. He then lay down to fast and dream for three days and nights. In this state of dreamy privation he hoped to entertain a spiritual visitor—a manitou—the guide who would teach him his future and life's work. Often no manitou appeared until the last moment. Sometimes no manitou appeared at all, and the youth would have to await his majority until he tried again...and succeeded.

For this boy, one thousand years ago, a great manitou appeared on the first night. Into the glow of the boy's small fire stepped a beautiful, strong young man, dressed all in green and yellow. The young man signaled to the boy to come wrestle with him. All night the boy wrestled with the manitou, like Jacob with the Angel. At dawn, the young man disappeared.

The manitou returned the next night and they wrestled again.

On the third night the young man finally spoke. He told the boy to overcome him and to kill and bury him on the spot. The boy was then to return throughout the summer to pour water on the grave and keep it clean. In the fall the Great Spirit's gift to the people would appear. Grieving but obedient, the boy killed and buried the beautiful young man and tended his grave. A green shoot sprang from the ground and grew tall. It bore green-wrapped ears of maize, the gift of the Great Spirit to the people.

Clearly this is a myth, but it bears within it the truth about the introduction of this new crop in the northeastern corner of North America. Between nine hundred and one thousand years ago, the "three sisters"—maize, beans, and squash—became the staple foods of the Iroquois and Algonquian tribes of New England, New Jersey, and New York. The "three sisters" were planted together on tilled hillsides beneath bare, girdled trees. Beans provided the nitrogen maize needed; squash climbed the cornstalks and spread about, providing ground cover and some protection from the pilfering of animals. The "sisters" provided a balanced diet, for maize and beans together form valuable protein.

As in the lands to the south, the cultivation of maize had far-reaching effects on the peoples of the Northeast. Though the tribes continued to travel from camp to camp, especially in summer, they built more permanent villages surrounded by fields of the "three sisters." As their populations increased, sporadic violence, brush-fire wars, torture, and even occasional cannibalism occurred.

**PORTENTS**

In 1492 by the European calendar, three ocean-tossed sailing ships were crossing the Atlantic to a world completely unknown to them. Dreamers and shamans across the continent had warned of coming disruption and disaster. Prophecies had spoken of destroying gods or demons. A Sioux story foretold, "The White Long-legs is coming. Look around you at the things you see—the grass, the trees, the animals. The Iktome Hu-Hanska-Ska will take them all."

To most newly arrived Europeans, Native Americans would appear as demons or wild savages—inhuman, or only half human. In

*Left: Squash of many different shapes and sizes were widely grown as a staple food crop. Aside from their food value, they were also hollowed out for use as drinking vessels and ritual artefacts, including rattles.*

truth, as the Mohegan First Mother could have told them, natives and newcomers were of the same family. Neither the natives nor the newcomers, however, could imagine the results of this first encounter.

*Below: An ominous portent for the native peoples: King Ferdinand of Spain observes the arrival of his Italian navigator, Christopher Columbus, on a Caribbean island (now believed to have been Samana Cay) in an engraving dating from 1493.*

# First Contact and Conflict

Christopher Columbus landed on an island in the present-day Bahamas on October 12, 1492. Historians now believe that he landed on what is known today as Samana Cay. Columbus has been the subject of both admiration, enshrined as an icon of European skill and resolution, and blame, damned as the person who subjected millions of Native Americans to misery through their contact with Europeans. Most likely, Columbus deserves both less praise and less vilification. He was an audacious mariner, but others, including the Norse, had reached the Americas before him. His importance lies in the fact that after his landfall in 1492 there was increasing contact between Native Americans and Europeans.

*Opposite:* North and Meso-America circa 1500, with major tribes and the resources that supported their lifeways. European incursions during the sixteenth century are represented by the ships at the shores.

## MESO-AMERICA

Although Mexico is not now considered part of North America, the situation in Mexico in the 1500s must be examined to understand

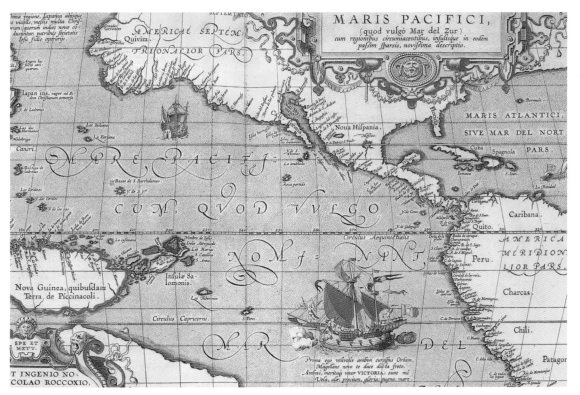

*Left and above:* European mapping of the New World advanced dramatically during the sixteenth century, beginning with the first known map of North America charted in 1500 by Juan de la Cosa, a shipmate of Columbus. The late-century map above shows a readily recognizable outline of the Americas, while the 1589 map of "Maris Pacifici," at left, by Ortelius, reveals the extent of European exploration along the Pacific Coast during the century.

developments in North America in subsequent centuries. Neither the native inhabitants nor the Europeans who came to the Americas observed the sharp political borders we do today. Anthropologists now regard most of Mexico as belonging to a still larger cultural area: Mesoamerica. This includes not only all of Mexico except its northern fringes but also Central America—Guatemala, Belize, El Salvador, Honduras, and parts of Nicaragua and Costa Rica. Of concern here, however, is the history of the people of central and northern Mexico, for they were the ones who influenced the history of both Native Americans and Europeans in North America.

*Below: Moctezoma was a skilled warrior who, from 1502, controlled the highly advanced Aztec Empire that dominated some five million people.*

RITR·DI·MOTEZVMA
CAVATO·DALL·ORIGINA
VENVTO·DAL·MESSICO
AL·SER·G.D.DI·TOSCA·

Before the arrival of the first Europeans, Mexico had seen the rise and fall of several Indian peoples, including the Olmec, Maya, and Toltec. These peoples had developed complex civilizations with intricate social orders, monumental architecture, sophisticated arts and crafts, and intellectual achievements including calendars and writing systems. At the time of the European arrival, the dominant people in Mexico were the Aztec. Originally a tribe known as Tenochca or Mexica from northern Mexico, they had migrated into the Valley of Mexico in the late 1100s. Once they settled down in the heartland of Mexico, they adopted many of the elements of such earlier cultures as the Toltec and Maya.

By about 1325 the Tenochca had founded two settlements on swampy islets in Lake Texcoco: Tenochtitlán and Tlatelolco. The former became the capital of the Tenochca and eventually the site of Mexico City. Gradually the Tenochca conquered most of the other tribes of central Mexico until, by 1500, they ruled an estimated five million people. During this period of conquest they changed their name to that of the "Aztec" in honor of their place of origin, which they called "Aztlan." Tenochtitlán, built on an island linked to the mainland by causeways, had a population of between 150,000 and 300,000 inhabitants. The city contained hundreds of monumental structures, a system of canals, and floating vegetable gardens known as *chinampas*. Because much of central and northern Mexico was relatively arid, control of water resources was crucial to any people who sought to assert power.

The Aztec were an extremely ambitious and warlike people. They established an elaborate commercial empire, controlling the trade not only of such valuable minerals as copper, gold, silver, jade, and turquoise, but also the exchange of basic foods such as beans, corn, papayas, squash, and turkeys. Beyond this assertion of commercial control, the Aztec constantly attacked the other peoples of central Mexico, taking not only their possessions but the people themselves as captives. Sometimes the captives were used as slaves for various enterprises but, more often and dramatically, they were taken for human sacrifice. The Aztec believed that their primary god, Huitzilopochtli, had to be placated by human blood. Aztec priests killed thousands of prisoners by tearing their hearts out in rites performed at the temple summits of pyramids. As a result of such practices—warfare, enslavement, and human sacrifice—the Aztec earned the enmity of the neighboring tribes of central Mexico.

While maintaining this harsh religion and relentless military aggression, the Aztec also developed one of the most advanced cultures in the New World. They had a system of writing and a calendar; they practiced metallurgy and other technologies; they operated elaborate urban, social, and religious institutions. Aztec society was dominated by a hierarchy of leaders from the priestly, military, and administrative classes. At the top of this rigidly hierarchical society was a priest-king known as the *tlacatecatl* ("chief of men"). In 1502 a new man succeeded to this high office: Moctezoma Xocoyotzin—known as Montezuma II by the Spanish and future generations.

The Aztec Empire first experienced foreign intrusion when Spaniards appeared along the eastern coast of Mexico as early as 1506. The encounter that would change the course of Mesoamerican history began with the arrival of Hernán Cortés in March 1519. Fortunately for the historian, the Aztec and other Indians of Mexico preserved their versions of the events that followed. They wrote these down in their own language, Nahuatl, as early as 1528 and recounted them to their Spanish masters in the decades that followed. Although the sequence of basic events does not differ from European accounts, it is the phrasings of the Aztec (as quoted here) that give a better impression of the true impact of the coming of the Spanish.

The Aztec were greatly influenced by omens; they saw almost all natural phenomena as portending something for their future. For years before 1519 they had been seeing lights in the sky, lightning bolts, comets, an unusual bird, and other phenomena, and their seers and magicians had been interpreting these as signs of a forthcoming crisis. *"To the natives, these marvels...signified that other peoples would be created to inhabit the earth."* Therefore, many of the Aztec were predisposed to yield to the strange newcomers arriving on their shores. Furthermore, the Aztec religion had long claimed that the god Quetzalcóatl would return from the east in a year of their cyclical calendar known

as "One Reed"—and 1519 was just such a year. Moctezoma himself, it was written, *"felt in his heart, He has appeared!...He will come here, to the place of his throne...for that is what he promised when he departed!"*

Cortés and about 500 Spanish soldiers landed along the east coast of the present-day Mexican province of Tabasco. They immediately set about to impose their will on the local people. A young Indian princess who knew both the Mayan and Aztec languages apparently volunteered to serve as an interpreter. She began by speaking to a Spaniard who had learned Mayan in captivity and eventually she learned Spanish. Her Indian name was something like Malinali, but the Spaniards baptized her with the name of Marina, then called her Doña Marina; to the Indians she became known as Malintzin, which the Spanish then turned into Malinche. Cortés soon took her as his mistress and she bore him a son. During the first few years Malinche played a crucial role in helping Cortés gain power over Moctezoma and the Aztec by conveying the demands of the Spanish and the wishes of the Aztec. Many Mexicans came to regard Malinche as a traitoress; even today the term "Malinchista" refers to a person who betrays her own people. By 1523 Cortés had Doña Marina married off to another

**Above:** *Silver was mined by the Aztec and other peoples farther south, as depicted in this engraving by Theodor de Bry. Witnessing the wealth of the Aztec Empire, the invading Spanish wanted to gain control of the sources of its minerals and precious metals.*

conquistador. Cortés later took his son back to Spain with him. Malinche died in 1551.

A few weeks after landing in Tabasco, Cortés moved north up the coast to establish his base at a site he named Veracruz. Long before this, word had been carried to Tenochtitlán of the unusual people *"of very light skin…all with long beards"* who had arrived on *"towers or small mountains floating on the waves of the sea."* Moctezoma and his religious advisers were naturally awed by the news of these extraordinary strangers. Moctezoma immediately commanded his finest craftsmen to make elaborate gifts of gold, valuable stones, and feathers. The gifts were quickly finished, and Moctezoma ordered five emissaries led by a priest to carry them to the foreigners. Moctezoma saw the rich goods not as bribes but as *"the treasure due to Quetzalcóatl."* When they arrived at the coast, the Aztec were taken aboard Cortés's ship and there presented him with the gifts. Cortés's response was to put the Indians in chains and then to fire off his cannon and firearms. It was clearly his intention to let the native people know that they would have no success if they chose to fight against the Spanish.

The messengers fled back to Tenochtitlán in terror and described to Moctezoma the men who *"dress in iron."* They were especially impressed by the horses: *"Their deer carry them on their backs…these deer are as tall as the roof of a house."* Upon hearing this, Moctezoma *"was filled with terror."* He sent out magicians to try to stop the foreigners with magic. He also sent captives who were sacrificed in the presence of the foreigners in an attempt to appease them, but this only filled the Spanish with disgust.

Cortés and his band set out to make their way from the coast to the capital. The Spaniards were quite graciously received by the Totonac and Zempoalan Indians as they passed through the towns of Zempoala, Quiahuitzlan, and Jalapa. The Spaniards met and defeated the Tlaxcalan and then discovered that these Indians hated the Aztec. With Malinche serving as translator and diplomat, Cortés enlisted about one thousand Tlaxcalan to reinforce his small band and continued his march toward the capital. More alarmed than ever, Moctezoma, with the intention of bribing the Spanish from proceeding, sent emissaries with even more elaborate gifts of gold. The Spaniards simply *"burst into smiles…they picked up the gold and fingered it like monkeys; they seemed to be transported by joy."* The sight of these treasures of gold, in fact, made the Spaniards even more determined to reach the Aztec capital, and they marched on. When word of this was brought to Moctezoma, he declared, *"We can do nothing but wait."*

Cortés's band entered the city on November 8, 1519. Even the most hardened Spanish soldiers marveled at the art and architecture of the Aztec capital. Moctezoma, believing Cortés to be the god Quetzalcóatl, received him with great honor. *"He presented many gifts to the Captain and his commanders, those who had come to make war."* Cortés assured Moctezoma that the Spanish *"have come to your house in Mexico as friends. There is nothing to fear."*

In fact, Cortés almost immediately placed Moctezoma under house arrest and seized gold and other royal treasures. In the eyes of the Aztec, who observed the Spanish looting everything they could lay their hands on, *"they were slaves of their own greed."* Meanwhile, as the Spanish continually demanded food and drink, the Indians *"brought them whatever they needed, but shook with fear as they did so."* With Moctezoma held prisoner and most of the other leaders having fled, Cortés and his men soon realized that the mass of Indians in the Aztec Empire were effectively powerless. In the months that followed, the Spanish proceeded to help themselves to anything they wanted.

Around mid-1520 Cortés left the capital and went to the coast to fight Pánfilo Narváez, who had come from Cuba to challenge his command. Only about eighty Spaniards and a few hundred Tlaxcaltec and other Indian allies

*Below:* Aztec warriors, as shown in the art illustrating various codices, were feared as ruthless foes.

remained in Tenochtitlán. While Cortés was absent, one of his impetuous lieutenants, Pedro de Alvarado, decided to attack the Aztec in Tenochtitlán during one of their great festivals: *"When the dance was loveliest and when song was linked to song, the Spaniards were seized with an urge to kill the celebrants....They posted guards so that no one could escape and then rushed to the Sacred Patio to slaughter the celebrants."* The exact number killed is not known, but it was evidently in the hundreds.

The Aztec rose up in fury and surrounded the Spanish and their Indian allies. Soon afterwards, Cortés, having defeated his Spanish rivals, returned to Tenochtitlán. With his enlarged band of warriors, he was able to force his way through the angry Aztec to join the besieged, and for several days they held off their attackers. It was during this time, evidently, that Moctezoma was killed. Whether he was assassinated by the Spanish or by his own angry subjects is not known, although the Aztec accused the Spanish of his murder.

Cortés, short of food and water and realizing that he and his band were seriously threatened by the overwhelming numbers of Aztec, decided to leave the city. On the night of June 30, Cortés led about two thousand Spaniards and their Indian allies in an attempt to sneak out across the canals and along the causeways. But an alarm was raised and Aztec warriors attacked them, *"loosing a storm of arrows at the fleeing army. The Spaniards also turned to shoot at the Aztec; they fired their crossbows and their arquebuses* [an early form of musket]*....The canal was soon choked with the bodies of men and horses;* [the Spanish] *filled the gap in the causeway with their own drowned bodies. Those who followed crossed to the other side by walking on the corpses."*

The surviving Spanish and their various Indian allies reached a nearby town where they rested. It is estimated that in their retreat they had lost at least half their number and almost all the treasures they had stolen from the Aztec. The retreat came to be known to the Spanish as the *noche triste*, "the sad night."

For the Aztec, it proved to be the start of a much longer period of sadness. By December 1520 Cortés had organized a large army that included his reinforced Spanish troops and his tribal allies: Tlaxcalan, Texcocan, Cholulan, Xochimilican, and Otomí. During this same period, the Aztec in Tenochtitlán suffered great losses from what they called the "hueyzahuatl"—a smallpox epidemic.

The Hispano-Indian army surrounded Tenochtitlán, and the city fell on August 13, 1521, after a seventy-five-day siege. The casualties of this unparalleled scene of death and destruction

*Above: The Mayan temple at Uxmal in the Yucatán peninsula was built around AD 1000. The Maya were among the sophisticated Mesoamerican cultures that pre-dated the Aztec Empire, leaving elements of their civilization to be adopted by the Aztec.*

were horrific. Some of the chroniclers assert that 240,000 Aztec—including almost all of the nobles—died, and that 30,000 of Cortés's Indian allies lost their lives in the struggle. The combined casualties of all subsequent wars between indigenous people and Europeans in North America over the next 350 years would not produce such a heavy death toll.

Cuauhtémoc, who had succeeded Moctezoma as *tlacatecatl*, surrendered to Cortés, saying, *"I have done everything in my power to save my kingdom from your hands. Since fortune has been against me, I now beg you to take my life. This would put an end to the kingship of Mexico, and it would be just and right, for you have already destroyed my city and killed my people."* Cuauhtémoc was later summarily executed. He remains an important Mexican hero to this day.

By 1522 the Aztec Empire was no more. It was replaced by the Spanish territory known as *Nueva España* or *Hispania Nova*, with its new capital of *Ciudad de Mexico* on the former site of Tenochtitlán. Cortés immediately began the process of imposing Spanish rule over much of present-day Mexico and Guatemala.

The Spanish moved quickly to enforce their rule by means of military garrisons, an administrative bureaucracy, Catholic missions, and colonial settlement. They were also quick to exploit the rich mineral and agricultural resources—silver mines in particular—of the vast new territory. Despite Spain's official policy forbidding slavery, the Spanish began to enslave the native people. Before the end of the 1500s, hundreds of thousands of Aztec and other native peoples of Mexico had died of brutal working conditions, starvation, and disease. The peoples of the New World had no immunity to such diseases as smallpox, mumps, and measles.

Great changes also occurred in the plant and animal ecology of *Nueva España*. If an Aztec of 1500 had been able to return to his homeland in 1600, he would have been amazed to see the enormity of the change in the landscape and animal life. The Spaniards planted orchards of imported peach, pear, orange, and lemon trees. They cultivated fields of wheat and brought thousands of horses, cattle, sheep, goats, hogs, and asses to Mexico. Within a single century, the government, religion, and landscape had all been radically altered.

The indigenous culture of Mexico was denigrated and marginalized, although it would never be completely suppressed. Even as they converted to Christianity, for example, many of the Mexican Indians combined the new faith with elements of indigenous religion. The most remarkable instance of this occurred at Guadaloupe, near Ciudad de Mexico, when an old peasant brought a *tilma* (cloak) to the Spanish bishop. The *tilma* bore an image of the Virgin Mary. This deeply impressed the bishop and the millions of people who have seen it since. The Miracle of Guadaloupe helped Spanish Catholicism to enter more deeply into the hearts of the Mexican people.

### THE NORTHEAST

The Northeast cultural area reached from Nova Scotia and the Canadian maritime provinces down the Atlantic seaboard to the border of Virginia, westward across Kentucky (with a dip into central Tennessee) to Illinois, and up the Mississippi valley to the land surrounding the Great Lakes and across southern Ontario and Quebec. The geographical and environmental features of this region are varied: ocean coasts and river valleys, rocky mountains and fertile flatlands, sweltering summers and freezing winters. The region is most particularly distinguished, however, by its extensive mixed forests of deciduous and coniferous trees.

*Below: The first meeting between Cortés and Moctezoma took place in Tenochtitlán on November 8, 1519, according to the European calendar. The Aztec calendar, which was based upon a fifty-two-year cycle, dated it as the year of "One Reed."*

In fact, the indigenous inhabitants of the area are often referred to as the Northeast Woodland Indians because so much of their way of life was linked to the forests, which provided not only material for dwellings, tools, and fuel, but also sheltered the many animals they hunted. The coastal Indians also depended heavily on marine life for food, while the inland peoples fished the lakes, rivers, and streams. Most also farmed to some extent.

The many tribes that inhabited this area in the 1500s can be divided into several major groups, each generally speaking the same or a closely related language, all of which in turn can be assigned to two major families, the Algonquian and the Iroquoian. One group of Algonquian speakers lived from Nova Scotia across New England, down the Hudson valley, on Long Island, and in the Delaware valley: these included, among others, the Micmac, Abenaki, Narraganset, Wampanoag, and Pequot. Another group of Algonquian speakers lived around the Great Lakes and included such tribes as the Algonkin, Menominee, Ottawa, and Potawatomi. A third group, the Prairie Algonquian, lived in the western reaches of this region and included the Fox, Illinois, Kickapoo, Miami, Sauk, and Shawnee. The Iroquoian speakers lived across much of New York State and the Canadian provinces of Quebec and Ontario, and included such tribes as the Mohawk, Oneida, Seneca, and Huron.

Sometime during the 1500s, possibly in the 1400s, many of the Iroquoian tribes formed several leagues or confederations. The best known of these, the League of the Hodeno-saunee—"People of the Longhouse"—eventually came to be known to English-speakers as the League of Five Nations. The five tribes were the Mohawk, Oneida, Onondaga, Cayuga, and Seneca. The details are unclear but the tradition is that a Huron named Dekanawidah ("peacemaker") inspired an Onondaga named Hiawatha to found the league in order to end the fighting among the Iroquoian tribes. They by no means gave up fighting other tribes, however. A council of fifty chiefs met periodically near present-day Canandaigua, New York, and made decisions regarding their external affairs. The tribes remained largely autonomous in the management of their internal affairs..

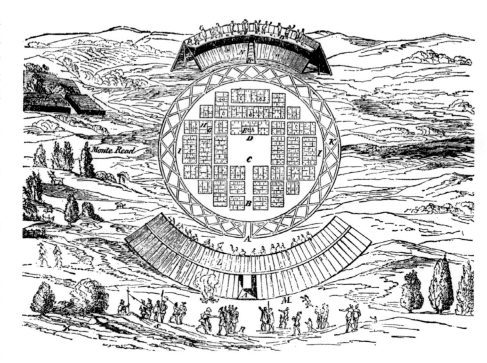

Many of the Northeastern tribes encountered groups of Europeans soon after 1500. As early as 1504, French, Portuguese, and Basque fishermen were already fishing off the coasts of Newfoundland and Nova Scotia, and some of them almost certainly made contact with the Algonquian tribes of the coast. These Europeans got on quite well with the native people because they traded items in return for the use of land for their fish-curing operations, for cutting wood for ship repairs and fires, and for access to supplies of food and water. Such sporadic contacts passed European diseases to the coastal tribes, although the extent of the resultant mortality is unknown. The fishermen were not interested in making claims or settlements on the land, but official expeditions sponsored by European powers would soon do both.

The Northeast Indians first encountered an official European expedition in 1524 during the voyage of Giovanni da Verrazzano, an Italian mariner in the service of the French king. After making his first landfall at Cape Fear, North Carolina, Verrazano sailed north along the coast, putting in and out of various havens and occasionally trading with the Indians. After sailing along the New Jersey coast, Verrazzano entered New York Bay as far as the narrows between Staten Island and Long Island. He observed people *"clad with feathers of fowls of divers colors"* but did not otherwise attempt to meet with them. He sailed into Narragansett Bay in Rhode Island and spent

*Above: The town of Hochelaga, the site of Montreal, as it appeared to French explorer Jacques Cartier in 1535.*

*Modus muniendi apud Mahikanenses.*

***Above:*** *This depiction of a Mahican village appeared in a map published in Amsterdam in 1650.*

***Below:*** *To Europeans, this area was sparsely populated, but a growing scarcity of resources had crowded the peoples of the Northeast along coasts and rivers. Confederacies formed in response to this pressure included the famous Iroquois League as well as those of the Delaware, Illinois, Abenaki, Wappinger, and the Council of the Three Fires (Ojibwa-Potowatomi-Ottawa).*

two weeks there in communication with the Wampanoag, *"is the goodliest people, and of the fairest conditions, that we have found in our voyage."* Verrazzano then continued sailing northeastward, going around Cape Cod and up the Maine coast, where he found the Abenaki *"of such crudity and evil manners, so barbarous."* The final insult came when the French departed and the locals displayed *"signs of discourtesy and disdain…such as exhibiting their bare behinds and laughing immoderately."* After cruising up as far as Cape Breton (and possibly to Newfoundland), Verrazzano sailed for France and reported his many discoveries to King François I.

The following year, in 1525, Estéban Gomez, a Portuguese mariner in the service of the king of Spain, sailed to the northeastern islands of Canada. He proceeded down the coast of Maine and at least as far south as Rhode Island, where he kidnapped a large number of Indians and

brought them back to Spain. Those who survived the voyage were freed, but they soon died. It was a common practice among the first Europeans who encountered the inhabitants of the New World to bring captives to Europe, where they were displayed as exotic specimens, employed as slaves, or trained as translators for future expeditions. During the 1500s few of these people ever returned to their homelands. Most succumbed to European diseases.

The natives of the Hochelaga (St. Lawrence) River valley met the next group of European intruders. Jacques Cartier made three voyages to the area for King François I of France. On his first voyage in 1534, Cartier encountered the Micmac on the Gaspé Peninsula and immediately traded metal knives, hatchets, beads, and other European items for furs. He also established close relations with the Laurentian Iroquois, whose chief, Donnaconna, allowed Cartier to take his two teenage sons, Taignoagny and Domagaya, back to France.

On his second voyage (1535–36), with the two brothers as guides, Cartier sailed into the river known locally as the Hochelaga. Cartier soon gave it a French name: the *St. Laurent.* He passed by the Indian villages of Ajoaste, Starnatum, Tailla, and Sitadin on the north shore of the river without landing, visited Stadacona (present-day Quebec City), and then proceeded to Hochelaga (present-day Montreal) where more than one thousand people greeted him. Cartier described the town as: *"Quite round*

*and inclosed with timbers in three rows in the style of a pyramid, crossed at the top, having the middle row in the style of a perpendicular line; then ranged with timbers laid along, well joined and tied in their manner, and is in height about two pikes."* The inhabitants of Hochelaga, he noted, were quite settled in their habits: *"they budge not from their country, and do not go about like those of Canada."*

Cartier was perhaps the first European to sample tobacco. He noted that the native people *"say that it keeps them healthy and warm, and they never go without having their said things. We have tried the same smoke, which, after being put into our mouths, seemed to be powder of pepper put theirin, it was so hot."*

Cartier wintered near Stadacona. In May 1536 he seized Donnaconna, the two brothers, and three other men, and sailed off to France with them, bringing four children who had been given to him as "gifts."

Of the ten Cartier brought back to France, none lived long enough to set foot in Canada again, but Cartier returned with a third expedition. In August 1541 he sailed up the St. Lawrence and established a settlement between Stadacona and Hochelaga. Over the winter the French were attacked. Cartier left in June 1542 to return to France. Just as Cartier was leaving Newfoundland, Jean-François de la Roque, sieur de Roberval, arrived with 150 French would-be colonists. But after a disastrous winter along the St. Lawrence, Roberval and the colonists returned to France.

As the 1500s ended, the peoples of the Northeast, depleted in numbers by the diseases transmitted unwittingly by the explorers, could well believe that the intruders from across the ocean would not attempt to settle in their land. Within a few years they would learn otherwise.

## THE SOUTHEAST

The Southeastern Woodlands cultural area extended from present-day Virginia down the Atlantic coast to the tip of Florida, across the states bordering the Gulf of Mexico into eastern Texas and then across parts of Oklahoma, Arkansas, Tennessee, Kentucky, West Virginia, and Maryland. Like the Northeast Woodlands area, it was heavily forested, but its climate is both warmer and wetter; it also offers a variety of environments with its long ocean coast and numerous inland rivers, fertile plains, and several mountain ranges. By the 1500s most of the inhabitants of the region were engaged in some form of farming, but they also hunted, fished, and gathered plants.

The many tribes scattered throughout this area exhibited a wide cultural diversity and belonged to numerous language families. In the northeastern coastal section reaching south from the Chesapeake Bay to Cape Hatteras lived Iroquoian speakers: the Meherrin, Nottaway, and Tuscarora. Sharing this territory were also some Algonquian speakers such as the Powhatan, Secotan, and Weapemeoc. Tribes including the Apalachee, Choctaw, Chickasaw, and Muskogee (Creek) spoke languages of the Muskogean family. Several other tribes, including the Natchez, the Caddo, and the Atakapa,

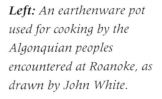

spoke languages that do not appear to be directly related to other families.

The Southeastern peoples had a clear sense of social organization and government. There were numerous tribes, which were often grouped together into confederations or chiefdoms. Some of the large chiefdoms were ruled by women. The paramount ruler of Cofitachiqui (called the "Lady of Cofitachiqui"), held a principality along the Savannah River (her name has not been preserved). Unfortunately, most of what we know about the chiefdoms depends on the written

*Left: Jacques Cartier opened the way for the creation of the colony of Nouvelle France, centered along the St. Lawrence River.*

*Left: An earthenware pot used for cooking by the Algonquian peoples encountered at Roanoke, as drawn by John White.*

**Above:** *Many of the natives who resisted the Spaniards led by Hernando de Soto suffered mutilation and death at the hands of Europeans.*

The most significant expedition to follow that of Ponce de León was that of Hernando de Soto. A veteran of Pizarro's conquest of the Incan Empire in Peru, de Soto landed at or near the village of Ozita in Tampa Bay in May 1539. He had with him more than 600 men, more than 200 horses, and many dogs and pigs. The animals at first terrified the Indians, who had never before seen their like.

It was immediately clear that de Soto was determined to conquer. He quickly killed two Timucua and seized the primary village of the Ozita chiefdom. This was only the start of his ruthless journey. Although romanticized by many Spanish reports, it was in fact a procession of brutal aggressions.

As they marched northward the Spaniards attacked and killed, stealing corn and sometimes destroying villages. The Spaniards seized chiefs and notables as hostages and put hundreds of men in chains and collars to serve as porters. Scores of women were also taken for the pleasure of the Spanish men.

Some of the most poignant echoes of the cruelty of de Soto and his men have come to us from different chiefs in what is now Florida. After de Soto sent a threatening message to the chief of Ocale, he is reported as responding: *"To me you are professional vagabonds who wander from place to place, gaining your livelihood by robbing, sacking, and murdering people who have given you no offense. I want no manner of friendship or peace with people such as you."*

De Soto also sent a message to the chief of the Napituca in northern Florida, warning him not to resist, or he would suffer the same fate that had already fallen upon Indians to the south. The chief of Napituca responded to the interpreter and de Soto's hostages as follows:

*"These Spaniards are the same people who committed cruelties against us in the past* [Pánfilo de Narváez's army]. *They are demons, not sons of the Sun and Moon, for they go about killing and robbing. They do not bring their own women, but prefer to possess the wives and daughters of others. They are not content to colonize a particular piece of land because they take such pleasure in being vagabonds, living on the labor of others. They are thieves and murderers. Warn them not to enter my land, for no matter how brave they are, they shall never leave it, for I shall destroy them all. Half of them I will bake, and the other half I shall boil."*

accounts of the European adventurers and invaders who entered the Southeast. Were it not for the beautiful illustrations drawn by John White (English) and Jacques Le Moyne (French), we would have little understanding of what the villages and chiefdoms of the region looked like in their heyday.

The inhabitants of this area, along with those of the Southwest, most directly felt the impact of the European arrival in North America during the 1500s. Juan Ponce de León was among the first, arriving in Florida in 1513. It is well known that he was searching for the legendary Fountain of Youth; few people know that he was also seeking to enslave local natives. He and his men landed somewhere between the sites of the present-day towns of Daytona Beach and St. Augustine, where they were met by hostile Timucua Indians. After brief skirmishes the Spanish went back to their ships. They then sailed down the eastern coast and around the southern tip of Florida. Landing on the western coast, perhaps at present-day Charlotte Harbor, they fought off some hostile Calusa. Although the Spanish then conducted peaceful trading with the Calusa, another fight broke out and ended with the Spanish fleeing Florida.

Ponce de León returned to Florida in 1521, intent on establishing a colony for Spain. He landed on the west coast, probably near Charlotte Harbor. The Spanish were attacked almost immediately, and Ponce de León was wounded by an arrow; the Spaniards retreated to Cuba, where he soon died.

The Napituca chieftain promised his people that the earth would open and swallow the Spaniards. When the chief's magic powers failed to destroy the invaders, he allowed de Soto to enter his village (located near present-day Live Oak, Florida). He then plotted against the Spanish, and a major battle ensued. Most of the Indians were killed or drowned. The chief of Uriutina, who survived the battle—the chief of Napituca did not—sent a message to the people of his villages saying:

*"Wherefore, what I enjoin upon them and ask is, that they do not, out of regard for me or for any one else, have anything to do with these Christians who are devils and will prove mightier than they; and that they may be assured that as for me, if I have to die, it will be as a brave man."*

De Soto continued on this destructive course as he led his men north into Florida through the chiefdoms of Ozita, Ocale, and Apalachee, delivering the sad fate that had befallen the people of Napituca to many other Southeastern Indians. The Spaniards wintered at the village of Apalachee (within present-day Tallahassee). Departing from Apalachee the following spring, they advanced into Georgia, bringing ruin to such villages as Capachiqui, Tao, Ichisi, Altamaha, Ocute, and Coafqui. The marauding Spaniards then turned to the area of present-day western North and South Carolina and eastern Tennessee, through such villages as Hymahi, Cofitachiqui, Talimeco, Ilasi, Coste, Tali, and Satapo. The "Lady of Cofitachiqui" was seized from her village and taken hostage. She was then forced to march on foot alongside the Spanish troops.

Along the way de Soto fought several battles and lost dozens of his men, scores of horses, hundreds of pigs, and most of his supplies. The largest battle was fought on October 18, 1540, between the Spaniards and the warriors of the chief Tuscaloosa at Maliba, near present-day Selma, Alabama. After the bloody conflict, which raged for almost a full day, the Spaniards counted twenty-two killed and 250 wounded. The Indians had lost 2,500 warriors. The clash at Maliba was one of the largest-scale battles ever fought between Europeans and Native Americans. The results of the fighting clearly demonstrated the great advantage held by the Spanish in their possession of swords, guns, horses, and armor.

De Soto then entered into the area of present-day Mississippi, advancing through the towns of Chicaza and Quizquiz. He reached the Mississippi River on May 8, 1541. Some of the locals called the mighty river "Chucagua." The Spaniards called it "Rio del Spirito Santo." De Soto and his remaining soldiers then entered present-day Arkansas and visited or attacked villages including Casqui, Pacaha, Coligua, and Tanico. Arriving on the western bank of the Mississippi River, de Soto died of a fever at Guachoya on May 21, 1542. His expedition had been catastrophic for the Spaniards as well as the countless thousands of Native Americans they had met. One of the tragedies of the sixteenth century was the virtual disappearance of the tribal chiefdoms of the Southeast. De Soto's march and the arrival of European diseases combined to bring an abrupt end to a vibrant native culture.

The next major encounter between Native Americans and Europeans came when French Protestants, called Huguenots, decided to establish a colony in the region. Led by Jean Ribaut, the first group sailed in 1562. They landed near the mouth of the St. Johns River in northern Florida and met a tribe of friendly Indians led by Chief Saturiba. Ribaut erected a stone column to claim the land for France, and then proceeded to sail north along the coast before selecting present-day Parris Island, South

*Below: Theodor de Bry, who sketched many sixteenth-century New World scenes, observed of the Florida natives that: "In order to preserve the flesh of animals, they prepare them in the following way: four strong forked stakes are planted in the ground over which are laid more sticks, forming a greating to take the animals and fish."*

*Right:* The mound city at Cahokia was already abandoned about AD 1450, indicating that the Mississippian Culture was already in decline when Ponce de Leon arrived in present-day Florida. De Soto's long campaign of threat and massacre probably did not kill as many natives as the diseases the Spanish brought or the famine caused by the food supplies they took away.

Carolina, as the site of his colony, which he named Charlesfort. The French were received there by Maccoa of the Cusabo tribe. After establishing good relations, Ribaut returned to France to collect more supplies and colonists. His return was delayed, and the French at Charlesfort began to run short of food. The French obtained maize and beans from Chief Ouade and then built a ship to return home.

In 1564 René de Laudonnière returned with new French Protestants to try again. Jacques le Moyne de Morgues, an artist, went along to record the new sights. This time they established their settlement, named Fort Caroline, on the St. Johns River, about ten miles east of present-day Jacksonville, Florida. The French resumed good relations with Chief Saturiba, who remembered Ribaut's visit in 1562.

*Right:* The French expedition at Port Royal in 1562–65. "Prom Lupi" (Wolf's Point) marks the place where fleeing local tribespeople left behind a wolf's whelp. The map depicts abundant resources surrounding the settlements; fish and shellfish were also plentiful.

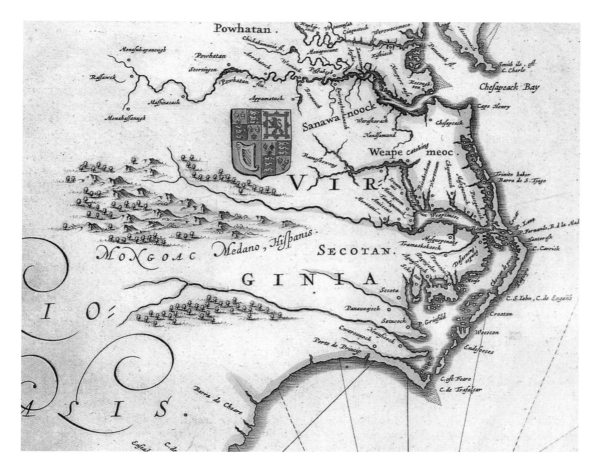

*Left: This Dutch map was based on the surveys and illustrations of John White and Jacques le Moynes de Morgues during the 1560s. The "lost colony" of Roanoke was founded on an island between North Carolina's coast and the barrier islands.*

The French made the mistake of choosing sides in a war among the Indian tribes. Initially they sided with Chief Holata Outina ("king of many kings"), and thereby alienated Chief Saturiba. They were drawn into a battle between Outina and one of his rivals. Then, in the spring of 1565, the French began to run short of food. The Indians demanded arms in payment for meat, and in April the desperate French seized Chief Outina and demanded corn as ransom. They received a little corn, but several other chiefs begged them to execute Outina, since they found him to be a tyrant. The French chose not to do so.

In August 1565 Ribaut arrived with supplies and reinforcements. He found many of the colonists ill and Fort Caroline practically in ruins. Making the situation even more grave, the Spanish had learned of the French attempt to settle on what they regarded as their territory, and a Spanish naval expedition arrived on the heels of Ribaut.

The Spanish and the French fought each other along the Florida coast throughout September. During this period the Spanish leader, Pedro Menendez de Aviles, established Fort San Augustin on the Florida coast near the Timucuan village of Seloy. Before the end of September, the Spanish had killed 250 French. On October 12 the Spanish trapped and killed another 150, including Ribaut. None of their native friends had been able to help the French against the power of the Spanish. Nevertheless, when a new French expedition arrived in Florida in 1567 to avenge the destruction of Fort Caroline, the Saturiba came to its aid. This last French venture was no more than a raid, and its leaders were unable to establish any settlement.

The Southeastern region experienced yet another major intrusion before the close of the sixteenth century. This was the attempt by some English adventurers to establish a colony at Roanoke Island along the coast of North Carolina. "Roanoke," derived from the local name of this small island, has been affirmed to be the first Indian word to enter the English language. Privately sponsored by Sir Walter Raleigh, the first exploratory expedition arrived in two vessels in 1584. The English were befriended by the local Indians, an Algonquian group ruled by Chief Wingina and his brother Granganimeo. The Indians even allowed two tribal members, Manteo and Wanchese, to make the journey to England to be trained as interpreters.

The first colonists arrived on Roanoke Island in July 1585. Some 108 of them—including the artist John White, who had also been with Martin Frobisher in Newfoundland—were left there, and the ships sailed off to England to collect more people and supplies.

Relations with the local people were at first friendly. Chief Wingina had allowed the English to lease some land on Roanoke Island, and they built a settlement there. An English chronicler reported, *"We found these people gentle, loving and faithful, lacking all guile and treachery. It was as if they lived in a golden age of their own."* This amicable beginning lasted for only a brief time. The English colonists destroyed the village of Secotan after the Indians did not produce a silver cup that had been either lost or stolen.

On June 1, 1586, Chief Wingina was killed by the English in a skirmish fought outside the town of Dasemunkapeuc on the mainland. The English colonists were extremely fortunate to be picked up by Sir Francis Drake and carried back with his party to England.

Within days after their departure, more English ships arrived with colonists and supplies. When they learned what had happened, most of the colonists decided to return to England; only fifteen chose to stay. In May 1587 yet another group of colonists sailed from England, now led by the artist-explorer John White. Arriving at Roanoke Island in July, they found no trace of the fifteen. In August, a baby girl was born to John White's daughter, Eleanor Dare. The baby was named Virginia in honor of the English name for the region. That same month John White and several others sailed back to England for more supplies, leaving 119 men, women, and children. White did not return until August 1590, three years later. Not one of the 119 colonists, including White's family, was found. The only trace of them was a word carved on a post, CROATOAN, the name of a nearby island inhabited by friendly Indians. Due to stormy weather, White was unable to visit the island, and the English sailed away. The mystery of the "lost colony" was never resolved, but it was assumed that the colonists were either killed or absorbed into the local culture. (Today, the Lumbee of North Carolina trace their ancestry in part to the lost colonists.)

This left the Spanish in Florida as the only Europeans in the Southeast. For the rest of the century they labored to establish control over at least the coastal areas. Pedro Menendez de Aviles, who was based at San Augustin, established a series of forts and colonies from Tampa Bay on the western coast of Florida all the way around the peninsula and up as far as the Chesapeake Bay. After his departure in 1572 his successors continued the struggle, and the story of the years between 1565 and 1600 in this region was one of virtually constant hostilities between the indigenous people and the Spanish. When the Spanish were not killing Indians, enslaving them, or destroying their

*Right: This map shows the colony of Roanoke and the Indian village of Dasemunkapeuc. The shipwrecks along the sandbars of the treacherous Outer Banks indicate the dangers of negotiating this stretch of the coastline, which became known as "the Graveyard of the Atlantic." The protected inner waters, however, were fertile fishing grounds for Native Americans, shown here in their dugout vessels.*

crops and villages, they were attempting to convert them to Christianity. There is no denying that the Native Americans could be equally vicious, but they were fighting to retain what had always been theirs. Disease also claimed many victims, and the native population was much reduced by the century's end.

As the 1500s drew to a close, the Spanish remained the only Europeans entrenched in the Southeast. Whether the European intruders were Spanish, French, or English, Catholic or Protestant, gold seekers or colonists, all of them had failed to treat the Native Americans they encountered with respect or dignity.

## THE GREAT PLAINS

The Great Plains cultural area extends from the southern portions of the Canadian provinces of Manitoba, Saskatchewan, and Alberta all the way down through central Texas. From the Mississippi River valley at its eastern limit, the region reaches west to the Rocky Mountains. Although there are stands of trees along its river valleys, the country is mostly grassland, which once sustained vast herds of bison. The terrain is mostly flat, but the area does contain some mountain ranges, including the Black Hills in South Dakota and Wyoming, and the Ozark Mountains in Arkansas.

The story of the inhabitants of the Great Plains differs considerably from that of all the other cultural areas. When the first contacts were made between Native Americans and Europeans in the 1500s, the tribes living there were not for the most part the ones who would later figure so prominently in the history of the region. Not only were the tribes different, but the way of life on the plains would change greatly in the following centuries. In the 1500s, although several of the tribes were semi-nomadic, many of the inhabitants were farmers settled in villages concentrated along river valleys. These included the Mandan and Hidatsa, who spoke languages of the Siouan family, and the Caddo, Wichita, Pawnee, and Arikara, who spoke languages of the Caddoan family. Only a few tribes depended on hunting bison and wild game; these included the Blackfoot (Nizitapi), who spoke an Algonquian language, and the Eastern Shoshoni, who spoke an Uto-Aztecan language.

The Great Plains dwellers encountered very few Europeans during the sixteenth century. The first contact was probably made by Álvar Núñez Cabeza de Vaca, who had been a member of the Spaniard Pánfilo de Narváez's 1528 expedition along the Gulf of Mexico. After a series of disasters, Cabeza de Vaca's ships were driven ashore on an island on the northeast coast of Texas. After living there for six years among the Indians, Cabeza de Vaca and three companions, including the Moor Estéban, took off for the west, hoping to join up with other Spaniards, or at least to reach the Pacific. As they journeyed across the plains of south-central Texas, they met one tribe after another and attracted Native American followers by appearing to be possessed of magical powers. After crossing the Pecos River, Cabeza de Vaca and his band finally passed into the territory of the Southwestern Indians.

Similar brief contacts occurred in 1541 when Francisco Vásquez de Coronado led an expedition in search of Quivira, a land reputed to be rich in gold. Crossing the Great Plains in northwestern Texas near present-day Amarillo, he encountered the Querecho and Teya, who hunted bison. He then advanced into central Kansas and the territory of the Wichita tribe on the Arkansas River. Coronado and his men were the first Europeans to see and describe the herds of bison. Pedro de Castenada reported, *"They have very long beards, like goats, and when they are running they throw their heads back with the beard dragging on the ground."* Castenada marveled at the physical expanse of the plains and the enormous numbers of buffalo.

Coronado sought the gold and other precious materials that had been the lure for many of the early Spanish explorers. Finding none, he executed the Indian guide who had insisted they would find great riches in Quivira. He then headed back to the Pueblo Indian country.

Although it would be many decades before the peoples of the Great Plains were to meet other Europeans, the lives of these Native Americans would be dramatically changed with the arrival of a European import—the horse—in the 1690s. Even during the sixteenth century, though, European diseases penetrated far beyond the routes of the explorers and probably affected some of the Plains peoples through transmission along trading routes.

*Overleaf: Prior to the coming of the horse, most of the peoples of this area were semi-sedentary farmers who had lived along the few rivers for an extended period. The Eastern Shoshoni had only recently left the Plateau and the "Eastern Apache" wandered on foot the area from Wyoming to northern New Mexico, where they were preyed upon by the Jumano. The Navajo, too, were recent arrivals, but the date is still a matter of controversy.*

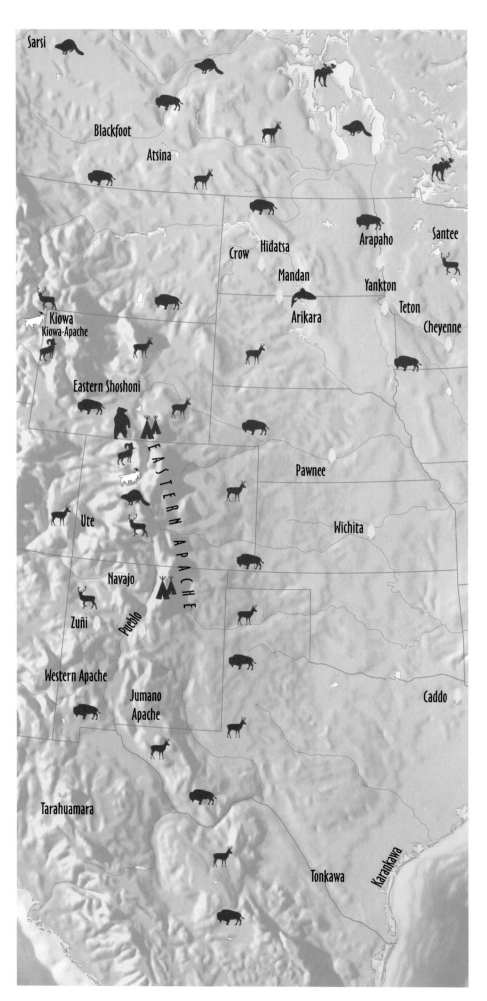

Sarsi

Blackfoot

Atsina

Crow   Hidatsa   Arapaho   Santee

Mandan   Yankton

Arikara   Teton

Kiowa   Cheyenne
Kiowa-Apache

Eastern Shoshoni

E A S T E R N   A P A C H E

Ute   Pawnee

Navajo   Wichita

Zuñi   Pueblo

Western Apache

Jumano   Caddo
Apache

Tarahuamara

Tonkawa   Karankawa

## THE SOUTHWEST

The Southwest cultural area differs from the other cultural regions considered here in that most of it lies in Mexico. Only its northern part lies in the United States—almost all of Arizona and New Mexico, as well as the borderlands of California, Nevada, Utah, Colorado, Oklahoma, and Texas. The terrain varies widely, from the rugged Mogollon Mountains of New Mexico to the desert land around the Gulfs of Mexico and California, from the deep canyons along the Colorado River to the vast tablelands throughout the region. Although the topography of the region is diversified, rainfall throughout the area is low, in most places less than twenty inches and often less than four inches annually. This low rainfall determines the area's vegetation—mainly western evergreen like pinyon or juniper at the better-watered high altitudes, and cactus, mesquite, and various desert shrubs in the lower, more arid regions.

Many of the Indians of this area were probably descended from peoples who had come up from Mexico, or who at least had been greatly influenced by Meso-American culture. These early inhabitants included the Anasazi, the Hohokam, and the Mogollon. The tribes living in the area in the sixteenth century can be divided into two main groups—one, more settled and agrarian peoples, and the other, nomadic and often more aggressive. In the region that is now the United States, the agrarian tribes included Pueblo peoples such as the Hopi, Zuñi, Keres, Tiwa, and Towa, and desert peoples such as the Hualapai, Havasupai, Mohave, Yuma, and Pima. The nomadic tribes included the widespread Apache and the Karankawa of southwestern Texas. The well-known Navajo arrived from the north only around AD 1000. They spoke a language closely related to those of the Athabascan Indians of Subarctic Canada. Initially nomadic, they soon settled down to farming and eventually (after European contact) to raising sheep.

Because their territories bordered *Nueva España*, the native peoples of the American Southwest soon felt the Spanish presence. The actual first contacts were unintended, made by Álvar Núñez Cabeza de Vaca and his companions, who included Estéban the Moor, when they journeyed across the Great Plains and into the Southwest (see previous section).

After spending a number of years in North America, Cabeza de Vaca and his companions arrived in Ciudad de Mexico in 1536. They recounted stories that they had been told of Indian cities of great wealth that lay to the north of the region they had crossed. Aroused by these reports, the Spanish viceroy in Mexico commissioned an exploratory expedition guided by Estéban the Moor and headed by a Franciscan priest, Marcos de Niza. As they moved northward toward the land of the Pueblo peoples—so named by the Spanish, with their word for "town"—Marcos did in fact begin to see products of the Pueblo Indians, including turquoise, blankets, and buffalo hides. Estéban, who had gone ahead, arrived in Zuñi territory near present-day Gallup, New Mexico. Feeling threatened by his arrogant behavior, the Indians killed him. Receiving word of this, Marcos apparently proceeded as far as the pueblo of Hawikuh south of Gallup and then turned back. In Ciudad de Mexico, Marcos told even grander tales of what he called the "Seven Cities of Cibola."

Encouraged by these tales, Francisco Vásquez de Coronado, governor of *Nueva Galicia*, a province of *Nueva España*, set out in 1540 with some 400 Spaniards and about 1,300 Indians.

For the next two years Coronado and his men searched throughout present-day Arizona and New Mexico. When Coronado came to the Zuñi villages near Gallup, New Mexico, he decided that they were the legendary Cibola, although he found no gold or other riches there. When Coronado attempted to impose Spanish rule over the Indians, the Zuñi of the Hawikuh pueblo attacked his group, but the Spanish soon defeated them and pushed northward.

During the following months, Coronado and his men overpowered all the Native Americans they encountered and forced them to accept Coronado's terms for peace. Also at this time, Coronado sent some of his men off on separate expeditions. One detachment visited the Pueblo Indians of Acoma and Pecos and also the villages at Taos, all in New Mexico. Another party went into the Zuñi villages of Arizona, and still another group went farther west and became the first Europeans to see the Grand Canyon. They did not descend to the floor of the canyon.

The Spanish chronicler Pedro de Castenada reported that the *"country of the terraced houses"* (pueblos) contained sixty-six villages which were distributed among thirteen different provinces. He listed the Indian names of the

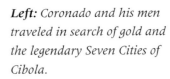

*Left: A traditional Pima basket.*

*Left: Coronado and his men traveled in search of gold and the legendary Seven Cities of Cibola.*

provinces as Cibola, Tusayan, Acuco (later known as "Acoma"), Tiguex, Tutahaco, Quirix, Ximena, Cicuye, Hemes, Aguas Calientes, and Yupueyungue. Castenada made a special study of the twelve villages of the province of Tiguex and observed:

*"They are governed by the opinions of the elders. They all work together to build the villages, the women being engaged in making the mixture and the walls, while the men bring the wood and put it in place....Before they are married the young men serve the whole village in general, and fetch the wood that is needed for use, putting it in a pile in the court-yard of the villages, from which the women take it to carry to their houses."*

Castenada went on to offer his theory that *"these people* [the Pueblo Indians], *since they are so few, and their manners, government, and habits are so different from all the nations that have been seen and discovered in these western regions, must come from that part of Greater India, the coast of which lies to the west of this country."* He was neither the first nor the last European to think this.

Relations between the Spanish party and native peoples deteriorated during the winter of 1540–41 as Coronado compelled the Indians

**Below:** *A Hopi ceremony at the sacred spring at Middle Mesa in present-day Arizona. Although this is a nineteenth-century photograph, such ceremonial and ritual practices among the settled Pueblo peoples have their roots dating back many centuries.*

to feed and shelter the Spanish force, which by then had grown to several thousand men. In the spring of 1541 Coronado set off in search of another reported golden land, Quivira. He led an expedition across northwestern Texas and onto the Great Plains in present-day Kansas. Failing to discover any gold or other riches, Coronado fell back to the pueblo country and, after spending another winter there, returned to Mexico in 1542.

During Coronado's absence, one of his lieutenants, Garcia Lopez de Cárdenas, allowed his men to commit all kinds of atrocities against the people of Tiguex Pueblo—stealing their food and clothing, raping their women, burning captives alive. Not surprisingly, the Tiguex fought back. When Coronado returned from the Great Plains, he joined Cárdenas in attacking the Tiguex settlements. After destroying the pueblos, he enslaved all surviving Tiguex, effectively wiping them out as a people. Although the Spanish authorities would accuse Coronado of mistreating the Indians, and Cárdenas would actually be tried and judged guilty of cruelty to them, an unfortunate pattern had been established: the Spaniards would

thenceforward use all force at their disposal to take and do whatever they wanted.

Coronado declared his expedition a success in that he had lost relatively few of his men. But it was also clear that the lands to the north of Mexico did not offer the riches for which the Spanish had so fervently hoped. The Spanish made no immediate moves to follow up on Coronado's expedition. Two small parties went north in 1581 and 1590, but neither led to any significant colonization.

The next major movement of Europeans into the Southwest was led by Juan de Oñate, who had been named governor and captain general of a new province there, which was to be called *Nueva Mexico.* A Spanish Basque, Oñate had married a woman who was both a granddaughter of Hernán Cortés and a great-granddaughter of Moctezoma. Because of both his marriage and lineage, Oñate has sometimes been called the "last conquistador."

Oñate set off for the pueblo country in January 1598 with 400 men, 130 families, 83 carts, and about 7,000 cattle. He was determined to establish his rule over an estimated 40,000 Indians. Arriving in the upper Rio Grande, he quickly seized any of the pueblos and all the food supplies he wanted. Many of his men unscrupulously attacked the natives, stealing their goods and raping the women. At the same time, a detachment under Juan de Zaldivar so

abused the people of the Acoma pueblo—often called the "sky city"—that they rose up and killed Zaldivar and twelve of his men.

Determined to punish the Acoma people, Oñate deployed his cannon against them and demolished the pueblo. Many natives were killed. Seventy men were captured and mutilated and were then placed in servitude along with some 500 women and children who had been seized. The Spanish reports noted that two Indians escaped from the massacre and were later seized and imprisoned. The unhappy captives barricaded themselves in their jail and reportedly called out:

*"Castilians, if you are not yet satisfied with the blood you have shed, and if you must still wreak your vengeance upon us, we will grant you this satisfaction. Send us two sharp daggers, and we will cut our throats and die here. We would prefer this rather than have it said that we died at the hands of such infamous dogs as you."*

Despite these hostilities, Oñate wrote glowing reports of his discoveries. More Spanish colonists began to appear in the upper Rio Grande, where they found conditions to be so bad that most of them abandoned the region and returned south to Mexico. As the century ended, the prospects for the Spanish in this region of the New World did not appear very promising. Prospects for the Native Americans here would prove to be much worse.

*Right:* *Beginning in the mid-sixteenth century, Spanish records often name any group that was not Puebloan "Apache." (Due to the large number of small locations important in this region, each map of it is limited primarily to those groups and locations discussed in the chapter in which it appears.)*

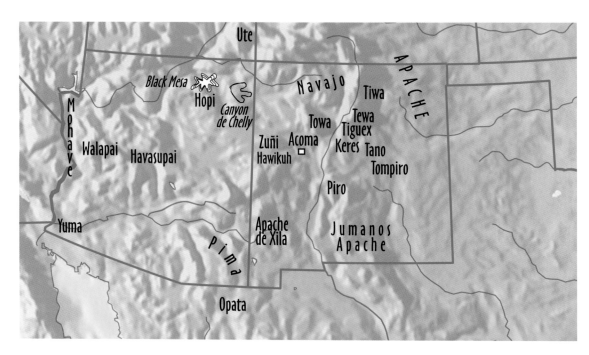

## CALIFORNIA

The California cultural area extends some fifteen hundred miles, covering most of the modern state of California down through the Mexican territory named Baja California. Mountains run along almost the entire area, close to the coast of California, and more to the center of Baja California. The northern region receives considerably more rainfall than the region south of Los Angeles. There are also more rivers in northern and central California.

In the 1500s a great variety of tribes speaking many different languages inhabited this area. The Yurok, Hupa, Wappo, Shasta, and Salina lived in the northern and central region; in the central area were such tribes as the Pantwin, Miwok, and Maidu; down in Baja California were tribes including the Akwa'ala, Nakipa, Cochimi, and Waicura. Given the extent of the area and its varied environments, there were inevitably considerable cultural differences among these peoples. Those to the north sometimes had lifestyles similar to those of their immediate neighbors, the Northwest Coast Indians; those to the east shared cultural traits with the peoples of the Columbia Plateau, the Great Basin, and the Southwest.

Virtually all the California peoples shared the plentiful and diverse plant and animal life that sustained a relatively dense population without the need for agriculture. They particularly depended on acorns, but they also gathered nuts, berries, fruits, tubers, and other wild plants. There were fish and shellfish and sea mammals; there were deer, elk, hare, quail, waterfowl, and other small game. This abundance made it possible for the many tribes across this area to thrive in relatively isolated villages, each group keeping much to itself. They had comparatively simple social structures and a basic material culture, with basketry among their finest achievements.

The appearance of several European expeditions surprised the California coastal peoples during the 1500s. The first known contact was probably made by Francisco de Ulloa, who cruised up the coast of southern California, perhaps as far as San Diego. Nothing is known of his dealings with the native people. In 1542 Juan Rodríguez Cabrillo led an expedition along the coast of California. On Catalina Island, the natives greeted Cabrillo and his party with singing and dancing. They proceeded on to visit the Chumash along the Santa Barbara Channel. The Spaniards reported many well-populated villages and noted their solid houses and well-made canoes and dugouts. It is believed that Cabrillo went as far north as Point Reyes, just north of San Francisco, and then sailed south to pass the winter near Santa Barbara, where he died, apparently from a wound that he had inflicted on himself while fighting Indians. Command of the expedition passed to a certain Ferrelo (or Ferrer), who sailed north again, possibly as far as Cape Mendocino, about 350 miles north of San Francisco, but none of this is known to have had any impact on the California peoples.

*Left: Miwok tribesmen hunting the plentiful deer in the vicinity of the village they called "Sagunte." Much later it would be called Mission Dolores, then Yerba Buena, and finally, San Francisco.*

The next recorded contact between the California peoples and Europeans occurred in 1579. The English mariner Sir Francis Drake sailed up along the coast of Baja California, then northwestward away from the coast before looping southeastward to make a landfall to the north of present-day San Francisco. Although his exact place of landing has never been determined, *"the fair and good bay"* to which he would later refer is generally agreed to be near what is today known as Drake's Bay.

Drake and some of his party went ashore and stayed from June 17 until July 23, 1579. The account they recorded of their contacts with the local Miwok was published in Richard Hakluyt's *The Principall Navigations* (London, 1589).

Soon after establishing a camp, the English received a group of natives led by the chief they called the King, *"a man of goodly stature & comely personage."* He was preceded by a scepter bearer, who *"began a song, observing his measures in a daunce, and that with a stately countenance, whom the King with his Garde, and every degree of persons following, did in like manner sing and daunce, saving onely the women, which daunced & kept silence."* The Indians proceeded to move among the Englishmen and performed bloody sacrifices by tearing at their own flesh, but the English tried to let them know they did not care for this practice. Later the Englishmen *"trevailed up into the Countrey to their villages, where wee found heardes of Deere by 1000 in a companie, being most large and fat of bodie."* They also falsely reported what so many of the early explorers had claimed and what their sponsors at home wanted to hear: *"There is no part of earth here to be taken up, wherein there is not a reasonable quantitie of gold or silver."*

The account states that the king and other leaders *"made several orations, or rather supplications, that* [Drake] *would take their province & kingdome into his hand and become their King, making signes that they would resign unto him their right and title of the whole land and become his subjects."* This seems likely to have been the Englishmen's interpretation of Indian offers of hospitality. In any case, before continuing his voyage around the world, Drake named the whole vast region Nova Albion and claimed it for England.

Ethnographers have only recently suggested that the Miwok probably believed Drake and his men to be people who had returned from the land of the dead. This belief would account for their acts of self-mutilation and their desire to please the European visitors. It would also explain one of the few key phrases of the Indian language that Drake and his men learned during their stay: *"Nocaro mu,"* which translated to *"touch me not."*

There were two more Spanish expeditions to the California coast during the sixteenth century—that of Pedro de Unamuno in 1587 and that of Sebastian Rodríguez Cirmenho (himself Portuguese) in 1590. Neither expedition had any known impact on the culture of the California Indians. All that lay well more than a century in the future.

*Right:* In this Edward Curtis photograph, a Klamath woman is gathering tules— a kind of bulrush— on Klamath Lake.

*Right:* In this Edward Curtis photograph, a Klamath woman is gathering tules— a kind of bulrush— on Klamath Lake.

## THE PLATEAU

The Plateau cultural area covers a territory of some 300,000 square miles, all of which is landlocked. It includes the southeastern corner of British Columbia, the northwestern corner of Montana, northern Idaho, eastern Washington, and an L-shaped strip extending across northeastern Oregon down through central Oregon and just barely reaching into northern California. On the east the area is flanked by the Rockies, and on the west by the Cascade Mountains; the area's northern limit is defined by forested hill country, while to the south it borders the desert of the Great Basin. Much of the area is a high plateau of largely treeless plains. Its distinguishing geographic features are its two major rivers, the Columbia and the Fraser, and their many tributaries.

Most of the more than two dozen tribes living in this area could be assigned to two language groups that were roughly divided at the Columbia River. Those to the south included the Klamath, Modoc, Numiipu (Nez Perce), Cayuse, Palouse, and Walla Walla; those to the north included the Sanpoil, Schitsu'Umish (Coeur d'Alene), Salish (Flathead), Spokane, Shuswap, and Lillooet. During the 1500s the plateau was sparsely inhabited. The people lived mostly along the banks of the many rivers, which supplied them with salmon—the main food source—as well as other fish like sturgeon and trout. Tubers, stem plants, and wild roots such as the camas were other important foods. Deer, elk, and antelope were also hunted.

The people who lived in this vast area differed in various ways; the Sanpoil of the central region, for instance, were a peaceful people, while the Klamath to the south were extremely aggressive. Yet all the Plateau peoples shared some cultural elements, such as earth lodges, root-gathering, and salmon fishing. In addition, they shared a religion based on the concept of guardian spirits and shamans, men and women who possessed the power to cure the sick and who also performed rites that appeared to give some control over events including hunting and the weather.

Because of their isolated and landlocked location, these peoples appear to have had no contact with white Europeans in the 1500s. But word traveled quickly among Native Americans, and it is likely that the Plateau peoples had

learned from their neighbors in the Northwest Coast and California regions that strange white people had begun to appear in unusual sea craft. Unlike most of the continent's native peoples, however, the Plateau Indians had another 200 years before these white people would begin to have any impact on their way of life, except for the fact that European diseases must have penetrated the region just as the rumors of "strange white people" had.

## THE GREAT BASIN

The Great Basin area, like the Plateau area to its north, is a completely landlocked region. Almost 500,000 square miles, it covers the southeastern part of Oregon, southern Idaho, practically all of Nevada and Utah, western Wyoming, western Colorado, a strip of eastern California, as well as small fringes of northern

Arizona and New Mexico. As its name suggests, it is a desert basin, almost entirely flanked by mountains; only its southwestern corner extends into more desert terrain. The mountains cut off much of the rainfall, and most of the water that drains down the mountain slopes into the basin disappears into "sinkholes." Many thousands of years ago there were numerous lakes here, but most of these had long since evaporated, leaving behind only a few with high salt content, the best known being Great Salt Lake, and some large alkaline flatlands.

Because of the limited rainfall, vegetation was relatively sparse, and the people who lived in this vast area obtained much of their food from whatever they could gather—seeds, grasses, berries, nuts, and roots. They also ate snakes, lizards, rodents, and insects. They hunted whatever small game they found—

rabbits, antelope, birds—and engaged in limited fishing. Because of the general sparseness of food sources, it is estimated that only about 30,000 people lived in the Great Basin at the opening of the sixteenth century.

Most of the inhabitants of this vast area belonged to three main groups—the Paiute, Shoshoni, and Ute. All these people spoke languages that belonged to the Uto-Aztecan family. As its name suggests, this family of languages is closely related to the language spoken by the Aztec, who by 1500 dominated the area of central and northern Mexico.

Because the Great Basin dwellers had to spend so much of their energy simply obtaining food, they had limited time for a relatively basic cultural life. Baskets were their most accomplished artefact, both in the aesthetic and technical sense. Among the favorite pastimes of the men were gambling with bone dice and betting on contests of skill. The people spent most of their lives in small family groups with little distinctive tribal identity. They were constantly moving about in search of sustenance. Among their few activities involving larger groups were periodic communal drives to capture antelope, rabbits, and even grasshoppers.

*Below: Colorful masks of the Northwestern peoples, painted with traditional designs featuring birds and animals.*

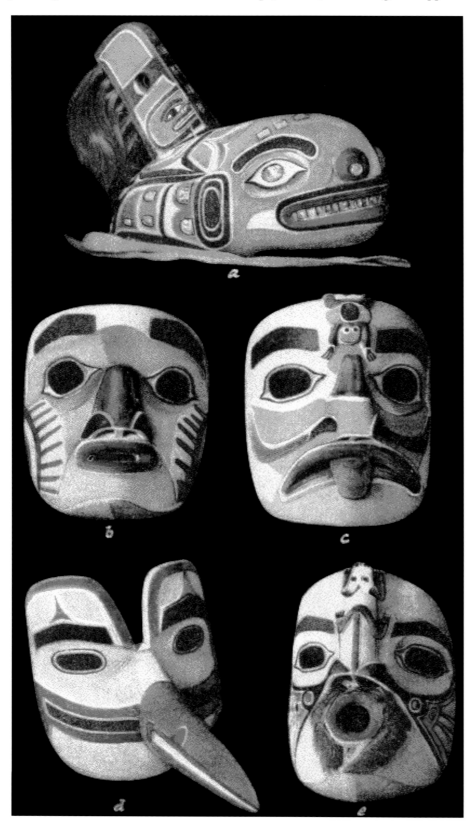

There is no record of any contacts between white Europeans and the Great Basin peoples in the 1500s, although tales about the Spanish who had entered the adjacent Southwest area, and probably diseases, may well have reached the Great Basin dwellers. As the 1600s dawned, it would be another two centuries before their way of life was drastically disturbed. Father Francisco Garcés would be the first European to enter the Great Basin—in 1775–76—as a Spanish missionary.

## THE NORTHWEST

This small but distinctive cultural area is a relatively narrow strip of coastal land, at its widest approximately 150 miles deep, extending some 2,000 miles from southern Alaska all the way to the northern boundary of California. A mountainous spine runs along most of this region, the mountains often dropping quite sharply to the sea. Countless inlets cut into the coastline and numerous islands lie along the shore. With many rivers and streams draining into the ocean, the inhabitants inevitably depended greatly on fishing, particularly on salmon. They also hunted whales and other sea mammals.

Because the Japanese Current warms the ocean here, the climate is more temperate than the latitude might suggest; this is also an extremely moist region with high rainfall that supports lush forests filled with birds and game. These forests also provided an inexhaustible supply of wood for houses, boats, and many other artefacts.

Thanks to these favorable environmental conditions, the region supported one of the densest concentrations of indigenous people in North America. It is estimated that some 200,000 people lived along the Northwest Coast at the beginning of the sixteenth century. Among others, they included the Tlingit, Haida, Eyda, Kwakiutl, Nootka, Coastal Salish, and Chinook. Blessed with a fertile environment, the peoples of the Northwest Coast maintained relatively complex and prosperous societies. They developed a unique institution known as the potlatch—a ritualized act of giving and the ceremonies surrounding it. By the time of European contact in later centuries, this cultural practice had developed into a complex ritual by which the status of adult males and their families was measured in the amount of material possessions they could give to others. The potlatch was usually associated with feasts at which men gave away both food and their possessions; in some tribes, the potlatch also involved songs, dances, and other rituals. Beyond its social functions, the potlatch was a way of distributing food and other possessions within a group.

The institution of the potlatch functioned within a more hierarchical society than was common among other North American tribes. There were distinct differences between chiefs, "nobles," and commoners; some tribes also maintained slaves—not only prisoners of war but even some of their own tribal members who had fallen into debt. The peoples of the Northwest Coast were also prone to aggression and engaged in warfare; some fought primarily to kill perceived enemies, others more to acquire slaves and various kinds of booty—in particular the distinctive dugout boats carved from cedar logs.

There is no record of contact between Europeans and the Indians of the Northwest Coast during the 1500s. These tribes went their way, undisturbed and unaware of what lay ahead in the centuries to come.

*Left:* A colorful carved and painted Kwakiutl mask.

*Left:* Traditional face painting of the warlike Tlingit, depicted here in a nineteenth-century Annual Report of the Bureau of American Ethnology.

## THE ARCTIC

At the beginning of the sixteenth century the people living across the Arctic region of North America were in many respects just as they would remain for the next four centuries. They called themselves Inuit, meaning simply "the people," but from the 1600s on they would become known to English-speakers as Eskimo. "Eskimo" was a word that Europeans took from the Algonquian name for this people, a word that means "raw meat eater." The Inuit territory extended some 4,000 miles from the coasts and islands of northwestern Alaska across the islands and shores of northernmost and northeastern Canada all the way to the coast of Greenland. In addition to sharing the same physical characteristics, which anthropologists designate as Mongoloid, they spoke closely related languages of the Inuit-Aleut family. (The Aleut, immediate relatives of the Inuit, lived on the long chain of islands extending west and south of Alaska and are regarded as Arctic Indians.) The Inuit population probably remained stable at about 75,000 during the 1500s.

Although all Inuit shared much of the same culture, various groups would eventually be assigned names that reflected their geographic locales, such as North Alaskan Eskimo, or Mackenzie Eskimo (of the Yukon region), or Labrador Eskimo. One major cultural difference, however, was in their form of dwellings. Although many of those who lived in the central region of northern Canada used igloos made of snow blocks, those in the far west and far east tended to live in ground level or semi-submerged houses made of various combinations of wood, sod, turf, or stone. Most Inuit groups depended on their dogs and fished and hunted, but whereas some almost exclusively fished and hunted sea mammals like whales, seals, and walrus, others depended more on land mammals including bear and caribou. One group known as the Caribou Eskimo were an inland people who lived west of the Hudson Bay and depended almost exclusively on caribou and freshwater fish. Another special group lived in the Coronation Gulf region of Canada (near Victoria Island) and came to be known as the Copper Eskimo. These Inuit gathered copper nuggets found on the ground and hammered them unsmelted into tools.

Throughout the 1500s very few Inuit had any direct contact with Europeans, and Inuit culture and lifeways remained essentially unchanged. The exceptions were just that—brief, isolated incidents. Some Norwegian and Danish fishermen probably had some dealings with the Inuit of Greenland and northeastern Canada. Other exceptional encounters arose from the three voyages of English mariner Martin Frobisher in 1576–78 in search of a "northwest passage" to the Pacific. While sailing around Baffin Island, Frobisher occasionally came into contact with the Inuit of the Nugumiut tribe, with whom he traded and sometimes skirmished. Frobisher was once struck by an iron-tipped Inuit arrow, proof that these Inuit had had contact with other Europeans. Frobisher brought four Inuit back to England, where they soon died.

During the expedition, the English artist John White painted the first depiction of Inuit people, faithfully showing their kayaks and clothing. For their part, the Inuit of the area they called Tin-nu-jok-ping-oo-se-ong—the English called it Frobisher's Strait—preserved some mementoes such as red bricks and brass rings. They also created a vivid and unfavorable impression of Frobisher in their oral history, which would be reported to an American Arctic explorer in 1861.

Other exceptional contacts occurred between the Inuit and the Portuguese, Basque, and French fishermen and whalers who began to

*Below: A sketch depicting the traditional igloo, dwellings made by the Central Inuit peoples of the Canadian Arctic.*

appear in the waters off northeastern Canada during the first years of the sixteenth century. The Europeans had far more advanced ships and certain technologies—guns and gunpowder chief among them—but the Inuit had superior tools and skills for deep-sea whaling. There was also some trading, as the Inuit had furs and sealskins greatly desired by Europeans, while the Europeans had metal wares, glass beads, and other articles valued by the Inuit. Although this trade did not immediately transform the Inuit way of life, they did initiate a relationship that would slowly develop between the Inuit and Europeans.

## THE SUBARCTIC

The various tribes in the Subarctic culture area inhabited a vast region that stretches from Alaska across much of Canada all the way to Newfoundland. Some lived along the Cook Inlet coast of Alaska, others along the Hudson Bay, some along the Gulf of St. Lawrence, and some along the shores of Newfoundland. Most, however, inhabited the interior territory marked by rivers, streams, lakes, ponds, swamps, and bogs. Although there are some mountains, particularly in the western reaches, it is for the most part flat or gently rolling terrain. The area is covered mainly with coniferous trees (pine, spruce, fir) mixed with some birch, aspen, and willow.

The many Subarctic tribes have been assigned to two main groups on the basis of their languages, with the dividing line approximately at the Churchill River, which runs southwest from the Hudson Bay. Those to the west belonged to the Athabaskan group and include such tribes as the Ahtena, Beaver, Chipewyan, Hare, Ingalik, Kutchin, Tagish, and Yellowknife. Those to the east belonged to the Algonquian group and included the Cree, Montagnais, Naskapi, and Northern Ojibwa, among others. The Beothuk of Newfoundland are regarded as an exception, for their language appears unrelated to the other two groups.

In the early 1500s, the native people of this vast region were few in number, perhaps no more than 150,000, living for the most part in small, scattered settlements. They relied on fishing and hunting for most of their food—large game such as caribou and moose, small game such as beaver, mink, and hare. Wherever possible they also foraged for plants. A few, such as the Montagnais and the Kutchin, may even have practiced some basic agriculture, or at least encouraged wild plants that were native to their area. Those who relied on caribou were seasonally nomadic, for they had to follow the caribou as they migrated back and forth between the taiga (forest) and tundra. All of these people used the fur and hides of various mammals for clothing.

These furs would become the main point of interaction between the people of the Subarctic and the Europeans during the later 1500s. The first contacts, however, occurred between the Indians and the European fishermen and whalers who began to operate off the northeast coast of Canada during the early 1500s. Spanish Basques had set up a large whaling station at Red Bay in Labrador by around 1543. The Basques hunted both bowhead and right whales almost to extinction.

English, French, and Portuguese fishermen soon followed these fishermen to the continent. By the end of the 1500s, a steady stream of Europeans came to take whales and walrus, cod and many other species of fish along the North American coast. But the most influential contact began when Jacques Cartier of France sailed up the Hochelaga River—which he renamed the St. Laurent—on his three voyages between 1534 and 1542. Although most of his contacts were with Laurentian Iroquois, Cartier also met some Subarctic peoples, particularly the Montagnais. These latter people instantly grasped the advantages of trading with Europeans, and by around 1560 the Montagnais had established a trading center at Tadoussac, located at the mouth of the Saguenay River on the Gulf of St. Lawrence. Tadoussac prospered as hundreds of European ships put in each summer to exchange European goods for furs. It was this trade, specifically with the French, that in the next century would have the greatest impact on the lifeways of Subarctic peoples.

*Left: Inuit snow goggles, used to protect the eyes and face from snow blindness and the harsh elements.*

55

Aleut
Pacific Inuit
Bering Sea Inuit
North Alaska Inuit
Tanaina
Tanana
Kutchin
Mackenzie Inuit
Hare
Copper Inuit
Central Inuit
Polar Inuit
West Greenland Inuit
East Greenland Inuit
Baffin Island Inuit
Eyak
Tutchone
Kaska
Dogrib
Yellowknife
Caribou Inuit
Labrador Inuit
Tlingit
Etchareottine
Beaver
Chipewyan
Montagnais
Naskapi
Beothuk
Haida
Tsimshian
Nootka
Kwakiutl
Sarsi
Cree
Cree
Tadoussac
Stadacona
Micmac
Chinook
Kutenai
Blackfoot
Atsina
Assiniboine
Arapaho
Ojibwa
Ojibwa
Algonquian
Abenaki
Yakima
Nez Perce
Salish
Hidatsa
Mandan
Arikara
Santee
Menominee
Ottawa
Hochelaga
Cayuse
Crow
Yankton
Teton
Cheyenne
Chiwere
Potowatomi?
Sauk?
Fox?
Huron
Iroquois
Shawmut
Patuxet
Pequot
Klamath
Modoc
Bannock
N. Shoshoni
Kiowa
E. Shoshoni
Miami
Illinois
Kickapoo
Neutral
Erie
Delaware
Manahata
Hupa
Pomo
Miwok
Ute
Pawnee
Dhegiha
Shawnee
Tutelo
Powhatan
Paspahegh
Yokuts
S. Paiute
Navajo
Wichita
Yuchi
Cherokee
Catawba
Tuscarora
Dasemunkapeuc
Chumash
Hopi
Zuñi
Pueblo
E. Apache
W. Apache
Jumano
Caddo
Chickasaw
Creek
Confed-
eracy
Yuma
Pima
Natchez
Choctaw
Timucua
Tarahuamara
Achusi
Calusa
Tonkawa
Aztec
Maya

# Accommodation, Exchange, and Warfare

## 1600–1700

During the sixteenth century, most peoples of North America had remained relatively undisturbed by the incursions of explorers to the New World. Foreign disease and hostile encounters with the visitors had blighted and ended lives, but most knew little or nothing of these matters: across the continent, they continued to follow the lifeways handed down through countless earlier generations. In the new century, however, change would affect many more people—and the change would prove permanent.

### THE NORTHEAST

At the beginning of the seventeenth century the many tribes of the Northeast region had little sense of impending change. With the exception of the Iroquois League formed in the late 1500s, the tribes had continued their regular modes of life, which had developed over hundreds of years. The Micmac continued to rely on fishing; the Narraganset, Pequot, and others drew sustenance from fishing, hunting, and horticulture. Maple sap was gathered every spring and boiled into sugar. All the materials necessary to make weapons and utensils could be found in the great forests that spread west from Virginia to the Mississippi valley and north to Maine and southeastern Canada.

Native American independence was soon imperiled by the arrival of several groups of Europeans. To the St. Lawrence region came the French, while English settlers arrived in present-day Massachusetts, Connecticut, and Rhode Island. Dutch merchants colonized a narrow body of land along the Hudson River, and Swedish settlers occupied land in what is now Delaware. From such small beginnings, these European groups established what became known as "Nouvelle France" (New France), "New England," "Nieuw Nederlandsch" (the New Netherlands), and "Nye Swerige" (New Sweden), respectively.

Explorers and founders including Samuel de Champlain, Captain John Smith, Henry

*Opposite: The continent in 1600.*

*Below: Samuel de Champlain founded Quebec at a narrow point on the St. Lawrence River on the site of the former Laurentian Iroquois town of Stadacona.*

*Above: Champlain's* habitation *at Quebec was well designed to meet the harsh conditions of the severe Canadian winter.*

Between 1603 and 1616 Champlain made at least seven voyages of exploration to the Northeast. He discovered many rivers and lakes, including Lac St. Louis (Lake Ontario), Lac des Hurons (Lake Huron) and Lac Champlain (Lake Champlain). In 1608 he founded Quebec on the site of the Indian village of Stadacona. This settlement became the capital of Nouvelle France. Champlain was eager to find a route through the continent to Asia, and he was paid to promote French trade.

Champlain learned that French knowledge of the St. Lawrence area was out of date. When Jacques Cartier had visited there in 1535, he had met Laurentian Iroquois who lived at Stadacona and Hochelaga as well as numerous smaller villages. Champlain found no trace of the Laurentian Iroquois. The area was dominated instead by the Montagnais on the north bank of the St. Lawrence. The disappearance of the Laurentian Indians is a mystery that remains unresolved. It is possible that they succumbed to European diseases introduced by Cartier and his men, but it is also conceivable that they were wiped out in an Indian war.

A skilled sailor and cartographer, Champlain accurately mapped the Atlantic coast from the Bay of Fundy to Cape Cod. He also strove to cement alliances with Algonquian tribes and the Huron against the growing—and brutal—strength of the great Iroquois League. In 1609 he routed a party of Iroquois on behalf of his Algonquian allies in a battle fought at the head of Lake Champlain. Believed to be the first time that firearms were

Hudson, and Peter Minuit led the way. European companies in search of wealth followed them. These early arrivals did not find North America's gold, but the companies found a substitute in what became a lucrative trade in beaver pelts and other furs and in fish and game.

Nouvelle France was the first important European colony to be established on the vast North American continent. In 1603 Samuel de Champlain claimed for France territory that was home to the Algonquian tribes of the Great Lakes, including the Ottawa and Ojibwa; the Maritimes, home to the Abenaki, Penobscot, and Micmac, among others; and the Subarctic, inhabited mainly by the Cree and Montagnais. The French claim included the St. Lawrence River valley and the Great Lakes.

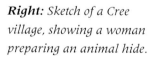

*Right: Sketch of a Cree village, showing a woman preparing an animal hide.*

used against the Iroquois, the battle ignited animosity between them and the French that would last for as long as 150 years.

The military and political presence of the Iroquois League formed late in the previous century was the key to the balance of power in the Northeast. Made up of five tribes—the Cayuga, Mohawk, Onondaga, Oneida, and Seneca—the confederation was an unusual arrangement in native North America. The Iroquois confederacy abolished capital punishment and provided for the welfare of all members of the five tribes—men, women, and children. It also mandated women's rights, and its later constitution would specify: *"The lineal descent of the people of the five Nations shall run in the female line. Women shall be considered the progenitors of the Nation. They shall own the land and the soil."*

Champlain's hostility towards the Iroquois was the result of their interference with his flourishing fur-trade network. His indigenous allies, the Huron and Algonquian, were essential middlemen in the fur trade, without whom success and wealth would have been impossible to achieve. In exchange for guns, knives, axes, and liquor, the Indians traded beaver pelts and other prized furs.

Champlain was also one of the few explorers who strongly supported the efforts of Jesuit priests in the area. The Jesuits were excellent allies for the traders. They carried out their work with respect for the peoples they sought to convert. The Jesuits learned the native languages and used local imagery and metaphor in order to encourage them to make the leap to Christianity. Understanding that confrontation was not practical, the Jesuits attempted to remain relatively tolerant of local cultures and customs, as long as they did not conflict with Christian dogma.

Tensions soon developed, however, between even the most hospitable native people and the settlers and priests in Nouvelle France. Smallpox broke out in devastating waves in the 1620s, 1630s, and 1640s among the peoples of the Saint Laurence region. Although some of the missionaries themselves died from it, many of the Huron blamed the disease on the Jesuit priests, believing it to be the result of sorcery the missionaries were practicing against them. The priests were never entirely safe from such accusations, although the Huron

were in general accommodating people. The Mother Superior in charge of a hospital that was established in 1639 observed: *"The patience of our sick astonishes me. I have seen many whose bodies are entirely covered with smallpox, and in a burning fever, complaining no more than if they were not sick, strictly obeying the physician, and showing gratitude for the slightest service rendered them."*

If the local people had some reason to believe that new suffering had come with the new religion, they also began to question its teachings.

In spite of the efforts of the Jesuits to promote peace, economic greed brought upheaval even to the remote areas of Nouvelle France. The Beaver Wars were precipitated by the overtrapping of beaver. The aggressive Iroquois began pushing north and west into Huron territory searching for pelts for their allies, who at that time were the Dutch. The Iroquois

*Above:* Warfare among the different native nations of Lower Canada was fueled by two major causes: religious conflict and competition for the beaver trade.

*Below:* The diseases brought by the Europeans were devastating to the indigenous peoples. Here the Florentine Codex depicts the agonizing experience of Mesoamericans dying of smallpox, to which they had no immunity. The disease decimated native nations across the continent.

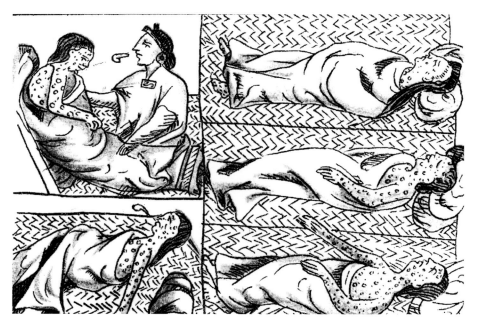

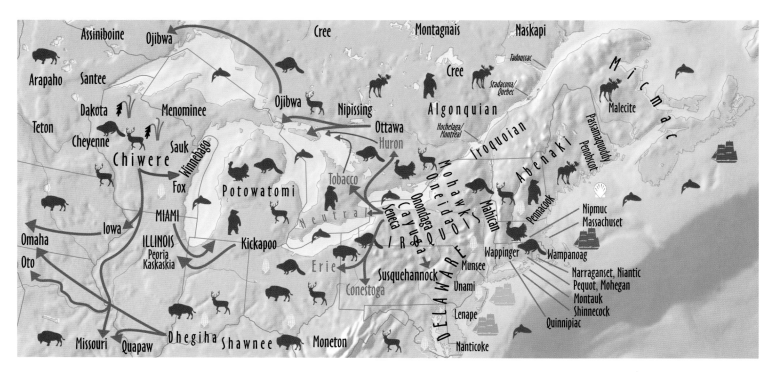

terrorized the southern and western regions of Nouvelle France. The league then turned on the Indian allies of the French and ultimately destroyed entire tribes. The Huron were foremost among these; the Iroquois attacked them savagely in 1648–49. The Huron were then driven out of their territory and many committed suicide rather than allow the Iroquois to torture them. Some Huron fled westward and became known as the Wyandot.

Although missionary work practically ceased in Iroquoian areas, neither ridicule, superstition, torture, nor martyrdom could check the zealous Jesuits in their pursuit of converts. By the end of the 1600s the Jesuits could be found from the mouth of the St. Lawrence all the way to Wisconsin. In 1650 Father Paul Ragueneau wrote:

*"When I ascended the great River [St. Lawrence], only thirteen years ago, I had seen it bordered with large numbers of people of the Algonquian tongue, who knew no God. These, in the midst of their unbelief, looked upon themselves as the Gods of the earth, for the reason that nothing was lacking to them in the richness of their fisheries, their hunting-grounds, and the traffic which they carried on with allied nations;...Since they have embraced the faith, and adored the Cross of Jesus Christ, he has given them as their lot, a portion of that Cross, verily, a heavy one, having made them a prey to miseries, torments, and cruel deaths; in a word, they are a people wiped off from the face of the earth."*

It appears that the Native American peoples had little idea that the priests, traders, and settlers who continued to infiltrate the landscape would so drastically alter their culture. In many ways, they seemed more amused than threatened by the inept and demanding lifestyles of their white counterparts. A member of the Micmac tribe pointed out to a Frenchman:

*Opposite, above:* European colonies taxed coastal resources, starving nearby peoples, and brought diseases that decimated Northeastern nations. Prompted by the Hudson River fur trade, the Iroquois sought new fur-hunting territory by annihilating neighboring nations, forcing the Ottawa, Nipissing, and the surviving Huron and Tobacco westward. The migrations of the Kickapoo, Chiwere, and the Dhegiha all began around the time of the Iroquois massacre of the Erie in 1654.

*"I am greatly astonished that the French have so little cleverness….Why risk thy life and thy property every year, and why venture thyself with such risk, in any season whatsoever, to the storms and tempests of the sea in order to come to a strange and barbarous country which thou considerest the poorest and least fortunate of the world?…As to us, we find all our riches and all our conveniences among ourselves…: there is no Indian who does not consider himself infinitely more happy and more powerful than the French."*

*Left and opposite, below:* Iroquois corn-husk False Face dancers from what is now central New York State.

"New England" was the second European colony created in the Northeast region. It began on the coast of present-day Massachusetts. Captain John Smith, who had played an important role in the founding of the Virginia colony, mapped and charted much of the coast in 1614. He marked in particular a secluded harbor that Champlain had seen in 1605—Champlain had called the harbor Cap St. Louis; Smith named it Plimoth. Situated there was the native town of Patuxet, which had around 2,000 inhabitants at the time of Champlain's visit.

In 1620 a small band of English nonconformists who were known as the Pilgrims organized an unchartered joint-stock company financed by a group of businessmen. They sailed on the *Mayflower* and arrived off Patuxet in December. They discovered a deserted town surrounded by corn fields that had been left fallow for several years. Only later did the Pilgrims learn that a deadly pestilence—believed to be an epidemic of bubonic plague—had swept through the coastal towns of the area in 1617, leaving as many as 90 percent of the inhabitants dead. This area had been occupied by roughly 3,000 Massachuset living in twenty coastal villages, until the epidemic virtually wiped out the tribe (most of the surviving Massachuset succumbed to an outbreak of smallpox in 1633). The plague had most likely been caused by contact between the local villagers and European fishermen, or perhaps explorers in the parties of Champlain and Smith. It is also claimed that the bubonic plague epidemic in Florida of 1613–17 had spread northward as far as New England.

The misfortune of the natives was seen as a boon to the settlers, who took over the deserted town and the cleared farmland surrounding it. Even so, the settlers were unprepared for the harsh winter and were unskilled in the food-gathering techniques necessary for survival. Half the Pilgrims perished during the first winter. More would have starved had it not been for a stranger who appeared in March 1621 to help them: He is known as Tisquantum, or Squanto.

There were few more widely traveled persons at the time—either Native American or European—than Squanto. In 1614 an English slaver, Thomas Hunt, had treacherously kidnapped him from his home of Patuxet—then still the prosperous town of around 2,000 people that Champlain had seen—and sold him into slavery in Malaga, Spain. Due to the intervention of some friars, he was freed. Squanto somehow made his way to England. He found work with John Slany, the treasurer of the Newfoundland Company. He then traveled to Newfoundland and back, and later had an opportunity to go to New England as a guide for another captain. It was then that he returned to his home of Patuxet and discovered that not only his family but his entire village had been wiped out. When the Pilgrims arrived, Squanto offered to help them; he continued to do so until his death in 1624.

Another true friend to the Pilgrims was Wasamegin— meaning "Yellow Feather." He is better known as Massasoit—the grand sachem of the Wampanoag. Massasoit and the English settlers, most notably the well-educated and ironic Winslow, remained friends even after repeated English violations of Wampanoag territory and liberties.

The Wampanoag lived in what is now Massachusetts and Rhode Island. They were both farmers and fishermen. At the time of the arrival of the Pilgrims in 1620, Wasamegin faced a

*Right: Iroquois chieftains were known for their oratorical skill, as well as their fighting ability.*

new and difficult situation. Between 1616 and 1618, disease introduced by the white traders had wiped out many of his people. In addition, the Wampanoag had been feuding with the neighboring Narraganset over trading rights in the Narragansett Bay area; the Narraganset— from the Narragansett Bay in what is now known as Rhode Island—had prevailed.

Wasamegin regarded the newly arrived Pilgrims as his potential allies against the Narraganset, who understandably resented Wasamegin's friendship with the English settlers. The Narraganset captured Wasamegin in 1621, but the English demanded his release. The Narraganset sachem Canonicus backed down and set him free. This initial incident taught the English that they could play the Native Americans against each other—and they would continue to do so.

The Pilgrims were followed in 1629 by the Puritans, another group of English separatists. The Puritans came ashore at Naumkeag, which they soon renamed Salem. Looking for a more promising site and a better harbor, they moved southward to a peninsula known locally as Shawmut. The new settlement, which they named Boston, soon became the capital of the Puritan enclave. The Puritans made few efforts to convert Native Americans to Christianity. Minister John Eliot was an important exception. He prepared an Indian catechism, translated the Bible into Algonquian—it was the first Bible to be published in North America—and wrote an Indian grammar and primer. Eliot also created "villages" in which the native people could learn to be more "civilized." In these "praying villages" they were forced to wear uncomfortable European-style clothing, to eat only with European utensils, and to devote themselves to learning their catechism for hours on end.

The Pekawatawo (Pequot), meaning "the destroyers," were the first major casualties of the Puritan migration inland. They lived on the western boundary of Narraganset land in what is now called Connecticut—named after the

Iroquois word for the river there. The Narraganset had repulsed an earlier invasion of Pequot that had taken place while the Narraganset were busy subduing the Wampanoag. But they were thoroughly routed, and no further hostile encounters occurred between the tribes until the 1630s. For many years the Pequot and Narraganset had been trading courteously with the Dutch, who had not settled in their territory, but were merely interested in trading. As the English presence dramatically expanded, however, the Dutch influence declined.

By 1635 English settlement was approaching the boundaries of Pequot territory. Some alert Pequot leaders became aware of how the English had incited war among the tribes of Massachusetts. Roger Williams, who earlier had been expelled from the Massachusetts Bay colony for advocating separation of church and state, was one of the few friends to the Indians. Williams worked tirelessly to promote alliances among tribes as well as between natives and white settlers. He learned to speak Algonquian and wrote the *Key to the Indian Languages* in 1643. He also wholly respected Indian territorial claims. But when the deaths of two scurrilous English traders, Captain John Stone and John Oldham, were blamed on the Pequot, hostilities began to escalate out of control. Even Roger Williams's attempts to mediate on behalf of the natives failed.

In 1637 the Narraganset were forced to choose between two adversaries: the Pequot and the English Puritans. The Pequot urged an alliance among Native Americans, but the Narraganset refused and decided instead to cast their lot with the English.

The Pequot War of 1636–37 was the first major war between Europeans and Native Americans in the Northeast. The ferocity of the European style of fighting dismayed the native people, who had no previous experience of this new kind of barbarism. As a Lenape leader explained to an English colonist in the mid-seventeenth century:

*"We are minded to live at Peace: If we intend at any time to make War upon you, we will let you know of it, and the Reasons why we make War with you; and if you make us satisfaction for the Injury done us for which the War is intended then we will not make War on you. And if you intend at any time*

*to make War on us, we would have you let us know of it, and the Reasons for which you make War on us, and then if we do not make satisfaction for the Injury done unto you, then you may make War on us, otherwise you ought not to do it."*

Some English chroniclers expressed disgust at what they perceived as the natives' *"feeble manner…[that] did hardly deserve the name of fighting."* Apparently, when they fought, there was a lot of noise and leaping and arrows flying, but very few deaths. *"When a man is wounded…they soone retire and save the wounded."*

But this was not the case with the English style of fighting, as the Pequot soon discovered. Only rarely were prisoners taken during the

**Left:** *Dedicated totally to their calling, French missionaries risked torture and death to evangelize the tribes along the Great Lakes.*

**Overleaf:** *This 1675 "Mapp of New England" shows the natural resources of the region and the territories controlled by various native nations, as well as English coastal settlements and incursions inland. Two years later, the reference to "King Phillips Country" would disappear from English maps. Dutch settlements along the Hudson River are shown at left, but there is no reference to the Delaware and other peoples with whom the Dutch traded.*

**Below:** *Missionaries traveled great distances into the interior by canoe and dog-sled.*

The manner of the Indian Fortifications
Town Houses and Dwelling places

A Mapp
of
New ENGLAND
by
John Seller Hydrographer
To the King
And are to bee Sold at his
Shop at the Hermitage in Wappin
And by John Hills
In Exchange Alley in Cornhill
London

Ornat.mo Prudent.moq. Domino
ROBERTO THOMSON
Armigero
Hanc Novæ Angliæ Tabulam
D.D.D. Johannes Seller.

Poanntack

N

E

N

W

Connecticut River

C O N E C T I

Hadley

Nope Isle

Whales Isle

New Albanie
Fishers point
Isle Beares

North Hampton

C

Kates kill

East reach

C U T

Cheeapie River

Dearsfield
Springfield

Bakers reach

E

N

G

Winser
Hartford

Moricans or
Pistol Point
The Straights

Raulph Johnstons kill
Vls Isle

Magdalens Isle
Shystons

C O L O N Y

Wethersfield
Midletown

P

Ninicrofts

Great Espouck

The Conecticuts

Country

little Espouck

The Waoranack Country

Norwich
Country

Tames kantes
Keyes Isle
Seppinos kill

L

A

N

Narat shoe

The Mouhegans Country

Narraganset
Guilford
Saybrook
New London

Fishers reach
hook
high reach
cooks reach

H U D S O N S   R I V E R

Allamanuck
Alphacken
Mechalteck
Seach kill
Wellgate

Greenwich
Stanford
Norwalk
Chichister
Stanfield

Shatford
Milford
New Hewen
Branford
Guilford

Fishers Isle

Salmakatperach

West Chester
Freedland

N

Archpelago

T h e

S o u n d s

New Yorke

Manhatton

Plumb Isle

attacks, and then just a few girls who could be sold as slaves. The decisive and deadly assault on the principal Pequot village was carried out as a pre-dawn surprise attack. All the inhabitants were killed: women, children, grandparents, and infants. William Bradford, who was not present at the battle, described the English reaction to the carnage as follows:

*"It was a fearful sight to see them thus frying in the fire and the streams of blood quenching the same, and horrible was the stink and stench thereof; but the victory seemed a sweet sacrifice, and they gave the praise thereof to God…*[who gave] *them so speedy a victory."*

Even the Narraganset, who had been persuaded to fight alongside the English, recoiled in horror during this ferocious attack and refused to take part in it. The English afterwards chided the Narraganset for this reaction, calling them cowards and traitors.

After their raid on the principal Pequot village, the English settlers continued to attack the dispossessed and starving Pequot indiscriminately, destroying the Pequot as a fighting force and putting their villages to flames. What was later vaingloriously titled the "Pequot War" came to a halt only when the English were satisfied that almost the entire Pequot tribe had been annihilated. The year was 1637.

From an estimated population of 2,200 in the early 1600s, around one-third were killed in the war and almost all survivors were taken captive, many sold into slavery. The last few survivors dispersed. Three-and-a-half centuries would pass before the Pequot resurfaced. The word "Pequot" was eliminated from the map, the name of the Pequot River was changed to the "Thames," and the village of Pequot was renamed "New London." As allies of the Pequot, the Niantic were also destroyed during the Pequot War; the survivors fled and settled with the Narraganset.

Betrayals and misunderstandings between Native Americans and English settlers continued while English governors and soldiers applied all their diplomatic skills to set the natives off against each other. The English were masters at fomenting hostilities among their rivals, which deflected the general, pervasive threat against themselves. Thus the Narraganset domain was steadily reduced. The Niantic sachem Ninigret (Janemo), in the meantime, became increasingly independent of the Narraganset co-sachems, Canonicus and Miantonomi, Canonicus's more vigilant nephew. Worried about the English encroachment, Miantonomi had begun taking over leadership of the Narraganset from his peace-loving uncle.

In 1638 the English of Massachusetts and Connecticut signed the Hartford treaty with the Narraganset and Mohegan. The agreement obligated the tribes to refer any dispute between themselves to the English, whose decision would be binding. Miantonomi was unhappy with the treaty. In 1642 he visited a Montauk tribe located in eastern Long Island and spoke of the need for Indian unification and resistance: *"For so are we all Indians as the English are* [all one people]. *And say brother to one another, So must we be one as they are. Otherwise we shall all be gone shortly, for you know our fathers had plenty of deer and skins, our plains were full of deer, as also our woods, and of turkeys, and our coves full of fish and fowl. But these English have gotten our land. They with scythes cut down the grass and with axes fell the trees. Their cows and horses eat the grass and their hogs spoil our clam banks and we shall all be starved."*

In 1643 the Mohegan routed Miantonomi and a band of Narraganset in a skirmish. An Englishman had loaned a heavy suit of armor to Miantonomi, supposedly to protect him in battle. Hampered by the heavy armor, Miantonomi was unable to escape. He was captured and killed by the Mohegan upon orders of his former allies, the United Colonies of New England. The Narraganset presence in the area was thus effectively diminished.

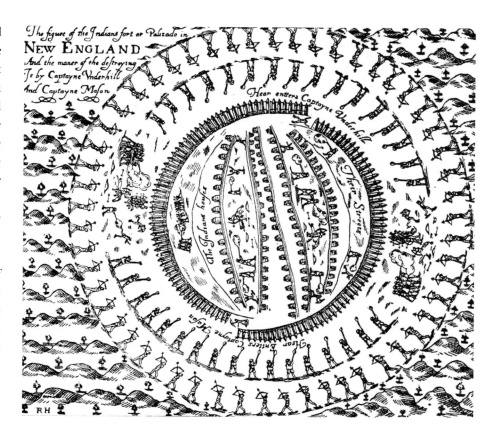

The death in 1661 of Massasoit, the peace-loving grand sachem of the Wampanoag, opened the door to large-scale conflict. Massasoit's second son Metacomet—"King Philip"—took over leadership of the Wampanoag. He was dismayed by the loss of his people's land to the English and also by the

*Below: One of many bloody battles fought between Metacomet's warriors and the English forces during 1675.*

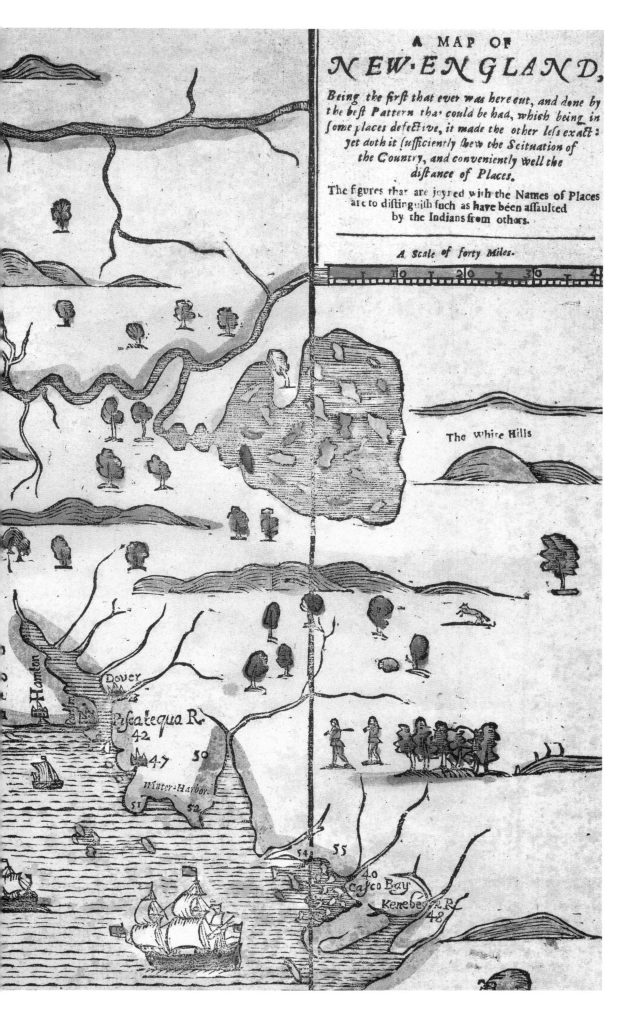

A MAP OF
NEW-ENGLAND,

*Being the first that ever was here cut, and done by
the best Pattern that could be had, which being in
some places defective, it made the other less exact:
yet doth it sufficiently shew the Scituation of
the Country, and conveniently well the
distance of Places.*

*The figures that are joyned with the Names of Places
are to distinguish such as have been assaulted
by the Indians from others.*

*A Scale of forty Miles.*

The White Hills

Hamton

Dover

Piscatequa R.
42

47    50

Winter-Harbor.
51    52

55

40
Casco Bay
Kenebegk R.
48

**Left:** *This "Map of New England" is a woodcut originally made to accompany William Hubbard's treatise on King Philip's War,* Narrative of the Troubles with the Indians in New England, *published in Boston in 1677. Rotated 90° from the now-familiar orientation so that North is to the right, it shows territories held by the coastal Algonquian nations like the Narraganset and Puritan towns including Springfield and New London (built on the site of a Pequot village). The Connecticut River is drawn to scale, but the size of the Merrimack River is exaggerated.*

*Above: Metacomet, a brave and inspiring leader, was among the first to seek a confederacy of tribes as a means of resisting the Europeans.*

apparently insatiable demands of the English settlers for more territory. By 1675 the English population in New England had risen to around 35,000, while the native population had declined dramatically. The Pequot War had accounted for perhaps 1,000 deaths, and the total number of other deaths in combat is not known, but disease had wiped out far greater numbers: aside from the 1617 plague, there were epidemics of measles and smallpox in 1633; scarlet fever in 1637; further outbreaks of smallpox in 1649, 1662, and 1669; measles in 1658; influenza in 1647 and 1675; and diphtheria in 1659. The extent of the human death toll from these epidemics is not known, but the population had probably declined to one-third or less of what it had been in 1600.

It remains unclear whether Metacomet deliberately planned the fighting that became "King Philip's War" or whether it was forced upon him by the actions of the Massachusetts settlers. Open hostilities broke out between Metacomet's warriors and the English settlers in the summer of 1675. Metacomet sheltered the Wampanoag women and children in a Narraganset fort near what is now South Kingston, Rhode Island. The allied tribes then wiped out the frontier towns of Swansea, Medfield, Groton, Lancaster, and Brookfield, and continued westward.

The war spread rapidly and became the most destructive in the history of New England. Hundreds of colonists were killed, their villages destroyed, and their farms burned. *"Know by*

*this paper that the Indians that thou has provoked to wrath and anger will war these twenty-one years, if you will,"* read a note left by a kidnapped Indian boy in Medfield, Massachusetts. He ran away to join Metacomet when the war began. *"There are many Indians yett. We come three hundred at this time. You must consider that the Indians loose nothing but their lives. You must loose your fair houses and cattle."*

Metacomet sought an alliance with the Mahican and Mohawk, who lived in what are now the Housatonic and Hudson River valleys. He was unprepared, however, for the intertribal animosities that still existed. Earlier in the century the Mohawk had pushed the Mahican out of the Hudson valley. Although the Mahican were generally peaceful and hospitable, they could not forgive this event.

The Mahican reception of Metacomet was lukewarm, but they allowed him to camp in the northwestern part of their lands, close to Mohawk territory. The winter was bitterly cold and the Wampanoag suffered severe hardship. The situation worsened when Edmund Andros, the English governor of New York, persuaded the Mohawk to attack Metacomet's camp. Blocked by their enemies to the west, the Wampanoag were forced to retreat eastward toward an inevitable defeat.

Back in Narraganset country, the colonial militia had discovered the location of the fort where Metacomet had sheltered the women and children of the tribe. The colonists surrounded the fort and put it to the torch. Between 300 and 1,000 Narraganset warriors perished; the losses of women and children are unknown, but they were probably very heavy. This horrific battle—the so-called Great Swamp Fight—broke the spirit of many of Metacomet's followers.

Over 1,000 white settlers were killed in the war, and more than 3,000 Native Americans perished. Metacomet himself was killed in August 1676. He was beheaded and drawn and quartered, and his head was stuck on a pike at Plymouth where it remained on display for twenty-five years. Most of his surviving followers were executed or sold as slaves in the West Indies.

King Philip's War marked the end of Native American resistance in southern New England. The war also underscored the importance of the Iroquois League, which had played a crucial role in the failure of the Indian resistance.

The European influx dramatically affected the lives of the Native Americans living farther south as well. In 1609 Henry Hudson, sailing on behalf of the Netherlands, discovered the river that bears his name. The Dutch traded on good terms with the people of the area, but when the first Dutch settlers arrived on Manahata ("Manhattan") in 1624, land disputes became inevitable. The island was purchased in 1626 for the equivalent of twenty-four dollars, and "Nieuw Amsterdam" became a leading trading community. Nieuw Nederlandsch was founded in 1626.

The Dutch colony enjoyed good relations with the local people during its early years, remaining neutral in most intertribal disputes. The Dutch also founded Fort Orange (later Albany) at the confluence of the Hudson and Mohawk Rivers. This trading post became a magnet for the Iroquois who brought furs to trade with the Dutch there. Indian–Dutch relations soured from 1639 when a new Dutch governor, Wilhelm Kieft, incited a series of wars with the people of the lower Hudson valley. The worst Dutch treatment of natives occurred at Pavonia (now Jersey City, New Jersey) in 1643. Wappinger, pursued by Mohawk, sought refuge in Pavonia and nearby New Amsterdam. Kieft refused to shelter the Wappinger and urged his Mohawk allies to attack them. The Mohawk killed about seventy Wappinger tribesmen. The governor then turned on the surprised survivors, most of them women and children, and murdered them all.

The Dutch colony endured several Indian wars. The Dutch turned their eyes southward and sought to overcome what they saw as a Swedish threat to their sovereignty. The colony of Nye Swerige had a shorter life. The first Swedish colonists sailed up the Delaware River in 1638 and founded a colony that grew to only about 200 people. The Swedes had generally good relations with the Native Americans of that region; they took care to purchase the land they settled on. Nye Swerige was conquered by soldiers from Nieuw Nederlandsch in 1655. The Dutch themselves were subsequently conquered by an English force in 1664. Nieuw Amsterdam

*Above: The Dutch settlers of Nieuw Nederlandsch conducted a brisk trade with the Wappinger, Mohawk, and other local nations, chiefly Delaware peoples. For almost a century, their Fort Orange (later Albany) was the center of the fur trade.*

became New York in honor of James the Duke of York, and the four European colonies were reduced to two: Nouvelle France and New England.

The long series of conflicts known as the French and Indian Wars began in 1689. Nouvelle France and New England were drawn into the war by their parent countries. The people who lived between the French and English colonists—the Abenaki and Iroquois in particular—became involved. The French colony had the advantage of a strong central government, while the English settlers, although far more numerous, were divided, independent, quarrelsome, and vindictive. In 1689 Nouvelle France had only about 12,000 inhabitants, while the English population already surpassed 200,000. Because of this disparity, the French were careful to form strong alliances with the Micmac and Abenaki.

The French failed in their efforts to make amends to the Iroquois. In 1684 the Onondaga orator Garangula addressed Governor La Barre of Nouvelle France: *"We carried the English into our Lakes, to traffick there with the Utawawas and Quatoghies, as the Adirondacks brought the French to our Castles, to carry on a Trade which the English say is theirs. We are born free. We neither depend upon Yonnondio* [the Iroquois name for the French governor] *nor Corlaer* [their name for the English governor of New York]. *We may go where we please, and carry with us whom we please, and buy and sell what we please."*

**A RECORD OF WAR**

The sequence of illustrations and symbols below shows a tribal record of a battle in the French and Indian Wars conducted on behalf of the French.

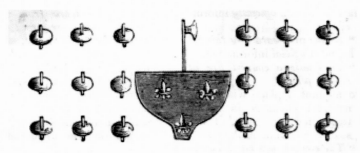

1. Each figure represents the number ten; together they signify that 180 Native Americans declared war with the French, represented by the hatchet over the arms of France.

2. The bird taking flight from a rock symbolizes their departure from Montreal, and the moon over the deer shows the date as the first quarter of the buck moon, or July.

3. They traveled by water using canoes, each hut representing a night spent on the journey. According to this illustration, the trip took twenty-one days.

4. When they disembarked upon the shore, they traveled on land for seven more days, illustrated by the appearance of a foot and the number of huts they passed.

5. They reached their enemies at sunrise, shown by the location of the sun, and lay in wait for three days, represented by the hand pointing over the three huts.

6. The hole in the building shows that they broke in and took their enemies—who numbered twelve times ten, or 120—by surprise, as shown by the sleeping figure.

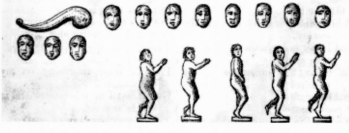

7. Using clubs, they killed eleven of their enemies (represented by the number of heads) and took five prisoners (the number of figures shown standing on pedestals).

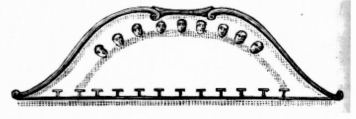

8. The nine heads in the bow, a tribal emblem of honor, show that they lost nine men in battle, while the empty pedestals mean none were taken prisoner.

A new French governor, the Comte de Frontenac, arrived in Quebec in 1689. After learning that war had been declared in Europe, he sent three French and Indian war parties south against English settlements in New York and New England. In response, the English, who realized Quebec's strategic importance to Nouvelle France, attempted to conquer the city, but suffered a humiliating repulse in 1690.

The war then settled into a series of raids. In 1696 Frontenac led a large French force into the land of the Five Nations. His show of force allowed Nouvelle France to end the war with an appearance of victory. The Iroquois had lost many warriors in the seven years of conflict. From then on they sought to be neutral in the wars between French and English colonists.

At the end of the seventeenth century both Nouvelle France and New England were firmly established; Nieuw Nederlandsch had subdued Nye Swerige and then had itself fallen to an English force. As the century came to a close, the Iroquois were still the most formidable Native American group in the Northeast. Their location in up-colony New York made them the middlemen in the fur trade and gave them leverage in the rivalry between Nouvelle France and New England.

## THE SOUTHEAST

Approximately one million Native Americans are estimated to have inhabited the Southeast at the beginning of the seventeenth century. Their lifeways had been strongly influenced by Mesoamerican culture. Advanced farming and skillful hunting provided the material basis for their settlements and complex political forms. They cultivated corn, squash, and sunflowers. Game was also plentiful. However, diseases introduced by de Soto's sixteenth-century march had brought epidemics to the area. Many had died before much could be recorded in detail about their culture.

The large Powhatan confederacy consisted of around thirty tribes that were based in the area of present-day Virginia. Wahunsonacock or "Powhatan," as he was known to the settlers, had inherited the great chiefdoms of Powhatan, Arrohateck, Appamattuck, Pamunkey, and Mataponi. He had then conquered or absorbed others to achieve his paramount chiefdom. Wahunsonacock's title was *mamantowick* (paramount chief); his subordinate chiefs were known as *weroances*. Wahunsonacock, who was more than sixty years old at the time of the first contact between his people and the English settlers in 1607, was initially friendly with the colonists. He was well aware of the

*Left: While the Powhatan fought wars of self-preservation with British colonists, the Tutelo, their ancient enemy, were being pushed southward by Iroquois incursions. The Yamasee, on the other hand, moved north to be closer to the British traders at Charles Town. Far to the northwest, the Dhegiha moved down the Ohio to the Mississippi and split into the Quapaw ("downstream") and Omaha ("upstream").*

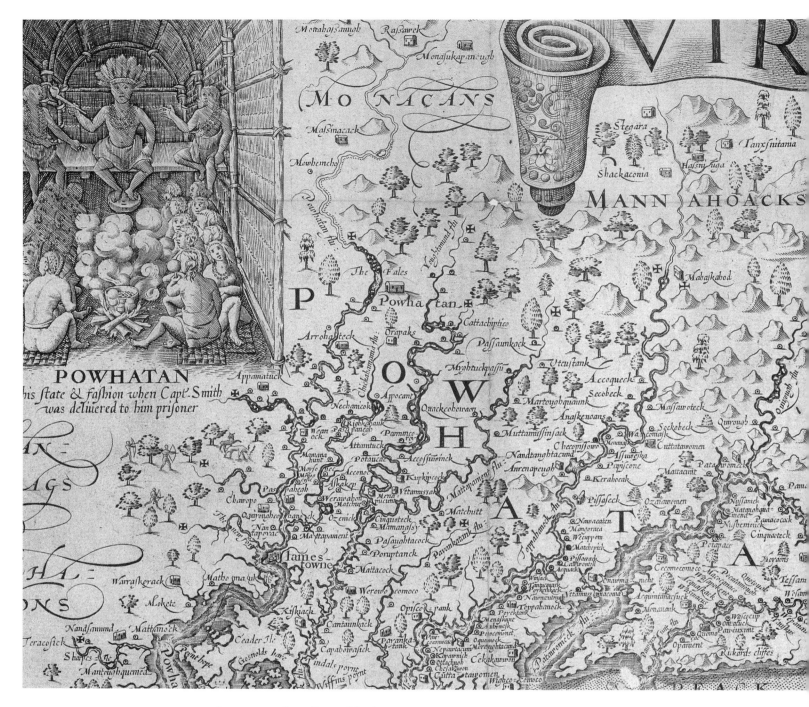

advantages of trading with the "coat-wearing people," as the Algonquian referred to the English—they also called them "cutthroats."

The English colonists who entered the Chesapeake Bay in 1607 chose to settle on a peninsula jutting into the James River where they established James Towne (later changed to Jamestown). The colonists had been sent by the London Company, just as the Spanish had been sent to Mesoamerica during the sixteenth century, in search of precious mineral ores and new sources of wealth.

The appearance of English settlers did not at the outset frighten the Powhatan tribes. The colonists were under strict orders *"to not*

*disturb the natives."* The directors of the Virginia Company of London, the primary backer of the Jamestown settlement, believed that it would be more profitable and less costly to befriend Wahunsonacock than to fight him. The settlers built Jamestown on a marshy peninsula that had been occupied only as a summer camp by the locals.

Wowinchopunck was the *weroance* of the town of Paspahegh, located close to Jamestown. Wowinchopunck opened hostilities against the English soon after their arrival. The English chroniclers reported that the Paspahegh were always their most fierce enemies. But Powhatan called on his subordinates to cease

*Left: John Smith's map of Powhatan country (the English Virginia) was first published in 1612. It depicts hundreds of thriving villages with such names as Kecoughtan, Quiyough-cohanock, and Arrchatek, many of which would soon disappear. The legend at upper left reads: "POWHATAN Held this State & fashion when Capt. Smith was delivered to him prisoner" [1607].*

fighting the English, and an uneasy truce was established between the two peoples.

In his dealings with the Jamestown colony, Wahunsonacock was obliged to interact with a rapid succession of English governors. Maria Wingfield was followed by Captain John Smith, who was succeeded by George Percy. Percy was replaced by Thomas Dale, who yielded the governorship to Thomas de la Warr in 1610.

Wahunsonacock said to Captain John Smith: *"Why should you take by force from us that which you can obtain by love? Why should you destroy us who have provided you with food?…I am not so simple as not to know that it is better to eat good meat, be well, and sleep quietly with my women and children, to laugh and be merry with the English, and being their friend, to have copper hatchets and whatever else I want…."* Wahunsonacock would find that Smith was actually more willing to "live and let live" than the governors who followed him.

In August 1610 Governor de la Warr sent soldiers to attack the town of Paspahegh when the Paspahegh refused to turn over deserters from Jamestown who had settled there. The town was torched, and the native plantations were destroyed. George Percy, de la Warr's second in command, recounted the sport of eliminating the offspring of the queen (the wife of Wowinchopunck): *"It was Agreed upon to putt the Children to deathe the which was effected by*

***Above:*** *Smith made a number of treaties with members of the Powhatan confederacy, as illustrated in this later engraving.*

***Right:*** *This eighteenth-century portrait shows Matoaka (Pocahontas) as "the Lady Rebecca" acclaimed by London society in 1617.*

*throwinge them overboard shoteinge owtt their Braynes in the water."* Afterwards, the queen was treated more gently: She was merely stabbed to death. This set off three years of open warfare between the English and the Powhatan. Wowinchopunck was killed in a skirmish in 1611, depriving the Powhatan tribes of one of their most aggressive warrior leaders.

Two years later several other settlers who had gone to live with the local villagers were hunted down and forcibly returned on the orders of Governor Thomas Dale: *"Some he appointed to be hanged, Some burned, Some to be broken upon wheles, others to be staked and some to be shott to deathe."* Dale also kidnapped and held hostage Wahusonacock's beloved daughter Matoaka (Pocahontas), who was only

seventeen years old at the time. A "weakness" that the founding colonial leaders quickly perceived in the native people—and exploited—was the terrible grief shown by parents when their children were taken from them. It was a simple matter to kidnap a child before entering a village and thus to begin negotiations with a strong advantage. This was especially true in the case of Wahunsonacock, who had as many as 100 wives and, consequently, a great number of children.

But the case of Matoaka was unusual. She tried to reconcile her father with the colonists, for she had been friendly with some of them as a young girl. Within a year she had been baptized as "the Lady Rebecca," and in 1613 she married an English widower named John Rolfe, in the first of only three recorded weddings between English and Powhatan during the seventeenth century. The marriage helped to establish a fragile harmony. The Virginia Company of London organized a voyage to England for the couple, hoping the publicity would help the company's finances. Of all the prominent Native Americans who visited Europe, Matoaka made the strongest impression. *"La belle sauvage"* was presented to King James I, and a courtier wrote that she *"did not only accustom herself to civility, but still carried herself as the daughter of a King, and was accordingly respected…by…persons of Honor."* Matoaka died of smallpox before she was able to return home. She was twenty-one years old.

Matoaka's infant son, Thomas, remained in England until he was in his twenties. His father, John Rolfe, initiated the cultivation of tobacco in Virginia. The tobacco trade developed into a highly lucrative business that the Virginia Company of London promoted heavily in England, where tobacco quickly caught on. People snorted, chewed, or smoked tobacco everywhere. They consumed it at meals, in classes, in church, and even in bed. King James grew so outraged with the habit that he issued a declaration called *A Counterblast to Tobacco.*

But the demand for tobacco grew rapidly. Not only were new plantations required to meet the soaring demand, but the cultivation of tobacco quickly exhausted the soil, and new fields had to be opened every two or three years. It was easier to appropriate native fields than to clear new land from scratch. Liquor

tore at the fabric of Powhatan society; disease continued to destroy entire villages; raiding and sporadic bursts of fighting broke out between the natives and the English settlers.

When Wahusonacock died a year after his daughter, his brother Opechancanough, who had been the *werowance* of the Pamunkey, took over leadership of the chiefdom. Believing that the English colonists were a serious threat to the very survival of the Powhatan, Opechancanough was not as conciliatory as Wahusonacock had been. Many of his people agreed with him; they held the English responsible for the serious epidemics that struck the tribes in 1617 and 1619. Not all the other tribes trusted him, however, and some resented the demands he made of them. Opechancanough did his best to unite the tribes in a surprise attack on the English, but the Patawomeck remained friendly with the English, the Potomac River people were neutral, and the Rappahannock, although supportive, did not want to participate in the actual attack.

Opechancanough launched his surprise assault on March 22, 1622. One quarter of the colonists—between 400 and 500 people—were killed on that day. The attack outraged the English because just one week earlier Opechancanough had assured them that *"the Skye should sooner fall than Peace be broken."* But Opechancanough did not follow up on his success. He believed that the English would see

the folly of remaining in Virginia and that they would soon decide to depart.

Instead of returning to England as Opechancanough had hoped, the English settlers seized

*Above: This illustration (c. 1670) is the first known depiction of the tobacco-curing process in colonial Virginia.*

*Left: An illustration by John White of a Florida woman of unknown tribe. Despite the distance, the bubonic plague epidemic that halved Florida's native population (1613–17) spread to the Virginia colony by 1617, and smallpox was also rampant.*

*Smith taketh the King of Pamavnkee prisoner 1608*

capture, but he eluded the English and remained in control of his people. The English relentlessly suppressed the Virginia-based tribes throughout the decade following Opechancanough's surprise attack, and he was forced to make peace with the settlers in 1632.

As the years passed, more settlers arrived and more land was required for their plantations. Even more than before, the main tension between the English and Native Americans now became an issue of land. The colonists had taken the Powhatan farmlands on the James River; after 1632 the Powhatan lost more farmland on the lower York River. In 1640 the richest farmland of all, on the Rappahannock and Potomac Rivers, was snatched from them and the Powhatan could no longer freely come and go between the forest where they had always hunted and the rivers where they had always fished, for now the land of the settlers lay between the two.

An uneasy "peace" reigned until 1644 when Opechancanough, who had by then reached his nineties and was blind and crippled, made one final attempt to oust the settlers. In another carefully planned surprise attack, between 400 and 500 of the English settlers were killed on a single bloody day, April 18, 1644. Although this was roughly the same number as had been killed in the massacre twenty years earlier, the colonial population in Virginia had since grown fourfold to about 8,000, and the percentage of deaths among the settlers was dramatically smaller.

The white settlers quickly retaliated. Old Opechancanough was captured and imprisoned in a small cage to be mocked by the English; he was eventually shot in the back. This time the Powhatan chiefdom finally came to an end. The English made a new treaty with a puppet leader named Necotowance, who accepted the status of a vassal, something that neither Powhatan nor Opechancanough would have agreed to in their lifetimes. The remnants of the Powhatan tribes were assigned to areas that became smaller and smaller, until there was no land left for them at all.

on the surprise attack as a justification to annihilate the Powhatan. For the next two years they pursued them mercilessly. Many losses occurred when the Powhatan were promised peace and persuaded to return to their villages, where they were then trapped and gruesomely massacred. A reward was offered up for Opechancanough's

When the first 104 English settlers arrived at Jamestown in 1607, the population of the Powhatan Chiefdom was estimated to be about 14,000, already reduced by disease to only a fraction of its number before the arrival of

Europeans in the previous century. By the end of the seventeenth century the English population in Virginia had grown to almost 60,000. Fewer than 600 Powhatan survived.

Native Americans living to the south of Virginia encountered English settlers somewhat later in the century. Between twenty-five and thirty tribes lived in South Carolina at the time of their first contact with Europeans. The most important of these during that period were the Cherokee, Catawba, and Yamasee. The colonial period from 1663 to 1729, known as the proprietary period, began when King Charles II of England granted eight lords proprietorship of the territory called "Carolina," which included today's North and South Carolina. English settlers founded Charles Town in 1670. Carolina became the southernmost English colony and the closest to Spanish Florida. Political strife and wars with the native people slowed the colony's growth. In the beginning the economy of the new colony was based on furs and pelts from trade and on forest products such as lumber, resin, and turpentine. As the seventeenth century came to an end, experiments with rice cultivation had proved successful, and rice became the leading crop of colonial Carolina.

During this period of its history, Carolina became the colony most known for its mixed population; there were more African slaves and Native Americans in the colony than Europeans. The English settlers pitted native groups against each other, and many Native Americans were sold into slavery on the auction block in Charles Town. Virulent smallpox and other epidemics destroyed entire tribes, and alcoholism proved almost as destructive. Unscrupulous traders encouraged alcohol abuse among the native people for the distinct advantage it yielded in negotiations with them.

Even so, as the century came to a close, the Southeastern peoples still controlled 90 percent of the territory they had held a century earlier. With the exception of the Powhatan, few Native Americans of the Southeast had yet witnessed the destructive power of English guns, and none could foresee that they would slowly be caught in a vise between Spanish Florida, the English coastal colonies, and what would become French Louisiana to the west.

*Left: Theodor de Bry sketched this image of the Powhatan performing a ritual dance at "a great and solemn feast whereunto their neighbours of the towns adjoining repair from all parts, every man attired in the most strange fashion they can devise."*

*Opposite: Finally splitting from the Hidatsa, the Crow migrated southwestward, where they met and befriended the Kiowa and their sub-tribe, the Kiowa-Apache, who were migrating eastward. The Comanche also began to divide from the Eastern (Wind River) Shoshoni about this time. From the Northeast (q.v.), the Chiwerean and Dhegihan peoples migrated along the rivers of the Central Plains.*

*Right: The great buffalo herds of the Plains were stalked on foot before the horse was introduced to North America.*

## THE GREAT PLAINS

At the start of the seventeenth century the peoples of the Great Plains still lived as they always had. They shared the vast, fertile land with more than sixty million buffalo. The Indians hunted, fished in the rivers, and lived in communal farming villages. The Mandan, Hidatsa, Caddo, Wichita, Pawnee, and Arikara farmed in the river valleys. The Blackfoot (Nizitapi), Apache, and Eastern Shoshoni were primarily hunters.

Those who lived along the major rivers were the first to feel the impact of the arrival of French explorers. In 1672 Louis Jolliet, a French-Canadian explorer, journeyed to the west to find the "great western river" described by the Illinois. Accompanied by Father Jacques Marquette, he left Michilimackinac in May 1673 and followed the Fox and Wisconsin Rivers to the Mississippi. The Frenchmen canoed down the Mississippi as far as the Arkansas River, encountering many hospitable tribes on the way. Through their adventure, French authorities became aware of the possibilities that existed for expansion and trade in the Mississippi River valley.

Soon after this first exploration by white Europeans, the French fur trader and explorer Rene Robert Cavelier, sieur de La Salle, became

consumed with the ambition to discover the mythical route to the Orient through the interior of North America. Some contemporaries described La Salle as a courageous and resourceful visionary, while others saw him as quixotic and obsessed with the desire for fame.

La Salle's travels took him farther west and south until April 1682, when he reached the mouth of the Mississippi. On behalf of France, he laid claim to the entire Mississippi River valley, which he named Louisiana. This territory stretched from the Illinois country to the Gulf of Mexico, and extended west toward present-day New Mexico. In 1686 one of La Salle's

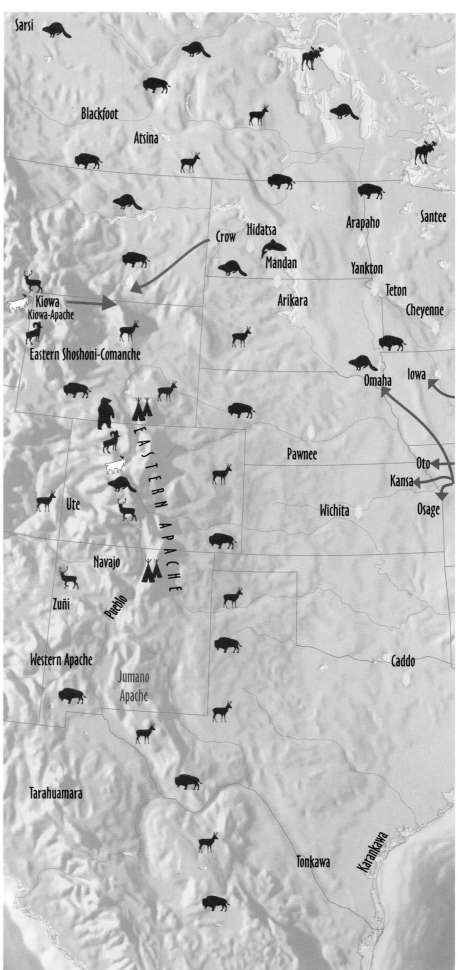

*Right: An engraving depicting a village devastated by disease, a factor that began to cause a death toll on the Plains during the seventeenth century.*

aides, Henri de Tonty, established Aux Ares, the first permanent white settlement in Arkansas, near to the mouth of the Arkansas River. Louis Hennepin, a Franciscan Recollect friar, was his chaplain and was with him when their party was captured by the Sioux, who held them for several months before another explorer, Daniel Greysolon Dulhut ('Duluth'), rescued them. Hennepin eventually returned to Europe, where he published dramatic accounts of his travels. Although Hennepin's accounts were not altogether truthful, they had a great impact in France and stimulated French interest in exploring the Gulf Coast region.

La Salle obtained men and ships in France. He sailed into the Gulf of Mexico, hoping to penetrate Spanish territory and exploit the mines he expected to find. But he missed the mouth of the Mississippi River and ended up in Texas, where he was murdered by mutineers. Explorers who followed La Salle sought to create a new French colony in Louisiana. In 1699 Pierre Le Moyne d'Iberville sailed across the Gulf of Mexico and made the first successful French navigation of the Mississippi Delta. His younger brother founded Nouvelle Orleans (New Orleans) in 1718.

These discoveries were doubtless glorious and exciting for the Europeans, but there was another side to the story: the succession of explorers brought smallpox and other epidemics to the Great Plains. Estimates vary as to how many died from these European diseases.

The lives of many Great Plains peoples changed shortly after the Pueblo Revolt of 1680 in the Southwest. When the Spaniards were forced to abandon their settlements in New Mexico, they left many horses behind. It was probably the Ute who first introduced the horse to the Comanche, and the strange beasts were quickly adopted by other tribes. Groups of Comanche began moving south, whether in search of more buffalo or more horses is disputed. After forming an alliance with the Ute, they occupied the central plains of eastern Colorado and western Kansas between the Platte and Arkansas Rivers and began to drive the Plains Apache from the region. The first contacts between the Comanche and Europeans are believed to have occurred in New Mexico at the very end of the century, when a group of Comanche visited a trade fair in Taos with some Ute. Although this meeting is undocumented, the Comanche were definitely known to the Spanish in present-day New Mexico by 1706.

Horses were so much a part of their lives that the Comanche came to believe that they had possessed horses even before the Spanish. As mounted warriors they enjoyed a tremendous advantage in warfare, and buffalo hunting became much more effective than the methods they had used formerly. Comanche riding skills became legendary. However, the Comanche were very hard on their mounts and never mastered the art of selective horse breeding.

## THE SOUTHWEST

By the early seventeeth century, the Spanish had implemented a two-part agenda for the northern frontier of New Mexico: the development of a mission system and the creation of an outpost to protect northern New Spain from incursions by other European powers. Throughout the seventeenth century, disease, natural factors, and human impact would combine and recombine to cause Native American migrations, turn horticulturalists into nomads, and precipitate the abandonment of half of the Rio Grande pueblos. Of the 134 pueblos that Don Juan de Oñate recorded between 1598 and 1601, only 43 would remain in 1640 and only 20 would be occupied in 1707.

The seventeenth century opened with a drought in 1601. Short of supplies, the newly established Spanish colony took to raiding native villages for additional food. While cornfields lay parched and withering, Governor Juan de Oñate condoned the plundering of the pueblos and even the torture of the natives to obtain their last supplies.

Naturally, in a desert environment, additional droughts occurred throughout the century, with the mid-1630s experiencing a prolonged dry period. The summer of 1659 brought another severe famine: Three years passed without a harvest, and consequently, there was a severe loss of livestock. A prolonged and widespread cycle of drought began in 1666 with the ensuing famine conditions continuing into 1672. By 1668 many natives had perished, and records indicate that among Las Humanas at least 450 died of starvation. Also suffering deprivation, the eastern Apache overran Las Humanas Pueblo at harvest time in 1670. Experiencing similar conditions, the Navajo and the Salinero and La Casa Fuerte Apache operating west of the Rio Grande raided pueblo and Spanish settlements for food.

It should be noted that early Spanish records apply the term "Apache" (probably derived from the Zuñi *apachu*, for enemy) to various Apachean groups. Confusion arises when both enemies and trading partners are identified as "Apache." Usually, different bands were meant; sometimes, the same band at different times.

A severe epizootic epidemic broke out among the Spanish livestock, decimating the colony's flocks and herds, especially their horses. Seeking replacement stock for their own depleted herds, the South Plains Apache began raiding for horses in 1672. As conditions deteriorated during this prolonged period of drought, the southern New Mexico Piro and Salinas pueblos as well as nearby Spanish settlements came under attack by the Apache. In the years following 1670, six Piro and Salinas pueblos perished, victims of famine, war, disease, and drought.

Yet another poor harvest occurred in 1681, and a drought beginning in 1683 lasted nine more years, bringing a total of two decades of drought and famine to the region.

The resultant malnutrition from these prolonged drought cycles greatly weakened the surviving native populations. Neither were the colonists immune from these conditions, and their constant demands for additional food further depleted the native supplies, frequently leaving them to die of starvation. This chronic malnutrition left the Puebloans even more vulnerable to the diseases that had come north with the Spanish settlers.

*Below: A Hopi village, photographed in the late nineteenth century. The Hopi suffered severe population loss in the seventeenth century as a result of disease, drought, internecine conflicts with the Apache, and depredations by Spanish conquistadors and colonists.*

*Right:* The sacred Corn
Twins, near Walpi,
a Hopi burial ground.

While the pre-Columbian native populations had not existed in a disease-free environment, local diseases provided no immunity against the infectious imports from Europe. Although the first Spanish record of disease in the Southwest is in 1630, Dobyns suggests the possibility that the 1520–24 smallpox hemispheric pandemic may have reached the pueblos from Mexico. Introduced into Mexico shortly after Cortés landed in 1518, the disease could have traveled via native trade routes from the Valley of Mexico northward to the Zuñi village of Hawikuh and from there eastward to other trade centers such as Pecos.

In support of this thesis, Jesuit records for New Spain (Mexico) of the late sixteenth and early seventeenth centuries include reports by the first missionaries to reach various settlements in northern Mexico of mass graves and worship of local deities whose primary attributes consisted of specific disease symptoms. In addition, the earliest Spanish *entradas* (expeditions) into the Southwest could have introduced such diseases long before permanent Spanish settlements were built.

Widespread outbreaks of smallpox and scarlet fever occurred between 1636 and 1641. It has been estimated that 20,000 deaths resulted, reducing the native population from 60,000 to 40,000, a one-third decline in population in just five years. An unidentified but lethal epidemic, documented simply as "La Peste," also swept through the area in 1640, killing another 3,000 persons. Between 1645 and 1647 an epidemic of malaria raged throughout the Southwest and northern New Spain.

Trade routes have long been considered major vectors for the introduction and spread of disease throughout the Southwest. The tri-yearly supply train from Mexico City to the colony has been credited with importing disease as well as trade items.

In all probability, native trade networks also played a role in spreading disease far from centers of Spanish settlement. Archaeological data show that several native trading centers were abandoned by 1650, all within a year or so of an epidemic, suggesting that the traders themselves may have been importing disease into their own pueblos. Las Colinas, a Piman-speaking trade center, and Chavez Pass, which had trade contact with the Pacific coast, were both abandoned by 1650. Tuzigoot, through which shells culled from the Gulf of California were imported, also ceased operations about that time. Although it was not abandoned, Pecos, an eastern trade center near Santa Fe, lost almost 40 percent of its native population between 1622 and 1641.

The second half of the century began with another smallpox outbreak in 1652. The decade of the 1660s had influenza outbreaks, while pestilence and death raged from 1670 to 1680. Estimates in 1638 had recorded the native

occurred during these years. Prior to 1692, while groups of Spanish were attempting to re-establish control, they frequently encountered starving groups of natives in the hills above abandoned and burned villages, suggesting disease, drought, and/or famine had stalked the area in the intervening years. The Zuñi, for example, had retreated from six villages to Corn Mesa, but when they returned, they had only enough people to populate one village.

Given all these factors, not only the population but the general health of the native population had declined dramatically during the seventeenth century.

Following the rapid and severe population decline, the Pueblo cultures would have experienced a destabilization of their economic and political infrastructure. Local healers would have been unable to help their people, and social bonds would have fractured with the death of key persons. Faced with such massive and prolonged upheaval, the pueblos would have been hard-pressed to maintain a cohesive society.

Sanctioned by the 1573 colonization laws, the native peoples, after swearing loyalty to the Spanish crown, owed tribute with a percentage due to the crown. In resource-poor New Mexico, however, this was impossible, and whatever tribute was collected went to the colonists.

An *encomienda*, the right to collect tribute from the natives, was awarded to a soldier in proportion to his rank and service. Governor Oñate would award an entire tribute-paying

population at 40,000; by 1670 those estimates had dropped to 17,000. The Spanish census just prior to the Revolt of 1680 placed the Hopi at 14,000, *"but pestilense consumed them."*

Because many mission and government records were destroyed in the Revolt of 1680, significant information about the preceding years has been lost. An additional hiatus in the records exists for the twelve years between 1680 and the Reconquest in 1692 when the Spanish returned to the area. However, given the previous evidence of the virulence of small-pox among the Puebloans, epidemics probably

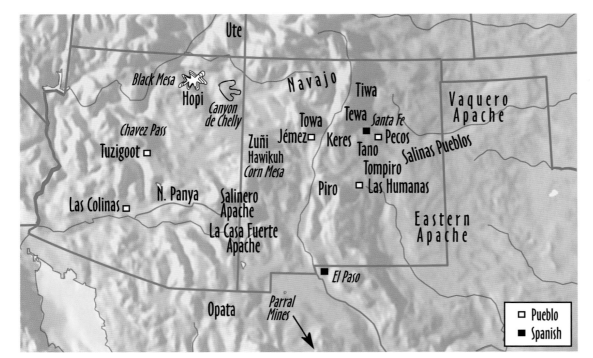

*Left: Records for this period began to reflect the variety of Apache groups. Male native prisoners were beginning to be sent south to work the Parral Mines, while women and children were enslaved in Spanish haciendas. The 1680 Pueblo Revolt drove the Spanish back temporarily to El Paso.*

pueblo or a fractional part thereof to a soldier. Tribute was usually maize and blankets or skins, and was intended as the personal income of the *encomiendero*. In no legal sense did the system entitle the recipient to use either native lands or labor. In spite of that, lack of governmental enforcement meant that other forms of available wealth, native labor, and land were expropriated almost immediately.

If the tribute of food was slow to arrive, the starving colonists turned to pillaging native supplies. These endless demands for tribute forced a change in the trading habits of the eastern pueblos with the Apache. Formerly trading primarily for buffalo meat and only occasionally for hides, under the incessant demands for tribute, hides came to dominate native trading. As a consequence, a meat shortage in these pueblos led to a poorer overall diet.

The natural consequences of the *encomienda* system led to an immediate loss of food for the Puebloans. Losing not only the produce they had invested time and energy cultivating, the additional labor demands by both the colonists and the friars denied them sufficient time for their own daily requirements. These conditions led to starvation in drought years and contributed to death rates during epidemics. Prior to 1643, *encomienda* had been assessed by household. However, following the severe population decline, it had been

changed to an individual level. Faced with this impossible burden, many natives fled the settlements and joined the nomadic Apache on the southern Plains.

Although slavery had been outlawed in 1542 in all Spanish possessions under the New Laws, and again in 1680 in the Recompilation of the Laws of the Indies, local conditions on the northern frontier evolved to permit and even encourage its practice. Throughout the colony, the Spanish were attempting to force their religion and culture upon an unreceptive population. Under Spanish law, anyone who resisted either Spanish rule or the rule of Catholicism (i.e., "Foes of Christ") was liable to a ten- to twenty-year sentence of servitude. Therefore, by characterizing a military action as a "just war" against those who "resisted" Spanish rule or the Catholic Church, the Spanish could legally condemn their prisoners to virtual slavery for such a period. As labor needs soared, this concept came to justify the slaving raids conducted against any native group. Women and children captives were usually allocated to Spanish households as menials, while the adult males were normally sent to the Parral mines in northern Mexico. After the 1599 attack on Ácoma (which had previously pledged loyalty to the Spanish crown), for example, upwards of 500 men, women, and children were sentenced to twenty years of servitude.

While charged with converting the natives to Catholicism rather than enslaving them, the Franciscan friars were forced to accept slavery as the only possible means to realize their grandiose plans to erect huge churches and elaborate mission compounds. Even after construction, substantial labor was required to maintain these buildings.

As early as 1600, raids were conducted primarily with the aim of taking prisoners. Such was the fate of the Tompiro Pueblos, which were attacked to obtain domestic menials.

During his tenure as governor, Don Juan de Eulate (1618–25) condoned not only forced labor/slavery, but also the kidnapping of "orphan" children left homeless as a result of epidemics. To reward loyalty among the colonists, the governor would issue "*vales,*" slips of paper giving the recipient the right to steal an "orphan" wherever he might find one. As a result of this policy, many pueblo children were kidnapped and made menials in Spanish homes.

In 1638, Governor Luis de Rosas used the pretext of a "just war" to launch a slaving raid against the Vaquero Apache on the southern Plains. The 100 captives taken were either placed in the governor's personal textile mill or shipped south to the Parral mines. A year later, eighty Ute were captured and enslaved. Both the labor crisis and slave raids continued into the 1640s.

Attempting to terminate these intolerable conditions, several pueblos as well as the Apache planned a revolt in 1649. Discovered before it could be implemented, the leaders were executed; many were sentenced to slavery.

Government-sponsored slaving raids, thinly disguised as punitive expeditions to ensure control over the Apache, continued under Governor Mendízabal, and seventy Apache captured in 1659 were promptly placed in the governor's personal service. Each Spanish raid, however, provoked a retaliatory raid by the offended Apache, leading to constant war and turmoil within the colony.

By 1668, a time of severe drought and famine, a new threat emerged west of the Rio Grande from raiding by hungry Salineros and La Casa Fuerte Apache as well as Navajo, against both Spanish and Puebloan settlements. As victims of a common enemy, Spanish and Pueblo troops united in an effort to destroy their enemies' crops. This alliance led to incessant raiding and counter-raiding until, by 1669, all of New Mexico was at war with the Apache.

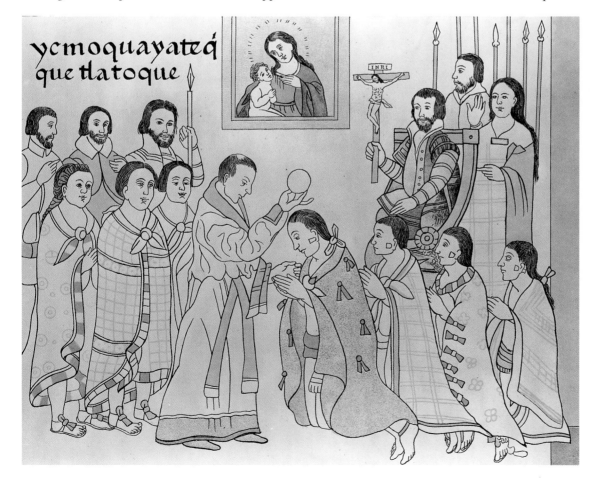

ycmoquayateq que tlatoque

**Left:** *Four native converts receive holy communion from a Spanish priest in this illustration from Mexico. While some conversions were apparently genuine, others were made under duress, for fear of Spanish reprisals.*

This policy of employing Pueblo auxiliaries in the colony's defense led to schisms within and among the native groups involved. As auxiliaries were primarily Christian converts, their presence within their own villages tended to split their pueblos into Christian and traditionalist factions. As soldiers under Spanish control, they also created enmity between their own pueblos and those pueblos that they attacked. The resultant internal stresses within and among the various pueblos prevented any large-scale unification among them.

Besides seeing action against local pueblos, these auxiliaries were used in the 1659 series of campaigns conducted against the Apache. When nomadic tribes raided the pueblos, seeking horses and food in times of famine, these forces were part of the retaliatory slaving raids. During the severe famine years around 1668, Pueblo and Spanish forces united against both the southern Apache and Navajo.

The year 1680 became a colonial watershed. Following decades of drought, famine, and disease, plus boundless Spanish demands for tribute and labor, the Pueblos and some Apache finally united in common cause and, on August 10, revolted. Quickly killing many colonists and driving out the survivors, the Puebloans proceeded to destroy every last vestige of the Spanish occupation.

The Puebloan unity eventually faltered, however. In 1692, under the leadership of Diego de Vargas, the Spanish were successful in re-establishing the colony in the Rio Grande valley. Their first objective was the recapture of the government center at Santa Fe. Once again, Pecos, Keres, and Jémez auxiliaries fought alongside the Spanish. By 1693 Santa Fe had been recaptured. Of its Pueblo defenders, 81 died: 9 in battle; 2 by suicide; and 70 by execution. Around 400 were sentenced to serve as slaves for ten years. In February 1694, when

**Below:** *Petroglyphs from Utah's arid Sego Canyon depicting Barrier Canyon-style spirit figures, anthropomorphic images, and abstract symbols.*

the Spanish marched on Black Mesa determined to destroy the remaining Pueblo forces entrenched there, Pecos, Keres, and Jémez forces accompanied them again.

In June 1696 another revolt was attempted by Jémez and the northern pueblos of Tewa, Tano, and Tiwa. A six-month campaign was required to suppress this revolt, and Pecos troops again served beside the Spanish.

Throughout the century, these native forces aided the Spanish for a variety of reasons, including personal survival, unity against a common enemy, and their common religion. However, their presence divided the pueblos, weakened their defenses against a common foe, and provided the Spanish with military strength they never could have mustered alone.

Later in 1693, the Apache returned to Pecos wishing to resume their former trading partnerships. And so it was business as usual again. However, some new changes and policies were to emerge as a result of the Pueblo Revolt of 1680.

Mexico City had come to several decisions about its northern frontier. It was considered imperative to retake New Mexico and establish a strong colony there. French interests had split Florida from New Mexico and now threatened New Spain's eastern borders. The valuable silver mines in northern Mexico had to be protected with a buffer zone. Finally, Spanish arms must never be humiliated again for fear of encouraging similar revolts in other Spanish possessions.

As the century closed, Spain had come to stay in New Mexico. The previous Franciscan theocracy had died with the Revolt, and government policy would now rule the colony. The *encomienda* system would be replaced by *repartimiento* (redistribution). Nomadic raiding would escalate, and it would be some time before the Spanish recognized that the French were involved in the raids. International power struggles had come to New Spain and would cease only with the Spanish acquisition of Louisiana in 1763.

*Above: Barrier Canyon-style shamanic spirit figures at Sego Canyon.*

## THE GREAT BASIN

In the early seventeenth century, in the dry, harsh environment of the Great Basin, the Paiute, Shoshoni, Ute, and other tribes of the region continued to forage for food—any food that could be found. The threat of starvation was always present. Coyotes were not eaten because they were believed to be endowed with supernatural power, and hunting buffalo on foot was both difficult and dangerous. When rabbits or antelope were available, bands of hunters worked together, directed by an "antelope shaman" or "rabbit boss." Men wearing antelope headdresses sang songs to lure the animals into ambushes where hunters lay in wait for them. Piñon nuts ripened in the fall, and in a good season enough were collected for a year or more. Infestations of grasshoppers were welcomed; the insects were boiled, roasted, or pounded into a paste to be dried for future consumption. Women did most of the gathering and preserving of food; they stored their provisions in grass-lined pits.

The peoples of the Great Basin lived in small family units with little in the way of formal leadership or religion. Shamanism was an important part of life. As well as helping in hunting antelope and rabbit, a shaman could heal the sick and could appeal to the spirit world on behalf of the people.

Only after the Pueblo Rebellion of 1680, when horses left behind by the defeated Spaniards appeared in the Great Basin, did their lives begin to change, so far as we can surmise. Horses became indispensable to the Ute and

Shoshoni, who soon increased their contact with the Comanche and other tribes. It is probable that smallpox and other diseases were also transmitted to the Great Basin during the seventeenth century, but there is little documentation on impact. However, the inhabitants of this bleak area, surrounded by forbidding mountains on all sides, were left undisturbed by Europeans until well into the next century.

## CALIFORNIA

The diversity of the California region fostered a wide variety of cultures. The Hupa, Yurok, and Karok in the north resembled the creative and complex Northwest culture groups; the Maidu, Miwok, and Pantwin in the east shared the simpler traits of the Plateau and the Great Basin peoples; and in the south lived the Akwa'ala, Cochimi, and Kamia—some of the peoples here were farmers.

Native lifeways in this region had, apparently, been scarcely affected by Sir Francis Drake's tour in the previous century. But when Martin de Aquilar explored the coasts of northern California and Oregon for Spain in 1603, twenty-four years after Drake's visit, there was little doubt that disease had already taken a heavy toll in the area.

More would soon follow. In 1602 and 1603 Sebastian Vizcaino led an expedition of three ships up and down the coast. Frequent stops were recorded and many friendly encounters with Native Americans described. Unfortunately, there were serious illnesses among the sailors. At one point during the voyage Vizcaino wrote, "[the ship] *seemed more like a hospital than a ship of the armada.*" Fortunately (for the Spanish sailors), Indians helped nurse the sick back to health and, Vizcaino reported, *"showed them all the kindness possible."* While some of the sailors were suffering from scurvy, others doubtless had contagious diseases to which the California peoples would have no immunity.

In the official histories throughout the seventeenth century, California remained a land apart from the New World. Even Nicolas Sanson's elaborate map of the North American continent, drawn in 1650, still represented California as an island. Eusebio Kino, a mission priest based in Pimeria Alta, wondered whether California was part of the mainland

*Below: Southern California tribes were renowned for their elaborate featherwork and reed weaving, as seen in these regional headdresses.*

when Cocomaricopas, of the Yuman tribes, sent him some Pacific blue abalone shells that could not have been found in the gulf. Father Kino concluded that the Yuman must have had some way to reach the Pacific on the opposite coast and that California must be a peninsula attached to the mainland.

Many boats probably voyaged up and down the California "peninsula" after Vizcaino, but these voyages, and their consequences for the indigenous people, are undocumented. Some European explorers were respectful toward native cultures; others were not so sympathetic. Inevitably, these encounters led to the introduction and spread of disease.

## THE PLATEAU

The numerous small groups inhabiting this high, relatively well-watered, wooded region did not alter their lifeways during the seventeenth century. They continued to subsist on an abundance of fruits and game and on salmon, which they harvested from the upper reaches of the Columbia and Fraser Rivers.

There was little farming in this region. Elaborate traps were used to catch fish—especially salmon, the most important source of food—which they ate both fresh and dried. Plant and animal foods rounded out the diet: nuts, seeds, deer, elk, and rabbit. The plant fibers of grasses, rushes, and reeds were used in basketry. The weavers of this region were famous for the variety of items they created,

including containers, bedding, house coverings, sandals, cradles, and mats.

Most Plateau people lived in settled village communities. Some large and productive fishing sites were shared among villages. A chief—either male or female—governed each village. Some chiefs were chosen, while others inherited the title. No chief, however, was more than a principal advisor or speaker; a council assisted the leader and limited his or her power.

The tribes in the central area, such as the Sanpoil, were generally peaceful and avoided confrontation. On the other hand, the Klamath, who lived on the southwestern edge of the Plateau, were warriors as well as hunters.

Across the Plateau area, people believed the spirit world had a supreme impact on their lives. Spirits took the form of animals, plant life, or sacred places. It was essential for everyone to have a spirit helper whom they would seek out on "vision quests." Not only shamans but many ordinary tribespeople were in touch with the supernatural world. When a personal spirit did not help, shamans were always available to deflect bad luck and cure ill health.

Remaining ignorant of fur trappers, missionaries, and pioneers, the Kutenai, Colville, Spokane, Shuswap, and Lillooet in the north, and the Klamath, Modoc, Nez Perce (Numiipu), Cayuse, Palouse, and Walla Walla in the south continued to live as they had for centuries. Horses scarcely penetrated this region until well into the next century.

## THE NORTHWEST

Throughout the seventeenth century, in the mild climate and dense forests of this region, people continued to gather shellfish, to fish and harvest salmon, and to hunt seals, otter, sea lions, and dolphins from spring through fall. In winter they turned to the mountains to hunt beaver, otter, marten, muskrat, bear, and elk. In this abundant region there was plenty of time for leisure and for the pursuit of traditional skills and crafts. The Haida in the north were accomplished wood carvers, the Cmyan (Tsimshian) were renowned sculptors of bone and ivory, the Kwakiutl were sculptors and skilled sailors, the Tlingit conducted a brisk trade with their southern counterparts.

The lives of the inhabitants of this area did not change discernibly during the seventeenth century. The villages, which consisted of 100 or more people, remained largely independent of each other. Of all the cultures in North America at the time, those of the Northwest were the most hierarchical. Social status was based on an individual's relationship to the leader of the community. Individual and group wealth—measured by various possessions including blankets, shells, canoes, and copper—were also important indicators of social position, as was reflected in their renowned potlatch ceremonies.

Religion was based on a strong faith in mythical ancestors. Dramatic ceremonies involving spirit quests and encounters were common. Highly stylized representations of the spirits were depicted not only on totem poles but also on intricately carved house façades, ornate boat prows, masks, and blankets. Not until the following century would invading settlers all but destroy these extraordinary accomplishments and rich cultural traditions. Little is known as to whether European diseases penetrated this region during the seventeenth century, or whether other factors caused migrations or population change.

*Below:* The coastal peoples of the Northwestern culture area relied on the abundant marine life as their main source of food. Their seaworthy canoes were elaborately ornamented with carving and paintwork.

### THE SUBARCTIC

In the early 1600s the Micmac and French visited Newfoundland to take advantage of the plentiful fishing along its coast in the summer. The elusive indigenous Beothuk were amiable hosts until a French fisherman shot a Beothuk in 1613. The Beothuk responded furiously, slaughtering thirty-seven French fishermen. The French then formed an alliance with the Micmac to drive the Beothuk from the region, persuading the Micmac to settle permanently in southern Newfoundland and providing them with firearms. The Beothuk were relentlessly driven inland.

Initially, the Europeans were attracted by the rich fisheries in the area. Intrepid Basque fishermen had been taking rich catches of cod off the northeast coast for more than a century. Deep-sea whaling was practiced so extensively in the 1600s that the expertise and greed of the Basque fishermen nearly drove the right whale and the bow whale to extinction.

Fur trapping in the interior quickly became even more profitable than fishing. The fur trade was the catalyst for the European invasion of the region, and the French and the English struggled to dominate the interior. As beaver, the most desirable commodity, became increasingly scarce in the eastern coastal region, the traders steadily moved inland.

As the essential middlemen of the fur trade, Native Americans were perceived both as a necessity and a hindrance to this lucrative commerce. As trading increased, demands on both sides intensified: knives, axes, guns, iron pots, and—disastrously—brandy and rum were exchanged for the precious pelts.

While the French were ousting the Beothuk from their homeland, fledgling English settle-ments sprang up along the eastern coast of Newfoundland, adding to the pressures on the Beothuk. Competition between France and England over Beothuk territory grew increasingly hostile. The French attacked several English settlements during 1627–28, but the English successfully resisted them. During the 1650s the French countered the English presence by encouraging a permanent settlement of Basque fishermen at Placentia, forcing them to reside there under French jurisdiction. The Basques rebelled in 1660 and murdered the French governor, but the French regained control, and in 1662 sent soldiers to Newfoundland. The English held on to St. John's and continued to strengthen their forts against attacks by Dutch pioneers and pirates as well as French settlers.

King William of England and King Louis XIV of France went to war against each other in 1689. King William's War was characterized by small, sporadic raids against isolated English settlements. These confrontations terrorized the inhabitants, but the outcome of the war remained undecided. The fighting continued

*Above:* A depiction of a northern Subarctic buffalo hunt.

*Below:* The Hudson's Bay Company established itself in the Subarctic from east to west by building such fortified trading posts as Fort Yukon, depicted here in 1847 after the beaver trade had passed its peak.

*Right:* Cree families built hide-covered tipis as their summer dwellings and traveled the waterways of the Hudson's Bay area in canoes. The Cree began migrating westward late in the seventeenth century because of pressures on their land caused by the fur trade.

*Right:* Cree families built hide-covered tipis as their summer dwellings and traveled the waterways of the Hudson's Bay area in canoes. The Cree began migrating westward late in the seventeenth century because of pressures on their land caused by the fur trade.

until the fall of 1696, when Pierre Le Moyne d'Iberville's army of French soldiers, Abenaki, and Placentia conscripts methodically destroyed all the English settlements along the southern shore of Newfoundland and captured St. John's. By this time the Beothuk had moved into the interior and may not even have been aware of the struggle over their homeland. The Treaty at Ryswick ended the war indecisively in 1697 and St. John's was restored to England.

Many French fur companies were granted monopoly privileges by the French monarchy even before they established their permanent settlements in the Subarctic region. Beaver pelts radically altered hat fashions in Europe. The entire process from trapping the beaver until the arrival of pelts in Europe took approximately two years. Workers in Europe removed long hairs from the pelts. They saved the soft short hairs, which were matted into felt for the manufacture of the new, highly coveted waterproof top hat.

Pelts of wolf, mink, bear, otter, raccoon, muskrat, and even squirrel were less valuable, but nevertheless useful. The more expensive furs lined the insides of European coats (it was considered barbaric in Europe for fur to be worn on the outside unless it had been processed into felt). At the beginning of the 1600s fur was a luxury item in Europe. As the century wore on, furs became so plentiful that prices dropped dramatically and even the middle classes could

afford them, profitably expanding the market despite their reduced cost.

In 1670 King Charles II granted a charter to *"the Governor and Company of Adventurers of England trading into Hudson's Bay,"* giving them *"the sole trade and commerce"* and ownership of *"all the lands and territories"* of the Hudson Bay region. The English were unaware of the vastness of this area: The territory was larger than the combined total of all other European land claims in North America. Until 1870 the Hudson's Bay Company would remain the European proprietor of the territory, which was called Rupert's Land in honor of Prince Rupert of the Rhine. The Hudson's Bay Company founded Rupert House and Moose Fort in James Bay. Even more important was their establishment of Fort Seven and York Fort, the principal trading post on the west side of Hudson Bay, in 1684.

In the early years of the Hudson's Bay enterprise, the native peoples perceived little threat from the minor intrusions into their huge territory. However, despite the apparent benefits of trade, it was not long before it disrupted their lifeways radically; disease and alcohol destroyed many lives. An exodus from the region began, some Cree and Ojibwa moving south to the Great Plains to hunt bison.

The Hudson's Bay enterprise was well-organized and strictly commercial. The paid laborers were kept under strict contract, with wages held for them in eastern towns. Many drank to ward off the seemingly endless loneliness and cold; bathing was virtually out of the question; and few had respect for the native men and women they encountered.

There were some exceptions. One was young Henry Kelsey, who in 1690–92 traveled with the Cree, in whose company he was very comfortable. They took him as far as the great prairies of western Canada. Explorations such as his were, however, rare. To avoid having to travel any farther than necessary, most Europeans encouraged the native traders to approach the bayside posts.

Europeans had no interest in settling this harsh land: They sought only to exploit the apparently limitless supply of fur. Had they left their alcohol and diseases at home, their impact on the Subarctic peoples would perhaps have been less destructive.

## THE ARCTIC

As they had for centuries, the Inuit and Aleut hunted seal and walrus, whale and porpoise, caribou and bear. They plied the frigid seas in boats of sealskin and wood or bone, and roved across the icebound expanses in sleds with runners of bone or ivory. The seal-oil lamp, the only lamp known in the Americas at the time, was the center of the Eskimo household. With its carefully trimmed wick of moss floating in a saucer of whale or seal oil, the lamp was used for light, heat, and cooking in their shelters, of snow, ice tents, or wood.

The Inuit traveled in small bands of perhaps forty to fifty people, including ten to fifteen hunters and the elderly and children. The primary social unit was the family. There were strong customs and taboos, but no laws. The Inuit believed that humans and animals existed in a mystical relationship. Animals were believed to have souls or spirits and to allow humans to hunt and kill them. Taboos prohibited mixing meat from land and sea mammals, either in meals or by using the same tools to hunt them.

Shamanism was of paramount importance in daily life. Human souls were sometimes lost or stolen, requiring the healing services of a shaman for their recovery. Shamans were respected and feared, for the Inuit were anxious about disease and illness, believing that these were caused by the neglect of important

rituals. Fixing a broken bone, however, was something every adult knew how to do.

The climate was bitterly cold, the terrain rugged and forbidding. In the Inuit language, "winter" is synonymous with "hunger." Cannibalism was not unknown; triage was necessary in their relentless struggle for survival. But in spite of the formidable challenges their environment presented, these people produced decorative work in bone and ivory. They were reputed to be hospitable, warm, happy, gregarious people.

Iron tools and weapons were already prevalent among the Arctic peoples, implying that there had been prior contact with Europeans. But the inhospitable land and harsh climate would protect them for some time to come from the curiosity and intrusion of Europeans, including the Russians.

*Below: An Inuit mother and child dressed in the thick clothing of fur and hide essential to survival in the frigid Arctic.*

Polar Inuit

North Alaska Inuit

Bering Sea Inuit

Aleut

Pacific Inuit    Tanaina    Tanana

Eyak    Tutchone

Kaska

Tlingit

Haida    Tsimshian

Nootka    Kwakiutl

Chinook    Yakima    Nez Perce
Cayuse
Klamath    Bannock
Hupa    Modoc    N. Shoshoni
Pomo    N. Paiute
Miwok    Ute
Yokut    S. Paiute    Navajo
Chumash    Hopi
Yuma    Pima    Zuni    Pueblo
W. Apache    E. Apache

Tarahuamara

Mackenzie Inuit    Central Inuit

Kutchin

Hare    Copper Inuit    West Greenland
Inuit
Baffin Island    East Greenland Inuit
Inuit

Dogrib    Yellowknife    Caribou Inuit

Etchareottine

Beaver

Chipewyan    York Fort/
Fort Bourbon    Labrador Inuit

Sarsi    Albany
Fort

Blackfoot    Cree    Montagnais    Naskapi    Beothuk

Kutenai    Atsina    Cree    Micmac
Salish    Arapaho    Assiniboine    Ojibwa
Crow    Ojibwa    Michilimackinac    Algonquian    Abenaki
Hidatsa    Santee    Menominee    Ottawa
Mandan    Yankton    Teton    Sauk    Huron
Arikara    Cheyenne    Winnebago    Iroquois
Bannock    Kiowa    Fox    Potowatomi    Neutral
N. Shoshoni    Iowa    Kickapoo    Erie    Delaware
E. Shoshoni    Omaha    Illinois    Miami
Comanche    Pawnee    Tutelo
Oto    Osage    Shawnee    Powhatan
Wichita    Yuchi    Cherokee    Tuscarora
Chickasaw    Creek    Catawba
Caddo    Quapaw    Confederacy
Choctaw    Timucua
Natchez
Tonkawa    Calusa

Maya

# Homelands Seized and Ceded

## 1700–1800

As the eighteenth century opened, most Native Americans still could not foresee what the rising tide of Europeans was going to do to their homelands and people. Some had already seen their lands occupied, some had already seen their populations decimated by disease, some had even fought several wars. But throughout the 1600s, most nations had been able to maintain their own independence and their integrity as cultures; with a few exceptions—in the colonial settlements along the Atlantic coast and in the Southwestern lands occupied by the Spanish—Native Americans still possessed most of their ancestral lands. Indeed, there were still many who had never seen a white person, and many more who had little direct contact with the white people.

What lay ahead in the 1700s might best be expressed by certain statistics: In 1700, the population of non-native people throughout what is now the continental United States was about 500,000. By the year 1800, that figure had risen to some 4,000,000. During that time, although firm figures are not known, it may be fairly estimated that the Native American population was cut in half, possibly from about 2,000,000 to 1,000,000. The rise of the settled population is easily explained by the constant stream of immigrants and the importation of African slaves: By 1750, African slaves are estimated to have comprised some 20 percent of the non-native population of what was soon to become the United States.

The decline of the indigenous population is more problematic. Warfare accounts for many of the deaths, but as deadly as such wars were,

it is now generally believed that diseases were responsible to a much greater degree for the decline in the native populations. Many of the epidemics of such diseases as smallpox, measles, influenza, typhus, or diphtheria were relatively localized, but there were also some that are known to have swept across much of the North American continent.

The spread of deadly diseases would continue to wreak devastation among Native Americans through the eighteenth century. In 1713–15, a measles epidemic moved throughout the continent. In 1715–21, a smallpox epidemic wiped out people on a wide swath from New England to Texas. In 1729–33 another smallpox epidemic struck; in 1736, diphtheria swept through many tribes; and in 1761, there was an influenza epidemic. A further smallpox epidemic struck the continent in 1779–83. The point about such epidemics is that they moved silently and widely among Native Americans, even affecting many who had no

*Opposite: North America in 1700.*

*Below: Wealthy English philanthropist James Oglethorpe, who established the colony of Georgia, meeting Creek chiefs in 1732.*

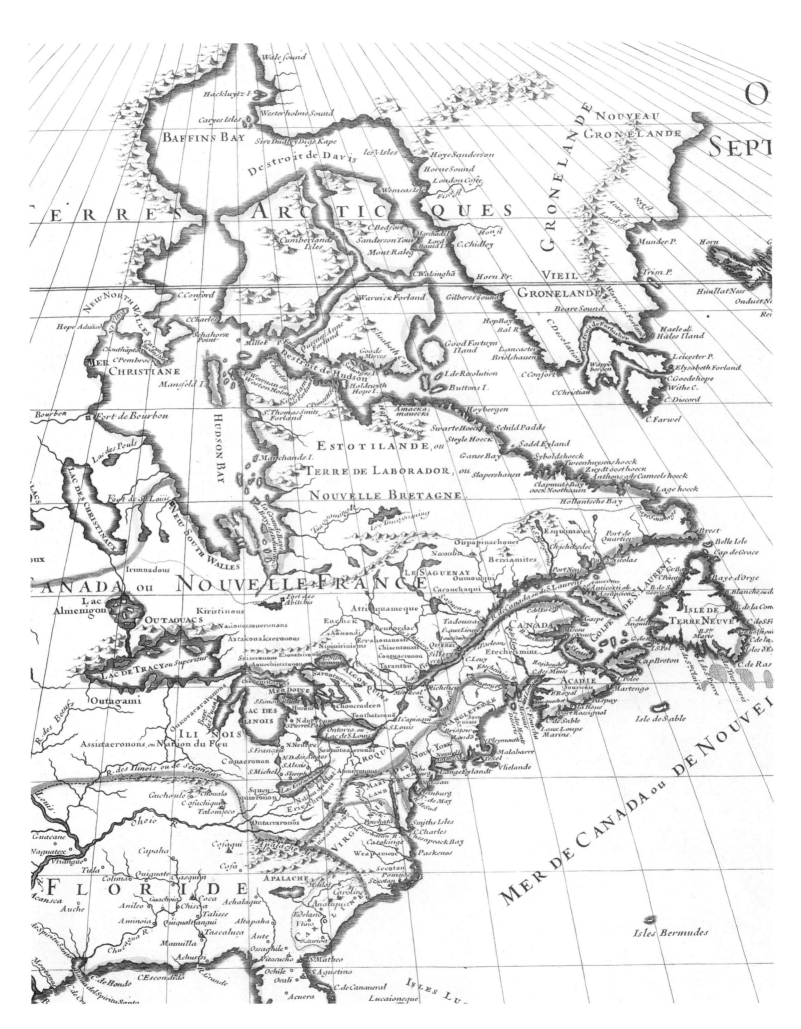

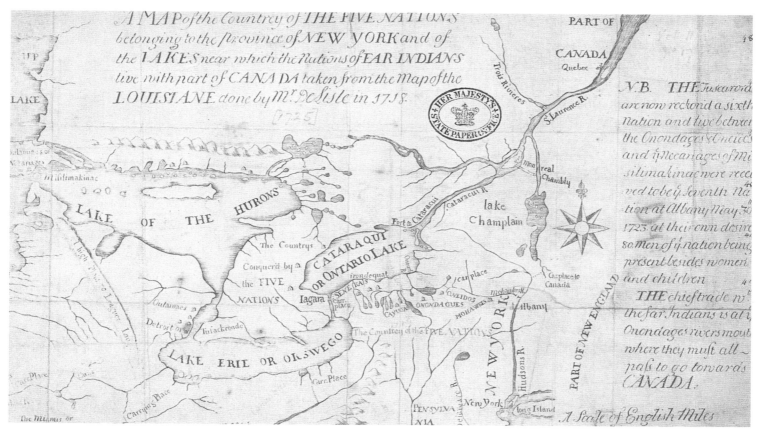

direct contact with Europeans. And not only did such virulent diseases kill, they sapped the morale and spirit of native survivors and onlookers who had no biological or scientific defenses to fight these imported diseases, against which traditional remedies and healing practices had no effect.

## THE NORTHEAST

The peoples of the Northeastern woodlands had been among the first to bear the brunt of both the European arms and diseases. Here especially, the sheer numbers of new people throughout the 1700s were pressing greatly on the established tribes. Not only did these newcomers take more and more land for their settlements and cultivated fields and domesticated animals, they wiped out wild animals regarded as dangerous, they hunted and trapped for flesh and pelts, and they fished the streams and lakes. They also introduced alcohol and venereal disease, all the while forcing many native people to convert to Christianity, abandoning or weakening their own traditions. Throughout the 1700s, broken treaties and unscrupulous traders continued to deprive the Northeastern peoples of their lands and goods. Another major factor was the almost constant migrations of tribes, whether forced by colonists, driven by scarcity of traditional food sources or intertribal wars, or moving west to find new beaver territory. Such movements only aggravated the "uprootedness" of the tribes. These factors have been described earlier.

But perhaps the distinguishing characteristic of the 1700s, especially in the Northeast region, was the fact that native nations became

*Above:* A map of Iroquois country, circa 1723, headed "the Five Nations" but including a note on the Tuscarora joining the League.

*Opposite:* This 1719 map was based on an earlier atlas by Guillaume de L'Isle, the most notable French cartographer of the early eighteenth century. According to this map, the English colonies have scarcely encroached on Iroquois territory, which is depicted here as part of Nouvelle France, while the area of the Southeast under Spanish influence— Florida—is extensive.

*Left:* This map appeared in Emma Willard's 1845 History of the United States, *illustrating the supposed locations of Native American tribes prior to European contact.*

involved in the wars that the Europeans were constantly fighting for control of the New World. As long as rival European colonial powers fought over land in the New World, native nations could often negotiate arrangements that best suited their own interests if they held the balance of power between the rivals. The Abenaki, for example, occupied lands east of Lake Champlain and northward into Nova Scotia. Squeezed between the Micmac and French settlements of New France to the north and the English settlements of New England to the south, the Abenaki performed a continual dance of negotiation with each European power. In 1705 the French, in an attempt to impress the Abenaki, took Chief Assacumbuit to France, where he was knighted by King Louis XIV. The Abenaki, however, were even more impressed by the French trappers, traders, and priests. With their adoption of local customs and their apparent lack of interest in possessing land for permanent settlement, these Frenchmen found more acceptance among the

Abenaki than the English farmers and fishermen, who were constantly pressing claims to land and to exclusive farming and fishing rights.

The Algonquian bands, resident in the Ottawa valley of Quebec and Ontario, also sided with the French, although they shifted their allegiance to the British after the defeat of the French in 1763. The Illinois were another tribe that cast their lot with the French, but this did them little good, as the Illinois were constantly under attack by such other tribes as the Fox, Miami, Sauk, and Kickapoo; by 1800, the Illinois were a greatly reduced and powerless people. The Kickapoo had originally fought the encroaching French but by 1729 had established an alliance; with the defeat of the French in 1763, the Kickapoo transferred their allegiance to the Spanish, then later sided with the British against the United States. None of these shifts resulted in their securing any permanent settlements or concessions.

The Anishinabe—better known by their band names including the Ojibwa and Chippewa—

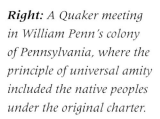

*Right: A Quaker meeting in William Penn's colony of Pennsylvania, where the principle of universal amity included the native peoples under the original charter.*

lived across the southern tier of Canada from Hudson's Bay to the Great Lakes. They sided with the British in both their war against the French and in the American Revolution; as a result they lost most of their land in the United States and were broken up into small bands. The Fox and Sauk also sided with the British against the French, but their numbers were greatly cut down by warfare and disease and they were constantly moving about the far reaches of the Northeast during the century.

Another large group of Northeastern peoples were the Lenape; the colonists called their best-known tribe the Delaware, because of their base around the Delaware River. Many of the Delaware had moved up into Pennsylvania to take advantage of the peaceful and, for the most part, just policies established by William Penn and the Quakers during the 1600s. Under Penn's leadership, Pennsylvania was the only English colony that consistently dealt fairly with the native peoples within its borders. By the 1720s, however, through an alliance with the government of Pennsylvania, powerful Iroquois leaders dominated the native peoples of the Pennsylvania region, including the Shawnee and Conoy, as well as the Delaware. The Iroquois continued to act as power brokers in the colony and persuaded other native groups to yield to English expansion. Then in 1737, through deceit and misrepresentation, the infamous "Walking Purchase" took many square miles away from the Delaware Lenape: William Penn's son Thomas convinced some Delaware chiefs to sign a deed granting the colony as much land as a man could walk across in a day and a half. The Pennsylvanians then cleared a path through the forest and sent not one but a team of three runners. In a petition to the magistrates of Pennsylvania the Delaware expressed their outrage:

*"We pray that you would take Notice of the Great Wrong We Receive in Our Lands, here are about 100 [English] families Settled On it for what Reason they Cant tell. They tell them that Thomas Penn has sold them the Land Which We think must be Very Strange that T. Penn Should Sell him that which was never his for We never Sold him this land."*

Their protest was to no avail. Gradually pushed out of more and more land, weakened by disease and warfare, and pressured by the Iroquois, the Delaware had moved into west-

ern Pennsylvania and the Ohio valley by the 1750s. There they would be among the first of the native nations to join the French in attacking the English frontier in Pennsylvania.

Undoubtedly the main actors among the Northeastern peoples during this century were the Iroquois, who at least since the 1500s had formed what became known as the League of Five Nations. These included the Mohawk, Oneida, Onondaga, Cayuga, and Seneca. By 1700 the Iroquois were weary of war and were seeking a position of neutrality in the conflicts between the English and the French, with their Abenaki allies. *"The enemy has brought us to a very low condition,"* said an Iroquois spokesman. In 1701, in exchange for English protection against French, Huron, and Micmac raids, the Iroquois agreed to deed to England's king *"all the land where the beaver hunting is, which we won with the sword."* The Iroquois pledged to remain neutral in all future wars between France and England, while at the same time pleading with French and English delegates to reconcile their differences and establish a lasting peace: *"Come, then, to some arrangement, both of you."*

This Iroquois agreement to remain neutral in the event of war between France and England allowed them to maintain the balance of power in the Northeast for many years. If at any time the Five Nations—they became six in 1722 when the Tuscarora moved up from North Carolina after the disastrous Tuscarora War

**Left:** *The powerful Iroquois League, with its skilled hunters and trappers, played a prominent role in Northeastern power politics and trade during the 1700s.*

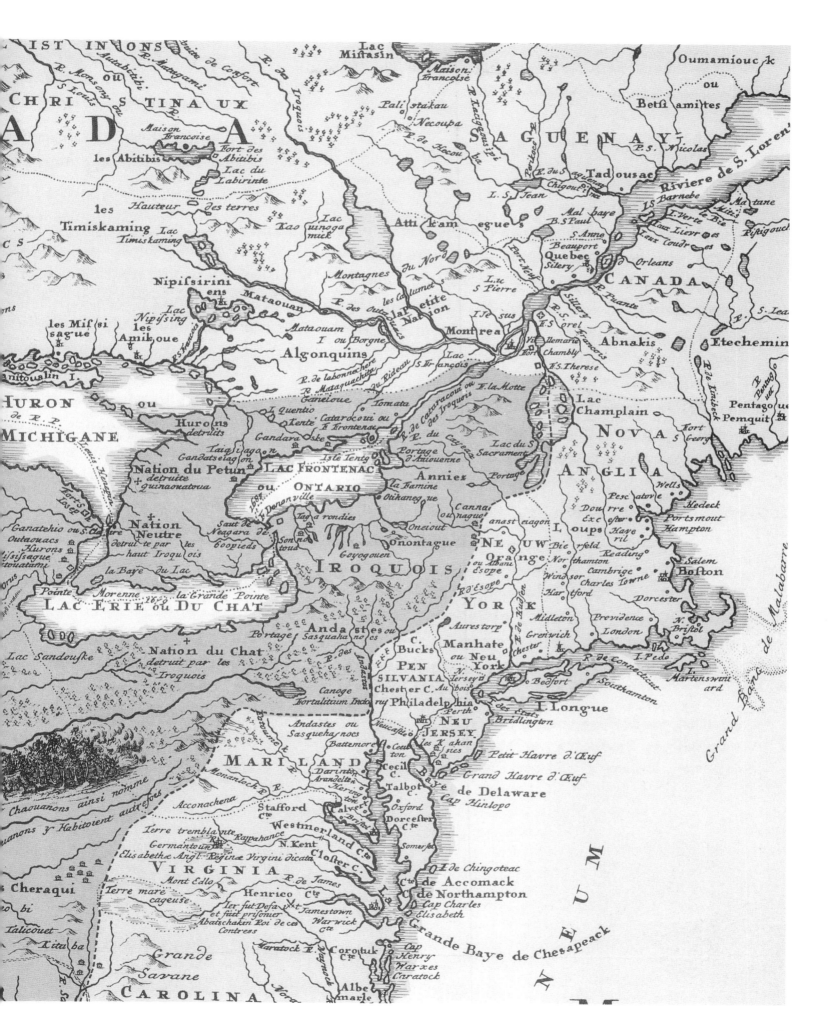

against the colonists (1711–13)—had decided to abandon their position of neutrality, they could possibly have brought about the fall of either New France or the New York colony.

The second in the series of French and Indian wars began in 1702. Called Queen Anne's War in America, in Europe it was known as the War of the Spanish Succession. French leaders devised a new strategy to avoid angering the Iroquois and disturbing their neutrality. In an attempt to intimidate the New England colonies and to force them to pull back their settlements instead of expanding them, the French intensified their hit-and-run attacks on vulnerable English frontier towns, but in most cases skirted Iroquois territory. Because their military forces were not numerous, the French needed native support to carry out their strategy successfully; thus most raids included many allied warriors led by a small number of French officers. The Abenaki, for example, joined a French raid to avenge an earlier English massacre of Abenaki leaders during their attendance at an Anglo-Indian peace conference.

The ruthless attacks on isolated villages outraged the English settlers and reinforced the belief held by many that the native people were "savages." In bloody attacks like the one on Deerfield, Massachusetts, in 1704, the marauders captured many English settlers. The French

placed some of these captives into French Catholic households, but awarded others among them to their Caughnawaga Mohawk allies to compensate for the loss of family members or for use as servants.

Throughout the remaining fifty years of the French and Indian wars, the taking of captives remained a policy of the French and their allies. In 1758 the Seneca captured fifteen-year-old Mary Jemison (Dickewamis). She lived the rest of her life among them and as an elderly woman dictated the story of her life. Her account provides important insights into the lives of the Seneca.

By 1709 Queen Anne's War had continued for six years, and no end was in sight. Colonel Francis Nicholson developed a plan to end the war. His plan required English naval support. The colonel persuaded a Mahican chief and three chiefs of the Canajoharie Mohawk to sail to London to plead before the queen for her support of a bold strike at New France. The impressive speeches of Chiefs Nicholas Etakoam, Cenelitonoro (John Laughing), Sayenqueraghta (Brant Vanishing Smoke), and Theyanoquin (or Hendrick) on behalf of Nicholson's plan convinced Queen Anne to finance it. Theyanoquin and his fellow chiefs were accustomed to according great respect, but not subservience, to powerful women; the

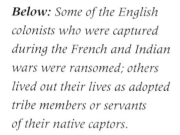

**Below:** *Some of the English colonists who were captured during the French and Indian wars were ransomed; others lived out their lives as adopted tribe members or servants of their native captors.*

*Left:* French Christian missionaries to the Northeastern tribes made converts through their willingness to respect all that was perceived as good in the indigenous cultures. English Protestants, who repudiated native beliefs as barbaric, even demonic, were less successful.

Iroquois tribes practiced matrilineal descent. Theyanoquin reminded the queen of the great sacrifices the Iroquois had made on her behalf and on behalf of her colonies during the war and suggested an equal exchange: *"The Reduction of Canada is of such Weight, that after the effecting thereof, we should have free Hunting, and a great Trade with our Great Queen's Children."*

The expedition was approved and funded, but the British effort came to grief in 1711 on the shoals of the Gulf of St. Lawrence. About 700 British lives were lost and the campaign was called off. Although Nicholson's plan had failed, Queen Anne's War ended in 1713 on terms favorable to England. France yielded Newfoundland and Hudson's Bay to the English, and thirty years of peace followed—the longest interruption of hostilities during the French and Indian wars.

Normal trading practices were restored throughout most of the Northeast during this thirty-year interlude of peace, while both England and France worked steadily to build forts and to strengthen defensive positions in anticipation of future wars. The French raised an enormous stone fortress—Fort Louisbourg—on Cape Breton Island, and were confident that its strength and location would guarantee their control of the St. Lawrence River passage into the interior. The French also strengthened their

defenses in the Great Lakes region, throughout the Ohio River valley, and down the Mississippi River to the newly established seaport of New Orleans, developing an arc of fortifications to contain the English colonies along the eastern seaboard.

These developments threatened the Iroquois. One Iroquois chief protested to the English in the 1730s: *"It is as if you on one side and the French on the other will press us out of our lands. We are like dumb people not knowing what ails us."* And some years later, in 1744, at the outbreak of King George's War, a Mohawk spokesman told the English: *"All the Six Nations who are your brethren are scattered....A great number are gone to Canada and elsewhere, and those that are left we imagine will soon be gone."* In Canada, the Ottawa had been devastated by European diseases; the Huron population, conquered by the Iroquois in 1650 and badly affected by diseases, was reduced by half. While the Iroquois appeared to retain their original strength, the series of wars in the region had destroyed many of their principal settlements. Many Iroquois had abandoned the longhouse shelters and lived in European-style cabins, buying goods at trading posts and working for English settlers. What territory was left to them was splintered from land that European farmers and lumbermen had either

**Above:** *Archaeological evidence shows that some of New England's native peoples produced pottery by firing clay vessels in kilns of burning logs.*

**Right:** *The Connecticut Mohegan Samson Occum became an advocate for Native American rights after his conversion to Christianity during New England's Great Awakening, one of several eighteenth-century religious revivals.*

purchased or stolen from them. *"Our hearts grieve us when we consider what small parcel of land is remaining to us,"* observed several Mohawk chiefs.

Some colonial leaders were interested in instilling European culture in the Iroquois through education and sought to convert them to English forms of Protestantism. In 1744 the Iroquois were invited to send some of their youth to Virginia to be educated. Unlike the Roman Catholic priests of New France, Protestant missionaries were only occasionally successful in these efforts. Their attempts were seen as a threat to traditional lifeways and as a cynical part of a larger English program of land acquisition. Some religious movements among the English colonists—such as the Great Awakening of the 1740s—did, however, affect the native peoples. Some, like the adoptive Mohawk Eunice Williams and her husband, joined in the popular religious revival meetings that occurred throughout the colonies, especially in New

England. Those who were drawn to the Christian faith—either through the dramatic words spoken at these large assemblies or through the more humble instruction of missionaries—usually assumed other European cultural traits and became more-or-less assimilated into colonial society. Samson Occum, a Connecticut Mohegan, was converted during the Great Awakening. He became a well-known teacher and minister, and spoke out against abuses visited on Native Americans by Christian Europeans. In 1764 Occum went to England to raise money for a Christian school for Native Americans started by Eleazar Wheelock. Ten years later the American Continental Congress voted funds to support the school, which was eventually named Dartmouth College.

King George's War was an offshoot of the War of the Austrian Succession, which broke out in Europe in late 1740. The war reached North America in 1744, where once again Britain and France struggled for control of the

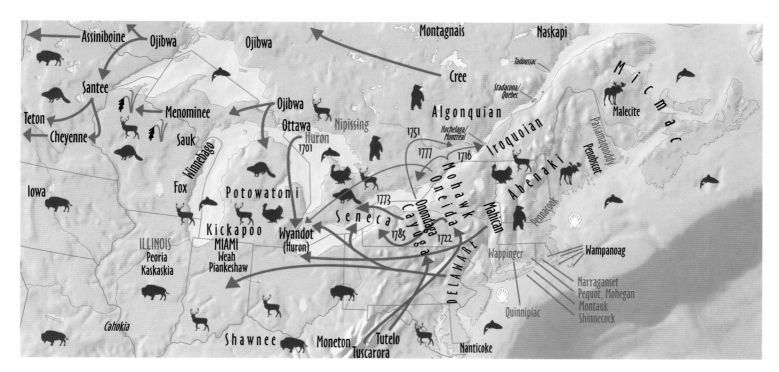

continent. An important British objective was the capture of the French stronghold of Louisbourg on Cape Breton Island in the Gulf of St. Lawrence. Native American tribes were less involved in this war than in the prior conflicts between France and Britain, perhaps because the frontiers of English settlement had expanded. Nevertheless, both sides conducted bloody cross-border raids with the help of Native American allies.

The final act of the drawn-out series of Anglo-French wars in North America began in the spring of 1754, where the Allegheny and Monongahela Rivers join to create the Ohio River in western Pennsylvania. "The Forks," as the junction was known, was coveted by both English and French as a strategic point of primary importance, because it controlled access to the upper reaches of the Ohio River system and thence to the Ohio valley and was also the key to inland routes to the Great Lakes region.

For native peoples, this new locus of conflict represented a major and significant shift of European attention from the coastal regions and the Anglo-French border in the north to formerly uncontested lands. After forty years of relative peace, the worst fears of the Six Nations of the Iroquois were realized as the two colonial powers collided in the struggle for mastery of North America. The French immediately began to threaten native land and villages near the newly constructed French forts on the Great Lakes. The English feared that the

Iroquois might abandon their neutrality and form an alliance with the French as they advanced. The Ohio valley—claimed by both the British colony of Virginia and New France—soon became the scene of brush-fire wars between the French and the indigenous Delaware and Ottawa.

The respected colonial statesman Benjamin Franklin called an emergency meeting of English colonial representatives and Delaware and Iroquois leaders at Albany in the early summer of 1754. Among the Iroquois leaders was the chief Theyanoquin (Hendrick) of the Canajoharie Mohawk, a Christian preacher and friend of the English. At the Albany Congress, Franklin proposed that all the colonies unite to meet the French threat. Besides proposing a style of intercolonial cooperation similar to the practices of the Iroquois League, Franklin urged that colonial policies toward native peoples be consistent and fair. The treaties and agreements negotiated between individual colonies and the various native nations had created a confusing, inconsistent, and frequently unworkable and destructive patchwork of relationships.

Iroquois leaders at the Albany Congress strongly expressed their fears that the English would not help to protect them from the French. Theyanoquin addressed the Congress:

*"We do now solemnly renew and brighten the Covenant Chain with our Brethren on the Continent. The Governor of Virginia and the Governor of Canada are both quarreling about lands which*

*Above: Seeking allies, the French offered several nations lands under their protection. Remnants of the Huron and others moved to Detroit and, under pressure from New York colonists, half the Mohawk moved to the vicinity of Montreal. The Onondaga also moved to Canada in 1751. Convinced their lands had become tainted by the colonists, the Delaware moved west, two groups turning north into Canada. Slaving raids by Southern colonists forced the Tuscarora and the Tutelo north to the protection of the Iroquois League. Trading with the British on Hudson Bay, the Cree exhausted beaver and moose populations around James Bay, forcing them to migrate westward, as did the Ojibwa, to new trapping grounds. The Ojibwa swept around Lake Superior, forcing the Assiniboine, Santee, Teton, and Cheyenne onto the Plains. The Iroquois League split over whom to support in the Revolutionary War.*

belong to us…[and] *the Governors of Virginia and Pennsylvania have made paths through our Country to Trade and built houses* [there] *without acquainting us with it."*

Discussions at the Albany Congress were unproductive. With no agreement for a strong, consistent approach to land claims and boundaries, any hope for an Albany "Plan of Union" vanished. The Six Nations left Albany with thirty wagonloads of gifts, but the representatives of the English colonies left with unallayed fears of the gathering strength of New France.

In 1755 the French and their native allies destroyed a British force under General Edward Braddock en route to seize a French fort at the Forks. The French and Indian War, known also as the Seven Years' War, was officially declared in 1756, and securing the strategic inland forts in the heart of Indian territory became a primary British objective. Theyanoquin and the Canajoharie Mohawks, key players in this drama, worked closely with William Johnson, a successful British trader and one of their firmest friends and allies.

Johnson had been living in the central New York area since 1738 and had married Gonwatsijayenna (Mary Brant), the sister of Chief Thayendanegea (Joseph Brant) of the Canajoharie Mohawk. Born of Christian Mohawk parents, "Molly" and Joseph Brant were educated both in English schools and in the Mohawk tradition. The family network of Johnson and the Brants became the most powerful force in the central New York area, able not only to mobilize Iroquois forces, but to negotiate on their behalf.

Johnson spoke the Mohawk language and was given the name Warraghiyagey, "man who understands great things." When the French and Indian wars resumed, Johnson was named Superintendent of Indian Affairs in the northern colonies, and Molly Brant served as liaison to the Iroquois and assisted in negotiations. Johnson's base in the Mohawk valley placed him and his native colleagues in the heart of the war zone as an army from New France began moving down Lake Champlain. Governor Vaudreuil of New France had the tentative support of two southern Iroquois nations, the Seneca and Cayuga, who felt most pressured by the French buildup on their western borders.

The French stronghold of Fort St. Frédéric (Crown Point), located at a narrows in Lake Champlain, was the primary British objective. In 1755, backed by the Canajoharie Mohawk, Johnson prepared an attack on the fort held by the French and their Caughnawaga Mohawk allies. Learning of the pending attack, the French forces moved out from the fort to confront the British and their Iroquois allies (mobilized by Johnson and Hendrick) near Lake George. In a clever maneuver, the Mohawk controlled the outcome of the Battle of Lake George. The Canajoharie Mohawk secretly persuaded the Caughnawaga Mohawk to refuse to attack them and their British allies, and the French were left unsupported. This was considered an important British victory, halting the French in their advance, although the fort still remained in French hands. Theyanoquin died in the battle.

The tactics of the Canajoharie Mohawk at Crown Point were applied in 1759 against the French at Fort Niagara. Messages and wampum moved back and forth between the combined forces positioned outside the fort and those inside who were allied with the French. Once the Native Americans on both sides decided not to participate, the plans of both the French and British commanders collapsed, since they each then had far fewer troops than they had counted on. Only when the British were able to block a French force attempting to relieve it did Fort Niagara fall into British hands.

The official declaration of war between Britain and France in May 1756 reached a country that had changed greatly since the outbreak in 1689 of the first French and Indian war. The ability of native nations to broker the balance of power in the Northeast, and their ability to play France against Britain to their own advantage, was greatly reduced. The British colonial population had more than quadrupled, to 1.2 million, while the population of New France (including Louisiana) had never increased to much more than 80,000. The rapid growth of the British population created pressures that led to unceasing British encroachment on native land. In the French and Indian War, the last in the series of French and Indian wars, the traditional Iroquois neutrality broke under the twin pressures of this British colonial expansion and increased French military activity along the shores of the Great Lakes and throughout the Ohio valley. While the Seneca leaned toward the French, the strong Canajoharie Mohawk nation now anticipated a British victory in North America that would effectively eliminate France's power and influence in the region. With that in view, the Canajoharie Mohawk abandoned their traditional neutrality and joined forces with the potential victors to benefit in the victory as well.

fiercely fought struggle to protect native homelands from seizure by the British, a struggle separate from the Anglo-French rivalry in North America. In April 1763 a Great Council of all the northwestern nations was held in a field near Fort Detroit. Pontiac called for unity to save their land, and by May a majority of the nations had combined to attack all British forts in the region simultaneously. Warriors quickly took nine British forts, forced the aban-

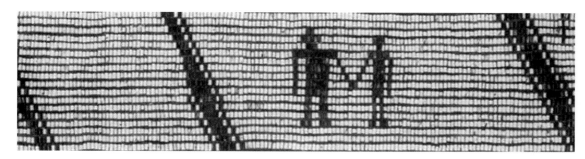

*Left: An Iroquois wampum belt of shell beads, patterned to serve as a tribal record and a means of intertribal communication.*

In a rapid sequence of events, the British forces were rewarded with the fall of Fort Niagara on the Great Lakes, the capture of Fort Louisbourg, the dramatic conquest of Quebec, and the occupation of Montreal. By 1760 New France was effectively under British control, although a formal end to the war would not come until three years later, when fighting in Europe between the two colonial powers would finally cease.

With the fall of New France, British-American settlers began to pour into the frontier territory over the Appalachian Mountains. Treaties between native nations and the French were ignored or "reinterpreted," and the nations beyond the mountains—the Delaware, Shawnee, Ottawa, and Seneca—began to fight back. Chief among the resisters was Pontiac (or Ponteach), an Ottawa leader in the Michigan territory, who was able to unite the native nations on the frontier. Pontiac's people had been allied with the French for many years. There had been few French settlers and the French had imposed no restrictions on hunting grounds. Observing the British occupation of Fort Detroit and the rapid movement of English settlers into the "Northwest Territory" of Ohio, Michigan, Indiana, and Illinois, Pontiac organized a crusade to prevent his people from being overwhelmed by the British tide.

After the fall of Quebec and Montreal, the French were no longer in any position to aid the Ottawa leader. Pontiac's War became a

donment of the tenth, and held Detroit in a stranglehold siege. Only the forts at Detroit, Niagara, and Pittsburgh held out against Pontiac's forces.

This was achieved through Pontiac's leadership and clever strategies that included deception, not just assault, and closing down the British supply lines. Fort Detroit survived the siege begun on May 7, 1763, because reinforcements and supplies arrived by ship across Lake Erie. Pontiac abandoned the siege only after the signing of the Treaty of Paris in 1763, which formally ended the French and Indian War. A French commander urged Pontiac to lift the siege and to agree to peace because there could be no future French support for his cause.

It has been claimed that the siege of another British fort, Fort Pitt (Pittsburgh), was broken through "germ warfare." All that is known for sure is that General Jeffrey Amherst, commander of the British forces in North America, wrote to Colonel Henry Bouquet, the officer leading a relief column towards Fort Pitt: *"Could it not be contrived to send the Small Pox among those disaffected tribes of Indians? We must on this occasion use every stratagem in our power to reduce them."* Bouquet agreed that blankets infected with smallpox might be distributed to the Indians, but it has never been proven that he carried out this plan. However, it has been claimed that an officer within Fort Pitt, Capt. Simeon Ecuyer, did send a present of two infected blankets and an infected handkerchief

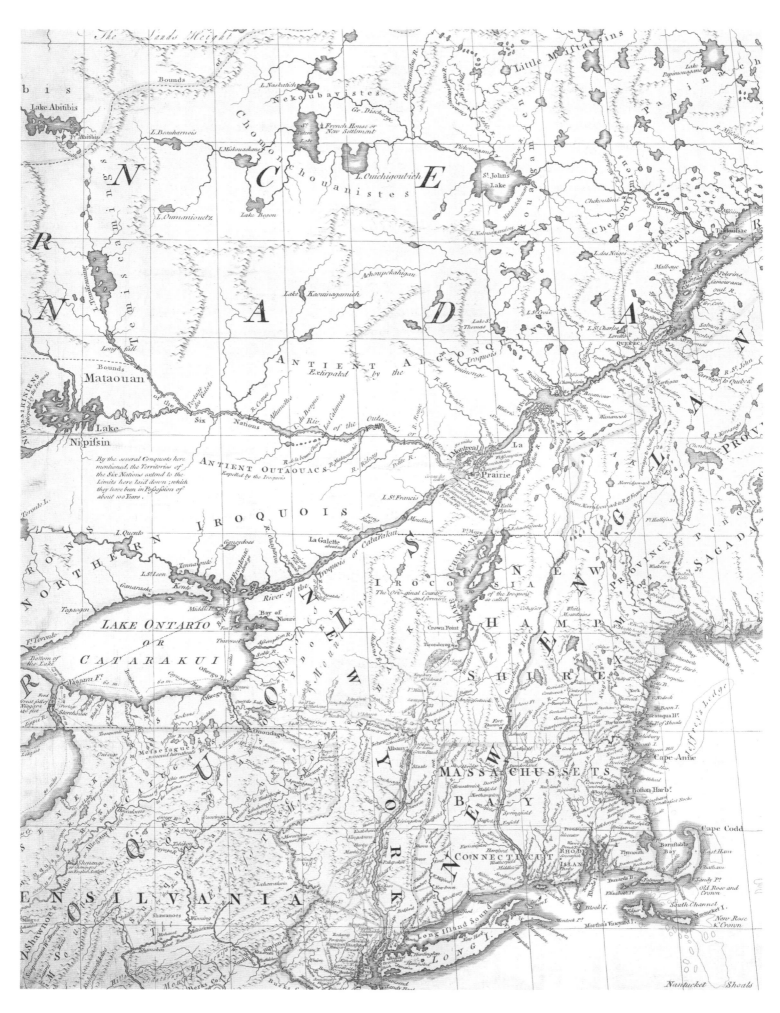

to the Delaware outside the fort. The siege was ended by Bouquet's force in August.

Once Pontiac had abandoned the fight to push back the British from the Northwest Territory, he became an advocate of peace and worked to improve relations with the new settlers. In response to Pontiac's War, the British government announced the Proclamation Act of 1763. This prohibited settlers from moving into lands across the mountains, which were designated Indian lands. The Proclamation Act turned out to be unenforceable, however. Boundaries drawn in London existed only on paper, and both Native Americans and colonists crossed them at will.

Britain, France, and Spain were the signatories of the 1783 Treaty of Paris. All of Canada and all territory east of the Mississippi River became British territory. This included Florida, relinquished by the Spanish who had entered late into the war as an ally of France. All French territory west of the Mississippi River was given to Spain. The balance of power in North America had dramatically and permanently changed overnight, leaving the native nations at a loss. They could no longer manipulate ambitious colonial rivals to their own advantage. Instead, they were now forced to hold their own against a united power whose colonial population was soaring and which no longer needed to court native loyalties.

In the brief decade between the end of the French and Indian War and the beginning of the American Revolution, the Northeastern nations struggled to retain their land and to create effective alliances among themselves. Change came too quickly, however, and native peoples came under pressure from every side. The Treaty of Fort Stanwix in 1768 illustrates their problems during this period. A native leader commented, *"Let us make a line for the benefit of our children that they may have lands which cannot be taken from them and let us doing that show the king that we are generous, and that we will leave him land enough for his people, then he will regard us and take better care that his people do not cheat us."*

The treaty line finally agreed upon was defined by the Ohio River. All the land beyond its northern bank—the Northwest Territory— would remain forever Native American and would be closed to further colonial settlement.

***Opposite:** Detail of the influential 1755 map of the "British and French Dominions in North America" by American John Mitchell. It was used to determine boundaries in the 1783 Peace of Paris. Note the annotation at center left: "By the several conquests here mentioned, the Territories of the Six Nations extend to the limits here laid down; which they have been in Possession of about 100 years." Near Lake Champlain, another note reads: "Irocoisia: The Original Country of the Iroquois and formerly so called."*

***Below:** The Ottawa leader Pontiac (Ponteach) fought to preserve native lands west of the Appalachians.*

Within a short time, however, the Ohio River boundary was ignored by English settlers. Governor Dunmore of Virginia even encouraged violation of the border.

While events along the Atlantic coast accelerated the movement toward American independence, the beleagured nations of the trans-Appalachian northwest struggled with the continuing encroachments of land speculators and farmers on their lands, which in 1774 finally provoked "Lord Dunmore's War," a series of bloody raids, attacks, and counterattacks by English settlers in the Ohio valley.

Lord Dunmore's War broke out around Fort Pitt at the Forks, as the Shawnee, Ottawa, and their allies tried to prevent the colonists from moving into the Kentucky territory. Kentucky was claimed by the colony of Virginia. Under the terms of the Treaty of Fort Stanwix, native peoples were obliged to relinquish control of its territory since it lay south of the designated Ohio River boundary.

To prevent the colonists from flagrantly crossing the Ohio River to start their farms in Indian territory, Shawnee leader Wynepuechsika, or Cornstalk, organized the peoples of the Ohio River valley. Defeated in battle, Cornstalk arrived with a flag of truce at the 1774 treaty negotiations at Chillicothe, Ohio, only to be jailed and then killed by colonial soldiers. In the course of the conflict several other important native leaders were killed.

Finding themselves at the mercy of the colonies—or the "thirteen fires"—native peoples became involved in various pre-Revolutionary events. The British urged the Iroquois to remain neutral. Once the Declaration of Independence was announced, the native nations began to break into groups supporting either the colonies or the British. The Passamaquoddy of Maine and several small groups chose to aid the colonists. Inland, the Iroquois abandoned neutrality. By the end of the French and Indian wars their population and power had been greatly reduced. They had been further decimated by an epidemic that had swept through the Onondaga Nation, killing most of its leaders. Native Americans fought against each other in most western engagements of the American Revolution. Throughout the Revolution the colonists emulated native warrior tactics, adopting ambushes rather than maneuvering in open fields according to the customary forms of engagement of classic European warfare.

In the early years of the War for Independence both British and Americans hoped to secure native support. The colonial leaders could offer nothing more than promises. The British, for their part, reminded the Iroquois of the covenant chain and the long history of official alliances between the native nations and the British government. The Six Nations were uneasy with the new Anglo-American rivalry, preferring to remain neutral and to be left in peace. Much of the Revolution, however, was intensely fought in their territory, making neutrality nearly impossible to maintain.

Mohawk chief Joseph Brant became a key figure during the American Revolution. Joseph's sister, Molly Brant, also exerted great influence over the affairs of the Iroquois. A colonial leader wrote, "*The Indians pay her great respect and I am afraid her influence will give us some trouble, for we are informed that she is working strongly to prevent the meeting at Albany, being intirely in the Interests of Guy Johnson.*"

When Brant returned to North America from a diplomatic visit to London in 1776, the War for Independence was well under way. He raised his own troops, Brant's Volunteers, composed of Mohawk and British loyalists, and began to fight and plan strategies with British military leaders. The unity of the Six Nations had by this time been broken, with the Mohawk, Onondaga, Cayuga, and Seneca renewing the covenant chain with the British, while the Oneida and Tuscarora were persuaded by a colonial Moravian missionary to remain neutral. It seemed to the four British allies that they would fare better under British rule than under independent American states bent on expansion.

The first major test of the new alliance was the Battle of Oriskany, in which the British and Iroquois inflicted heavy casualties on the colonists and prevented reinforcements from reaching Fort Stanwix, although the fort itself held firm against them. The aftermath of this battle set Iroquois against Iroquois as British-allied Iroquois put villages of the neutral Oneida to flames. Raids throughout the Mohawk and Wyoming valleys were led by the Seneca chief Kiantw'ka (or Cornplanter) and the elder Kaientkwahton (Old Smoke). In 1778 their

Seneca and Cayuga warriors, with assistance from some British loyalists, destroyed eight forts and burned nearly 1,000 homes. Because of his notoriety, Joseph Brant was blamed for all the devastating and barbarous attacks throughout New York. While Brant led many of the destructive raids, he was not present at some of the most horrible, like the massacre of innocent women and children in Cherry Valley.

The terrorist raids throughout New York outraged General George Washington and prompted him to order Major General John Sullivan to eliminate the Iroquois threat by any means necessary. Sullivan's troops destroyed every native village, orchard, and field they could find, adding their own barbarism to the list of war atrocities. More than 5,000 Iroquois refugees fled to Fort Niagara, where they barely survived a harsh winter. The population of the four nations was reduced to one half of its pre-war number, and only two villages were left untouched. Seneca Mary Jemison remembered: "*A part of our corn they burnt and threw the remainder into the river. They burnt our houses, killed what few cattle and horses they could find, destroyed our fruit trees and left nothing but the bare soil and timber....Accordingly we all returned, but what were our feelings when we found that there was not a mouthful of any kind of sustenance left, not even enough to keep a child one day from perishing with hunger.*" The villages and lands of the Iroquois nations never recovered from the devastation. However, Brant, Cornplanter, and other leaders continued to strike deep into New York's heartland until 1783, when a peace treaty ended the War for Independence.

*Below:* Detail of a map from the Eighteenth Annual Report of the Bureau of American Ethnology illustrating the Pennsylvania cession under Article 3 of the 1784 treaty between the new United States and the Six Nations, setting the new western boundary of the Six Nations.

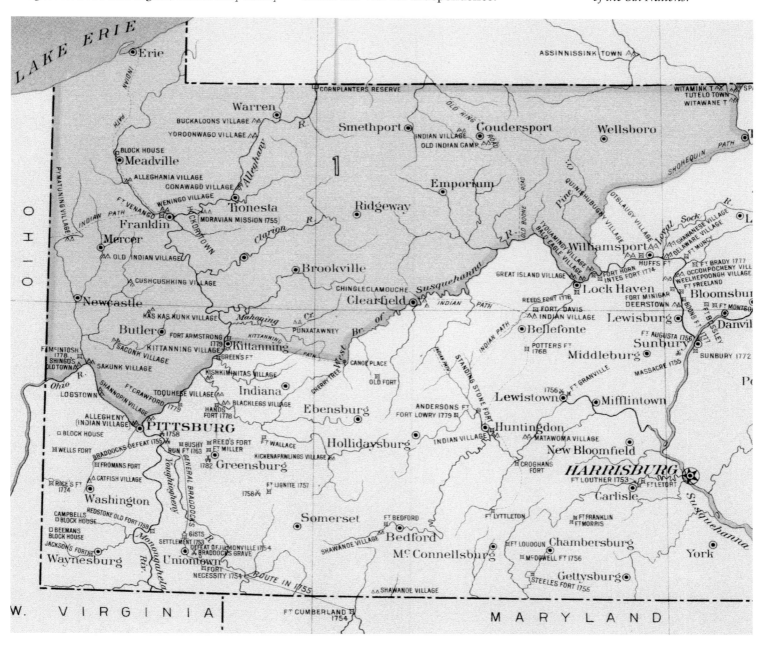

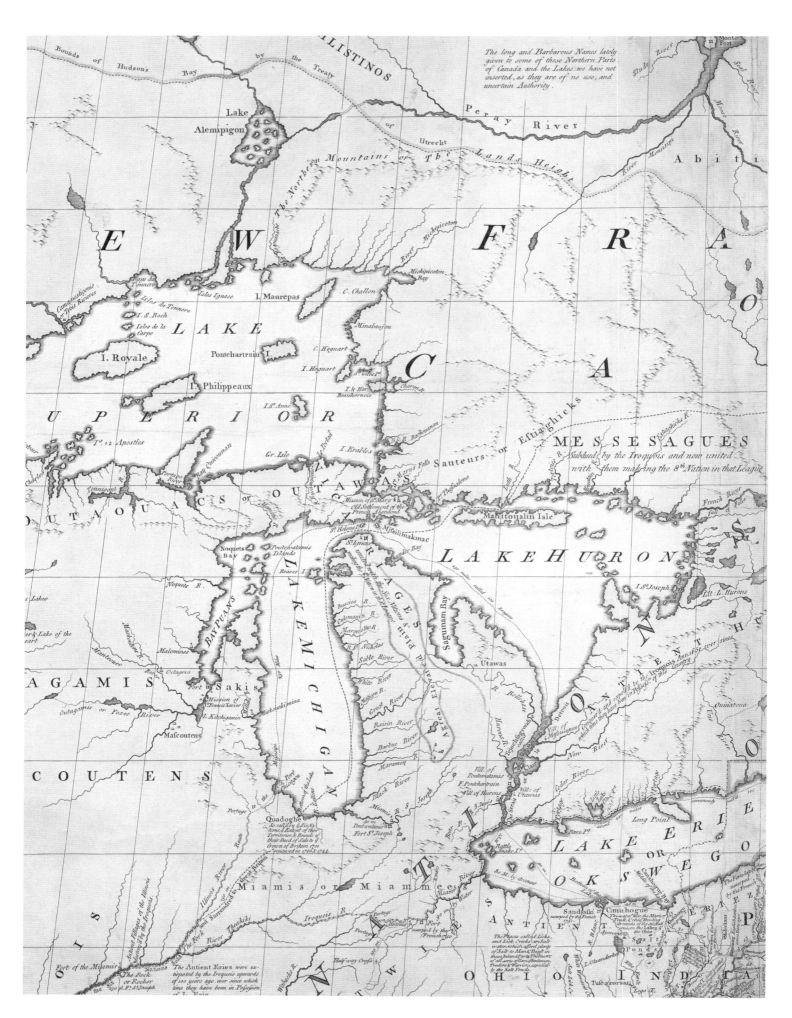

The Treaty of Paris ceded all land south of Canada and west to the Mississippi River to the newly independent American states. Florida was returned to Spain. A new Treaty of Fort Stanwix was negotiated in 1784 between the western native nations and the victorious American states. All Native American claims to the Northwest Territory were overturned, and, no longer recognized as sovereign nations, the native people were treated as common residents of the new United States. In 1785 Chief Brant and other native leaders led an exodus into Canada to join four earlier settlements of Mohawk exiles. As compensation for their alliance with the British during the American Revolution, they were given more than 600,000 acres between Lakes Erie and Ontario to create the Six Nations Reserve.

While Brant led his people into exile in 1785, the situation remained critical in the Northwest Territory as Miami Chief Michikinikwa, or Little Turtle, organized raids throughout the Ohio valley against the new flood of American settlers. An expedition was sent to halt the raids, but the American troops were lured into ambushes by Little Turtle and were easily defeated. A second attempt to destroy Miami resistance was led by General St. Clair, governor of the Northwest territories. Like Pontiac a clever tactician, Little Turtle drew St. Clair and his forces deeper into native territory, where they were surrounded by Little Turtle's warriors. More than 600 American troops were killed, about 300 were wounded, and the remainder made a desperate retreat to safety. The result was one of the single worst defeats of its forces by native warriors in the history of the United States—far worse than the defeat of Custer in 1876.

Peace talks at Sandusky, Ohio, were a failure, with native nations refusing to relinquish the Ohio River as the boundary of Indian territory. A third, stronger, and carefully organized expedition against Little Turtle set out. Some 3,000 well-trained and -equipped men led by General Anthony Wayne headed into Indian territory once again, building support forts along the way. In 1794 Little Turtle, unable to dislodge Wayne and his troops from Fort Recovery, and anticipating defeat by Wayne's strong force, proposed peace talks. Little Turtle observed to his men:

*"We have beaten the enemy twice under separate commanders. We cannot expect the same good fortune always to attend us. The Americans are now led by a chief who never sleeps; the night and the day are alike to him…we have never been able to surprise him. Think well of it. There is something whispers [to] me, it would be prudent to listen to his offers of peace."*

Little Turtle's warriors rejected his proposal, selected a new leader in his place, and the native forces were led into a disastrous battle at Fallen Timbers near Fort Miami. Nearly all were killed, their villages and crops were put to the torch, and the uprising begun by Little Turtle came to an end. In the Treaty of Greenville in 1795, 1,100 native leaders agreed to give up all of Ohio and much of Indiana. At Greenville, an Indian leader declared: *"We do now, and will henceforth, acknowledge the fifteen United States of America to be our father.… [We] must call them brothers no more."* General Anthony Wayne responded: *"I now adopt you all, in the name of the President of the Fifteen great fires of America."*

Thus ended the eighteenth century for the native nations of the Northeast. Their circumstances had dramatically and irreversibly changed since 1700, when they had been sovereign nations in control of most of the hundreds of millions of acres of woodlands and river valleys in the Northeast between the Atlantic Ocean and the Mississippi River.

**Opposite:** *The Great Lakes region from John Mitchell's 1755 map. The Ottawa, Sauk, and Fox are among those shown as retaining independent status, while Iroquois-controlled lands include the former Erie, Huron, "Messesagues" (Missisauga, an Ojibwa subgroup), and "Nicariages" (Necariages, an Ottawa clan or subgroup).*

**Left:** *The imposing Seneca chief Cornplanter was allied with his fellow tribesman, Red Jacket, on the British side against the American Revolutionists.*

## THE SOUTHEAST

At the beginning of the eighteenth century some of the native nations of the Southeast were as powerful as the English and Spanish colonies on their borders. Several factors would alter that status—including slavery. The slave trade was big business, and not only the trade in African slaves. The Indian slave trade also boomed in the eighteenth century. Charles Town, South Carolina, was the center of a slave trade in native peoples, and Charles Town businessmen were the major profiteers. As early as 1708 the English population of the Carolinas (5,300) was almost outnumbered by the presence there of 2,900 African and 1,400 Native American slaves. Applying the same practices that had been successfully used to expand the slave trade in Africa, the Charles Town traders encouraged the subjugation of weaker coastal native groups by stronger groups—many of whom were former enemies of the colonists—and supplied the dominant native nations with weapons and trade goods in exchange for captives. In 1702, for example, the Chickasaw killed or captured 2,300 Choctaw and sold the survivors to slave traders.

Most Native American slaves were sent to work the plantations of the West Indies, but many were put to work on cattle ranches and rice and indigo plantations in the Carolinas. Some were also sent north to New York and New England. Continual battles were fueled by the requirements of the slave trade, and some Native Americans perceived the ultimate danger of continuing to cooperate with it.

English slave traders initiated massive raids into Spanish Florida, bringing back perhaps 12,000 native people to be sold at the Charles Town slave auctions. Even though many of the Carolina proprietors in London opposed the Indian slave trade and tried to halt it, they were unable to control the actions of the Charles Town traders. In the Carolina colonies themselves there was no significant resistance to the abuse or enslavement of native people.

Probably the most powerful inland native group in the region was the Creek (also known as Muskogee). For many years they preserved a balance of power through a loose confederation of native peoples similar to the Iroquois League to the north. The Creek played off English interests on the Atlantic coast against Spanish settlements in Florida and along the coasts of Alabama and Mississippi, and against French interests in the Mississippi River valley. The primary objective of the Creek was to confine the English to the Atlantic seaboard and to prevent their domination of the lower South. Manipulating the intense rivalry among the colonial powers to their own advantage, the Creek negotiated preferential trade agreements with each European country. In their pursuit of weapons and trade items, they remained close to the European trade centers in the South, even though this proximity threatened their way of life. They soon became very wealthy and powerful, but their dependence on the trade system deepened. Armed with European weapons, they fought the Choctaw of Alabama and Mississippi as well as the Spanish in Florida and along the Gulf Coast.

*Right:* The Choctaw in present-day Mississippi were affected by the incursions of the Spanish, French, and Americans during the eighteenth century.

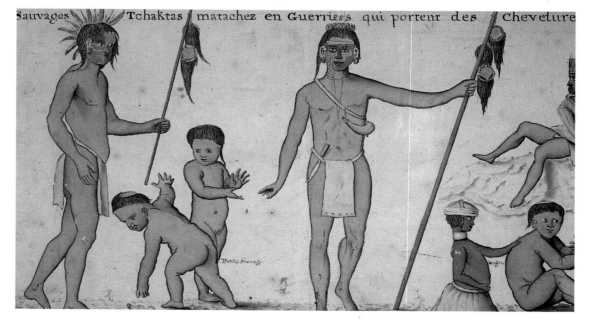

**Left:** *Attacks by the colonists on the Tuscarora and Tutelo were directed at taking land and enslaving natives. The Tuscarora began migrating north to the protection of the Oneida and the Iroquois League around 1713. The Tutelo moved to Fort Christanna, having been promised protection from slavers there. When that promise proved false, the Tutelo sought protection from the Cayuga and moved north around 1740. The British and the Creek Confederacy made war against the Apalachee twice, finally defeating them in 1704 and selling many of the survivors into slavery. Those who remained took refuge with the Mobile. With the Apalachee gone, the British and Creek were able to launch attacks on the Timucua. The Yamasee War of 1715 resulted in their utter defeat and the Yamasee were forced to retreat to Spanish Florida. The Natchez, too, were virtually annihilated in their war with the French. When a few survivors took refuge with the Huoma, the French attacked that nation as well.*

The demise of the Apalachee and Timucua in the early eighteenth century opened lands for settlement by Creek peoples under pressure from British colonization in the Carolinas. The first Creeks to migrate south, the Oconee were called *Sim-in-oli*—"Wild Ones" in Muskogee. Initially settling down to farming on Florida's Alachua Plain, they were called "Siminole" by Euroamericans as early as 1773. They absorbed remnants of the Yamasee and other defeated nations, growing to about 5,000 by 1817.

The Tuscarora were a large coastal farming nation that had lost many of its children to slave traders. More and more of their land was seized for the expansion of English settlements, and the Tuscarora finally rose in revolt against the British. In 1712, some 900 Creek, Yamasee, Cherokee, and Catawba allies and 33 settlers mounted a fierce attack on the Tuscarora fort of Nooherooka (Neoheroka), bringing an end to the Tuscarora War. In that battle alone, more than 500 of the Tuscarora were killed or taken into slavery. By the end of the war more than 1,000 of the Tusacarora had been killed and at least 700 had been enslaved. Although the Tuscarora were granted a reservation in North Carolina, many of them moved northward during the following years to join their Iroquoian-speaking relatives in northern New York. In 1722, as mentioned, they were accepted into the Iroquois League as the Sixth Nation.

The Yamasee had allied with the English in the Tuscarora War to defeat the weaker nation and share in the rich harvest of slaves that would bring them valued trade goods. But in 1715 the Yamasee themselves rose against the British in a series of Yamasee Wars that involved fifteen native nations and nearly succeeded in driving the British out of the Southeast. The Yamasee were greatly in debt to the British traders, owing them several years' worth of deerskins. At the same time, the French along the Mississippi River, who traded with the Creek, encouraged attacks on all parts of the western Carolina frontier, which forced the English to retreat into Charles Town. Creek chief Brims coordinated these attacks, believing that the British could be completely driven from the land if the native nations combined their forces. The Yamasee and Creek then sought an alliance with the large and powerful Cherokee nation for a combined attack on Charles Town to force the British from the region altogether.

The decision of the Cherokee leaders was crucial to the native alliance. After a lengthy debate within the nation between the pro- and anti-British factions, the Cherokee decided to

**Above:** *Few Americans are aware that both Africans and Native Americans were sold at auction in Southern slave markets.*

support the British against the other nations. With expansive promises from the British for the trade goods they so desired, the Cherokee agreed to declare war on the Creek, for otherwise *"they should have no way in geting of Slaves to buy ammunition and clothing."* In 1730 seven Cherokee leaders—including the powerful Attakullakulla, or Onacona (Little Carpenter)—were taken to England to sign a treaty with King George II. At the beginning of the American War for Independence, however, Attakullakulla broke with other Cherokee and raised troops for the American patriots.

As the alliance of nations collapsed in the face of combined Cherokee and British strength, the Creek pulled back from the coastline into Alabama and maintained their ties with the French, while the Yamasee retreated into Florida. Brims was a master diplomat. He used his two sons as emissaries, sending one to the Spanish and the other to the British to represent the Creek, and he maintained diplomatic relations with such northern nations as the Seneca. It was not unusual for Brims to send his sons and other representatives to Charles Town, London, or Mexico City. For many years after the Yamasee Wars, Brims managed to preserve the neutrality of the Creek nation amidst all of the competing powers—both native and European—that encircled the nation in the heart of the Southeast. After Brims died in the 1730s the Creek were able to maintain their neutrality even when the Anglo-French rivalry ignited into wars. In the 1740s the British put intense pressure on them to expel the French from the region. Malatchi, Brims'

youngest son, adroitly maintained Creek sovereignty in spite of British threats to withdraw all trade. In 1747 he simply informed the British that they would not be allowed to build forts in Creek territory and that there would be no military support for any advances on the French or Spanish. He then personally visited St. Augustine and a major French fort to inform the Spanish and the French of British attempts to gain Creek support.

In 1718 New France expanded in the Mississippi River valley, establishing the first permanent fort at New Orleans, which they built on the former site of a Choctaw village called Chinchuba, the Choctaw word for "alligator." The Natchez peoples of the area were in constant conflict with the French, however, and in 1729 they attacked and were temporarily victorious. Unhappily for the Natchez, though, the Choctaw nation made an alliance with the French and burned Natchez villages. More than 1,000 Natchez were killed and at least 400 others were captured and sold into slavery. The surviving Natchez fled.

The Chickasaw faced the same French threat in the lower Mississippi River valley but were able to prevent French troops from destroying their towns. They repeatedly repulsed heavy French attacks between 1736 and 1753 and remained undefeated throughout the French and Indian wars.

After the failure of the largest nations to unite and expel the British, native peoples in the Southeast were trapped in intensified trade dependency and slave trade relationships. The most destructive weapon used by the British was trade—all kinds of trade. Intertribal warfare increased, and all were weakened by warfare, slavery, and European diseases. As coastal groups dwindled in number and moved away, settlers moved onto their land. After the seven Cherokee leaders signed the treaty with King George II in 1730, the British presence in the Southeast became secure.

As one of the larger native nations in eastern North America, the Cherokee played a pivotal role in the power politics of the South, especially after the Yamasee Wars. At first they benefited little from their alliance with Britain. English traders regularly cheated them, and through their contacts with the English the Cherokee suffered a devastating epidemic of smallpox that killed some 11,000 in the late 1730s. In 1748 the South Carolinians failed to honor their alliance with the Cherokee, doing nothing to aid them against a Creek attack. This provoked Cherokee retaliation against some of their English trading partners.

In self-protection, Cherokee leaders kept communication open with the French so that the British would not take their relationship for granted. With the colonial population in many remote areas outnumbered perhaps ten to one by native peoples, the British were sensitive to the danger of losing Cherokee support, without which they had no buffer between themselves and the French and their Choctaw allies. From 1750 until the end of the French and Indian War, South Carolina offered lavish gifts and favorable trade agreements to preserve friendship with the Cherokee and to ensure Creek neutrality. Faced with this need to maintain good relations with the Southeastern peoples and the simultaneous decline in the native population, along with the increased trade in African slaves, by 1750 colonial trade in Indian slaves had virtually disappeared in the Southeast. Deerskins, a primary trade commodity since earliest contact, were now being exported briskly: In 1750, 100,000 deerskins passed through the hands of traders in Charles Town.

Nanyehi (Nancy Ward)—the Ghighau, "Beloved Woman of the Cherokee"—was a major figure among the Cherokee during this period. In a battle with the Creek, Nanyehi fought with Cherokee warriors and was credited with helping turn the tide of battle to victory. Widely respected, she was a significant peacemaker as well, at times warning English settlers of forthcoming Cherokee attacks and meeting with Cherokee chiefs to urge peace with the colonists.

As the French and Indian War unfolded in the 1750s, the Cherokee nation was in a pivotal position to control the outcome of British colonial efforts against growing French strength throughout the Great Lakes region and in the Mississippi River valley. The governor of Virginia worked for two years to secure Cherokee support for George Washington's expedition to the Forks in Pennsylvania to dislodge the French, but the promised Cherokee warriors never arrived. Washington's troops were forced under

siege to surrender, but were allowed an honorable retreat. This was the beginning of a delicate balancing act in the Southeast in which Cherokee leaders assumed control, because the sparse British population along the seacoast had little power to confront the strength of the French and their allies without support.

Following Washington's defeat, the British government commissioned General Edward Braddock to lead a force across the Appalachian Mountains in 1755 to expel the French from the region of the Forks, the gateway to the large frontier territory claimed by the English colony of Virginia. Virginia tried again to negotiate Cherokee support for this critical mission, but in the end French and allied troops ambushed and destroyed Braddock's forces. Only eight Native Americans fought with Braddock, while half of the victorious enemy force was Indian. The dramatic victory of the French and their allies at the battle of the Monongahela confirmed colonial Americans in their conviction that native rather than European war tactics were required to win battles on American terrain.

In 1758 and 1759 a series of back-country skirmishes between the Cherokee and British settlers developed into the Cherokee Rebellion. As relations with the British worsened, the Cherokee nation began to look to the French for supplies and to the Creek for military help. Since the Creek often hinted that they might lean more toward the French, or even join in alliance with the Cherokee Nation, the British urgently presented them with lavish gifts to preserve their neutrality during the Cherokee Rebellion. As the Cherokee Rebellion continued, the governor of South Carolina sent an invasion force into Cherokee territory to cut off French supplies and put a stop to the attacks. Onitositah, or Corn Tassel, made clear the Cherokee sentiments:

*"Let us examine the facts of your present eruption into our country, and we shall discover your pretensions on that ground. What did you do? You marched into our territories…you killed a few scattered and defenseless individuals, spread fire and desolation wherever you pleased, and returned again to your own habitations.…Again, were we to inquire by what law or authority you set up a claim, I answer, none! Your laws extend not into our country, nor ever did."*

Remembering too well the failure of the Cherokee nation to support them in the

**Overleaf:** *Detail of John Mitchell's 1755 map showing the dominance of the Creek Nation over a wide area of the Southeast.*

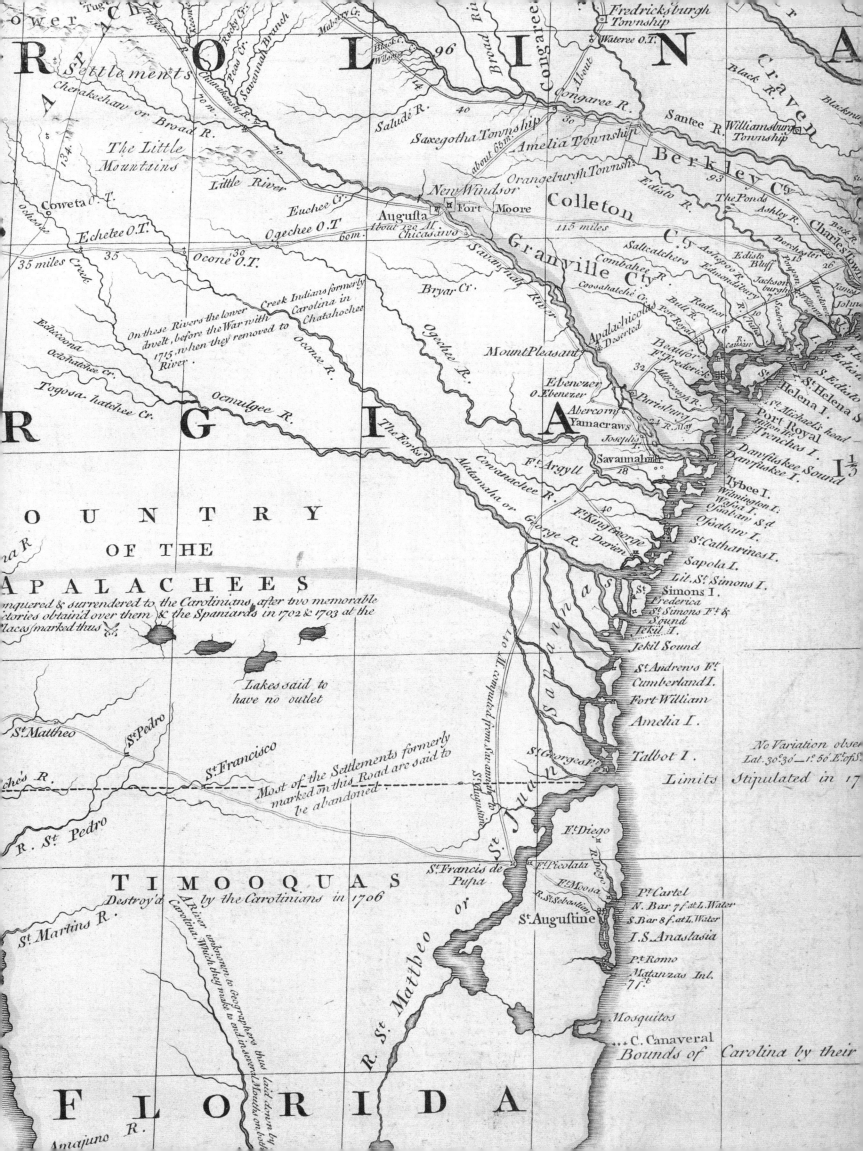

Yamasee Wars, the Creek finally scorned the Cherokee plea for help during the Rebellion. British troops were organized to crush the uprising, but even a large expedition by Lord Jeffrey Amherst failed in the unfamiliar and difficult terrain. In 1761 an outbreak of small-pox weakened the Cherokee, and the British destroyed villages and crops, finally forcing an end to the Rebellion.

Until the end of the French and Indian War in 1763, the Creek, Cherokee, and Catawba had remained strong nations, between them confining European settlement to a strip of coastline less than 100 miles deep. By the mid-1700s their leaders had become skillful diplomats capable of negotiating advantageous trade agreements and able to hold their people and land together against great pressures.

When the Treaty of Paris ended the French and Indian War, however, the Southern nations lost their favorable negotiating position. The French withdrew from North America, leaving the British in a commanding position, and yielded the port of New Orleans to Spain. The Choctaw, their former allies, were left exposed and hoping that France would retake portions of North America. Meanwhile, the British colonies had become more united, more populous, and stronger economically. They disregarded previous treaties and established new trade laws with Native Americans: Prices increased; there were no more gifts; no rum was offered; fewer weapons were made available; and the quality of supplies was poorer.

The boundaries of native lands were consistently ignored, and violence flared against intruding settlers throughout the South after 1763. The Creek failed in their efforts to unite the native nations of the Southeast to join in Pontiac's War in the Northwest Territory.

Prior to the eighteenth century, the Spanish mission system had become well established in Florida and the lower Southeast, but the population of Spanish settlers was never very large. After the Treaty of 1763 Florida became British territory, and the Spanish settlers withdrew from the area, taking allied Indians—who numbered less than 100 at the time—with them to Cuba. One of the few documented cases of the extinction of a Native American people occurred in 1767. The Spanish archives in Guanabacoa, Cuba, recorded the death of Juan

Alonso Cabale (1709–67). He seems to have been the last of the Timucua, who had numbered as many as 200,000 at the time of their first contact with Europeans.

Georgia had been made a colony in 1733 to serve as a buffer between the English seaboard colonies to the north and the Spanish in Florida. It was a rough-and-tumble colony, sparsely populated with European outcasts and debtors under the leadership of the idealistic James Oglethorpe, who had prohibited slavery in the colony until pressure forced its acceptance in 1749. Upon his arrival in Georgia, Oglethorpe immediately sought an alliance with the powerful Creek. Following a pattern that had been proven successful elsewhere, he took a dozen of the most important Creek leaders to London to meet with King George II, including the aged chief Tomochichi, who asked the king to promise them *"a fair and substantial basis for trade,…free repair of firearms, and the prohibition of rum."*

Oglethorpe also named Mary Musgrove (Matthews-Bosomworth) to be his Superintendent of Indian Affairs. Coosaponakeesa, "Creek Mary," was an educated Anglo-Creek woman who, through seniority, eventually became the head of a powerful Creek matriarchy with claims to land and privilege in the region. Two of her three European husbands were successful businessmen, but they were secondary to Mary in influence. Oglethorpe used Mary as his primary interpreter and mediator with the Creek until her death in 1763.

Within the next ten years, pressures in the colonies precipitated the American Revolution. The Shawnee, Delaware, and Mohawk Nations sent representatives south to persuade the Cherokee, Creek, Choctaw, and Chickasaw to support the British against the American colonists. By 1776 Cherokee leader Tsiyu Gansini, or Dragging Canoe, was organizing raids in support of the British, attacking forts and settlements throughout the Appalachian back country. While the Chickasaw conducted attacks on the settlers in the Kentucky and Tennessee regions, the Choctaw and Creek aided the British in the lower Mississippi River valley. The southern revolutionaries organized militia armies to sweep through Cherokee lands, where they destroyed villages and crops, but Dragging Canoe and his supporters withdrew to Tennessee and continued their raids with British supplies and support: *"Our Nation was alone and surrounded....After we had lost some of our best warriors, we were forced to leave our towns and corn to be burned by them, and now we live in the grass as you see us...but we are not yet conquered."*

By 1780 the revolutionary militia's policy of total destruction had succeeded in suppressing the raids, and land concessions were demanded from the Cherokee. Cherokee leader Unsuckanail observed: *"The encroachments on this side of the line have entirely deprived us of our hunting grounds....When any of my young men are hunting on their own grounds, and meet the white people, they, the white people, order them off and claim our deer."*

In the lower Mississippi River valley, Britain's allies continued to operate when it suited their own interests rather than in unqualified support of the British objectives. Expeditions were freely abandoned when British arrangements or supplies were insufficient. In 1780 the Choctaw left the British unsupported at Mobile, allowing the Spanish fleet—who were allied to the American Revolutionaries—to take the town.

Tensions in the lower South increased after the end of the American Revolution. To satisfy the demands of Georgia settlers for Creek land, the state of Georgia declared war on the Creek Nation.

Several Creek chiefs were forced to accept a series of treaties between 1783 and 1786, but these were rejected by their people. To force agreement, the Georgia government then seized hostages. Into this vortex stepped Hippoilkmico, or Alexander McGillivray, son of a Scotsman and a woman of Creek and French descent. Despite his European education and service with the British during the American Revolution, McGillivray became a member of his mother's Wind Clan and his first loyalties remained to the Creek people. A skillful negotiator, McGillivray established an alliance with the Spanish in Florida, who had regained Florida in 1783 and who supplied him with arms to fight British expansion. He forcefully defended Creek land ownership:

*"We warned the Georgians of the dangerous consequences that would certainly attend the settling of the lands in question. Our just remonstrances were treated with contempt, and those lands were soon filled with settlers....We made another effort to awaken in them a sense of justice and equity; but, we found from experience, that entreaty could not prevail, and parties of warriors were sent out to drive off all intruders, but to shed no blood, only where self preservation made it necessary."*

McGillivray's greatest achievement was the Treaty of New York in 1790, when the Creek Nation bypassed the state of Georgia to negotiate directly with the new United States government. When he died in 1793, the Creek lost a powerful spokesman.

Relations between Native Americans and African Americans were complex throughout the eighteenth century, adding another layer to the many conflicts between native and other peoples. The trade in native slaves reached its peak in the Southern colonies in the early 1700s, but by the end of the Yamasee War in 1715 the African slave trade had begun to increase. Heavy importation of African slaves in the 1730s led to frequent slave uprisings. By 1761 the slave revolts had become so serious that further imports were halted for three years. In 1765, when 7,000 Africans were shipped to the South, more than 100 African slaves fled into the interior and attempted to create a new colony. Again, the importation of African slaves was temporarily halted.

The Europeans in the South had been greatly outnumbered by Native Americans and Africans throughout the development of the colonies and remained so into the early nineteenth century. Europeans feared that the two groups would unite against them, and they worked continuously and deliberately to divide

**Overleaf:** *Cherokee territory, as shown in Mitchell's 1755 map, "formally surrendred [sic] to the Crown of Britain at Westminster 1729." The Chickasaw are here described as "In Alliance and Subjection to the English." Despite these descriptions, the Five Civilized Tribes were powerful and could negotiate with Britain from a position of strength throughout the wars against the French.*

**Below:** *Much of Spanish Florida was sparsely populated by Europeans, and the region became a refuge for Southeastern peoples hard pressed by colonial encroachment.*

them with hatred. Native Americans were relocated away from plantations with large African slave populations. Treaties with the Creek, Cherokee, and other nations always included provisions demanding the return of runaway African slaves, and bounties were offered for their capture and return.

African slaves served in the South Carolina militia during the wars between the British and the Tuscarora, Yamasee, and Cherokee. During the Yamasee War, half the militia troops were African. In 1760, although South Carolina was desperate for more troops, only a small number of African slaves were conscripted to fight in the militia against the Cherokee in the Rebellion, because the population of African slaves was by that time so enormous that the colonists feared African rebellion as well.

In spite of their most strenuous efforts, the Europeans could not altogether suppress the natural sympathy that developed between the two victimized populations. The Tuscarora sheltered many fugitive slaves before the Tuscarora War in 1711, and refugee Africans fought on the Tuscarora side in that war. Runaway slaves fought alongside the Yamasee in the Yamasee Wars. When the wars ended, the Yamasee refused to return the African fugitives and actu-

ally joined them in raids on plantations to free African slaves and help them reach safety in Spanish Florida. A colony of free Africans was established near St. Augustine. When Governor Oglethorpe attacked St. Augustine in 1740, his force was defeated by combined Spanish, Native American, and African troops.

In the 1720s African slaves learned to speak Cherokee as well as English, Spanish, and French, and runaway African slaves frequently served as interpreters between native peoples and Europeans. There was, however, no unified attempt to expel the Europeans: Relationships were inconsistent, determined by changing circumstances in the unending struggle to survive.

## THE GREAT PLAINS

The introduction of firearms and the rapid adoption of horses were changes of revolutionary importance for the peoples of the Great Plains in the eighteenth century. The Spanish had forbidden trade in guns to native peoples in the seventeenth century, but the Apache seized some in defiance of this prohibition. When the Spanish were driven out of New Mexico by the Puebloans in 1680, the Apache took many of the animals left behind and became masterful horsemen. Guns also came to the Plains peoples through contact with neighboring native groups to the east, where trade with the French and British flourished.

Moving northward from New Mexico, the horse spread quickly throughout the Great Plains. By 1750 the Blackfoot in present-day Alberta used horses, and by 1770 so did the Sioux in Minnesota. Their cultures were totally changed by the advantages in transportation, hunting, and warfare brought by the introduction of horses. The use of horses transformed a number of settled native nations into nomadic peoples who followed the buffalo herds. After 1700 the Comanche moved out of their settlements in the Rocky Mountains: As mounted warriors, they became the rulers of the southern Great Plains, challenging the dominance of the Apache and forcing them to move into the desert Southwest.

In the northern Plains the combination of guns and horses intensified intertribal warfare over hunting grounds. The Cheyenne and Sioux dominated the northwest and central Plains. As the Cheyenne, Arapaho, and Sioux moved west of the Missouri River, they pressed the Kiowa and Comanche down into Colorado, Nebraska, and Texas. Fierce fighters, the Cheyenne struck at the Crow in Wyoming and Montana, and at the Pawnee in Nebraska.

Having pressed the Cheyenne and Arapaho onto the Plains, the Sioux continued that pressure, taking all of the Dakotas and reaching into Wyoming and Montana. The Nitzitapi (Blackfoot) Confederation rivaled the Sioux in size and power. Based in the northwest Plains, the Blackfoot hunted buffalo in Alberta and Saskatchewan. Once they too had sufficient guns and horses, they expanded their hunting territory south into Montana and sent horse raiders down as far as the Rio Grande.

Not all nations of the Great Plains abandoned agricultural village life with the introduction of the horse. The Pawnee, Wichita, Omaha, Mandan, and some Sioux maintained settled villages. In 1782 about half the Sioux people resided in Minnesota, where they harvested wild rice, raised crops, and hunted buffalo. These groups had become successful farmers, and some, like the Hidatsa, were gifted horticulturists who developed many different strains of corn and beans. The agricultural villages became important trade centers as the nomadic natives brought hides and dried meat to exchange for corn, guns, European textiles, and metal tools. But the village dwellers had to fortify their densely populated communities with palisades against the surprise raids of their trading partners—who occasionally seized the goods they wanted instead of bartering for them.

At the start of the eighteenth century, France and Spain nominally controlled most of the Great Plains. Actually, the Spanish had extended their mission system only as far as southern Texas, while the French exploited the rest of the territory primarily for its furs and hides.

During French control of the Louisiana Territory, a network was established to gather furs and skins similar to the one that prevailed in Canada. Since native cooperation was vital, the French distributed gifts to foster loyalty and friendship. Licensed traders traveled to the various villages to trade for and collect goods. The French were well aware that a general peace would benefit this enterprise, but they were unable to achieve it. They also knew that trading firearms was exacerbating tribal rivalries,

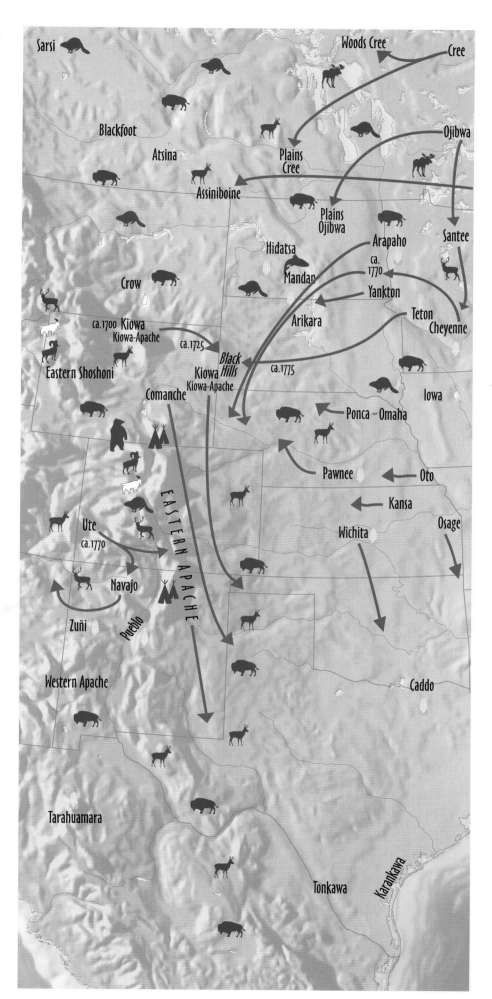

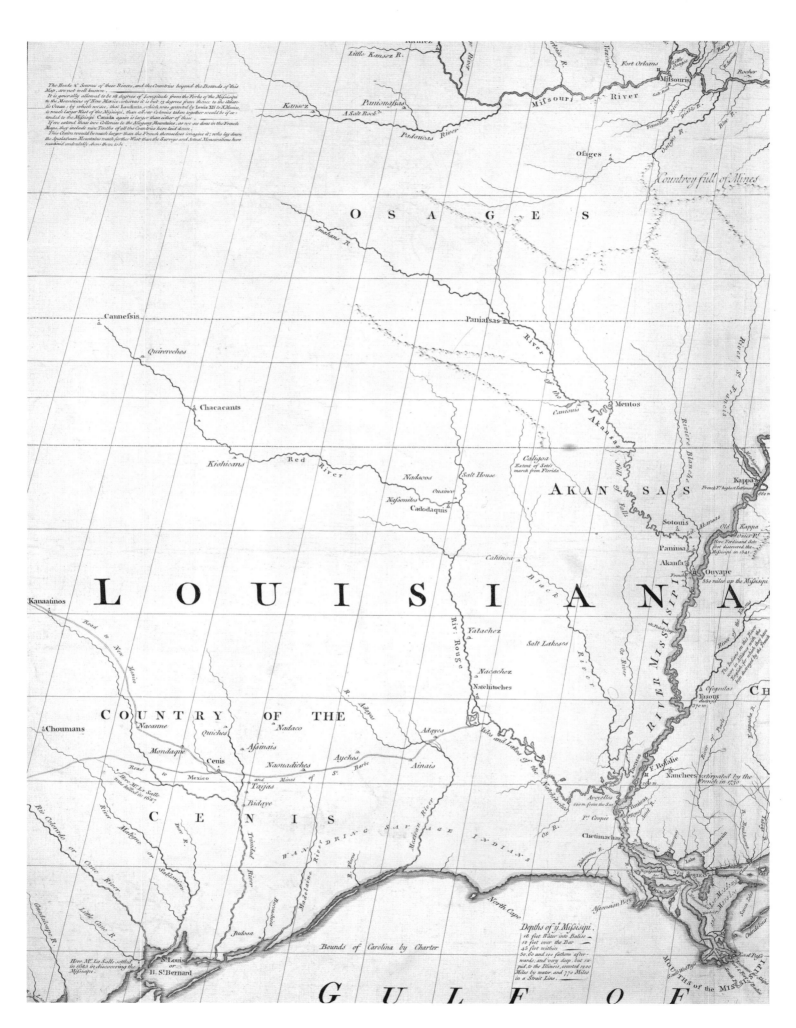

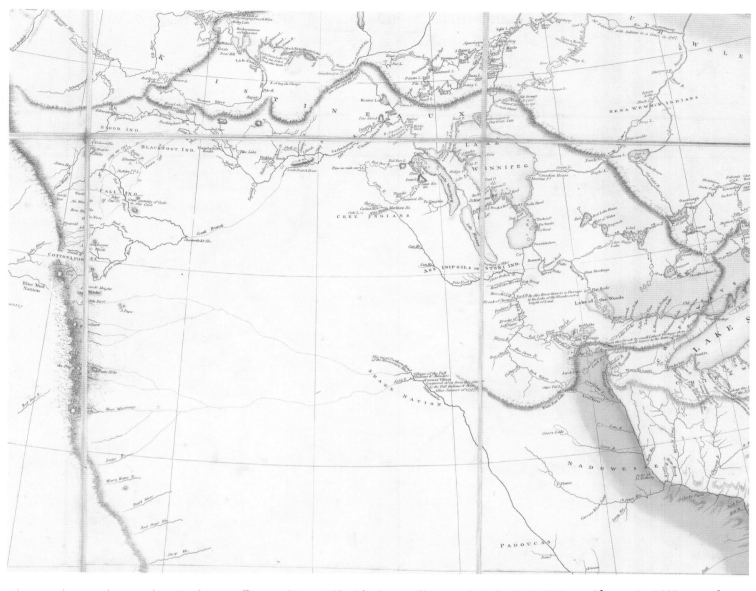

*Above:* An 1802 map of the northern Plains by A. Arrowsmith, commissioned by the Hudson's Bay Company.

*Left and opposite:* Two details of the Great Plains from Mitchell's 1755 map, parts of Louisiana Territory but as yet showing little Euroamerican incursion. The "Cenis," or Hasinai (a Caddoan group) are shown to the south, while the Sioux, "reckoned one of the most Populous Nations of Indians in North America," dominate the northeastern Plains.

129

but refusal to do so would only drive the natives to trade with the British, a situation to be avoided at all costs.

The Spanish acquired the Louisiana Territory in 1763, when the Seven Years' War ended, while the British got all the former French claims east of the Mississippi, Maintaining the French trading system as it was enabled the Spanish to benefit from it, but it proved impossible to establish a trade monopoly with the various tribes, particularly on the upper Mississippi and Missouri Rivers, where the British were making inroads.

Because the fur trade was based upon widely dispersed, free-roaming animals rather than agricultural products or mineral extraction, the policies Spain had instituted in New Mexico and New Spain were not viable in Louisiana. Instead, an uneasy alliance between natives and Spanish ensued, and the Spanish were unable to prevent all tribal raiding and killing. A particularly aggressive tribe, the Osage were never curbed completely, despite punitive trade embargoes and withholding of annual gifts. Accepting sham Osage avowals of contrition as satisfactory, the Spanish had a convenient excuse to ignore ongoing breaches of the peace. On that basis, they hoped to maintain the substantial Osage contribution to yearly revenues while forestalling British expansion into the area—all without a war with the natives which was not feasible economically, politically, or militarily. As a result, Spanish policy in the Louisiana Territory became an anomaly in the Spanish Empire.

*Below:* Two hornos— *beehive-shaped adobe ovens— at Rancho de las Golondrinas, a Spanish ranch founded in New Mexico during the early 1700s.*

## THE SOUTHWEST

The lessons of the Pueblo Revolt of 1680 as well as new domestic and international conditions and events ushered in changes in the new century. Concerns over the French presence on the eastern frontier would influence Spanish-Indian relations throughout the century.

The Franciscan theocracy and missionary zeal was gone, swept away by the harsh realities of frontier life. In its place were governmental policies that emphasized defense and revenue instead of missions and converts. Throughout the century, mission wealth would fall in proportion to the rise in wealth of the Spanish settlers.

The new government was given priority, and military funding would be greater than the grants to the missions. Few of the old families had returned after the 1680 revolt; the *encomiendero*-soldier was now replaced by salaried soldiery in garrisons, and the *encomienda* system was replaced by the *repartimiento* system of rotational labor.

Pueblo territory would also shrink as arable land became scarce. Prior to the eighteenth century, the fictitious Pueblo League had given each Pueblo the rights to all lands they habitually inhabited or tilled. As population fell fewer farmers tilled the land and nomadic raiders were easily able to force the abandonment of indefensible land. As the Puebloans lost control of these areas, they eventually fell into non-native hands.

Throughout the eighteenth century, the devastation of native populations by disease continued. Following their return in 1692, the Spanish settled the surviving natives into fewer, larger settlements. The resultant higher population density allowed disease levels to mount, from both increased crowding and poor sanitation practices. The resettlement pattern had a significant impact on the evolution of future epidemics. Initially, the epidemics infected a larger population base. However, the widely dispersed settlements, as well as governmental policy restricting travel by everyone, confined many epidemics to a single town. Even so, certain epidemics, such as the outbreaks of measles in 1728–29 and smallpox in 1780–81, were widespread and extremely lethal.

In 1719 smallpox erupted in Nambé Pueblo, and measles afflicted Jémez, Ácoma, and

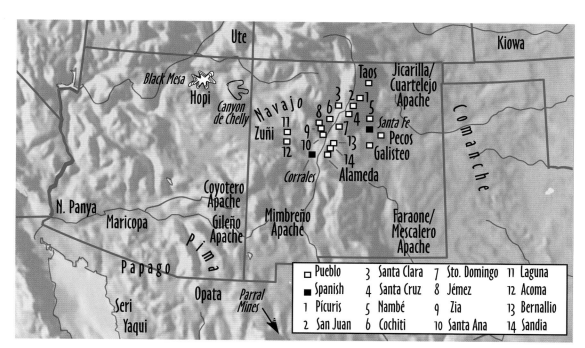

Map legend:

| □ Pueblo | 3 Santa Clara | 7 Sto. Domingo | 11 Laguna |
|----------|---------------|----------------|-----------|
| ■ Spanish | 4 Santa Cruz | 8 Jémez | 12 Acoma |
| 1 Pícuris | 5 Nambé | 9 Zia | 13 Bernallio |
| 2 San Juan | 6 Cochiti | 10 Santa Ana | 14 Sandia |

Galisteo in 1728 and 1729. As conditions worsened, Indians fled from Jémez, Zia, Santa Ana, and Cochiti Pueblos, probably taking the disease with them. Smallpox was again in Jémez, Santa Ana, and Santa Fe in 1733 and in Zuñi, where 200 died, in 1734. Pecos experienced a smallpox outbreak in 1738, and in an unnamed epidemic in 1748, fifteen children died. A major epidemic occurred in 1759, and in 1770 an unnamed disease fatal to children erupted in Santa Clara. Laguna had an outbreak of *La Peste* in 1772. The extremely destructive smallpox epidemic of 1780–81 hit Sandia, Bernalillo, Corrales, Alameda, Santa Clara, the Hopi, and Santo Domingo where more than 230 Puebloans died. On May 1, 1781, the governor reported 5,025 deaths from the disease—over 25 percent of the native population—the worst recorded epidemic to hit this area. A two-year drought, famine, and malnutrition preceding the epidemic almost certainly contributed to the high mortality levels. As a result of this depopulation, the number of missions was reduced to twenty. The century ended with another smallpox outbreak at Santa Cruz in 1799.

Nor were the southern Plains tribes exempt from these epidemics. Trading, raiding pueblos, and slaving raids brought these nomadic tribes into sufficient contact to ensure disease transmission. Consequently, they experienced outbreaks of smallpox in 1710 as well as the destructive epidemic of 1780–81. Many natives, desperate for a cure, sought conver-

sion and baptism, which were soon followed by last rites and death.

Prior to the 1780 smallpox outbreak among them, the Comanche had become a powerful tribe. However, greatly weakened by the epidemic, they were looking for peace by 1785 and formed an alliance with the Spanish in 1786. By 1790 they were trading at Pecos, and itinerant merchants had begun traveling into the southern Plains with their goods.

The colonial need for labor continued throughout the century, with the government and friars vying for control of the native labor force. Following the return of the Spanish in 1692, the Puebloans were no longer subjected to slave raiding by the Spanish. Instead, the "just war" for slaves was carried out against hostile Apache tribes.

However, the Puebloans did not completely escape labor conscription. The old *encomienda* system had been replaced by *repartimiento*, a rotational labor draft whose assignment center was located in Santa Fe. In addition, the demands for raw materials continued. The draft was run on a weekly basis, with men assigned to building, irrigation maintenance, and cultivation of the governor's and constables' fields. Women were assigned the domestic chores of husking corn, threshing wheat, grinding flour, and baking bread. Travel to Santa Fe for assignment was mandatory and no exceptions were made. Even pregnant women were not excused, and many aborted due to exhaustion from long travel on foot and heavy work demands.

Upon entering Santa Fe, Pueblo women also faced an additional danger from the Spanish. Frequently attacked and raped, they often became pregnant. So prevalent was this problem that as early as 1707, fourteen Pueblo governors complained to the Colonial Government about it.

By 1750 a change had occurred in Pueblo culture that would profoundly affect the lives of these violated women and their mixed-blood children. Although sexual liaisons between Spanish men and native women had been accepted and tolerated by the Puebloans for centuries, by the mid-eighteenth century these women came to be viewed as defiled and were frequently expelled from their villages along with their mixed-blood offspring. As a consequence of this marginalization, these women had few options available to them beyond entering Spanish households as menials or joining the nomadic tribes. Once expelled, these women, children, and future generations were lost forever to their nations.

In some cases when a woman gave birth to a light-skinned child, it was abandoned at the local mission, where it was recorded in the baptismal records as a *hijo de iglesia*, a child of the church. These children were then placed in Spanish homes where they were raised to become menials, draining yet more people from their native villages.

The labor draft had severe economic consequences for the general well-being of the Pueblos. The men were forced to leave their own fields untended while they completed their labor rotation. The resultant lower har-

vest yields led to fewer stored reserves for famine periods, higher levels of malnutrition, and higher mortality rates from starvation and disease. Worse, the crops they did harvest were frequently demanded in times of drought and famine by the Spanish. As a consequence of this cycle of declining harvest yields and Spanish theft, many natives were forced to join Spanish households as menials—the only survival option available to them.

In the early eighteenth century, international tensions developed between Spanish and French powers over control of the trans-Mississippi West. As native raiding intensified along the eastern borderlands of New Mexico, the Spanish did not comprehend the underlying causes until 1697, when reports began to arrive suggesting that interlopers on the southern Plains were inciting and abetting the increased raids. Finally realizing their vulnerability to a potential French-Indian coalition, Spain instituted policy changes that would create a vicious cycle of raiding. Intent on creating a buffer between themselves and the French, the Spanish now courted former enemies and turned them into allies, who were then urged to conduct slaving raids against the allies of the French.

Prior to 1694 the Spanish had attempted to discourage New Mexico natives from raiding other tribes for captives whom they then offered to the Spanish as slaves. However, in 1697, following a change in policy instituted to weaken the French allies, the Spanish began to trade willingly for Pawnee women and children, promptly enslaving them. As their new policy matured, New Mexico officials had, by 1706, become a prime market for slaves, horses, and weapons taken from the Pawnee, Wichita, Kansa, and other tribes along the Platte and Missouri Rivers.

By 1706 the French were ready to launch their campaign to acquire control of the trans-Mississippi West. From their trading posts in Illinois and along the Missouri River, they were arming and inciting Wichita, Pawnee, Kansa, Osage, and the southward-drifting Comanche into attacking Spanish and Pueblo settlements as well as any Apache groups under Spanish control. Working through intermediaries, the French encouraged the Faraone Apache, kin to the Mescalero, to intensify their accustomed

*Below: The introduction of domestic horses by the Spanish left an indelible imprint on the American West.*

hit-and-run raids on Pícuris and Pecos for horses and women and children.

These early slaving raids were so openly condoned that an official memo concerning a 1714–15 raid against the Faraone Apache specifically requested that women and children be spared. As the century progressed, the pueblos of Taos, San Juan, Nambé, Zia, Pecos, and Bernalillo became departure points for slaving raids and market places for the disposal of arriving captives. As early as 1702, baptismal records of the northern pueblos and towns begin to show Pawnee entries. By Catholic tradition, each captive was baptized before entering into a Spanish household as a menial laborer. Therefore, these records offer an excellent resource to estimate the extent of slaving operations, as well as the tribes from which captives were being taken at any point in time. These records also indicate that those baptized were exclusively tractable children and young women: prime candidates for slavery.

Male captives, on the other hand, were not baptized. Instead, they were sent into the very lucrative slave trade with the mining centers of Chihuahua, where the Parral mines had an insatiable need for laborers. Large numbers of Comanche were shipped there in 1716, and it is assumed that many Apache and eastern Plains natives also ended their lives in those mines.

With the end of the Seven Years' War in 1763, the French presence and threat in the Louisiana territory ended. However, raiding by the southern Plains tribes did not cease. In addition, French arms had made many tribes very powerful. Continuing their drift southward, the Ute and Comanche continued pushing the Jicarilla, Cuartelejo, and forerunners of the Mescalero Apache up against Spanish settlements, keeping the territory in turmoil.

To strengthen this trading system, a rendezvous network was established, based at Taos. Within the system, the most desirable trade commodity was captives from the southern Plains. Slaves became so important within the colony that social status was determined by slave ownership, and slaves could be used to discharge debt. So insatiable and indiscriminating was New Mexico's labor demand that even Spanish women and children captured in Mexico by western and southern Apache were purchased as menials for local households.

Aside from their immediate benefit to the Spanish, the policy of fostering intertribal warfare, slave raiding, and looting also sapped tribal strength and potential unity, weakening their enemies over the long term.

By the end of the century, however, these native alliances would also create Spanish dependence upon the southern Plains as a major source of slaves, armaments, horses, and meat for the colony.

During the first quarter of the eighteenth century, southern and western tribes began raiding the area west of the Rio Grande. In response the colonists launched punitive expeditions against hostile Western Apache, Seri, Yaqui, and occasionally even the Pima. Captives from these raids were sent to the ranches and mines of northern Mexico. Reacting against these slaving raids, the local tribes quickly plunged the entire frontier from the Gulf of California to the Rio Grande/Rio Conchos confluence into violence. Expanding their raiding territories, the well-mounted Apache bands struck deep into Sonora and Chihuahua. Attempting to counter this warfare, Opata and Pima auxiliaries joined the Spanish forces in retaliatory attacks. By 1748, forays were being conducted against the Apache and the Seri, with the Spanish raids reaching as far west as the Gila River in the next decade.

Making little effort to distinguish peaceful from hostile Apache, the Spanish struck indiscriminately at the Apache bands. One raid out of Tubac into the Santa Cruz valley of Arizona netted forty captives, who were distributed among the Spanish and Pima soldiers.

Following decades of this incessant raiding and warfare, by 1770 Sonora and Chihuahua were on the brink of ruin. To alleviate these conditions, a council was called in 1776, and preparations were launched to implement José de Gálvez's proposals for subduing the Apache. Basic to the plan was a military campaign against all hostile Apache. The traditional policy of creating alliances and then fostering intertribal warfare with the hostile groups was envisioned: Ultimately it was hoped the two sides would destroy each other. A third point was to attack the very social fabric of native culture through a trade in inferior guns and liquor. Initially this campaign would supply captives to the Spanish. The Apache would be forced into submission and then resettlement on a reservation. There their culture could be destroyed, and the remaining members would be assimilated into Mestizo society.

By 1786 this program for *reducción*, reduction, of the Apache was in place. A bonus was offered for each Apache killed, and captives could be retained by Spanish and Opata soldiers. The baptismal records for 1787 documented the campaign's success, showing numerous Apache children passing through the church on their way to slavery. A raid in October–November 1788 at the headwaters of the Gila River recorded 54 killed and 125 captured women and children.

So effective was this campaign that an estimated 6,000 Coyotero, Gileño, Mimbreño, and Faraone Apache were forced into submission. Herded onto *establecimientos de Paz* (peace establishments or reservations), these Apache were held there through the end of the century by a combination of force and fear of enslavement.

Until the late 1740s, the Navajo had been the object of missionary efforts. However, by the end of the 1750s, this program had collapsed as priorities shifted from missions to land acquisition. As Spanish settlers moved into the areas around Mount Taylor, Rio Abajo, and Rio Puerco in the East, seeking arable land, the Navajo initially felt no concern, hoping for allies against the Ute who preyed upon them. Instead, conflicts quickly developed between the two groups over the concept of land grants and the easy accessibility of livestock that promoted rustling.

Conditions deteriorated, and by late 1773 Governor Mendinueta, following traditional policy, had made a secret pact with the Ute to remain neutral while the Ute raided Navajo *rancherias*—small farming plots. Through this policy, the governor hoped the Ute raids would push the Navajo farther west, thereby freeing up additional land for Spanish settlement.

The Ute raids killed many Navajo, destroyed *rancherias*, and provided a steady stream of captives to the Taos trade fair. These raids also seemed to achieve Mendinueta's objective by forcing the Navajo to drift slowly toward Canyon de Chelly and the Chuska Mountains, and eventually into the Chinle drainage area of Arizona.

However, once the Navajo discovered Spanish complicity in the intensifying Ute raiding, they struck back at the Spanish settlements along the Rio Puerco and Rio Grande. Two Spanish retaliatory expeditions in 1774, made up primarily of Pueblo auxiliary troops, captured forty-six women and children. As payment to the troops, these Navajo ended up at Laguna, Ácoma, and around Albuquerque. Again, baptismal records document the fate of the young captives of Ute and Puebloan raiding.

The smoldering problems left from these slave raids, killings, and land grabs would reach a climax in the next century. The population losses to the Navajo people between 1680 and 1868 would be estimated at 1,000 dead and 1,600 baptisms, all representing people lost forever to the Navajo Nation.

For the Spanish colonists and the native peoples, the eighteenth century was one of raiding, slaving expeditions, retaliatory attacks, and shifting alliances. Frequent use of native auxiliary troops pitted native against native. Some Apache had been forced onto a reservation: In the next century, this would be the fate of all Southwestern native peoples. Pueblo populations continued to decline due to disease, labor draft demands, expulsion of "defiled" women, and abandonment of mixed-blood children. Similar population declines occurred among the nomadic tribes due to factors including disease, warfare, and slave raiding.

In an effort to increase production and tie the colony into a wider economic market, the Spanish crown abolished the *repartimiento* system on December 4, 1786.

**Below:** *Southwest detail of a 1719 map. Note the virtually indiscriminate use of the name "Apache" for all non-Puebloan Native Americans known to the Spanish, including the "Apaches de Navajo."*

## THE GREAT BASIN

The arrival of the horse in the Great Basin around the start of the eighteenth century was not always the advent it had been elsewhere. Because horses needed the scarce plants and water that people also required for sustenance, horses were seen as no more than a food animal by the Western Shoshoni and Paiute. Only those who migrated annually to hunt buffalo, like the Eastern Shoshoni and Ute, or those who lived in the moister northern Basin and southern Plateau, like the Northern Shoshoni and the Bannock, adopted their use as mounts for hunting and raiding.

The Eastern Shoshoni, from whom the Comanche would separate later in this century, had moved onto the Plains permanently, while the Northern Shoshoni continued to migrate annually from the salmon rivers of the northern Basin and southern Plateau to the buffalo ranges on both sides of the Rockies.

Beyond hunting buffalo, the horse was useful for raiding other nations. The Ute rode out of the Basin to attack the Navajo and Eastern Apache in the Southwest, driving the Apache southward and the Navajo westward, while the Shoshoni rode north to raid the Blackfoot on the northern Plains. Basin peoples who adopted the horse also adopted the Plains mode of dress, as well as other aspects of Plains culture.

New Mexican traders first entered the Great Basin after 1760, but documented little about the area. Father Francisco Garcés (1738–81) traveled 698.5 leagues (1,837 miles) by his own reckoning through the region between June and September 17, 1776, and left the first detailed account of it. Soon afterward, two other Franciscans penetrated the Great Basin. In July 1776, Fathers Francisco Atanasio Dominguez and Francisco Silvestre Velez de Escalante led a small expedition north from Santa Fe seeking a route to the missions in California. Returning in 1777 without having attained their goal, they painted an unflattering portrait of the region, declaring that only the Utah valley area was suitable for settlement. They found the bearded people they met (the Ute) of interest, however, and discovered the first Anasazi ruin located in present-day Colorado.

New Mexican traders continued to operate in the Basin through the century, but added little to the general knowledge of the region.

## CALIFORNIA

The California region remained relatively undisturbed during the early eighteenth century. Primarily hunters and gatherers, the local peoples lived in small mobile bands, spoke as many as 100 different dialects, and benefited from the mostly productive land and mild climate. Their only contacts with outsiders were those involving the ships that periodically explored along the coast in search of favorable harbors, fruit and other provisions, and—as if in warning of changes to come—slaves.

The Spanish colony of New Spain to the south continually expanded northward. By about 1760 the Spanish were alert to Russian seal hunting along the Pacific coast and sought to prop up the Spanish claim to the entire coast by establishing a chain of missions northward from Baja Califoria. Father Eusebio Kino had already spent many years establishing and maintaining missions in Baja California and in the Sonora region of northern New Spain. This intrepid Jesuit also explored the fringes of the

*Below: This 1719 map (a detail of the map also shown on page 134) demonstrates how little was known of the California region, especially to the north, in the early eighteenth century. No information is recorded on the Native Americans of the region.*

Sonora Desert in the Arizona region, looking for an overland route to the Pacific Ocean. To the Spanish imperial mind, it was only logical that Kino's missions should expand north from Baja (lower) California into Alta (upper) California, and that military presidios should be established alongside the missions to secure the Spanish claim to the territory.

It was not until 1769 that Father Junipero Serra, accompanied by a military governor, established at the fine harbor of San Diego the first Spanish Franciscan mission in California. The Spanish went on to create a total of twenty-two fortified missions between San Diego and San Francisco. They also founded Mission Dolores on the site of what had been a village known as Sagunte. The impact of this Spanish expansion on the California nations was immediate and devastating.

The Spanish empire had more than 150 years of experience in mission work among the pueblos of present-day Arizona and New Mexico, but the California peoples were very different from the Puebloans. They did not live in concentrated villages with strong agricultural traditions. Among the Puebloans, Spanish priests had from the beginning constructed mission complexes on the edge of each pueblo settlement, and the Puebloans remained in their traditional homes and retained their traditional culture and economies. In California the Spanish decided to build the missions and draw the scattered California native groups into permanent living quarters connected to them. Closely supervised, the "Mission Indians" were forcibly "civilized" in every aspect of their lives.

This process was totally destructive to the native nations of California. In the early years of the missions, people were drawn to them for food during droughts and by the prospect of an easier life. At first no one was compelled to move to the mission compounds, but as more food and supplies were needed for military forces stationed near the missions, Native Americans were coerced into residing within them.

At the missions, people lived either in dormitories for single adults or in small family dwellings attached to the mission compound. They ate in a communal kitchen, which interrupted normal family relationships and village rhythms. They lost touch with their religious cycles and their revered customs and patterns of leadership and responsibility. Sometimes distinct native groups speaking as many as five different languages were thrown together into a single compound. The Spanish imposed Roman Catholicism on the residents. Stripped of their traditional social structures and customs, and with no means to resist, the Mission Indians were soon trapped in a new, degrading, and completely alien style of life.

Suffering from European diseases and under an increasingly harsh regime of forced labor, the Mission Indians became utterly demoralized and declined in number to about 20 percent of their original population. Mission runaways were tracked down by Spanish soldiers, who beat and tortured them before returning them to the missions. A Kumeyaay man reported, *"We saw two men on horseback coming rapidly toward us; my relatives were immediately afraid and they fled with all speed...but already it was too late....When we arrived at the mission, they locked me in a room for a week....The interpreter told me that I should do as the father told me....I found a way to escape; but I was tracked and they caught me like a fox...and they carried me off to the mission torturing me on the road."*

Most of the Baja California missions were destroyed in 1734 by Native Americans and by descendants of English and Dutch pirates and shipwrecked Spanish crew members. Spanish archives record uprisings in Alta California in 1771, 1775, and 1776. The great Kumeyaay rebellion occurred at the San Diego Mission in 1775, with sporadic resistance the following year. The ringleaders of the revolt were captured and other runaways were hunted down. Soon after the revolt broke out, a special military unit sent to strengthen New Spain's northern colonial boundaries arrived overland from Arizona. The Spanish soldiers reinforced the garrisons of the local presidios, helped suppress the Indian revolt, and remained in place to prevent further uprisings.

## THE PLATEAU

During the eighteenth century, the native peoples of the Plateau region continued in their traditional lifeways. They remained dependent on fish—particularly salmon—and cama roots that were pounded into flour as the most important elements of their diet. They gathered in large trading fairs throughout the

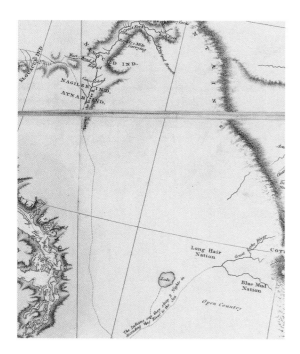

*Left: Even as late as 1795, little was known by outsiders about the Plateau peoples or geography. The annotation below the unnamed lake reads: "The Indians say they sleep 8 Nights in Ascending this River to the Sea."*

*Left: Even as late as 1795, little was known by outsiders about the Plateau peoples or geography. The annotation below the unnamed lake reads: "The Indians say they sleep 8 Nights in Ascending this River to the Sea."*

Plateau area. The peoples of this region were noteworthy for their many women leaders.

Although the Plateau peoples did not encounter Europeans during this century, they did welcome a significant newcomer—the horse. The Shoshoni brought the horse into the southern Plateau in the early eighteenth century, and horses were also evident in the Canadian part of the Plateau by the century's end. This development made the native groups more mobile and enabled them to follow the buffalo in their annual migration. Some began to adopt a Great Plains style of dress, with hide tunics and leggings, and adapted to living semi-nomadically in their traditional tipis instead of in settled pit-houses.

### THE NORTHWEST

When Captain James Cook dropped anchor in 1778 near present-day Vancouver, he was the first Englishman—although not the first Caucasian—to be seen by the native peoples of the Northwest. Since the mid-1700s, the Russian fur trade had been expanding in the Alaska region. As the stock of animals declined because of overhunting, the Russian hunters and trappers moved their operations farther down the Pacific coast, establishing a Russian American Company base and garrison near present-day Sitka in 1799. Russian contacts with the peoples of the Northwest region had been hostile from the beginning, since the fierce Tlingit had no intention of surrendering their favored hunting and fishing grounds.

In the course of his third major voyage of exploration, Cook had sailed to North America from Hawaii. He and his crew were welcomed warmly and with great ceremony. They found people living in culturally rich and economically stable communities along the Pacific coast. The Kwakiutl and Haida were skilled woodcarvers who created elaborate ceremonial masks, huge carved and painted seagoing dugouts, and tall totem poles. They lived in large wooden houses that faced the sea and celebrated their prosperity through a custom called potlatch, a periodic outpouring of gifts from the giver's most prized possessions.

Cook offered a variety of European trade goods in exchange for a large cargo of sea otter skins, which he then delivered to the Chinese port of Guangdong (Canton). Captain Cook learned at Guangdong what the Russians had already discovered: The Chinese greatly prized the luxurious sea otter pelts and were prepared to pay well for them.

When Cook's illustrated journals were published in 1784, five years after his death in Hawaii, they prompted a great rush of ships to the West Coast. The trade possibilities were obvious, and soon British ships were competing with American ships out of Boston. By 1785 a profitable trade was already in place between the Northwest and China, and in 1788 John Meare of the Hudson's Bay Company built the first trading post at Nootka Sound on land purchased from Chief Maguinna.

This commercial activity was worrisome to the Spanish, who saw their northern border in California threatened by the competing European traders. In fact, both Spain and Britain claimed several Northwest harbors and sent special ships to chart them. The Nootka harbor on the west side of Vancouver Island was especially disputed, and in 1789 the Spanish established a settlement and fort there, pushing the native people from the area and seizing rival ships in coastal waters. They abandoned the fort after six years, and the British took control of the region.

By the 1790s British and American ships had hauled away over 100,000 sea otter pelts. Ships wintered in Nootka Sound, and their crews maintained cordial relationships with nearby peoples, including the Haida of the Queen Charlotte Islands and the Kwakiutl

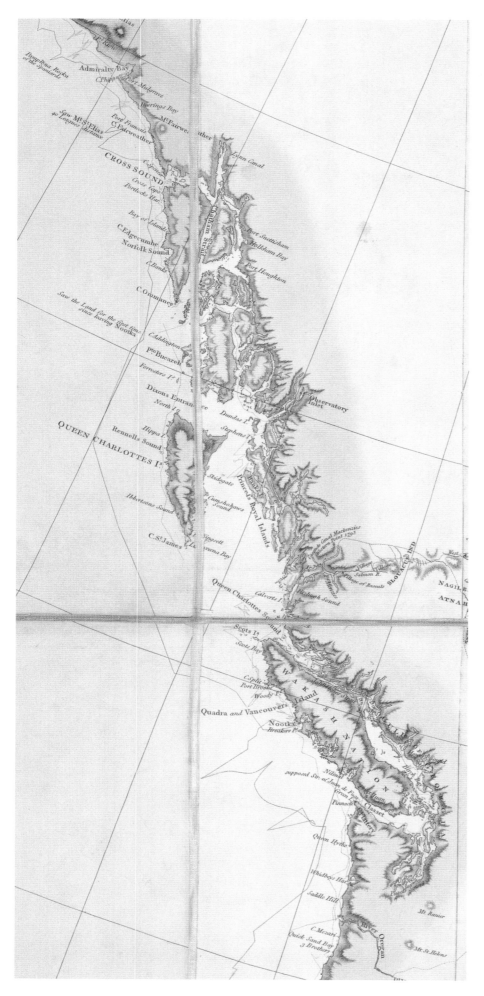

and Tlingit along the coast. Traders had to observe complex trading proprieties and adapt to native concepts of property. Native gift giving had a variety of nuances and implications, for the potlatch custom of lavish giving could celebrate an occasion, humiliate an enemy, or allow a person to overcome his shame. Those who received a gift were expected to return at least twice as much to the giver at the next potlatch.

In exchange for furs and products from the sea, the peoples of the Northwest desired metal of all kinds for tools or for ornamentation. European clothing for presentation at potlatch ceremonies, and ceramics, guns, and woolen blankets were also in demand. The native traders began to offer goods designed for export, such as beaded work, engraved copper plates, tools, jewelry, and wood carvings. After seeing sails on English ships, the coastal peoples devised ways to add sails to their dugouts. The Tlingit traded in elk hides, which were prized as body armor. The Tlingit also produced elegant blankets and shirts made of cedar bark fiber and the wool of mountain goats or sheep. They decorated these intricately, with traditional symbols and designs.

Not all exchange was beneficial, however. European diseases were quickly introduced to the coastal communities, from which they rapidly spread inland, killing many. There was also an active slave trade, for the Kwakiutl exchanged their captives for European goods, and the traders in their turn would sell these captives to other native peoples along the coast.

Because the outsiders did not come to settle permanently, and because they were not inclined to abuse the natives as the Russians had, the two cultures were able to maintain a relatively balanced and mutually beneficial relationship. Like the Iroquois and the large Southeastern native groups, the peoples of the Northwest were shrewd traders who understood how to play each trading nation off against the others. The Tlingit were especially energetic and clever traders and acted as middlemen for many other native groups.

There was only occasional violence between the Northwest native nations and the traders. This usually occurred when a trader had in some way humiliated a native leader. The arrival of the next ship might then be met with an attack rather than a welcome. Although there are no records documenting mortality figures from dieseases throughout this region during the eighteenth century, there are records of a smallpox epidemic in the 1770s, and it can be assumed that the consequent population decline was substantial. The increase in newly available goods—including alcohol—had also begun to erode traditional lifeways of the Northwestern peoples.

## THE SUBARCTIC

The fur trade of the Subarctic changed radically near the end of the seventeenth century with the establishment of British trading posts on Hudson Bay. No longer the middlemen between the Cree and the French along the St. Lawrence-Great Lakes trade corridor, the Ojibwa were now forced to obtain the better British goods through the Cree.

The first years of the eighteenth century, however, saw the depletion of both moose—the Cree staple—and beaver in their homeland on James Bay, forcing them to migrate westward. The Ojibwa, also seeking new beaver lands, pushed west while keeping the Cree to the north, where they came into contact—and conflict—with the Chipewyan, Etchareottine, Dogrib, and others.

When the Cree appeared, the Chipewyan had already pushed the Yellowknife northward from Great Slave Lake and away from the Coppermine River, where the natural copper nuggets from which they made their "yellow knives" were found. Practicing slavery, the Cree took Chipewyan women captive.

One such, named Thanadelthur, escaped and took shelter with Hudson's Bay Company traders at Fort York. Although her fluency in Cree was "indifferent," she was only the second Chipewyan speaker known to have reached the fort. James Knight, an executive of the company, saw in her a means of establishing peace between the Cree and the Chipewyan and of opening trade directly with the Chipewyan at a more northerly post.

Her reports of both "yellow mettle" and a great river to the northwest before her death in 1717 prompted Knight to send an expedition there in 1719. Although that attempt resulted in the loss of all ships and men, future searches for the fabled Northwest Passage would eventually explore the Canadian Northwest.

The Cree became strongly connected to the fur trade and followed the movement of the Hudson's Bay Company to the interior, where

*Opposite: Northwest coast detail of Arrowsmith's late eighteenth-century map commissioned by the Hudson's Bay Company.*

*Below: The western Subarctic, as shown on the same map.*

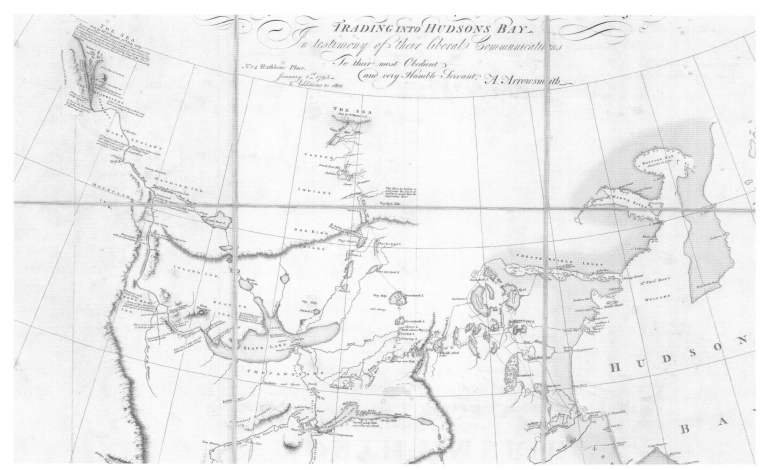

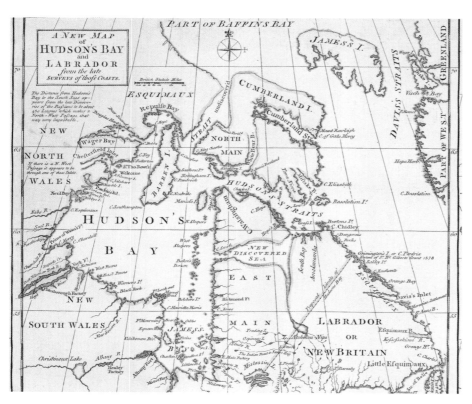

**Above:** *Hudson Bay and its surroundings, as depicted by John Mitchell in 1755. Note the references to the "Esquimaux," and, at left: "If there is a Northwest Passage it appears to be through one of these inlets."*

fur animals were still plentiful. The Ojibwa often intermarried with the Cree, and they expanded their territory north of the Great Lakes to build their trade with the Hudson's Bay Company, competing for a share of the trade. After the Treaty of Paris ended the French and Indian War in 1763, France lost its Canadian lands and the subsequent British monopoly of the fur trade strained relations on all sides.

Rivaling the Hudson's Bay Company, the North West Company entered the fur trade in 1778 and established its palisaded headquarters deep within the Subarctic interior at Lake Athabasca. Its organizers were independent French *voyageurs* and Scottish traders from Montreal, all prepared to compete fiercely with the Hudson's Bay Company for control of the inland trade. Many Métis—people of mixed French, Scottish, and Cree heritage—were employed by the North West Company. In order to deliver their goods to Montreal, the North West Company established more than 100 outposts, which were located at every important river junction throughout the northern Plains and Subarctic region, each within a day's canoe journey of the next.

Between 1769 and 1772 Matonabbee, a Chipewyan leader, guided Samuel Hearne as he explored the inland territory seeking the elusive inland waterway on behalf of the Hudson's Bay Company. While he failed to find the water-

way, Matonabbee led him to the shore of the Arctic Ocean. Hearne thus became the first European to arrive there by overland trail.

In 1789 a party of Native Americans and French *voyageurs* guided Alexander Mackenzie as he sought the inland passage for the North West Company. The British Parliament had by this time offered a sizable reward for the discovery—and proof—of a Northwest Passage. Mackenzie followed the river that would be named for him west until it flowed north into the Arctic Ocean. He discovered the enormity and complexity of this river basin, as large as all of Western Europe. He did not find the coveted trade route to the Pacific Ocean, but his guides had directed him all the way across the continent. In 1793 Mackenzie and his companions laboriously crossed the Rocky Mountains on foot to reach the Pacific. This journey revealed the great obstacles that stood in the way of trade routes to the West Coast. All these expeditions involved journeys of thousands of miles through a harsh climate and terrain laced with rivers and lakes previously known only to native peoples.

By 1799 the Hudson's Bay Company had opened a trading house on the edge of the Rocky Mountains for its growing trade routes and was conducting extensive mapping of the interior. The primary impact on the peoples of the Subarctic region was a shift from hunting for themselves to hunting and trapping for profit. They fought each other, overhunted, and soon became dependent on the trading companies for favorite goods. A smallpox epidemic swept through the territory from 1780 to 1782. Alcohol, used by the two companies in their competition for trade, became a deadly commodity. These factors led to the social and cultural collapse of many native nations.

**THE ARCTIC**

Throughout the eighteenth century, most of the residents of the Arctic—including the Inuit, Inupiat, Aleut, and Alutiiq—continued their age-old ways. These people inhabited an area with some 6,000 miles of coastline, and much of their sustenance depended on taking marine life, including whales, seals, and walrus, but some also hunted land animals. With the exception of the Aleut, almost all of these people from Siberia to Greenland now spoke closely relat-

languages. Along the northeastern coastlines, their few contacts with white Europeans—explorers, fishermen, whalers, and traders—were sometimes friendly, sometimes hostile, but in any case never more than transient. The first men from Britain's Hudson's Bay Company appeared on the northwestern shores of Hudson Bay in 1717 and almost immediately began to trade with the natives, paying with metal knives and axes, beads, tobacco, and eventually guns and ammunition.

There was little formal social organization among these various Arctic peoples: Most of the time, they went their own ways as nuclear families, occasionally combined into local groups or larger bands. In 1770 a group of Chipewyan, an aggressive Subarctic tribe, were guiding Hudson's Bay Company agent Samuel Hearne in his search for the best route for a Northwest Passage. When they got to the banks of the Churchill River, in the Far North, they came across a summer encampment of Inuit; during the night, the Chipewyan raided it, and killed every man, woman, and child.

In the far west of the Arctic—including the northern coast of Alaska and the Aleutian Islands—the Aleut and Alutiiq had a particularly unhappy encounter with white men. In 1728 a Russian expedition under Vitus Bering had discovered what would be called St. Lawrence Island, off the west-central coast of Alaska; fog prevented the Russians from seeing the mainland during this expedition. But in 1741, Bering led another expedition that sighted Mt. St. Elias, near the coast of southeastern Alaska; they landed on an offshore island (later named Kayak) and sailed home with some sea otter pelts. Russian fur hunters and traders soon appeared on the scene. Some of the Russians dealt fairly with the Aleut and Alutiiq, but other Russians made virtual slaves of them. On occasion, the Russians moved into an Aleut village, seized women and children as hostages, then demanded otter pelts as ransom. In 1763 some of the Aleut decided to revolt. They waited until five small Russian ships came within their waters, then attacked and destroyed four of the ships and killed most crew members. The Russians retaliated quickly. Ivan Soloviev, a navigator, led a force that destroyed numerous villages on several of the Aleutians, burnt much of the native hunting

equipment, and killed many. After this, the Aleut realized that resistance was futile.

In 1784 Gregory Shelikov, a Russian trader, established the first white settlement in Alaska, on Kodiak Island, off the southwest coast of Alaska, the main homeland of the Alutiiq. In 1799 the Russian government chartered the Russian-American Company to oversee the fur trade. Alexander Baranov was the manager, and he too, treated the Aleut harshly. Although he promised to make the Aleutian fur hunters more like partners in the fur trade, they were, in fact, treated like slaves. New diseases also took their usual devastating toll.

**Below:** *Children of the Subarctic nations learned to use snowshoes almost as early as they could walk.*

Aleut

Bering Sea Inuit

North Alaska Inuit

Pacific Inuit    Tanaina    Tanana

Eyak

Tlingit

Haida

Nootka

Kwakiutl

Tsimshian

Chinook    Yakima    Nez Perce
Cayuse

Klamath    Salish
Hupa    Modoc    Bannock
Pomo    N. Paiute    N. Shoshoni
Miwok
Yokut    S. Paiute    S. Ute
Chumash    N. Ute    E. Shoshoni

Yuma    Navajo
Hopi    Zuñi    Pueblo
Pima    W. Apache
E. Apache    Kiowa

Tarahuamara

Tonkawa

Kutchin

Mackenzie Inuit

Kutchin

Hare

Tutchone

Kaska

Etchareottine

Beaver

Copper Inuit

Dogrib

Yellowknife

Chipewyan

Sarsi

Kutenai    Blackfoot    Atsina
Assiniboine

Cree

Woods Cree

Plains
Cree

Hidatsa
Mandan    Yankton
Arikara

Crow

Teton

Arapaho

Cheyenne

Comanche

Central Inuit

Caribou Inuit

York
Factory

Albany
Factory

Cree

Northern
Ojibwa

Michilimackinac

Plains
Ojibwa    Ojibwa

Santee

Menominee
Sauk
Fox

Iowa

Omaha
Pawnee
Oto

Osage

Wichita

Caddo

Quapaw

Baffin Island
Inuit

Polar Inuit

West Greenland
Inuit

East Greenland Inuit

Labrador Inuit

Montagnais    Naskapi

Beothuk

Cree

Micmac

Algonquian    Abenaki

Iroquois

Potowatomi
Wyandot
Kickapoo
Miami
Delaware

Illinois

Shawnee

Yuchi    Cherokee

Chickasaw    Catawba
Natchez    Creek
Choctaw    Confed-
eracy

Seminole

Calusa

Maya

Winnebago

# Removal and "Manifest Destiny"

## 1800–1850

When the nineteenth century opened, Native Americans could have had no conception of what lay ahead during the coming 100 years. Although their population had already suffered a tremendous collapse—some scholars estimate the population had declined 95 percent since the first Europeans arrived—that was due mainly to the introduction of diseases against which Native Americans had neither genetic nor immune resistance. But in the nineteenth century, the continent's indigenous peoples would be subjected to a variety of assaults on every aspect of their existence. Disease would continue to take its toll, but organized military campaigns, constant skirmishes with settlers, "peaceful" removals, broken treaties, and many other offenses would contribute not only to the decline in their numbers but to the loss of their homelands and the destruction of their societies and cultures.

Although the line is not an absolutely solid one, it is both convenient and realistic to divide the accounting of this history at the midpoint of the century. The first fifty years saw primarily the end of the nations east of the Mississippi; the second fifty years is a separate story— mostly concerning the fate of those west of the Mississippi—although it is also true that the groundwork for the story of those western tribes was being laid by events that transpired during the first half of the century. In any case, a good place to start understanding both periods' events is with the respective population figures of the European-Americans and the Native Americans.

### AN EXPANDING U.S.A.

The surging population of the United States had caused great concern to some native leaders from early on. In 1750, the thirteen British colonies had contained a population of only some 1,170,760. But by 1800, the young United States (the original thirteen plus Vermont, Kentucky, and Tennessee) had 5,308,483 people, and it would grow to 9,638,453 in 1820 and then to a staggering 17,069,453 in 1840. Individual states and territories saw great population increases as well. Ohio, which became the seventeenth state in 1803, grew from 45,365 people in 1800 to 581,434 in 1820 and on to 1,519,467 in 1840. The state of Georgia, which would play such a prominent role in the process of Indian removal, grew from 162,686 in 1800 to 340,989 in 1820 and then on to 691,392 in 1840.

During these same years, the overall population of Native Americans was declining. Our best estimates suggest that there were around 1.4 million native North Americans in 1700, about 1.05 million in 1800, and that the number had fallen to 770,000 by 1850. Comparing these statistics, in 1840 the state of Ohio contained more Euroamericans than there were Native Americans on the entire North American continent. Little wonder that some native scouts would report to their tribes that the oncoming settlers were "like blades of grass," or "the stars in the night sky."

When the nineteenth century opened, it was apparent to most tribal peoples east of the Mississippi River that the growing United States posed a considerable threat to their land and lifeways. France had withdrawn from the continent some forty years earlier, and Spain would soon relinquish its fragile hold on the lower portion of the Mississippi River and then on Florida. Great Britain retained Canada, but there was as yet no substantial migration from the urban centers of Montreal and York (which later became Toronto). The Constitutional Act of 1791 had divided Quebec into the colonies of Lower Canada (present-day Quebec) and Upper Canada (present-day Ontario), while the vast expanse of land west and north of these colonies held no interest for settlers except for the Hudson's Bay Company, which continued to monopolize it for furs.

Clearly, though, the greatest pressure on Native Americans by 1800 was in the territory that lay between the Atlantic coast and the Mississippi River. In New England and along much of the northeastern foothills of the Appalachians, indigenous peoples had been all but pushed out—or at least compressed into small and powerless enclaves. But the first half of the nineteenth century would bring unprecedented loss and deprivation for many other tribes east of the Mississippi River. Almost all of their land and cultural heritage was lost dur-

ing these calamitous fifty years. While historians have recounted the tragedy of the Indians' fate in these eastern lands many times, it is still difficult to comprehend fully the devastation that occurred between 1800 and 1850. Native peoples of the East lost their land, livelihood, culture, and, ultimately, for many, their lives.

The native nations developed and employed a number of different strategies in response to the power of the young and expanding United States. Some tribes, notably the so-called Five Civilized Tribes of the Southeast, practiced adjustment and accommodation; many individuals tried to become more like the Euroamericans. Other tribes actively resisted; they tried to defeat or at least deflect the westward thrust of American settlers. Still others practiced a form of nonviolent resistance; they used the legal system of the United States in valiant efforts to maintain control of their ancestral lands.

A number of powerful and impressive chiefs emerged during this period. Tecumseh, William Weatherford, Black Hawk, and Osceola are only the best known of the freedom fighters. Other rulers employed spiritual leadership as a way

to counter the power of the whites in the East. To Tenskwatawa, better known to some as "The Prophet," a half century of Indian spiritual leadership culminated in a kind of resistance movement that embodied both spiritual and material forms of resistance to the infringing settlers. There were also leaders who urged accommodation of one sort or another; Chief John Ross and the linguist Sequoyah were among these.

## REMOVAL AS AN OPTION

Outright warfare, whether by large organized military units (the Creek War in the Southeast, the Seminole Wars in Florida, the Black Hawk War of the northern Mississippi valley) or by constant skirmishes between advancing settlers and the resident tribes, was to be a major means of eliminating Indians in the East. But another less publicized but no less devastating method was that of forced removals. Although these are most commonly associated with Andrew Jackson, it was actually another American president who first gave voice to this possibility. Thomas Jefferson was inaugurated as the third U.S. president in 1801. A man of great intellect and discernment, he was, by the standards of his time, sympathetic to the plight of native peoples. His second inaugural address, delivered in 1805, addressed the situation of the Native Americans directly: *"The aboriginal inhabitants of these countries I have regarded with the commiseration their history inspires."*

But well before he undertook his second term, Jefferson had come to believe that it might be desirable to remove many Indians to the west of the Mississippi River, where, he thought, they could live free from the influence of the Euroamerican population. On February 27, 1803, President Jefferson wrote in confidence to William Henry Harrison, then governor of the Indiana Territory:

*"In this way our settlements will gradually circumscribe and approach the Indians and they will in time either incorporate with us as citizens of the United States or remove beyond the Mississippi. The former is certainly the termination of their history most happy for themselves, but, in the whole course*

*of this, it is essential to cultivate their love. As to their fear, we presume that our strength and their weakness is now so visible that they must see we have only to shut our hand to crush them, and that all our liberalities to them proceed from motives of pure humanity only. Should any tribe be foolhardy enough to take up the hatchet at any time, the seizing of the whole country of that tribe, and driving them across the Mississippi, as the only condition of peace, would be an example to others, and a furtherance of our final consolidation."*

This letter indicates that Jefferson was the first American president to raise the specter of forced migration, one that would become a grim and terrible reality during the presidency of Andrew Jackson. Starting in 1830, the Jackson administration carried through a series of laws and treaties requiring the removal of most of the major tribes to west of the Mississippi. The full story of these removals belongs with the various tribes who were so tragically affected. But between these forced removals and the several wars, almost all native nations were effectively eliminated as significant participants east of the Mississippi River by the 1850s.

## WESTERN MOVEMENTS

At the very moment that Thomas Jefferson was writing to William Henry Harrison about removing the Indians to lands west of the Mississippi—with the implication that there they would be able to conduct their lives untroubled by European-Americans—he was undertaking something else that would also eventually seal the fate of the nations west of the Mississippi. That January, he had called for an expedition to explore the vast northern tier of the territory between the Mississippi and the Pacific. Jefferson's calm certainty in both these matters would be sustained by a number of events that soon coalesced to alter the balance of power in North America.

Most of the territory Jefferson had in mind in January 1803 had once "belonged" to Spain. But in 1800, French first consul Napoleon Bonaparte forced Spain to cede the territory between the Mississippi River and the Rocky

*Left: As governor of the Indiana Territory at the turn of the century, future president William Henry Harrison pursued an aggressive anti-native policy.*

*Right:* *Eastern North America in 1803 (this version was published in England in 1809). Non-native settlement was still confined largely to the coastal regions, but the area west of the Mississippi was by now better known to cartographers.*

*Right:* *Eastern North America in 1803 (this version was published in England in 1809). Non-native settlement was still confined largely to the coastal regions, but the area west of the Mississippi was by now better known to cartographers.*

Mountains secretly to France. Napoleon wanted to create a new French empire in North America, this time based along the Mississippi River; the French named this the Louisiana Territory. Events intervened to spoil Napoleon's plans. He was thwarted by a revolt of the native and enslaved population of the Caribbean island of Haiti. Thousands of French soldiers, including Napoleon's brother-in-law, died in the fighting and from an epidemic of yellow fever.

Meanwhile, Napoleon realized that he was soon about to become engaged in a war with Great Britain. As a result, Napoleon was looking for a means by which to extricate himself gracefully from the North American situation.

Once he learned of the cession of this territory to France, President Thomas Jefferson sent emissaries to Paris to offer to buy New Orleans and a small section of land around the city. Jefferson correctly perceived that New Orleans

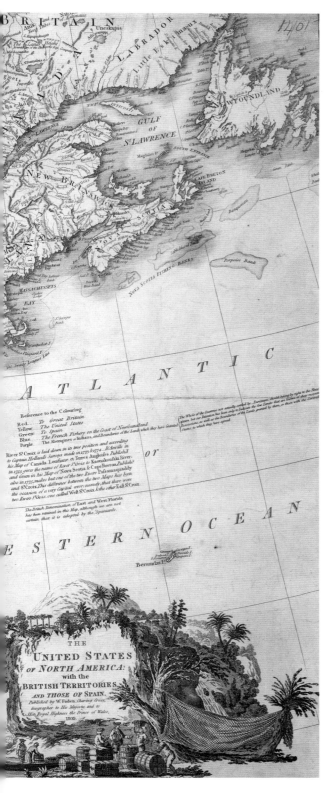

entire vast section of land that lay between the Mississippi River and the Rocky Mountains—that is, the land north of the equally vast southern tier still owned by Spain.

The negotiations and treaty-signing were of course unknown to any of the Native American peoples of that vast region: These included the Mandan, Hidatsa, Cheyenne, Sioux, and many others. Although it would be nearly eighty years before the young United States could fully make good its claim to control all this territory, the ultimate fate of these native peoples was to some extent sealed by the document signed in Paris on May 2, 1803.

In May 1804, an expedition set out from near St. Louis, Missouri, that would change forever the lives of the native nations west of the Mississippi. This expedition, the first crossing of the continent by white men, had been conceived of and authorized by none other than Thomas Jefferson. Although entwined with the hunger for the acquisition of land and wealth and a determination to secure the legal interests of the United States, the desire of Jefferson to explore and map the uncharted geography of the lands west of the Mississippi River was more than a merely pragmatic interest in surveying land and finding new territory for the transfer of the "troublesome Indian tribes" of the East. Jefferson also sought to fulfill the idealized vision of the educated eighteenth-century man: the discovery of the yet-undiscovered world.

Thomas Jefferson's dream was ambitious. He organized an expedition to discover a land passage to the Northwest, and he charged that expedition to collect every detail of knowledge—geological, botanical, zoological, archaeological, and ethnological—that could be gleaned along the way. Jefferson appointed his personal secretary, Meriwether Lewis, to command the expedition, with Lewis's friend and former subordinate William Clark accompanying as co-commander. Both men undertook special training to prepare for the expedition. Lewis was sent to Philadelphia to learn survival, scientific, and cartographic skills. William Clark was already a skilled mapmaker and an accomplished illustrator of mammals.

Lewis and Clark embarked on their journey from the shore of the Missouri River outside St. Louis. (The area they departed from was

was vital to the strategic interests of any party with an intention to enter and dominate the heartland of North America. The American envoys, James Monroe and Robert Livingston, were astounded when French Foreign Minister Talleyrand offered to sell not only New Orleans but the entire vaguely defined area referred to as the Louisiana Territory. The Americans negotiated with speed and came to terms with the French for $15 million for the

*Opposite: Great Lakes region detail from an early nineteenth-century map, in which the green boundary represents United States land and the red, British, after the 1783 treaty. The dominance of the Iroquois over the eastern part of this region is clear from the annotations, which identify the former territories of the Huron, Erie, Missisauga, and Nipissing, all conquered by the Iroquois. West of Lake Michigan are the Sioux, Ottawa, and Fox Nations.*

one of the most ancient and venerated of Native American sites; the burial grounds at Cahokia were only a few miles southeast of St. Louis, but they would not be uncovered until around 1811.) They headed northwest up the Missouri, then chose to winter over with the Mandan in present-day North Dakota. While there, Lewis and Clark met Toussaint Charbonneau, a French-Canadian fur trader, and his sixteen-year-old wife, Sacagawea ("Bird Woman"), a Shoshoni who had been taken captive years earlier and brought to the Mandan country. That winter she gave birth to a son by Charbonneau, but when the expedition set out that spring, she also went along as a guide and interpreter. The party continued west, crossing the Continental Divide and eventually reaching the Pacific Ocean at the mouth of the Columbia River in November of the same year. After wintering over there, the expedition made its way back to St. Louis, arriving on September 23, 1806.

American schoolchildren today know that Sacagawea performed a valuable service for the American explorers. But few today have much knowledge and appreciation of the great number and variety of native peoples Lewis and Clark encountered; time and circumstances did not permit the explorers to remain with these tribes long enough to document their ways of life. More importantly, in celebrating the epic journey and many achievements of the Lewis and Clark expedition, we can all too easily overlook what followed in its wake. Although a few individual Europeans—trappers, backwoodsmen, traders, and others—had previously made occasional contact with Native Americans in this vast territory, most of the native peoples living there had never met a white man. But shortly after Lewis and Clark arrived back in the East, Europeans would begin to move across and into this territory and have an impact beyond anything Native Americans could have imagined.

Even before Lewis and Clark returned, the U.S. Congress was passing legislation organizing the lands of the Louisiana Territory. Also before the explorers' return, Lt. Zebulon Pike conducted two expeditions, the first to explore the new territory, the second to explore the Southwest (still Spanish territory). Other government-sponsored expeditions soon followed,

but long before the government could organize the territory, private trappers and fur traders were moving into the region. Colorful individuals like Jedediah Strong Smith and Jim Bridger were carving out legendary reputations as explorers and guides. Preferred routes westward became known as "trails"—the Santa Fe Trail to the Southwest, the Oregon Trail to the Northwest. Small settlements begin to arise, and soon the U.S. was building forts in the territory (since 1812, renamed the Missouri Territory). The forts and the growing presence of the U.S. Army were justified at first as only to protect the new transients and settlers, but soon the army was taking a far more active role against the Native Americans. Meanwhile, an increasingly steady stream of European settlers was making its way westward: For many years, most westward migrants showed little interest in the vast territory between the Mississippi River and the Rocky Mountains; they headed directly for the Southwest or the Pacific Coast.

But one constant emerges: Gradually the Native Americans living in this territory—and indeed throughout the trans-Mississippi west—would experience the same cycle that had devastated their relatives to the East—endless skirmishes, full-scale wars, forced removals, broken treaties, disease, and hunger.

## THE NORTHEAST

Even as Lewis and Clark were expanding the scope of American vision of the continent, the main wave of American settlers had only reached the outskirts of the rich and fertile lands of the Ohio River valley. Numerous tribes displaced during the Revolutionary War had joined those with deeper roots in the lower Great Lakes region, which was now home to some survivors of the Iroquois league, some Algonquian tribes, the Ottawa, Ojibwa, and Delaware, as well as the Miami, Potowatomi, Kickapoo, Menominee, Illinois, Sauk, Fox, Winnebago, and Shawnee, among others. When in 1806 the U.S. Congress authorized funds for the construction of the Cumberland Road, which was to run west from Cumberland, Maryland, to aid migration to the Ohio River valley and beyond, the floodgates opened.

In the region watered by the Ohio, Wabash, Illinois, Scioto, Maumee, and Miami Rivers,

the American settlers soon encountered the combined power of two Shawnee brothers: Tenskwatawa and Tecumseh. Tenskwatawa and Tecumseh could hardly have been more different. The older brother, Tecumseh, had distinguished himself as a scout and a warrior at a young age; under Chief Blue Jacket, he had fought against the Americans in 1791 and 1792. Even the defeat at the Battle of Fallen Timbers had failed to daunt Tecumseh; his mark (or signature) was conspicuously absent from the Treaty of Grenville signed in 1795. By con-

trast, Tenskwatawa, the younger brother, had been known as an indolent youth, much given to drink and daydreaming.

The brothers joined forces around 1805 and began to develop their vision for creating a pan-Indian confederacy, one that would defend the lands and waters of all tribal peoples, not just one, against encroachment by the Americans. Tenskwatawa provided the spiritual basis for the hoped-for confederacy; Tecumseh was the orator and warrior who could bring the tribal peoples together.

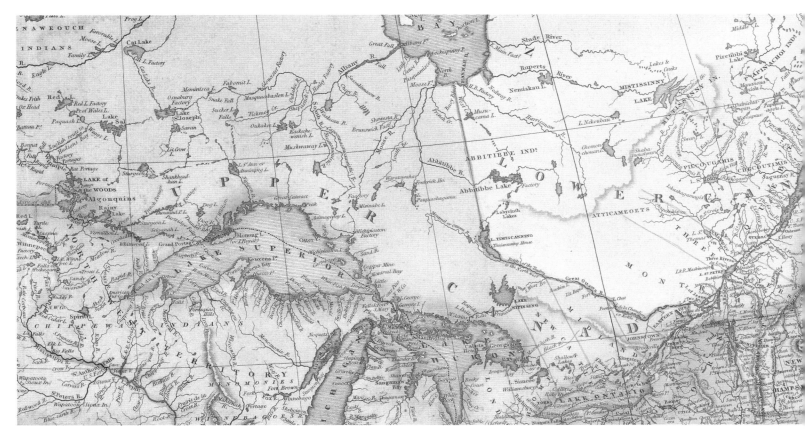

*Right: The Shawnee warrior Tecumseh created an Indian confederacy against U.S. incursions in the Midwest, but was defeated by Harrison's forces at the Battle of Tippecanoe in 1811.*

Like Metacomet and Pontiac before them, Tecumseh and Tenskwatawa encountered numerous difficulties in their attempt to bring tribal peoples together in a joint effort. Some of the difficulties were inherent in the tribal system; others were created by the pacifism or pessimism of some leaders who thought it was futile to resist the white Americans. Seeing the need to create a new optimistic spirit, the brothers began in 1808 to build a village at the confluence of the Tippecanoe and Wabash Rivers, near present-day Fort Wayne, Indiana. The settlers who learned of the village began to call it "Prophet's Town," after Tenskwatawa.

The Shawnee brothers met their match—and indeed their nemesis—in William Henry Harrison, governor of the Indiana Territory. Harrison deceived a group of chiefs into signing the 1809 Treaty of Fort Wayne, which granted more than 2.5 million acres of Indiana Territory and the recently admitted state of Ohio to settlers. Tecumseh and Tenskwatawa were infuriated by Harrison's trickery. Harrison suspected the brothers intended to block further settlement in the region and he twice summoned Tecumseh to appear at Fort Vincennes to justify his behavior. The Shawnee brothers attempted, unsuccessfully, to assuage Harrison's suspicions. Whether or not the issue would

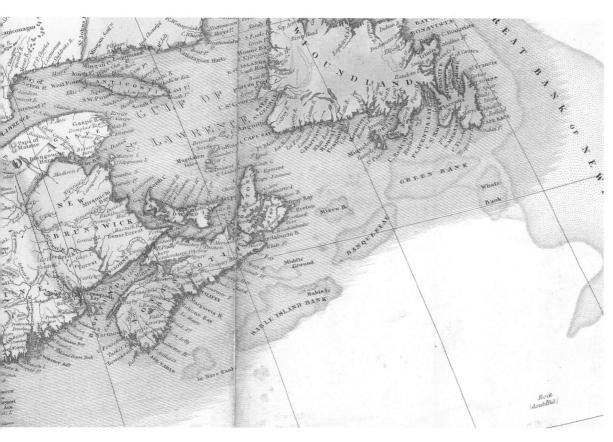

*Left:* Detail of the St. Lawrence and upper Great Lakes region in an influential 1822 map by Henry Schenck Tanner. Here, there is little sign of the former Iroquois presence, but the Menominee, Winnebago, and Chippewa (Ojibwa) figure prominently to the west of Lake Michigan.

have come to blows on its own is uncertain, but we do know that the onset of the War of 1812 brought conflict and war to the Ohio valley region.

British officers in Upper Canada (present-day Ontario) encouraged Tecumseh in his attempts to form an Indian confederacy. Tecumseh believed that the British presented much less of a menace than the Americans, who, he noted, were never satisfied with the amount of land they received, whether by treaty, by force, or by direct sale. By around 1810, Tecumseh had decided to throw in his lot with the British if it came to war.

In the summer of 1811, Tecumseh left Prophet's Town. He traveled south, hoping to persuade the Southeastern tribes to join his resistance movement. Tenskwatawa was left in charge of the growing Prophet's Town during Tecumseh's absence. In the early stage of his journey, Tecumseh met with both Choctaw and Chickasaw chiefs on the banks of the Tombigbee River in Mississippi. There he delivered his most famous speech:

*"Where today are the Pequot? Where are the Narraganset, the Mohawk, the Pocanet, and other powerful tribes of our people? They have vanished before the avarice and oppression of the white man, as snow before a summer sun."*

Continuing on his travels, Tecumseh spoke to the Cherokee and Creek peoples of the Southeast. Then he turned north and began to return to the Northeast. En route home, he experienced and survived perhaps the greatest earthquake of North American history, centered on New Madrid, Missouri, on December 16, 1811. The quake was fearfully strong; the Mississippi River itself ran backwards (northward) for several hours; forests were devastated; and Reelfoot Lake was created from a bend in the Great River. Some claim that the quake appeared to be beneficial, even providential, for Tecumseh. Apparently he had become exasperated by the Creek's indifference to his speeches and he had threatened to "stamp his foot" when he returned to his homeland. It has been suggested that the earthquake induced at least some of the Creek to fight in the upcoming Red Stick War of 1813–14.

Tecumseh returned to Prophet's Town, which was only a vestige of its former self. Learning of Tecumseh's mission to the Southeastern tribes, Governor William Henry Harrison had mustered a force of more than 1,000 American troops and had marched on Prophet's Town in Tecumseh's absence. The fateful Battle of Tippecanoe was fought on November 11, 1811, just east of Prophet's Town. Although the

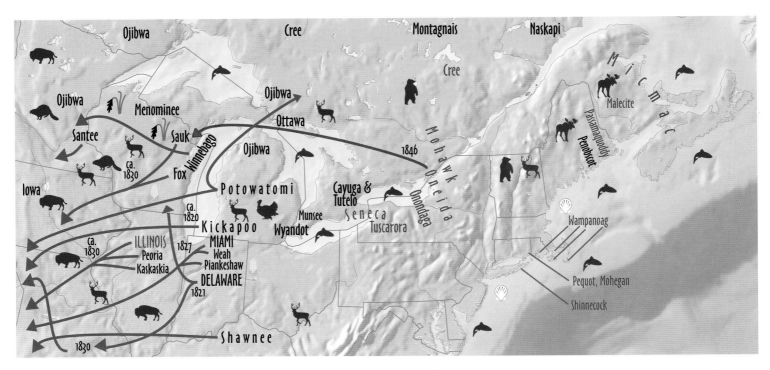

*Above: Before the Indian Removal Act became law, several nations moved west of the Mississippi voluntarily, hoping to avoid forced relocation to what would become Kansas and Oklahoma. Some of the Potowatomi moved to the Ojibwa territory in Canada. Although land in "Indian Territory" had been set aside for them, the Oneida moved instead to lands on Green Bay that had been obtained for them. By 1849 very few identifiable native nations were left in the Northeastern United States.*

Shawnee warriors inflicted serious casualties on Harrison's troops, they melted away after the battle, and Harrison was able to enter the town without another fight. He and his troops burned the town and destroyed the stores of food they could seek, thus ensuring a harsh and hungry winter for the survivors.

Tecumseh returned north to find the central part of his confederacy in ruins. It was a bitter blow to the proud leader. He parted ways with his brother and went to Upper Canada to seek assistance from the British.

On June 18, 1812, the United States declared war on Great Britain. For a long time historians have emphasized the naval issues, such as impressment, when seeking to determine the cause of the war. Today, historians generally agree that there were at least four main causes: impressment, British support for Tecumseh's confederacy, the presence of British forts on the American border, and the desire of American pioneers to take and hold British Canada. It was the "War Hawks" in the U.S. Congress who pushed through the declaration of war.

The start of the War of 1812 presented an opportunity the Northeastern peoples would not see again: that of one colonizing European power fighting against another and choosing to make alliances with Native Americans. Tecumseh entered an alliance with the British, led by General Isaac Brock. The two men were well matched; they were intrepid leaders who wanted to go on the offensive in spite of the

numerical odds against them. Brock gave Tecumseh the rank of brigadier-general in the British army.

Tecumseh and Brock masterminded and led a joint British-Indian force, which captured the American Fort Detroit. The 2,300-man American garrison surrendered without a fight after Tecumseh paraded his warriors past the fort again and again (in succession). It was the greatest British-Indian victory during the war and the single greatest surrender for American military forces prior to the surrender to the Japanese at Bataan in 1942.

There followed a brief period in which Tecumseh and his warriors harassed the American frontier settlements in Indiana and Ohio. Tecumseh's reputation grew, both as a skillful warrior and as a humane foe, after he saved American soldiers from a massacre at Fort Malden in 1813. But the tide turned against Tecumseh's people and their British allies that year. Brock was dead, replaced by the more timid General Henry Procter, and by late summer the allies were in full flight from Fort Detroit, with American troops in hot pursuit.

Tecumseh persuaded General Procter to make a stand at Moraviantown, on the banks of the Thames River in Ontario. There, on October 5, was fought one of the last major engagements in the Northeastern region. Approximately 1,000 Shawnee, Ottawa, Ojibwa, Delaware, Wyandot, Sauk, Fox, Kickapoo, Winnebago, and Potawatomi warriors fought beside the British. Faced by the size and strength of the American army, led by General Harrison, the British broke and ran soon after the battle began. Tecumseh and his warriors fought heroically but to no avail, and by the end of the day the Indian force was destroyed. Tecumseh fell dead on the field, but his body was never found. For the next twenty years, different American veterans of the battle would lay claim to having killed the great chief. One of the veterans, Richard Mentor Johnson, rose to become vice-president of the United States, based at least in part on his claim.

Peace was signed between the United States and Great Britain on December 24, 1814. The British made great efforts to protect their former allies. A clause of the treaty announced that the Americans were obliged to end *"hostilities with all the tribes or nations of Indians with whom they may be at war...*[and] *to restore to such tribes or nations, respectively, all the possessions, rights and privileges which they may have enjoyed or been entitled to in one thousand eight hundred and eleven, previous to such hostilities."*

The British efforts were to no avail. During 1815, most of the Northeastern tribes that had contributed to the British cause during the war came to peace terms with the United States. The treaties left no doubt as to who had emerged as the victor; lands and regions were stripped away and a new wave of American pioneers was poised to sweep into the entire upper Mississippi valley area. *"Old America is breaking up and moving westward,"* reported a chronicler in the latter part of the decade. Settler wagons rolled into Indian lands throughout the Mississippi valley, and those tribes still east of the great river suffered further losses of both population and land. Between the years 1810 and 1830, the white American population north of the Ohio River increased by 1,199,594.

The Northeastern peoples settled into a quiet despair during the decade and a half following the end of the war. There was no hope at all for those who had lost their land during Pontiac's War or Blue Jacket's War in the 1790s, and some smaller tribes, including the Peoria and Kaskaskia, accepted relocation terms from the federal government peacefully. But some tribal peoples who still retained sections—however small—of their territory, continued to hold out against the encroachment of settlers and

the new treaties. One band of Kickapoo, led by Mecina, refused to move westward with other members of the tribe in 1819. Mecina's band resisted for several months before being overwhelmed by federal fighting, while a second Kickapoo band led by Kennekuk outmaneuvered the government for many years by apparently agreeing to relocate, but providing constant reasons for delaying.

The Kickapoo ("people who move about") resettled many times. During this period they were still in motion. Originally from the Lake Erie region, they moved to southern Wisconsin and thence to Illinois. Due especially to the ceding of lands to the United States, the Kickapoo resettled continually between 1800 and 1850, with some clan members moving as far as Kansas, Texas, and northern Mexico. With the establishment for some of a permanent home in Kansas, where they still hold reservation rights today, the Kickapoo, along with the Delaware, Seneca, and others, were displaced to lands not too distant from the new homes of the Five Civilized Tribes.

Other recalcitrant tribes included the Winnebago, Sauk, and Fox. The Winnebago held land in the upper Mississippi valley that was coveted for its deposits of lead as well as for farmland. Skirmishes between Winnebago and settlers resulted in an 1827 battle with federal troops, after which they were forced to

*Left: In 1832 Sauk leader Black Hawk led the last of the Indian wars of the Old Northwest, a futile effort glorified as Black Hawk's War. He finally left his native Illinois for Iowa.*

surrender and submit to relocation westward. Those who managed to hold onto their fragile toehold in the Old Northwest hoped and looked for a savior, someone who might restore the balance that had been so disastrously altered by the War of 1812. Their hope came to center around Chief Black Hawk.

Ma-ka-tai-me-she-kia-kiak, or Black Hawk, was born at Saukenuk in 1767, near the confluence of the Rock and Mississippi Rivers in present-day Illinois. He became a Sauk chief and also provided leadership to a neighboring tribe, the Mesquakie, more commonly known as the Fox. Black Hawk supported the British cause during the War of 1812. When the war ended he returned to his village only to find that a rival chief, a pro-American named Keokuk (whose name means "He

*Below: In this 1828 map by James Wyld, the disputed Fox land east of the Mississippi is designated as "Lands ceded by the Sac and Fox Indians 3d November 1804"; this territory would be the focus of the Black Hawk War.*

Who Has Been Everywhere"), had usurped his leadership. Earlier, in 1804, an unauthorized treaty ceding land east of the Mississippi River had been signed but was not ratified. Black Hawk ignored it, and for many years there was an uneasy stand-off between the Americans and the Sauk and between Keokuk and Black Hawk. In 1830 Keokuk ceded all lands east of the Mississippi River to the Americans. With this cession, the seeds of the Black Hawk War were sown.

In the autumn of 1829 the Sauk left their village to hunt for food. They returned to find that American squatters had settled there. In 1831 the United States army continued to harass Black Hawk. Shortly thereafter Black Hawk reluctantly left his home with his band of followers and moved west of the Mississippi

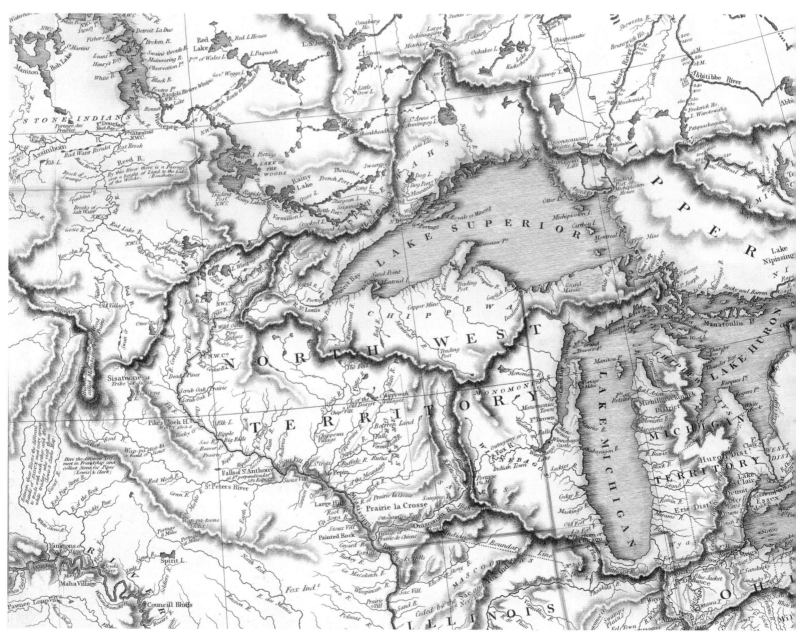

River to Iowa. He hoped to return to a life of farming and hunting, but he missed his home and was enraged by the actions of the white men. In a final act of resistance, he and his warriors, with the assistance of the Fox, attempted to recapture their traditional homeland. But Illinois militiamen and Army regulars, spurred on by President Andrew Jackson, pursued Black Hawk and his followers. In the Battle of Bad Axe (1832) Black Hawk's men were mercilessly slaughtered. He surrendered and was imprisoned at Fort Monroe. His farewell speech at Prairie du Chien reveals his oratorical skill:

*"You have taken me prisoner with all my warriors. I am much grieved, for I expected if I did not defeat you, to hold out much longer, and give you more trouble before I surrendered. I tried hard to bring you into ambush, I fought hard. But your guns were well aimed. The bullets flew like birds in the air, and whizzed by our ears like the wind through the trees in winter. My warriors fell around me; It began to look dismal. I saw my evil day at hand....That was the last sun that shone on Black-hawk."*

Black Hawk was paraded in full ceremonial dress in Washington, D.C., and New York City before being exiled to Iowa. He dictated his autobiography five years before his death on October 3, 1838, and was laid to rest in accordance with Sauk tradition: He was placed sitting on the ground with a cane supporting his hands. A bulwark of wood was placed around him and his body was left to the elements. During the following winter the body was stolen, but was later recovered in Quincy, Illinois. The bones were then buried under a marker.

### THE SOUTHEAST

The Southeastern tribes were in some disarray at the beginning of the new century, but they were hardly broken. Aside from the coastal groups that had been shattered and dispersed by warfare during the previous century, these peoples maintained a strong and resilient posture in the face of their situation. Some leaders saw the danger of being caught in a vise grip between the Spanish in Louisiana and Florida and the settlers of the young United States. But the peoples who had endured countless invaders and explorers since the time of Hernando de Soto were hardly likely to despair. They did not know that they would soon face an implacable foe.

If William Henry Harrison was the principal early nineteenth-century enemy of the peoples of the Northeast, then Andrew Jackson (1767–1845) became the scourge of those in the Southeast. Both before and during his presidency he concentrated on removing Native Americans to the west of the Mississippi River and beyond. Jackson felt no compunction about his actions: A seasoned fighter, he used all his intelligence, temperamental fervor, and ruthless nature to accomplish his goals.

A vivid picture of the Southeastern peoples had been painted through the words of William Bartram, a traveler and naturalist who had studied various villages between 1776 and 1778. Bartram first visited the Seminole of Florida, of whom he wrote:

*"They enjoy a superabundance of the necessaries and conveniences of life, with the security of person and property, the two great concerns of mankind.... They seem to be free from want or desires. No cruel enemy to dread; nothing to give them disquietude, but the gradual encroachments of the white people. Thus contented and undisturbed, they appear as blithe*

*Below: The Five Civilized Tribes' territory and the eastern Plains at the turn of the nineteenth century— before the specter of forced removals—from the map also shown in part on page 149. Note the reference to the "Antient Timookas," or Timucua, by now long extinct, and the "Remainder of the Natchez, Allies of the English," who were now located some distance north along the Mississippi from their former homelands, also marked on this map.*

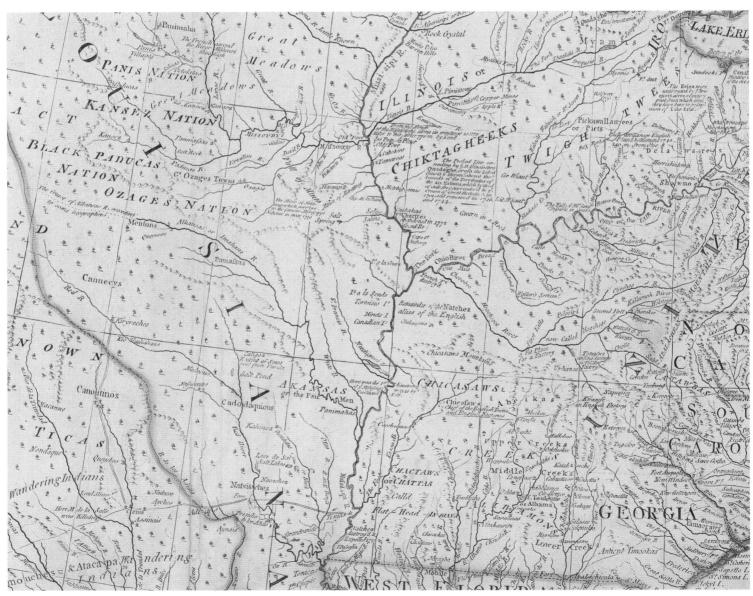

*and free as the birds of the air, and like them as volatile and active, tuneful and vociferous. The visage, action, and deportment of the Siminoles [sic], form the most striking picture of happiness in this life; joy, contentment, love, and friendship, without guile or affectation, seem inherent in them."*

Bartram then went north into the Cherokee country, listing forty-three principal towns, before continuing to describe and count fifty-five Creek towns, estimating their population at 11,000.

The settlers in Kentucky and Tennessee posed the greatest threat to the Southeastern peoples' security. The trickle of pioneers who had first made their way through the Appalachian Mountains at the time of Daniel Boone had swelled; it is estimated that the white American population south of the Cumberland River increased by 1,545,605 people between 1810 and 1830 alone. It was obvious that they would continue to press to the south and west. The question was, how best could Native Americans stop or deflect them?

There was a strong tendency toward accommodation. Five tribal groups—the Creek, Choctaw, Chickasaw, Cherokee, and Seminole—became known as the Five Civilized Tribes because of their willingness to adopt some of the white, European ways. Part of this desire for accommodation and acculturation came from the Indian Agent for the United States Benjamin Hawkins, while some of it came from the efforts of natives like Sequoyah, the Cherokee who spent nearly fifteen years creating his 86–character Cherokee syllabary.

The War of 1812 threatened to sunder completely the growing good relations between the Five Civilized Tribes and the American settlers. Tecumseh had made a point of visiting the Creek villages during his attempt to enlist Southeastern peoples' support for a united resistance in the autumn of 1811. Whether or not Tecumseh can be said to have played a major role in the Creek response to the situation the nation faced, after his visit the militant "Red Stick" faction of the Creek tribe began to prepare for war.

The principal leader of the Red Sticks, William Weatherford, was born in Polk County, Tennessee. The Red Stick War (1813–14), with William Weatherford (also known as Red Eagle) commanding his warriors, began because of incursions by white settlers into Creek territory and out of anger over the political land-removal stance of the United States. The Red Sticks mounted attacks against the White Sticks, who were allied with the United States. These attacks reached their most violent point with an attack (1813) on Fort Mims near Mobile, Alabama, in which some 250 Americans and their allies were killed. In 1814 William Weatherford, recognizing that his people needed to maintain everyday life but also had to be ready to defend themselves, described his methods of defending the Creek as follows: *"I would have raised corn on one bank of the river and fought them on the other."*

The attack on Fort Mims provided justification to the United States to crush the Red Stick Creek. Weatherford reorganized his forces. He knew that Andrew Jackson was on his way to confront him. After the attack on Fort Mims, while the Americans were waiting for Jackson's arrival to supplement their forces, many Creek leaders gave themselves up. But Weatherford, after hearing of these desertions, is quoted as saying: *"I will never give in as long as I have ten men to fight behind me."*

Jackson brought 3,000 men, including 500 White Sticks and Cherokee, to his invasion of the Red Stick territory. At the Battle of Horseshoe Bend on March 27, 1814, Jackson's army overwhelmed and defeated around 1,000 Creek warriors. The Creek suffered 557 killed on the battlefield and another 250 drowned or shot in the river. Tecumseh's plan for a confederation had failed and the Southeastern peoples were at the mercy of the United States government.

Weatherford escaped from Horseshoe Bend with some of his warriors. Andrew Jackson sent out word that Weatherford was to be brought to him "bound by deer thongs." Instead, Weatherford gave himself up to General Jackson, saying: *"I have come to ask for peace for my people, who desire it....If I had an army, I would yet fight; I would contend to the last; but I have none. My people are all gone. I can only weep over the misfortunes of my nation"*

Surprisingly, General Jackson let him go, promising to destroy him if he reappeared. As a result of the defeat of the Red Sticks, however, the terms of the Treaty of Fort Jackson (1814) demanded that the Creek Nation cede to the young United States between 14 and

22 million acres of land—historical sources differ on the amount—in Georgia and Alabama. Thirty-six native leaders signed the document, which included a "guilt clause": The leaders admitted that they had *"suffered themselves to be instigated to violations of their national honor and the principles of humanity by impostures [imposters] denominating themselves Prophets."* In this key sentence, the United States government served notice that no future leaders like Tecumseh and Tenskwatawa would be tolerated.

In 1830 the population of the United States reached 13 million. This was a prodigious expansion from the 4 million who had greeted that nation's independence in 1783. Seizing upon this population growth, Jackson and others began to agitate for the removal of the remaining tribal peoples in the Southeast. It would be no small feat. The East Cherokee census of 1825 showed there were 13,563 native Cherokee, 147 white men who had married into the nation, 73 white women who had married into the people, and 1,277 black slaves. This census, which was only for the east branch of the Cherokee, showed the substantial size and economic growth of these people. The census of 1826, which included all the Cherokee, shows that the Cherokee owned 22,000 cattle, 7,600 horses, 46,000 swine, 726 looms, 2,488 spinning wheels, 172 wagons, 2,943 plows, 10 saw mills, 31 grist mills, 62 blacksmith shops, 8 cotton machines, 18 schools, and 18 ferries.

Anxious to show that they were ready to adapt to the white man's ways, the Cherokee leaders met at their new capital town of New Echota (in northwest Alabama) and approved a written constitution on July 26, 1827. John Ross (1790–1866), who was only one-eighth Cherokee (and one-half Scottish), became the first president of the nation. Ross, whose original name was Tsan-Usdi, was a leading Cherokee chief, born in Turkey Town in the Cherokee Nation near Lookout Mountain, North Carolina. Ross, an enterprising leader, businessman, and planter, was one of the wealthiest of the Cherokee. He became and remained the most vocal and persistent defender of Native American rights of his time in the Southeast.

On February 21, 1828, Sequoyah (c. 1770–1843) and Elias Boudinot (1804–39) published the first edition of the *Cherokee Phoenix.*

Founded and published in the Indian Territory of present-day Oklahoma, the newspaper represented a tremendous step for the Cherokee as a people. No less keen an observer than Alexis de Tocqueville noted that the Cherokee went further, creating a written language and establishing a permanent form of government.

Their assimilation was greatly advanced by Sequoyah, who was the inventor of the Cherokee syllabary. Sequoyah was born in Taskigi, near present-day Vonore, Tennessee. His mother was Cherokee and his father, an American trader. Sequoyah was known as a farmer, trader, and hunter, and had also been a soldier, having served under General Andrew Jackson during the Creek War of 1813–14 (the Red Stick War).

The importance of Sequoyah's syllabary cannot be overestimated. After many linguistic experiments, he assigned a set of eight-six (later reduced to eighty-five) symbols representing basic sounds. The reading method was so adaptable and so easy to learn that by 1822, when Sequoyah visited relatives who had moved to the Arkansas Territory, communication by the written word had been established. The system flourished thereafter. Missionaries quickly adopted it, and by 1827 the syllabary had been cast into type in Boston.

Elias Boudinot, also known as Buck Watie, was born at Oothcaloga in the Cherokee Nation, in present-day northwest Georgia. He was educated at a Moravian mission school and was then invited with his cousin John Rindge to attend the Foreign Mission School

*Opposite: The Southeast, as represented on Tanner's 1822 map, prior to the Removal Act. The Five Civilized Tribes are shown in their homelands, except for the Cherokee, part of whose land grant of 1802 is indicated in Arkansas, at center left. Under the terms of the unenforced 1802 agreement between the federal government and the state of Georgia, the Cherokee were to leave their Georgia homelands: Not until 1838 would this relocation be enforced.*

*Left: The mixed-blood Cherokee, Sequoyah, also known as George Gist, developed the syllabary that enabled the Cherokee to read and write in their own language. He introduced it to tribal leaders in 1821.*

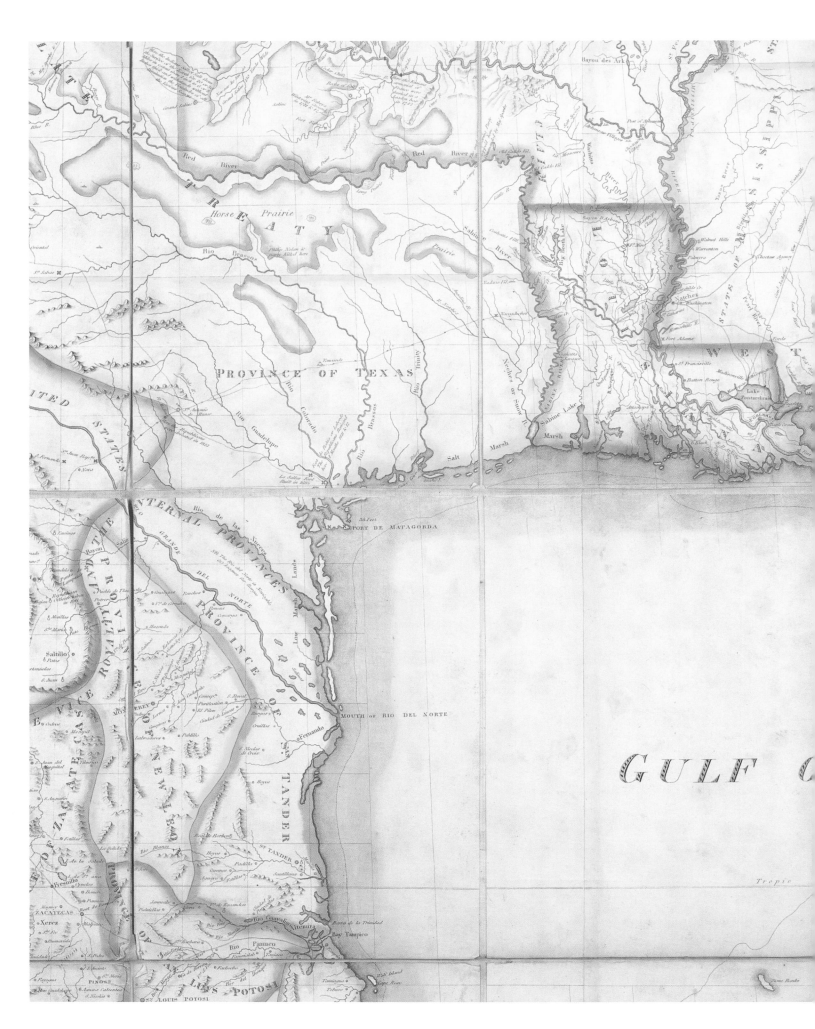

*Left:* Ominously, the existence of the Southeastern nations is scarcely acknowledged on Robinson's 1819 map. An east-west line running through Alabama and Georgia is annotated: "Indian boundary line agreeable to General Jackson's Treaty," referring to the 1814 Treaty of Fort Jackson, which demanded the cession of Creek lands after the Red Stick War.

in Cornwall, Connecticut (1818). He became the editor of the bilingual *Cherokee Phoenix* (c. 1828) but subsequently resigned due to official Cherokee censorship of the plans for Indian Removal. The leaders of the Cherokee felt that any internal dissent would betray their political weakness to the United States government.

The state of Georgia led the way in prompting for removal. In 1827 Wilson Lumpkin, a Georgia congressman, introduced a resolution in the U.S. House of Representatives, *"that the*

*Below: Robinson's 1819 map included several tables showing his informal census of various tribes known to Americans, with details of their trade goods. Here, he lists peoples "South of the Arkansas River."*

| A Table *exhibiting the Nations of Indians South of the Arkansas River who have intercourse with the Americans.* | | | |
|---|---|---|---|
| Names of The Nations | N° of Souls | Where Situate | Articles of Trade |
| Caddoque | 470 | Red River | Horses Mules Peltry &c |
| Yattassee | 84 | Bayou Pierre | Deer and Bear Skins |
| Nandakoe | 40 | Sabine R | D° |
| Adaize | 95 | Sabine | D° |
| Eyeish | 25 | D° | D° |
| Keychie | 170 | Trinity | Horses Mules and Peltry |
| Tachie | 80 | Sabine | Deer and Bear Skins |
| Nabedach | 80 | D° | D° |
| Bedie | 100 | Trinity | D° |
| Arcokisa | 235 | Mouth of Trinity | D° |
| Mayes | 200 | Guadalupe R | D° |
| Carankoua | 700 | Island | |
| Cance | 475 | Colorado | Deer and Bear Skins |
| Tankawa | 465 | Brasos & Trinity | Horses Mules and Peltry |
| Tawakenoe | 470 | Brasos | D° |
| Panee | 900 | Red River | D° |
| Hietan | 2450 | Red River and Arkansas | Horses and Mules |
| Natchitoches | 46 | Red River | |
| Biloxi | 47 | D° | |
| Appalache | 43 | Bayou Rapide | |
| Alabama | 100 | Bayou Boeuf and Red River | Deer and Bear Skins |
| Opelousas | 80 | Nementou | |
| Coshatta | 480 | Sabine | Deer and Bear Skins |
| Tunica | 70 | Bayou de Glaze | |
| Pascagoula | 70 | Red River | |
| Tensas | 115 | D° | |
| Washa | nearly extinct | | Bayou La Fourche |
| Choctaw | 250 | Washita and | Bayou Chico |
| Arkansas | 450 | Arkansas | Deer and Bear Skins |
| Total | 8786 | | |

*Committee on Indian Affairs be instructed to inquire into the expediency of providing, by law, for the removal of the various tribes of Indians who have located within the States and Territories of the United States to some eligible situation, west of the Mississippi River."* Lumpkin was and remained the single greatest advocate of Indian removal.

Andrew Jackson took office as the seventh American president in 1829. His forceful manner and dictatorial ways soon showed in his attitude to Indian removal, and debates began to ensue within the U.S. Congress. Jackson, who had hated both the British and Native Americans since his youth during the Revolutionary War, took up the gauntlet of Indian removal where Thomas Jefferson had left off twenty-five years earlier. In his inaugural address, Jackson declared it would be his *"sincere and constant desire to observe to the Indian tribes within our limits a just and liberal policy, and to give that humane and considerate attention to their rights and their wants which is consistent with the habits of our government and the feelings of our people."* Despite numerous and valiant efforts to amend or improve the bill, the fateful Indian Removal Bill was passed by the House of Representatives by a vote of 102 to 97 on May 26, 1830.

The Indian Removal Act provided authority for the efficient transfer of the native population to the west of the Mississippi. Throughout the 1830s and until 1860 the U.S. Army forcibly removed tribes from their homelands, initiating death marches never before recorded in American history.

In a fine speech laced with irony the Cherokee chief Speckled Snake responded "To A Message From President Andrew Jackson Concerning Indian Removal, 1830":

*"Brothers!…When the white man first came to these shores, the Muskogee gave him land;…and when the pale faces of the south made war on him, their young men drew the tomahawk, and protected his head from the scalping knife. But when the white man had warmed himself before the Indian's fire, and filled himself with the Indian's hominy, he became very large; he stopped not for the mountain tops, and his feet covered the plains and the valleys. His hands grasped the eastern and western sea.…With one foot he pushed the red man over the Oconee, and with the other he trampled down the graves of his fathers."*

As an adjunct to the removal policy, the state of Georgia pressured the government to enforce an 1802 agreement that guaranteed the removal of Native Americans from Georgia as compensation to the state for its cession of western territory to the United States. As much as Georgia welcomed the Indian Removal Act, the state also required that all U.S. citizens take an oath of allegiance to Georgia and obey its laws. Samuel Austin Worcester, a missionary to the Cherokee and a U.S. citizen, refused to swear allegiance to Georgia and argued against the state's policies. He was arrested, convicted, and jailed for four years. This missionary, a principal ally of Boudinot, helped translate the Bible into the Cherokee language. After being convicted and sentenced, Worcester sued the State of Georgia in 1832. The Supreme Court sided with Worcester and the Cherokee Nation in this case, declaring that only the federal courts had jurisdiction over Indian affairs and that states could not apply their own laws to Indian nations. Despite this legal victory, President Jackson refused to honor the decision. He made his famous statement: *"John Marshall has rendered his decision. Now let him enforce it."*

Although a defender of Cherokee rights, Elias Boudinot was prepared to accept removal. He felt that it would be in the interest of the Cherokee to negotiate a treaty that would define their rights during the process of removal. Boudinot's feelings were shared by his Cherokee cousin John Rindge and his cousin's father, Major Rindge, who believed that a treaty would help to protect them.

John Ross strongly disagreed with Boudinot, John Rindge, and Major Rindge. Although Ross negotiated for many years, he failed to prevent the application of the removal policy. When gold was discovered on Cherokee lands in 1832, Ross was unable to prevent the mass deportation of his people.

Avoiding the dissent of many Cherokee who sharply disagreed with them, Boudinot, John Rindge, and Major Rindge signed a secret agreement, the Treaty of New Echota, on December 29, 1835, ceding all Cherokee lands to the United States for a payment of $5 million. Although the treaty was signed without the authority of John Ross or the approval of most members of the Cherokee Nation, it sealed their fate. They were first transferred to

**Above:** *Robert Lindneux's well-known painting of the Cherokee Trail of Tears, during which the Southeastern tribe lost almost a quarter of its members.*

camps and then, prodded by U.S. troops, forced on a death march, now known as the Trail of Tears. Bitterly opposed to the false treaty, Ross led his people to their new home in present-day Oklahoma. The Trail of Tears cost the Cherokee Nation approximately one quarter of its members. It became one of the best-documented tragedies ever recorded in American history. In the disease-ridden camps, no provisions were made for shelter or sanitation; the water was polluted and food was scarce. The journey of deportation began at gunpoint in November of 1838. Pneumonia, smallpox, measles, malaria, cholera, and other mortal diseases were rampant among the deportees. Most made the journey on foot.

Although the Cherokee Trail of Tears is the most notorious such tragedy, the other mem-

bers of the Five Civilized Nations were also the victims of forced marches, disease, and death. In 1831 the Choctaw were forced to present-day eastern Oklahoma in a cruel winter march. Exposed to harsh winter weather and disease, exhausted and without shelter, they died by the thousands. They were forced to settle in disease-infested malarial marshes. Alexis de Tocqueville witnessed a group of Choctaw trying to get across the Mississippi River:

*"It was then the middle of winter, and the cold was unusually severe; the snow had frozen hard upon the ground, and the river was drifting huge masses of ice. The Indians had their families with them, and they brought in their train the wounded and the sick, with children newly born and old men upon the verge of death. They possessed neither tents nor wagons, but only their arms and some provisions. I saw them embark to pass the mighty river, and never will that solemn spectacle fade from my remembrance. No cry, no sob, was heard among the assembled crowd; all were silent. Their calamities were of ancient date, and they knew them to be irremediable."*

The Creek Nation was next. The Treaty of Washington, signed on March 24, 1832, provided for the removal of the proud Creek Nation: The majority were forced on an overland march to Oklahoma. The single worst catastrophe they endured came when the steam vessel *Monmouth* foundered in the Mississippi River, drowning 311 Creek.

According to many sources, the Chickasaw suffered the least during removal. They made preparations in advance and had inspected the territory west of the Mississippi River to which they were to be moved. They were transferred in a relatively orderly manner and allowed to bring their horses with them. Nevertheless, they suffered enormous casualties, as many as 500 Chickasaw dying of smallpox during the removal.

The Seminole of Florida suffered in a different way during the decade. The Seminole were part of the Creek Nation, including the lower Creek villagers, who had fled south as a result of white hostilities against Spanish Florida. Their forces were augmented by the retreating Red Stick and other tribes, including the Apalachi and Yamasee. From the eighteenth century until the 1820s the Seminole welcomed freed African Americans and runaway slaves, who became assimilated. Asi-Yahlo (or "Black Drink Singer"), better known as Osceola,

*Below:* Osceola, the courageous young Seminole leader who resisted U.S. efforts to remove his people from Florida and repudiated the specious treaties that many native nations had been tricked into signing.

S.CEOLA.
of Florida.

rawn on Stone
by Geo Catlin
from
ORIGINAL PORTRAIT
NEW YORK.
1838.

**Left:** *After the Red Stick War, the Creek Confederacy was broken. A few survivors escaped to Florida, where they joined the Seminole Nation, which had formed from the remnants of several defeated tribes. The Alabama fled instead to Texas, then a part of Mexico. Legally separating from the Cherokee Nation in 1819, a few Cherokee (sometimes called the Mountain Cherokee) formed a corporation to own their lands. In 1809 another group had moved to lands held by the Nation in Arkansas and became known as the Western Cherokee. When the Indian Removal Act came into force, the Mountain Cherokee were undisturbed, but both the Western Cherokee and the main body of the Nation were forcibly relocated to Oklahoma along with most of the other surviving nations. Only the Seminole were able to resist, fighting two wars with the United States.*

became the leader of the Seminole determined to resist removal. Born in the Creek country, he was of mixed English, Creek, and African American blood: Intermarriage among Native Americans, whites, and Africans was common in this region. As a young man in the Everglades of Florida, he was referred to as "Tallahassee Tustenugee," a war cry meaning "Warrior of Tallahassee Town."

The first Seminole War began in 1817 when the Red Stick Creek joined with the Seminole in Florida to prevent the United States from taking additional lands. General Andrew Jackson used this as an opportunity to crush Native American and African American settlements and to eliminate the Spanish outposts of St. Marks and Pensacola as well.

Partly as a result of Jackson's aggression, Spain ceded Florida to the United States in 1821. After the agreement of Moultrie Creek (1823), the Seminole were pressed to relocate to a reservation in central Florida. Other chiefs and their towns were permitted to stay on the Apalachicola and lower Chattahoochee Rivers. Others escaped to the Everglades and the swamps of southern Florida. The Treaty of Payne's Landing, signed on May 9, 1832, specified that those Seminole not in reservations would "consider" relocation to the west of the Mississippi River.

The First Seminole War eventually led only to the Second. The cotton farmers wanted the return of their slaves, and everyone appeared to want the land, even the swamps. This opened a period of negotiations and broken treaties. The next outbreak of war occurred in 1835, when the United States insisted that the Seminole move to Indian territory west of the Mississippi River.

Osceola, then thirty-one, resisted removal. He denied the validity of the Treaty of Payne's Landing, as well as the Treaty of Fort Gibson, signed in 1833. With regard to the Treaty of Payne's Landing (1832), one of a series of important documents edited by Woodbourne Potter offers an unexpected view of the Second Seminole War by "a Late Staff Officer," who said the following:

*"This land will soon be surveyed, sold to, and settled by the whites....Your laws will be set aside, your chiefs will cease to be chiefs; claims for debt and for your negroes would be set up against you by bad white men, or you would perhaps be charged with crimes affecting life; the claims against you...would be decided by the white man's law....Your condition, in a very few years, would be hopeless wretchedness....What a palpable violation of the third article in the treaty at Camp Moultrie, would the United States have committed by permitting such*

**Page 168:** *The arrival of tribes removed from the East put enormous pressure on the resources of the south-central Plains, forcing both the Chiwerean-Dhegihan peoples and the earlier occupants yet farther west. The virtual extinction of the Mandan by smallpox allowed the Arikara to expand into their territory. Without known conflict, the Cheyenne divided into the two groups known today.*

*Infringements upon the rights of these red men of the forest, who they had sacredly pledged themselves to protect and guard from injury!"*

Other documents recorded at this meeting referred to a number of confrontations between General Wiley Thompson (a federal agent for central Florida) and Osceola and other Seminole leaders. At the conference held at Fort King (1835), Thompson tried to impose the specifics of previous treaties, including those of Payne's Landing and Fort Gibson. The principal Seminole leaders refused to sign the documents, and Osceola is reported to have plunged his knife through the agreements.

Osceola rose to speak. *"My Brothers! The white people got some of our chiefs to sign a paper to give our lands to them, but our chiefs did not do as we told them to do; they have done wrong; we must do right. The agent tells us we must go away from the lands we live on—our homes, and the graves of our Fathers, and go over the big river among the bad Indians.…When the Great Spirit tells me to go with the white man, I go: but he tells me not to go."*

The Seminole fought courageously against the power of the United States. An American baggage train was attacked, and Wiley Thompson captured Osceola in the summer of 1835 and shackled him. Osceola said he would support removal and was released: He had no intention of agreeing to removal, but he needed to be free to organize his followers. Osceola killed a chief named Charley Emathla who supported removal and finally killed Wiley Thompson. After a successful ambush of army regulars by his supporters, Osceola was able to organize the First Battle of the Withlacoochee on New Year's Eve, 1835. This battle marked the official start of the Second Seminole War.

Numerous sources recount General Thomas S. Jessup's capture of Osceola in October 1837. Osceola and eighty warriors approached Fort Peyton, carrying a white flag of truce. Jessup's soldiers surrounded Osceola and captured him, provoking a great outcry. Osceola, who was ill with malaria, was first imprisoned at Fort Marion, near St. Augustine, and then moved to Fort Moultrie, South Carolina. Knowing that he was close to death, Osceola asked that his two wives (the first called Che-cho-ter, meaning "Morning Dew," and the second the daughter of a former slave) and his children be permitted to attend him. Osceola died at the age of thirty-four on January, 30, 1838, of complications of malaria and an abscess due to tonsillitis—then called quinsy.

The Second Seminole War continued until 1842, but most of the Seminole had been transferred west of the Mississippi River by 1839. More than 3,600 were settled in Indian Territory, an undefined area whose size and shape was determined by the government of the United States. As few as 400 remained in Florida. Most of these settled in the Big Cypress Swamp near Lake Okeechobee, while others secreted themselves in the Everglades. The Third Seminole War (1855–58) resulted in the removal of all but a handful of the Seminole to land across the Mississippi.

While removal saw the native population of the Southeast decline by many thousands during the first half of the nineteenth century, disease also played a major part in the devastation of these peoples. Measles and smallpox claimed many casualties, and a cholera epidemic of 1831–38 killed thousands more during the removals period. The lifeways described (albeit romanticized) in the late eighteenth century by Bartram were, by 1850, a mere memory in the Southeast.

## THE GREAT PLAINS

The Great Plains region reached what was probably its peak in terms of Native American population around 1800. Scattered over great distances, their collective number was perhaps 200,000 at this time (although this estimate is by no means precise). While Native Americans of most other regions had suffered substantial declines in population by 1800, several factors combined to make the Plains peoples exceptional in this respect. The most obvious change contributing to the overall population peak was the migration of several major groups to the region, each for its own reason or combination of reasons. In addition (although these tribes are not included in the population figure given above), the forcible relocation of the Southeastern tribes to the eastern fringes of the Plains added a large number of Native Americans new to the region.

The introduction of both horses and firearms had radically altered the lifeways of the Plains peoples, bringing some groups into the region from other bases, and contributing to the newly developing Plains culture. With the spread of the horse, some Plains tribes (including the Mandan and Hidatsa to the north and the Caddoan to the south) remained primarily agricultural, using horses to supplement their resources, while others abandoned their former settlements altogether, becoming nomadic hunting tribes. The Shoshoni, for example, originally inhabitants of the Great Basin, increased rapidly in population in the eighteenth century after adopting the horse and gradually migrating to the Great Plains, and were flourishing as never before when the new century opened. The horse not only made hunting much easier, making the buffalo a reliable food source, but increased mobility by providing far more effective transportation. The recently nomadic hunting tribes began raiding the settled villages, thus increasing the impact of these changes on all Native Americans on the Great Plains at the beginning of the nineteenth century.

The introduction of firearms to the region did not affect all Plains peoples uniformly. The Spanish did not allow arms trading with Native Americans, and the southern Plains peoples found guns less readily available than their northern counterparts—although they obtained a number of guns through raiding. The northern peoples, on the other hand, obtained guns relatively quickly, initially through trading with the French and British, later mainly through trade with the fur companies. Guns were useful both for hunting and in warfare. Some Plains peoples used guns equally for both purposes; others found the bow and arrow more efficient than guns in hunting game. During a buffalo hunt, for example, numerous arrows could be shot by a mounted hunting party moving swiftly through a herd. The hunters would then retrace their path and kill the wounded animals. By comparison, a single shot fired on horseback, followed by reloading before another could be fired, was cumbersome. In warfare, the gun was also used by mounted warriors, whereas the settled agricultural peoples employed it primarily for defense. By stationing guns behind the village pallisades, they became much less vulnerable to raiding parties.

The major peoples on the central Plains in the early nineteenth century included the Sioux, some of whom had migrated west as a result, initially, of increasing attacks by Ojibwa seeking new beaver territory. From their earlier Minnesota and northern Iowa base, the Sioux had gradually abandoned agriculture as

**Below:** *Robinson's 1819 listing for this region demonstrates the large Sioux population on the Plains at this time.*

| Names of Nations | Nº of Souls | Place of Residence | Articles of Commerce |
|---|---|---|---|
| Grand Osage | 2.300 | Osage River | Deer Bear Beaver Raccoon & Buffaloe Skins |
| Little Osage | 935 | Do | Dº |
| Kanza | 955 | Kan | Dº |
| Otto | 445 | Platte | Dº |
| Missouri | 300 | Dº | Dº |
| Grand Panie | 1.600 | Dº | Dº |
| Rep. Panie | 1.100 | Rep. Fork | Dº |
| Panie Loups | 1.000 | Wolf River | Dº |
| Maha | 600 | Dº | Dº |
| Poncar | 250 | Quicourre | Dº |
| Ricara | 3.000 | Missouri | Dº |
| Mandan | 1.250 | Dº | Dº |
| Ahwahhaway | 200 | Dº | Dº |
| Menetare | 2.500 | Dº | Dº |
| Ayauwai | 800 | River de Moin | Dº |
| Sauke | 2.000 | Mississippi | Dº |
| Fox | 1.200 | River de Moin | Dº |
| Winchago | 1.000 | St Peters River | Dº |
| Sioux | 9.500 | Dº | Dº |
| Chipeway | 5.300 | Source Mississippi | Dº |
| Teton | 4.600 | Missouri | Dº |
| Assinniboin | 1.000 | Dº | Dº |
| Cataka | 300 | Quicourre | Dº |
| Kites | 500 | Teton | Dº |
| Chayenne | 1.300 | Chayenne River | Dº |
| Wetapahato & Kiawa | 1.800 | River Platte | Dº |
| Castahana | 1.500 | Dº | Dº |
| Dotame | 120 | Chayenne | Dº |
| Yappe | 1.000 | Head Missouri | Unknown |
| Kechectsa | 4.000 | Dº | Dº |
| Kanenavish | 1.800 | Dº | Dº |
| Nemov | 600 | Mad. River | Dº |
| Black Foot | 3.500 | Marias River | Dº |
| Total | 58.255 | | |

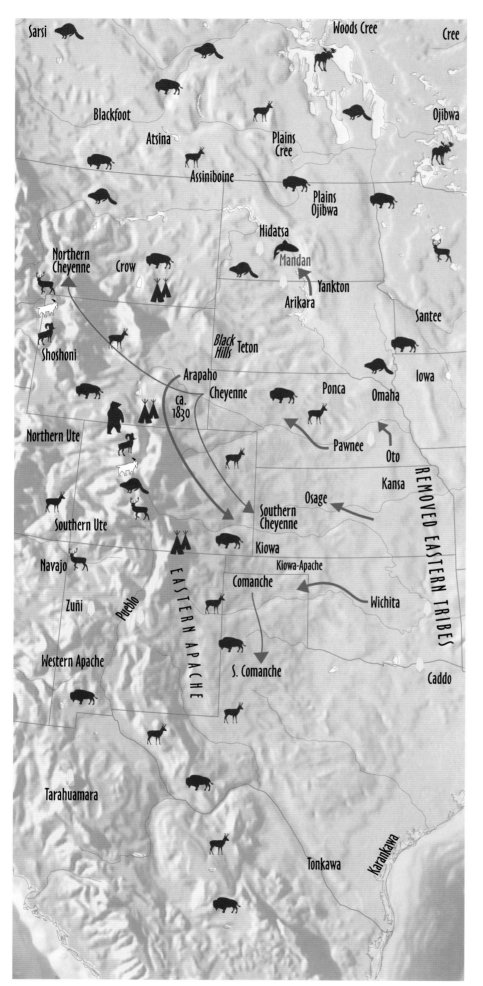

they became more dependent upon the horse, especially during the late eighteenth century. In turn, they pressured the Cheyenne, Omaha, Ponca, Kiowa, Crow, and Arikara, among others, through direct intertribal warfare, prompting migrations of some of these tribes toward the Great Plains, or farther west on the Plains. Sioux victories in war and success in hunting led to a large population expansion and, by 1800, they dominated the region through their larger numbers and alliances with other tribes throughout the northern and central Plains.

Population estimates for 1800 give the following figures for the central Plains: There were around 27,000 Sioux and about 10,000 Pawnee, who were also a major force. After them both in size and importance came the Cheyenne (3,500), the Arapaho (3,000), the Omaha (2,800), the Oto (1,800), the Iowa (1,100), the Ponca (800), and the Missouri, who numbered approximately 500.

Apart from the Shoshoni, the Blackfoot and Assiniboine tribes were dominant on the northern Plains; the former numbered around 30,000; the latter perhaps 10,000. The Cree and Crow each numbered 4,000; the Arikara, 3,800; the Mandan had 3,600; the Gros Ventre had 3,000; the Hidatsa numbered 2,500; and there were perhaps 800 Sarsi. Again, the dominant tribes had flourished largely as a result of adopting the horse and guns, increasing their effectiveness in hunting and raiding.

Another major factor, often overlooked, was the effect of epidemic disease on Great Plains demographics. In 1831 a smallpox epidemic broke out on the central Plains to devastating effect. At least 3,000 Pawnee died—some sources indicate that the outbreak reduced them to half of the total population in 1800—with the most serious inroads among the children and young adults. Prior to this, most central Plains tribes, not including the Pawnee, had been vaccinated against smallpox by independent fur companies. Although other tribes were affected by the epidemic, notably the Shawnee, Delaware, Osage, and Omaha, they did not suffer the losses incurred by the Pawnee. As a result, the Reverend Isaac McCoy, with other members of the religious community and perhaps the fur companies (who had a vested interest in native health), pressured Congress to pass the Vaccination Act in 1832.

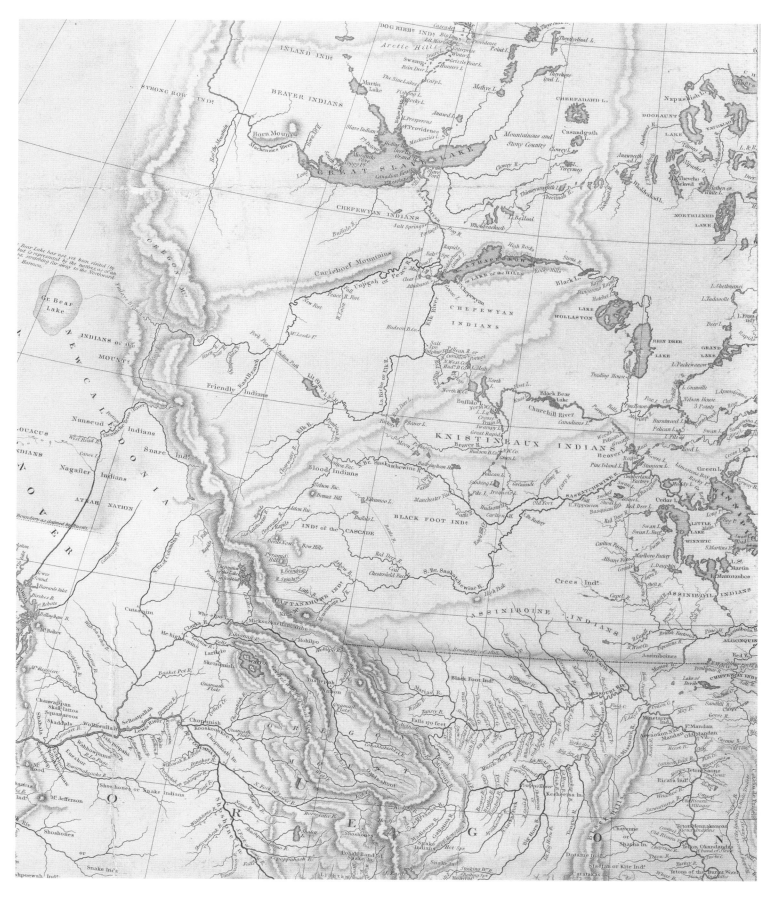

This legislation was followed by a campaign to immunize as many Missouri River tribes as possible under the auspices of the federal government. Partial success was achieved among the Iowa, Oto, Yankton, Yanktonai, Omaha, and Teton during 1832. Unfortunately, though, government follow-through was weak, and many tribes, including the Santee Sioux, refused to be vaccinated. The northern Plains area, above Fort Pierre, South Dakota, was the least protected.

*Above:* Detail of Tanner's 1822 map showing the northern Plains.

*Opposite: The northern Plains, now mapped in some detail, from the 1827 map by James Wyld.*

*Right: The Sioux warrior Slow Bull in the photograph "Prayer to the Great Mystery" by Edward S. Curtis, who preserved the visionary power of the Plains peoples in his memorable work.*

Consequently, when the crew and passengers of the American Fur Company steamboat *St. Peters* became infected with smallpox, and they disembarked at Fort Clark, North Dakota, on the east bank of the upper Missouri, the disease spread rapidly among the natives, decimating the nearby Mandan, whose population was reduced from some 1,600 to 125. Both the Arikara and the Hidatsa lost half their people in what soon became a pandemic, spread across the Plains by intertribal contact. Two other major tribes—the Assiniboine and the Blackfoot—were shattered. The balance of power among the Plains tribes was altered drastically during the years 1837–38. Other epidemics—of smallpox, cholera, and measles—broke out over the next two decades and took their toll along the upper Missouri.

Meanwhile, new tribes, notably from the Southeast, were being forcibly relocated to the Plains, especially to Oklahoma, which was designated Indian Territory by the Western Territory Bill of 1834, along with most of present-day Kansas and parts of Nebraska and eastern Colorado. Additional tribes were pushed westward by more powerful tribes searching for more productive beaver territory. As the trading network expanded westward, new trading centers required local supplies of buffalo hides and tallow as well as food. Those Sioux who had prospered as a result of their immunization against smallpox in 1832 took the lead in the buffalo-hide trade, raiding other villages and keeping the herds away from them.

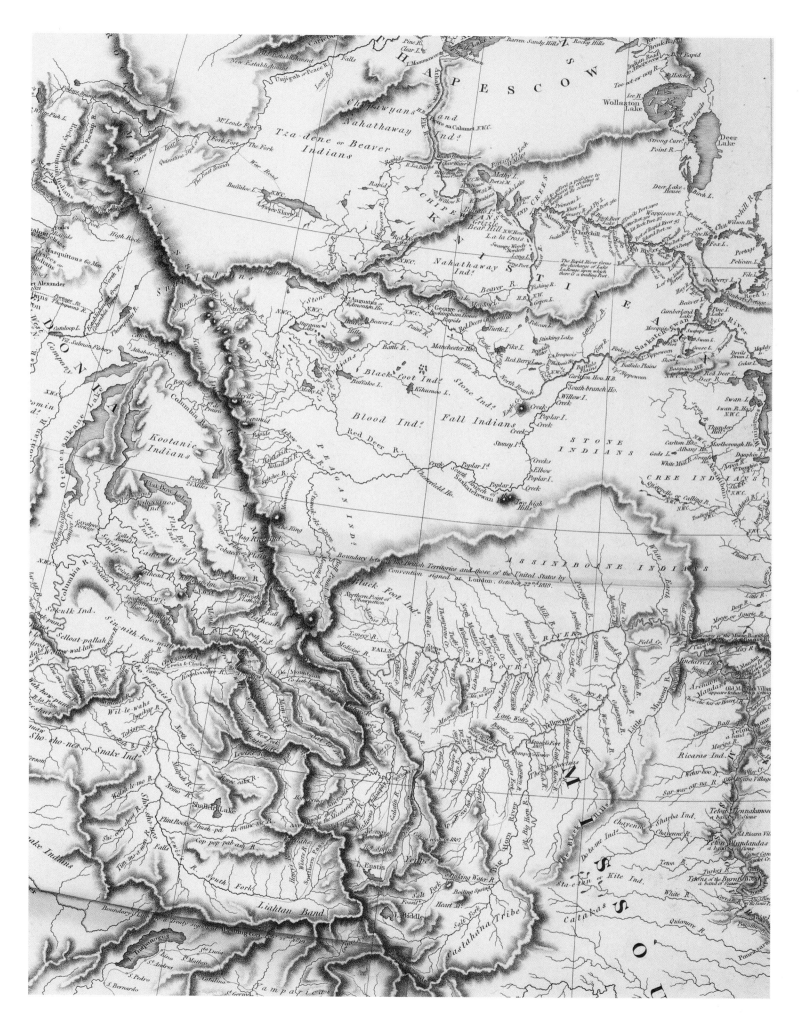

On the southern Plains, nomadic tribes including the Comanche, Kiowa, and various Apache bands were dominant. The Comanche numbered about 10,000—by far the largest tribe—extending across northern Texas and up toward southeastern Colorado. The U.S. military encountered them in 1829 while doing reconnaissance for the Santa Fe Trail: The Comanche attacked both travelers and settlers who invaded their territory at every opportunity. The Texas Rangers were formed specifically to contain the Comanche, who resisted with raids, ambushes, and every tactic they could devise until their final surrender in 1875. Needing to return to known locations at specific times to harvest crops made Southern Apache periodically vulnerable to Comanche attacks. The Eastern Apache, too, offered relentless, if hopeless, resistance to the increasing incursions of settlers and military installations into their southern Plains strongholds.

The flowering of the so-called "Plains culture" existed only for a relatively short time. It resulted from the evolution and elaboration of material and spiritual cultures among the newly arrived tribes. Their intertribal contact would stimulate the development of spectacular ceremonial dances, festivals, modes of dress, and techniques of warfare.

One widely diffused ritual was the Sun Dance, adopted by several tribes during the second half of the eighteenth century. Performed by twenty tribes in the nineteenth century, the ritual was most elaborate among the Arapaho, Cheyenne, and Oglala Sioux, suggesting that one of these tribes may have originated it. While many elements of the ceremony were common among all of these groups, its form, content, and objectives varied widely, as did the shape of the Sun Dance lodge, some being roofed or semiroofed while others used a tipi.

Military elements were common: sham battles around and counting coup upon the tree destined to be the center pole, and recounting combat successes during the rite. Sweat lodges, ritual bison hunts, Sun Dance dolls, buffalo skull altars, offerings of cloth, ritual torture, and flesh sacrifices figured prominently in various versions. The sacred number four, which represented the four directions, was symbol-

*Right:* The designated territories of the relocated nations on the eastern Plains after the Trail of Tears.

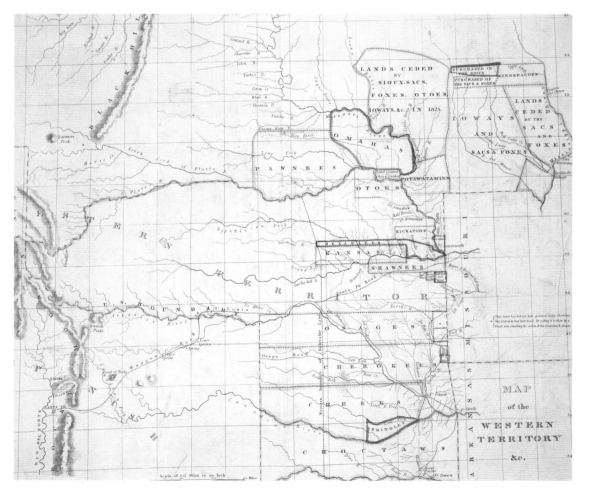

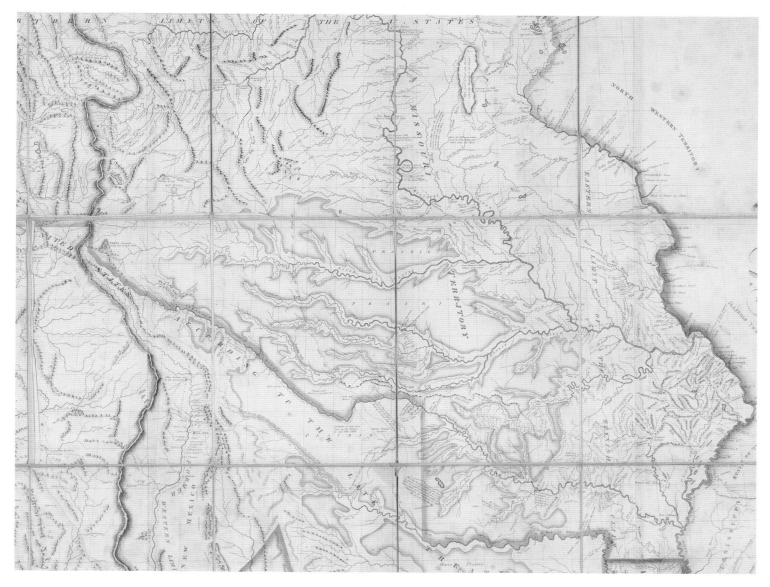

ized in the four-day duration of the ceremony and four repetitions of ritual actions.

Held during the summer, the ceremony was sponsored by an individual who had vowed to hold it during a personal crisis, as a result of a dream or vision, or from a desire for success, shamanic power, or revenge. In contrast, the dance's objective was often to ensure plentiful buffalo, wisdom, or tribal well-being; only among the Crow was an enemy's death the desired outcome.

Individual dancers hoped, through the rite's intense physical and mental exertions, to enter a trance state in which they might obtain personal power, wisdom, hunting and war success, health, or general tribal benefit. After the Sun Dance, the various bands separated, moving to different hunting territories.

Several other cultural traits were common among the Plains tribes, including various military societies that encouraged and engaged in horse raiding and warfare. The need for protection during these risky endeavors led young men to seek supernatural guidance and protection through vision quests. Successful quests frequently led to the creation of highly valued medicine bundles or shields. Because personal success in horse raiding, warfare, coup counting, and hunting led to power and influence within the tribe, supernatural aid was deemed imperative to achieve one's goals within a life fraught with dangers and uncertainty. Men failing to attain their own supernatural protection could occasionally purchase medicine bundles from those who had succeeded.

Although this period was particularly dynamic for the Plains tribes, developments east of the Mississippi River would forever change their lives and cultures. The next fifty years would see the last of the Indian wars, the closing of the western frontier, and the end of the Plains buffalo-hunting culture.

*Above:* John H. Robinson's 1819 map contains few references to Plains peoples.

## THE SOUTHWEST

The first half of the nineteenth century was a time of turbulence as a succession of three national governments ruled in the Southwest. Profitable slaving raids continued, exacerbated by scalp hunters. Native American groups fought each other either as independent raiders or as auxiliaries of national armies. Diseases ran rampant through pueblos and tribes. Due to increasing overall population, arable land would become a prominent issue.

In 1806–1807, Lt. Zebulon Pike led an expedition that explored the Southwest, even though it belonged to Spain. Pike led his expedition up the Missouri River, then cut westward across present-day Kansas and southern Nebraska and into Colorado (where he sighted what would become known as Pike's Peak), then proceeded down into New Mexico and the Rio Grande valley. Pike was taken prisoner by the Spanish but released and taken to the border of the United States in July 1807. As with the expedition of Lewis and Clark to the north, in the wake of Pike came American traders and settlers. But long before these "Yankees" began to play a role in this region, Native Americans and the Spanish had stirred up their own troubles.

*Below: The desert-dwelling Mohave were one of the few California tribes with a strong sense of tribal identity and a reputation as fierce warriors.*

As in previous centuries, disease continued to plague the Native Americans of New Mexico. Even after the devastating smallpox epidemic of 1781–82, New Mexico delayed instituting a vaccination program until 1805. Despite this measure, outbreaks of that disease and others continued throughout the 1800s.

The first nineteenth-century outbreak of smallpox was at Santa Clara Pueblo in 1800. In 1805, Santa Clara and Cochiti Pueblos and Santa Fe experienced a measles epidemic. Another smallpox outbreak occurred in 1815 and, in December 1816, eighteen adults died from the disease at Pecos Pueblo. Additional outbreaks occurred at San Juan and Santo Domingo Pueblos. The Pícuris death book of the period indicates an increase in deaths suggesting an appearance of the disease there as well. In 1826 seven children at Pecos died of smallpox, perhaps due to a lapse in the vaccination program. In the same year the Papago in Arizona experienced a measles epidemic. Another outbreak of smallpox occurred in 1831–32 in San Miguel de Vade. Pecos, located close to San Miguel de Vade, probably experienced this epidemic as well. This was a particularly virulent outbreak, affecting even many tribes on the upper Missouri River. Smallpox again broke out in 1840 in San Juan Pueblo, this time affecting only children.

As in previous centuries, several more native trading centers were abandoned as a result of disease during this half century. Pecos Pueblo, a victim of epidemics, raiding, drought, and famine, was abandoned in 1838. The Northern Panya trading center on the lower Colorado River, which had existed since the sixteenth century, was abandoned in 1827 as a result of the 1821–27 measles epidemic. Acting as couriers between Sonora and California, it is possible that the Northern Panya traders were first exposed to the measles in Sonoran villages and then brought the disease home, possibly even carrying it on trading expeditions into California. The resultant mortality rates in the Northern Panya Pueblo eventually led to their 1827 departure from the Colorado River area.

A general population decline also occurred around this trading center. Estimated at 10,000 inhabitants in 1775, the population had dropped to 1,000 by 1850. The severity of this mortality rate forced the survivors to amalgamate with the Maricopa tribe in 1840.

Prior to Mexican Independence in 1821, Spanish control along its northern frontier had been steadily weakening. The line of garrisons originally across northern Mexico were gradually abandoned, and with these closures came a loss of military presence and control. The Apache, previously intimidated into remaining on their reservation, silently slipped away and resumed their raiding.

Plagued by the same Apache raiding problems as the previous government, Mexican authorities decided to institute a modified version of Galvez's eighteenth-century plan. The Apache territory was to be divided into three zones, with headquarters at Janos for the Plains Apache, Santa Rita for the Mimbreño and Gileño, and the middle Gila valley for the Western Apache. A series of raids by Mexican forces led by Ramón Morales were begun against the Apache, culminating in the 1831 surrender of the Apache headmen at Santa Rita de Cobre in southwestern New Mexico.

Under the terms of surrender, rather than receiving government subsidies and food gratis as they had in the previous treaty, the Apache were now required to work for their subsistence. Expecting nomadic peoples to become subsistence farmers—a profound change in their culture—was a vain hope despite the treaty.

Additional problems arose as Yankee muskets and gun powder began finding their way into Rio Grande, Rio Pecos, and Texas trade centers, and from there, to the Apache. By 1831 this ready supply of reliable weapons had turned them into formidable adversaries who began raiding deep into Mexico. Thousands of heads of livestock as well as Mexican captives began flowing northward, the captives ending up either in native camps or at New Mexican trade centers as slaves.

So intense was this raiding that, by September 1835, the Mexican government felt forced to institute a bounty system: 100 pesos for a male scalp over fourteen years, 50 pesos for a female scalp, and 25 pesos for one of either sex under fourteen years. Although not initially conceived as such, the system lead to a policy of extermination and attracted bounty hunters who formed small groups specifically intended to hunt down the Apache.

James Kirker, an Anglo American who had amassed a force of Delaware, Shawnee, Mexicans, and mountain men, began attacking the Apache operating near the copper mines at Santa Rita de Cobre. Kirker's group proved so successful in subjugating the Apache that the Governor of Chihuahua invited him to come south into Mexico and operate from there. Enlarging his contingent to more than 200 men, Kirker hunted the Apache in Mexico from 1839 to 1845. When Kirker entered Chihuahua City in 1845, he had taken 182 scalps, 18 captives, and rescued 20 Mexican women and children from native captivity.

In response to the bounty system, the Apache intensified their raiding, attacking Mexican settlements between 1838 and 1845 and capturing scores of women and children who ultimately ended up at the trade centers of the Pecos and Rio Grande valleys.

**Above:** *Two views of the winter Antelope Dance at Oraibi Pueblo, a Hopi village in northeastern Arizona. Various animal dances begin at dawn in the pueblo communities, when those who impersonate the desired game animal come in from the hills to begin their ritual.*

Arable land had become scarce by the beginning of the nineteenth century, and Spanish settlements had been forced to expand away from the original colonial centers. The Navajo first began experiencing the resulting territorial encroachment around the Rio Puerco of the East. The ensuing conflicts escalated until 1804, when 1,000 Navajo warriors lay siege to the town of Cebolleta. The state militia was dispatched to lift the siege and, in the ensuing battle, fifty-seven Navajo men were killed and five women and children were taken captive, later to be sold as slaves.

Despite this victory, conditions continued to deteriorate until the Governor of New Mexico requested additional support from the Governor of Sonora. A force of Spanish soldiers and their Opata auxiliaries marched north to join the New Mexico militia.

To sustain the pressure on the Navajo, a winter campaign was launched. The end of this campaign came on January 17, 1805, in Canyon de Chelly, when the forces surprised a group of Navajo. In the ensuing battle, 115 elderly men and women were killed and 33 young women and children were taken captive. Eleven of these captives were handed over to the militiamen, while the rest were given to the Sonoran and Opata soldiers. The probable fate of these Navajo is suggested by entries in the baptismal records in early 1805, which list nearly a dozen "Apache" who had taken the first step to servitude.

In contrast to the persecution of the Navajo, the Spanish had, in 1786, formed a lasting alliance with the now armed and again powerful Comanche. In keeping with traditional policy of inciting intertribal warfare, the Spanish pledged their neutrality in any Comanche attacks upon the Navajo. Suspecting Spanish duplicity in the suddenly frequent Comanche raids, the Navajo were aggressively responding both to the raids and to land encroachment by 1818.

Although a treaty was signed a year later and an uneasy peace restored, the Spanish authorities would have preferred to eliminate the Navajo problem by forcing them into California, but, lacking the military strength to implement this plan, nothing was done.

When land and grazing rights violations recurred, new hostilities broke out. By 1822 the governor felt compelled to issue warnings to outlying areas to expect renewed attacks. When a large military campaign from Sonora and Chihuahua was planned to suppress these raids, the Navajo were temporarily intimidated into opening treaty negotiations. A major provision of this and all subsequent treaties would be the return of captives and stolen property. Without even waiting for a response from the Navajo, the campaign was launched: 50 warriors were killed and 36 women and children were taken captive.

By 1824 the Navajo found themselves surrounded by enemy Ute, Puebloans, and some Apache bands that were being used as auxiliary forces against them. In addition, payment to these soldiers would be in Navajo women

**Right:** *Continued Ute raiding, with Spanish approval, forced the Navajo to move westward and take refuge in the area in and around Canyon de Chelly, vacating lands the Spanish had wanted.*

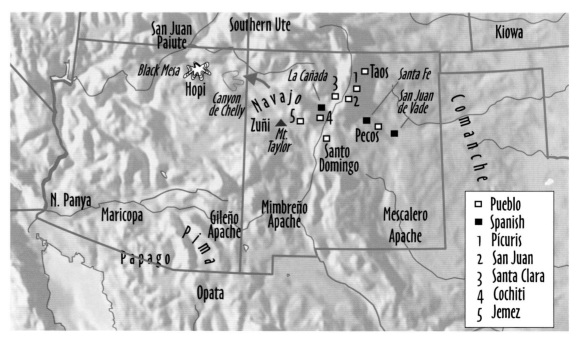

and children. The Navajo had become a major source of captives for the slave trade. The decade of the 1820s saw many sanctioned and clandestine raids on the Navajo, with 250 Navajo captives showing up in the baptismal records for that period.

The territory's economic system was also changing as hard currency began flowing into the area, and slaves no longer were exchanged for goods. The price for a Navajo child was 75 to 150 pesos; a three-month slaving expedition had become more profitable than subsistence agriculture.

As a result of the incessant raiding and pressures upon them, the Navajo had begun migrating slowly westward, occupying the Chuska Mountains and the Chinle drainage, and drifting toward Black Mesa, the Hopi homeland. Because of this movement, Black Mesa had become prime slaving territory by 1846. Realizing their isolated position, the Navajo formed alliances with other victims of the Spanish slave trade, including the San Juan Paiute in the north and the Gileño Apache in the south. As a consequence, an 1838 Mexican expedition pursuing some Navajo suddenly came under attack by Apache. Such Mexican adventures soon ceased, but for an entirely unrelated reason.

Shortly after Mexican Independence in 1821, American traders had appeared in Taos and Santa Fe, while American fur trappers ranged New Mexico's northern mountains. Soon after their arrival, the newcomers began sending reports back to the United States that were severely critical of the government of Mexico, the Mexican people, and the Mexican culture, all with the aim of stimulating the American public to demand expansion of American political control into the Southwest. This propaganda campaign eventually succeeded when the Mexican War broke out in 1846.

Brigadier General Stephen Watts Kearny, arriving to take possession of the territory for the United States in August of that year, promptly vowed American protection from native raids and theft of livestock. An initial American campaign against the Navajo quickly resulted in the Treaty of Ojo de Oso on November 22, 1846. The old hostilities would not be put to rest so easily, however, and the treaty neither produced a lasting peace nor halted livestock raiding. Outlying settlements and the Jémez, Santo Domingo, and Zuñi Pueblos were struck repeatedly. Civilian reprisal expeditions were mounted without official military sanction. The military undertook another punitive campaign, attacking Black Mesa on November 16, 1850, capturing livestock and taking 28 female and 24 male prisoners. Unrepentant, the Navajo mounted retaliatory raids.

With the signing of the Treaty of Guadalupe Hidalgo in 1848, the United States annexed the territory presently lying in Arizona, New Mexico, California, Nevada, and Utah, along with the all the problems endemic to the area: religious conflicts, labor shortages, and limited land and water resources. The familiar cycle of raiding continued under a new government pledged to halting it. United States efforts to this end by abolishing the underlying causes for the raids would continue for the next four decades.

One of the provisions of Guadalupe Hidalgo was that the United States guaranteed to halt Indian raids from American territory on Mexican settlements and prohibit the trading of the Mexican captives and livestock at New

*Below:* Detail of the Southwest from an 1819 map of Mexico, Louisiana, and the Missouri Territory by American cartographer John H. Robinson.

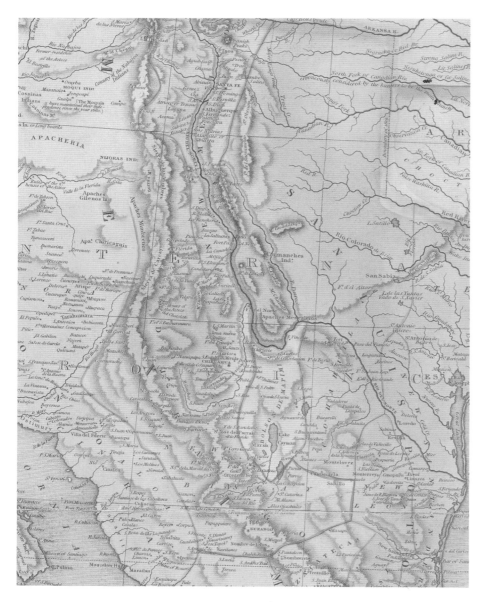

Mexican trade centers. Again, patterns established over centuries would not be broken as a result of this declaration of intent.

Nor were the Puebloans exempt from conflict with the new American government. During the Mexican War period (1845–48), the Missouri volunteers stationed in the Rio Grande valley began appropriating Puebloan crops and livestock, and kidnapping women. Infuriated, the Tiwa of Taos, aided by other Puebloans and some Mexicans, began attacking the offending Americans on January 19, 1847, eventually killing American Governor Charles Bent and twenty other Americans.

In response, 500 militiamen were assembled to march against the Puebloans. After an unsuccessful attempt to defeat the American army at La Cañada, the Puebloans retreated to Taos Pueblo. Artillery bombardment of the pueblo and church ultimately forced the defenders to flee into the hills, many of whom were shot during the retreat. Fifteen leaders were later tried and executed. In total, an estimated 200 Pueblo participants in this revolt were killed and many more wounded.

Both the causes of and the major participants in this revolt were eerily similar to those of the Pueblo Revolt of 1680. Seemingly, little had changed in the intervening 167 years, but the next fifty years would at last produce peace—if only on American terms.

**Above:** *The Southwest in Henry Schenck Tanner's 1822 map, with detailed annotations showing tribal locations. At top left, near Walpi, is written "The Moquis [Hopi] have maintained their independence since the year 1680."*

**Right:** *A depiction of the Antelope altar at Walpi, printed in the Nineteenth Annual Report of the Bureau of American Ethnology.*

## THE GREAT BASIN

After acquiring Louisiana, Spain needed native cooperation to sustain the lucrative fur trade there, pre-empting further slave raiding in that area. New Mexico now needed a new source of labor and began looking beyond their northern frontiers. Meanwhile, the acquisition of the horse by the loosely associated Ute bands had resulted in the unification of bands under war leaders like Chief Wasatch, who led by virtue of their ability to supply horses to their followers.

Although occassionally raiding California ranches and Central Plains tribes for mounts, the Ute usually got horses by bartering with the Spanish, initially trading buckskins, furs, and dried buffalo meat. Around 1800 the Ute began to offer only Paiute women and children. New Mexico had enacted laws that banned slave trading, but both the colony's labor needs and the secret Spanish agreement to allow Ute attacks on the Navajo led the New Mexicans to ignore traders who were illegally bartering horses and guns for captives.

By 1830 those traders had built a complex network from New Mexico to California along the Old Spanish Trail. Traveling from their New Mexican bases, the slavers sold guns to the Navajo and Ute for horses. They then contacted Paiute bands, who would often exchange a woman or a child for a horse, which they would use for food. The captives were taken on to California, often bound to the backs of mules, to be sold or traded for more horses. Slaves collected on the return trip were sold in New Mexico at the rate of $100 for a boy and between $150 and $200 for a healthy girl. Guns were purchased there, and the cycle was repeated.

Californians, also aware of native unrest due to slaving, attempted to outlaw the trade in 1824. Although California and New Mexico court records list a few prosecutions of slavers, the slave trade continued to grow throughout the mid–1840s.

"Uncle" Dick Wootton, a mountain man who had trapped in the Wasatch Mountains of Utah during the late 1830s, later recalled encountering Mexican slavers who were operating so openly in the area that they had carried furs back to Taos for him.

Referred to as "the Greatest Horse Thief in History," Walkara (1808?–55), the son of a Ute clan chief, rose to prominence after gaining control of the Great Basin slave trade. Raiding the Paiute for captives and California ranches for horses, he exacted tribute from the Paiute in the form of blankets, deerskins, and warriors. Those unable to meet his demands gave their women and children in payment.

New Mexican slavers who profited more by doing their own raiding began to weaken the monopoly of Walkara when, in 1847, the Mormons entered the Great Basin. Delighted with a new market, Walkara welcomed Brigham Young and his followers, encouraging them to build more settlements in the areas of southern Utah under his control.

The Mormons, however, refused, on religious grounds, to buy two Paiute children whom Walkara's brother, Arrapeen, offered. They quickly found themselves in a moral dilemma when Walkara threatened to shoot the captives unless they bought them. Trapped, the Mormons bought one child, but the second was indeed shot. Thereafter, the Ute used this threat to ensure the sale of their captives. Appalled by the slave traffic and the prospect of having their new Zion overrun by slave traders, the Mormons would soon enact—and enforce—laws against them.

Even the naive new American government in New Mexico, believing the Ute to be "friendlies," continued to issue permits to them for trading in the Great Basin to New Mexican traders based solely on their promise not to sell weapons or alcohol.

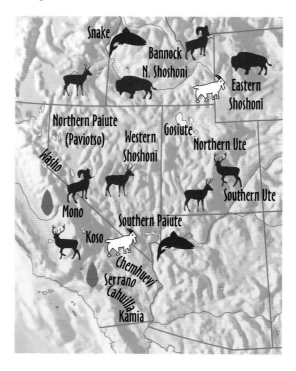

*Left:* Numic peoples entered this arid area from the eastern Sierra Nevada about AD 1000 and had populated it by AD 1450. Annual migrations of as many as 1,000 miles were needed to utilize scarce resources, especially water.

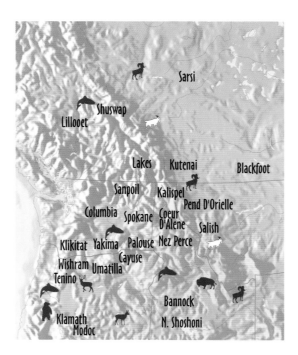

## THE PLATEAU

Life in the Plateau region remained relatively stable during the first half of the nineteenth century. This was in part because those who lived there were protected by the Columbia River Basin and by the Fraser River to the north, and were surrounded by a series of mountain ranges: the Rocky Mountains to the east, the Cascade Mountains to the west, as well as the Blue Mountains to the south. The peoples populating this area—the Cayuse, Coeur d'Alene, Klamath, Modoc, Nez Perce, Salish (or Flathead), Spokane, and Yakima, among many others—were seminomadic peoples who lived as hunters and gatherers. Population estimates compiled between 1780 and 1800 give a total of about 62,600 natives in the region.

Their early contacts with Europeans, though rare, exposed the Plateau peoples to devastating diseases including smallpox (there had been an epidemic in 1780 and there were numerous outbreaks in 1800–50), measles (1847), and outbreaks of scarlet fever, typhoid, typhus, and cholera. Although a vaccination against smallpox already existed by the turn of the nineteenth century, there were no doctors available in this region to dispense it.

When the Lewis and Clark expedition arrived at the Plateau (1805–1806), they encountered a variety of tribes including the Salish (whom Europeans called Flatheads). The reports from the Lewis and Clark expedition provided the first detailed physical description of the Plateau peoples, their culture, and their means of subsistence. Soon after the expedition, British traders—the North West Company and the Hudson's Bay Company—along with John Jacob Astor's American Fur Company began to explore the region looking for its trading potential and for a river that would lead them to the Pacific Ocean. (These companies had earlier established their bases in the Northwest Coast.) The Hudson's Bay Company established trading relations with the Klamath in 1829, and the traders also dealt with the Nez Perce and Cayuse. Although much of the game that sustained the fur trade would be greatly depleted by 1840, these incursions marked the "beginning of the end" for the traditional lifeways of the Plateau tribes, who experienced fresh exposure to disease as well as the intervention of missionaries.

A Table exhibiting the Position and numbers of the Indian nations West of the Rocky mountain on the Columbia River

| Names of Nations | N° of Souls | Place of Residence | Articles of Commerce |
|---|---|---|---|
| Clatsop | 200 | Pacific Ocean | Sea Otter |
| Chiltx | 800 | Whilby's Bay | D° |
| Chinnook | 400 | Columbia River | D° |
| Cathlahmah | 300 | D° | D° |
| Wakkiakume | 200 | D° | D° |
| Skilute | 2,500 | D° | D° |
| Quathlapootle | Unknown | | |
| Wappatoo | | | |
| Clackamus | 1,800 | Clackamus River | Unknown |
| Cathlapoortalh | 3,000 | Cathlapoeweah River | |
| Shahala | 1,000 | Columbia River | |
| Searcheep | 800 | D° | |
| Chillukkittequan | 2,600 | D° | |
| Wachhowpums | 1,000 | D° | |
| Echeloot | 1,000 | D° | |
| Eneeshur | 1,200 | D° | |
| Pishquitpahe | 2,600 | D° | |
| Sho-sho-nes | 10,000 | Multnomah River | |
| Sho-sho-nes | 4,000 | Lewis River | |
| Sho-sho-nes | 2,000 | Towarnahiooks | |
| Skaddats | 400 | Cataract River | |
| Squnnaroosse | 240 | D° | |
| Shallattos | 200 | D° | |
| Shanwappom | 400 | D° | |
| Wollawollah | 2,600 | Tapotote River | |
| Sokulk | 3,000 | Columbia River | |
| Chymnapum | 8,000 | Lewis River | |
| Willewah | 1,000 | Willewah River | |
| Pelush | 1,000 | Lewis River | |
| Sho-sho-nes | 1,800 | D° | |
| Cuthlahsh | 450 | Clarks River | |
| Hihighenimmo | 1,500 | D° | |
| Cutssahnim | 2,400 | Columbia | |
| Chimnahpum | 2,000 | Selostar | |
| Lartielo | 900 | Lartaw River | |
| Tushepah | 800 | Clarks River | |
| Total | 62,070 | Aggregate Am.t 129,111 | |

Among the Columbia River tribes, intertribal warfare that would escalate in the 1850s broke out initially as the Cayuse War of 1847–50 between the Cayuse and a group of missionaries at Waiilatpu led by Marcus and Narcissa Whitman. The incident began over an outbreak of measles, prompting a group of Cayuse to kill the Whitmans and twelve other missionaries for their perceived role in the epidemic. In retaliation, a volunteer army from Oregon Country attacked the Cayuse and other Plateau peoples. The war ended in 1850 with the surrender of the Cayuse most responsible for the incident; they were hanged, and the settlers declared that the Cayuse had forfeited all claims to their land.

This episode would disturb the former balance between the peoples of the region and strain their relations with the newly arriving settlers. The Oregon Trail had opened in 1842, and soon became one of the best-known and most-traveled routes for settlers moving to the West. The route began in Independence, Missouri, and followed rivers west to Oregon. In 1846 the British and the United States signed the Oregon Treaty, giving the United States all land below the 49th parallel. In 1848 the United States established the Territory of Oregon (which also included the present-day states of Idaho and Washington and part of Montana) and soon began relocating the native peoples away from these lush and productive lands. With the passage of the Donation Land Act of 1850, which gave 320 acres of free land in the territory to any male American citizen over eighteen, the floodgates of white settlement opened.

## CALIFORNIA

Approximate Native American population figures for the California culture area at the opening of the nineteenth century were compiled by the Spanish missions between 1770 and 1805. By their counts (which should be considered less reliable for the northern part of the region), there were now a total of around 196,300 Native Americans in the region. Some of the largest were the Yokut (18,000), the Wintun (12,000), the Miwok (11,000), the Chumash (10,000), and the Costanoan (10,000).

During the Spanish exploration and possession of California, diseases such as diphtheria, smallpox, measles, and cholera had decimated many tribes in the southern part of the region.

As it had in the Southwest, the Spanish *reducción*—reduction—program concentrated native converts into controllable settlements around missions. In these settlements, poor sanitation, contaminated food and water supplies, and overcrowded living quarters sped the spread of disease.

Mission records list epidemics of measles in 1821–22 and 1827–28. Death rates as high as 15 percent were recorded at San Buenaventura Mission in 1821. A probable outbreak of influenza hit the northern Chumash area in 1832, reducing the population by 16 percent. Smallpox raged throughout California in 1844. At La Purísima Concepción Mission, 150 of the 200 native residents died, while almost the entire native population at San Luis Obispo succumbed.

Moreover, the prevalence of syphilis among the "Mission Indians" caused many miscarriages and stillbirths, preventing their populations from rebounding to former levels.

The native survivors of these diseases fared poorly: Many had been compelled to work for

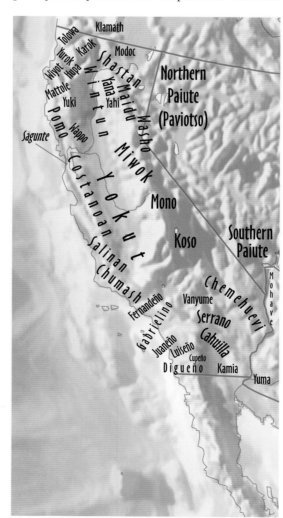

*Left: The California culture area strictly includes only that portion of the present state on the west side of the Sierra Nevada. One of the most stable areas of native North America, the groups shown occupied roughly the same areas from at least AD 500. By AD 1900, most had either become extinct or were confined to tiny reservations in or near their homelands.*

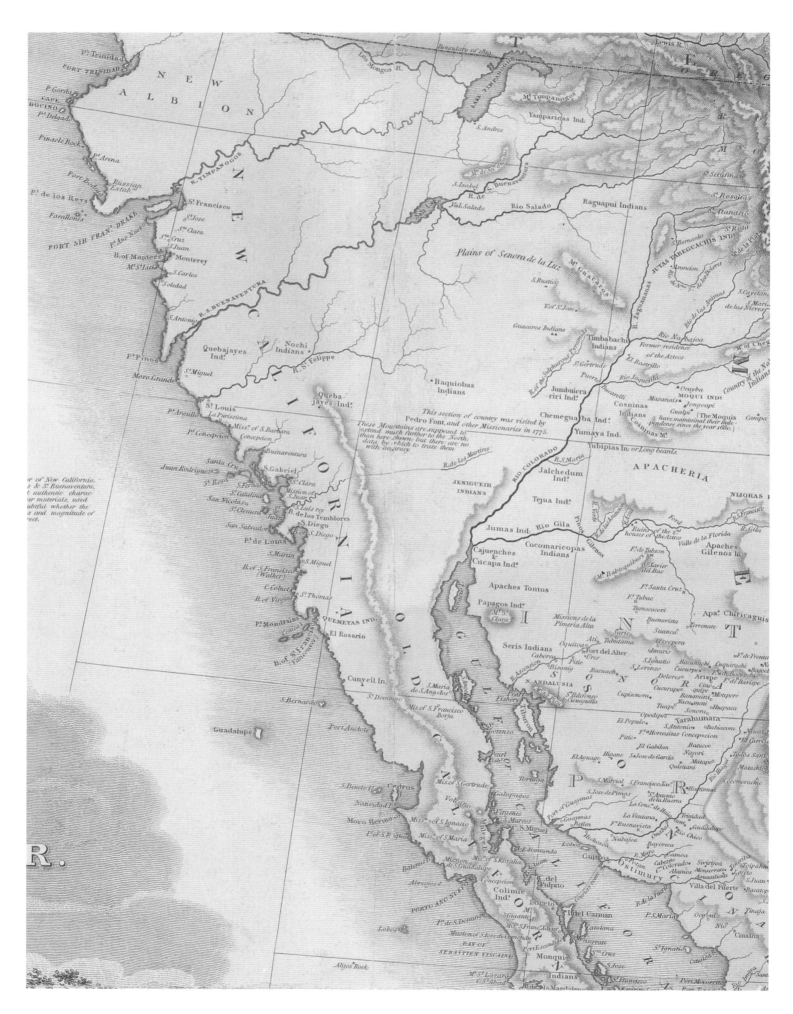

the Spanish missions, and they were treated by the Mexican authorities as slave labor, in conditions as described for the Southwest culture area. Although many thousands of Native Americans were baptized as Christians, this often meant simply that they could be removed from their villages at whim and were required to obey their Spanish masters. Most were not paid and were treated with extreme cruelty. In 1834, the Mexican government secularized the missions, and supposedly Native Americans were to receive half of the lands; in fact, the Mexican administrations kept all the land.

The California peoples responded in various ways. Some were passive; others tried to flee. Encoded messages from this period have survived in the stone work of the missions. The Spanish and Mexican administrations kept systematic records and controlled the territory with an iron grip; it was almost impossible to hide. Most native fugitives were caught and either killed or severely tortured. For the Native Americans within the California part of the Spanish mission area, the population had been reduced by at least half by the time the United States acquired California in 1848 as part of the settlement of the Mexican War.

The Spanish were not the only foreigners the California peoples had to fear. In the early nineteenth century the Russian Trading Company in Alaska expanded its operations farther south to compete with the Hudson's Bay Company. For a brief time (from the 1810s to the 1840s) they established land bases on the northern coast of California (founding Fort Ross in Bodega Bay in 1812) and on the offshore Farallon Islands. The Russians forced those Native Americans they encountered into labor, exact-

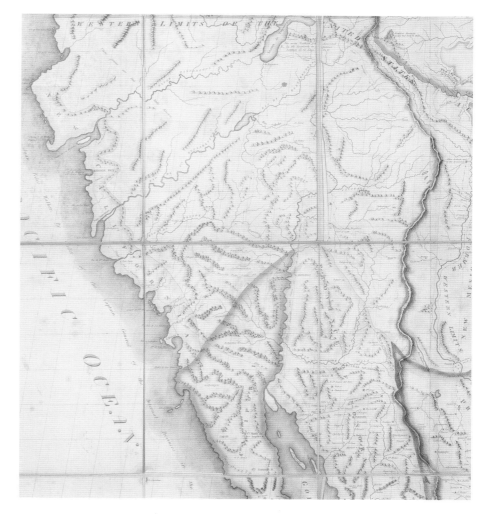

ing extreme punishment—even murder—to ensure control. The Pomo resisted the Russians, but were nevertheless greatly depleted.

The next event that would greatly impact the region was the discovery of gold at John Sutter's sawmill in January 1848. Soon after, hoards of gold seekers flooded into the area and quickly became determined to rid the region of its native population, and a new round of brutality would spell death for the natives of California.

## THE NORTHWEST

Russian, British, and American competition for the Northwest Coast fur trade radically increased native contact with foreigners during the early nineteenth century.

After the Russians established forts in Tlingit territory, it was not long before friction developed. Kodiak natives began harvesting sea otter pelts that the Tlingit had expected to collect and trade to the British. Russian promises to protect the Tlingit from their enemies and give them more goods in trade seemed hollow when the Russians refused to offer weapons

*Above:* In northern California, Robinson annotated his 1819 map: "These parts are but little known."

*Opposite:* Tanner's 1822 map also reveals that little was known of central and northern California, and virtually nothing of its native population.

*Left:* The 1848 gold strike at Sutter's Mill would spell doom for California's surviving native peoples.

and rum, as the Americans and British had. Eventually, hostilities broke out that the Russians were convinced had been fomented by the British and Americans, and, in 1802, the Old Sitka Fort was destroyed.

In 1804, with naval assistance, Baranov built a new fort at present-day Sitka. Sporadic hostilities continued, but a stable basis for trade evolved, with the Tlingit supplying fish, game, and even potatoes to the Russians.

The British came overland via the trading post networks of the Hudson's Bay and North West Companies. Many natives settled around these forts for convenience and protection from raids.

Arriving by sea, the American Fur Company established its post at Astoria, on the Columbia River, in 1811. While the Russian and British trade centered on sea mammal pelts, John Jacob Astor's men concentrated on the beaver

trade, which tended to exclude the nearby coastal peoples from involvement.

North of the Juan de Fuca Straits, a triangle trade arose: American clipper ships traded rum and molasses from the Caribbean for sea otter pelts to be sold in China. This then led to a co-operative venture in which Russian-controlled Aleut hunters supplied the furs for transport by faster American ships between 1803 and 1813.

Diseases from South America, Asia, and the Caribbean followed these new trade routes, introducing several devastating epidemics. Smallpox had first arrived in the 1770s, and natives recalled the abandonment of entire villages. Local outbreaks of the disease recurred in 1801, 1836–38, and 1853—roughly every generation. The 1836–38 outbreak is believed to have reached the area by both overland and sea routes. During this period, measles, influenza, dysentery, pertussis, tuberculosis, and venereal diseases appeared in rapid succession, spreading quickly through native populations.

The appearance of malaria in the lower Columbia River drainage in 1830 come close to

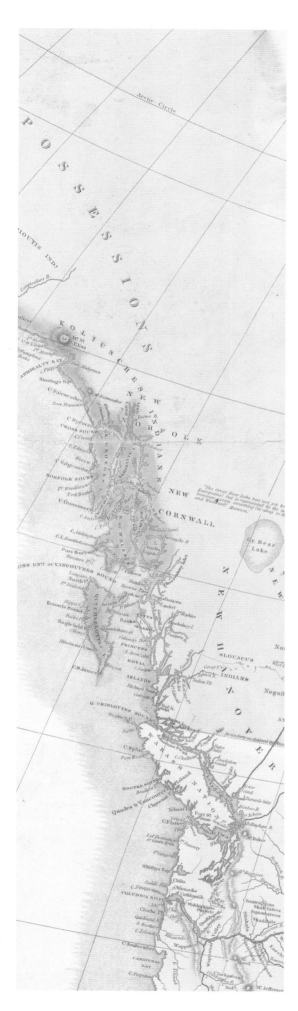

annihilating the Chinook and Kalapuya. Its debilitating effects caused many to die of secondary illnesses; miscarriages and stillbirths increased. Native remedies added to the mortality rate: Plunging into rivers to treat fever and taking sweat baths for chills often led to death.

Of the 18,250 natives living in the area before the epidemic, only 2,433 remained by 1840. Groups of Sahaptin, Klikitat, and Salish soon occupied lands along the Columbia River and in the Willamette valley left empty by the decline of the Chinook and Kalapuya.

Farther north, social disorder and upheaval ensued as hundreds of depopulated villages consolidated into far fewer settlements. Around Fort Rupert, for example, four Kwakiutl villages merged into one. Formerly independent entities with separate sets of titles and privileges, the new community was now faced with sorting out the relative ranking of the various titles.

Moreover, the sudden death of men of rank often resulted in the loss of ritual knowledge and estates left without designated heirs. The titles normally spread among many adult family members were now often inherited by a family's sole survivor, regardless of age: 658 titles were distributed among some 8,000 Kwakiutl in 1835, but among less than 2,300 in 1882, many such titles being held by children. By century's end, these economic and social changes would even influence the nature of the potlatch ceremony.

### THE ARCTIC

Policies in Alaska had begun to change with the creation of the Russian American Company in 1799. Where many fur traders had operated, the new company was granted a twenty-year monopoly. At each renewal of its charter, however, it was required to provide additional social services. Eventually, the territory's schools, medical services, even the church, would be supported by the Russian American Company. New policies dictated that natives would be employed to explore and chart the coastal waters and interior sections of Alaska. One native was even sent to the Hudson's Bay Company's Fort Yukon to spy on the competition.

Aleksandr Baranov, who became the chief manager of all Alaska under the new company, was concerned more with food supplies and competition from British and American

*Left: Tanner's 1822 map shows that non-native knowledge of the Northwest region was confined to a narrow coastal strip. Above Great Bear Lake is the notation that no European had yet visited the lake, but it was represented from Indian accounts of its size and location.*

traders than with social programs and exploration. Believing that securing Russia's North American colonies required expansion south, he had built new settlements in Tlingit territory at Yakutat and (Old) Sitka, sites chosen for their strategic importance as harbors that were favored by British and American traders.

To expand his tiny Russian force, Baranov recruited native warriors from nearby tribes including the Chugach, who saw the Russian expansion into Tlingit territory as revenge on their ancient enemies. Failing to gain enough volunteers, he used conscription, virtually stripping the Kodiak Archipelago of men. With these forces, he was now able to make trading forays as far south as San Diego and Baja California. However, this placed the Kodiak natives in dire straits. Lacking hunters, shortages of food and other essentials developed. Baranov used his control of supplies to force most Kodiak women, children, and elderly people to work for him in exchange for a bare subsistence.

To prevent British and American northward expansion, the Russian Navy often called at Alaskan ports. During such visits, inspections were conducted and inquiries made into any complaints registered about administration of the colony. Investigations into those reports

(substantiated by the clergy) of exploitation of the natives resulted in Baranov being officially censured in 1804–1805, 1810, and 1817, and finally removed in 1818. Many Aleut joined the Russian Orthodox Church in gratitude for the clergy's support.

Thereafter, senior naval officers were made governors of the territory. Previously, Baranov had used the difficulty of communicating with the government to justify his autocratic rule, but his military successors now used the same situation to justify doing nothing at all until instructions arrived.

**Below:** *The Aleutian Islands and Russian settlements along the coast of present-day Alaska, from Tanner's 1822 map.*

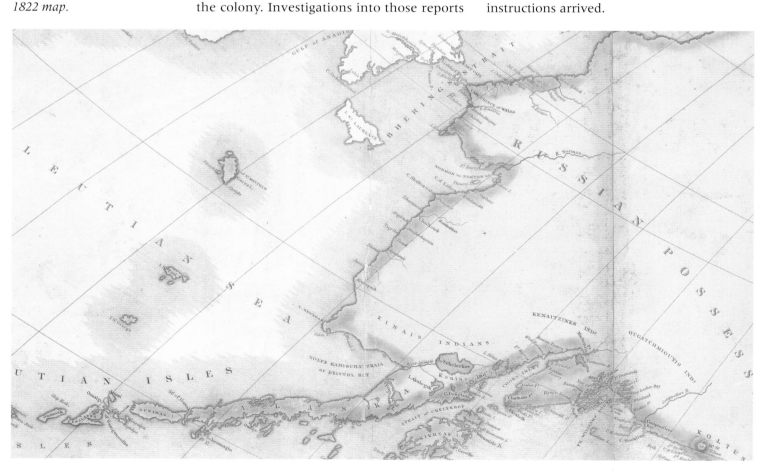

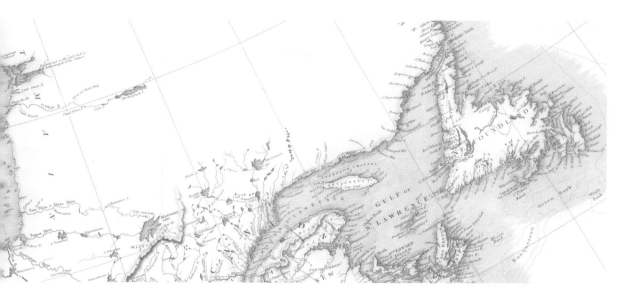

*Left: The eastern Subarctic in 1828, mapped by James Wyld. In this harsh region, only the trading routes were known. Very little detail is shown of the native nations of the region.*

New policies, however, protected the rights of all natives under Russian control by making them citizens of the Empire with the status of free peasants. This opened opportunities for education and social advancement, allowing some natives to rise to management.

The Russian American Company attempted a smallpox vaccination program in 1818, but it met with staunch native resistance. When the 1836–39 smallpox pandemic reached Alaska, native beliefs thwarted another vaccination program, and some one-third to one-half of the Aleutian and southern Alaskan natives died. Because the Russians appeared to be immune, the natives concluded that the disease had been introduced deliberately.

The discovery of the Northwest Pacific whaling grounds in 1838 led to vastly increased foreign contact with the Inuit north of the Bering Strait by 1850. Bowhead whales, a rich source of baleen ("whale bone"—actually cartilage—was used in the corsets at the time), were found to migrate from the Pacific into the Arctic Ocean in summer. Whalers plying the Beaufort Sea began to contact northern Inuit with increasing frequency. Inevitably, alcohol was traded and various diseases transmitted.

## THE SUBARCTIC

Intense competition between the Hudson's Bay Company and the North West Company for Subarctic furs marked the early nineteenth century. Violence, often resembling war, was fueled in part by increasing use of alcohol in the trade. Distilling spirits locally, York Factory's 1815 production of 3,300 gallons rose to more than 6,000 gallons by 1821.

By this time, declining profits made it obvious the competition had become mutually destructive. The companies merged to form a monopoly in Rupert's Land, abruptly enacting cost-cutting measures that reduced the amount of goods a native received for his skins.

In addition to requiring more effort to get enough pelts to obtain now-necessary amounts of trade goods, natives were faced with declining stocks of large game as well as fur-bearing animals. The resulting poorer diet and less adequate clothing weakened native health.

Among the Ojibwa who had migrated north into the territory of the Hudson's Bay Company, these factors combined to produce a leadership crisis as well as a rise in accusations of witchcraft to explain the higher frequency of illness. This distrust caused schisms between interdependent groups, making survival even more difficult.

Farther north, contagious diseases spread through the Eastern Dene in 1820. Also the first to contract smallpox in the 1838 pandemic, it spread from them to all the Dene by 1839. During the next twenty years, whooping cough (pertussis) would kill many of their children.

The illness and death of hunters and leaders in epidemics further curtailed food supplies, increasing susceptibility to disease; the Kutchin population dropped from some 5,400 in 1800 to around 900 by the 1860s.

Population declines among Dene groups may have made it impossible for some to operate caribou pounds or make fish nets, forcing them to forsake their traditional subsistence patterns and enter the fur trade. The loss of women to make necessary clothing may also have mandated this change in their lifeways.

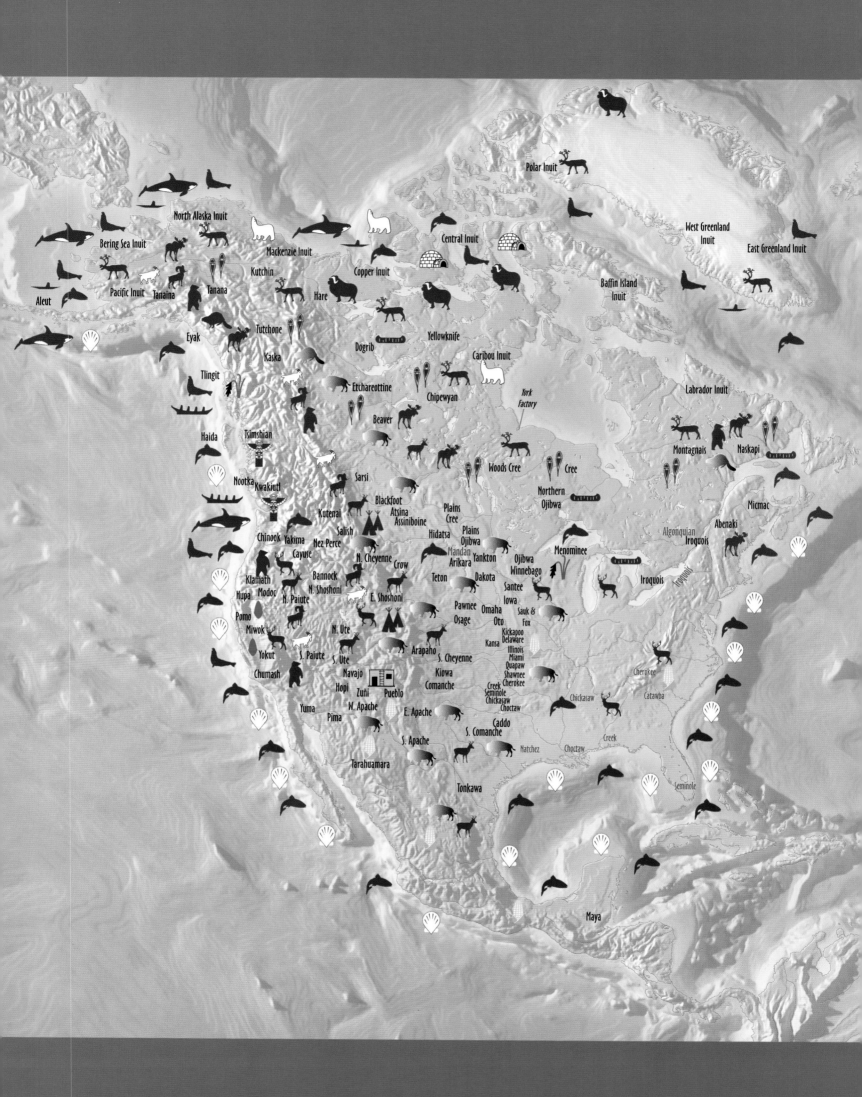

# "The Last Great Resistance"

## 1850–1900

The last fifty years of the nineteenth century witnessed social, political, and economic changes that profoundly transformed the lives of everyone living in North America, including the indigenous peoples.

During this period the United States emerged from a bloody civil war to become a unified, continental nation in transition from an agrarian to an industrial economy. In 1850 the "frontier" of American settlement (with the exception of pockets in Utah, Oregon, and California) lay east of the Great Plains. By 1900 the official recognition of a frontier line of settlement had been discarded. American citizens, including former slaves, along with European and Asian immigrants, had occupied and established governments throughout the territory from the Plains to the Pacific shore. In the East, technological innovation and business reorganization fostered the growth of industrial capitalism, while in the South, a culture based on racial segregation became more firmly entrenched. Throughout the nation, ideas of progress and Social Darwinism influenced private actions and government policy. To the north, where British colonies confederated in 1867 to form the Dominion of Canada, similar conditions existed, albeit on a lesser scale.

Wherever they lived, Native Americans of the late nineteenth century were affected by these developments. But, unlike their neighbors, Indians were also subject to concerted efforts by public agencies and private organizations to define, control, and reshape their lives. Tribally held lands continued to pass into non-native hands; the territory that remained for native use became part of government-administered reservations. The missionaries, reformers, and bureaucrats suppressed sacred ceremonies, replaced traditional social practices and cultural values with their own, and took over the education of Native American children. Agents eliminated, bypassed, or restructured native governing bodies to ensure the government's authority of its "wards." Supporting these measures (at least on federal reservations) was the constant threat to use military force against noncompliant natives.

Native responses to these policies and attitudes reflected the diversity—tribal and individual—that existed in Native America. Some defended their independence and way of life on the battlefield or in the courts. Many more (undoubtedly a majority) resisted unwanted intrusions in imaginative, subtle ways. Still others accepted, to some extent, the circumstances in which they found themselves and strove to be accepted by the dominant society. Those who were able to distanced themselves from whites and followed the old ways. All tried to survive.

Most did survive, but many did not. Over the course of the half-century, the native population of the United States decreased dramatically, giving rise to the popular notion that Indians were the "vanishing Americans." Although enumerations compiled by the Bureau of the Census, the Bureau of Indian Affairs, and other agencies were often incomplete, contradictory, and self-serving, a real decline in population was indeed occurring. A partial tally in 1850 revealed 400,764 Indians; ten years later, the census tabulated an aggregate population of 339,421. In 1890 the government reported an Indian population in the contiguous states and territories of 248,253. By 1900 the total had dropped to 237,196, its nadir. In that year,

*Opposite: Native North America in 1850, showing the Eastern nations virtually eliminated.*

Oklahoma (including Indian Territory) reported the highest number of Native Americans—64,445; Vermont reported the lowest: 5.

The causes of this decline were several. Warfare, both intertribal and between Native Americans and whites, accounts for some of the losses. Genocidal attacks by whites destroyed some specific communities, such as the Yahi of northern California. The removal or emigration of natives from their homelands and their inter-marriage with non-natives also reduced tribal rolls. But perhaps the most significant causes of decline were disease and the loss of traditional lifeways. Epidemic illnesses still swept through native camps and villages. The destruction of hunting grounds sometimes resulted in wide-spread starvation, and the introduction of unfa-miliar diets to reservation Indians often led to malnutrition and death. In 1890 journalist Thomas Tibbles observed some Lakota at

Rosebud Reservation in South Dakota *"actually diseased by this new, unnatural way of life. I saw many of them covered with running sores, others with scrofula. Often men in their early prime dropped dead in their tracks from stoppage of the circulation...caused by the thickened blood caused by excessive meat-eat-ing without the counteracting exercise to which Indian bodies had been used for centuries. Many Sioux women,"* he reported, *"were unable to bear chil-dren after their mid-twenties."*

Pretty Shield, a Crow medicine woman, remembered that when the buffalo disap-peared *"sickness came, strange sickness that nobody knew about."* The resultant illness and death *"would not have happened if we Crows had been living as we were intended to live. But how,"* she lamented, *"could we live in the old way when everything was gone?"*

Pretty Shield had grown to adulthood liv-ing the free life enjoyed by generations of her

*Below: The state of Missouri in an 1850 map by Cowperthwait. There was very little non-native settlement here until after the 1803 Louisiana Purchase. By 1812, when Missouri was made a territory of the U.S., it was known as the "Gateway to the West," becoming a state in 1821. By 1850, as shown in this map, the Eastern native nations had been removed to the west of Missouri, whose population in 1861 was 1,182,000 (including 144,000 slaves).*

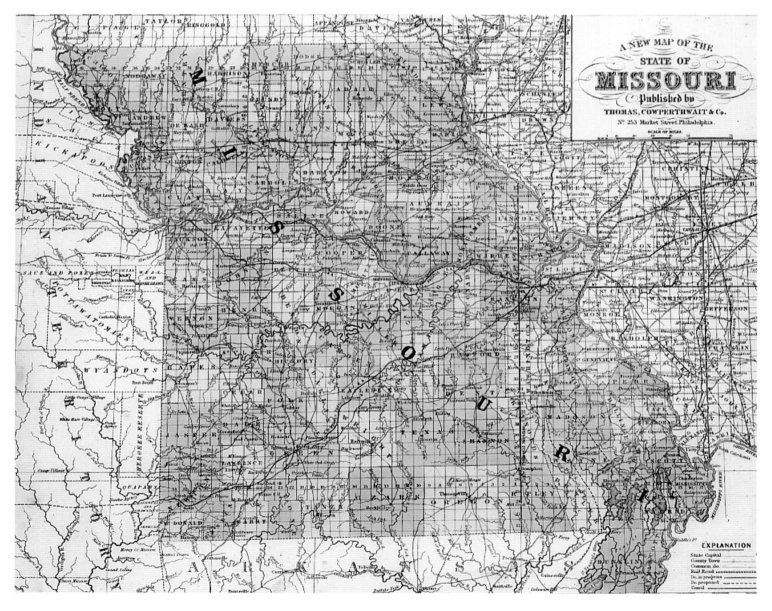

ancestors. So had her contemporary, the famous Crow Chief Plenty Coups. Recounting his life story, he reflected that *"when the buffalo went away the hearts of my people fell to the ground, and they could not lift them up again."* When Thomas Tibbles surveyed the Rosebud landscape, he concluded that it *"would bring to any sensitive soul a sense of complete desolation and degradation. And the Indians,"* he noted, *"are a sensitive race."*

Reservations (lands "reserved" for native occupation and use after purchases or cessions) had existed since the seventeenth century. The first was set aside in 1638 for the Quinnipiac in present-day New Haven, Connecticut. Other reservations soon followed in Massachusetts, Virginia, and elsewhere. After American independence, the federal government assumed exclusive jurisdiction over relations with tribes occupying the nation's commonly held territory. With a few exceptions (notably the Iroquois and Cherokee), tribes residing within the borders of the original thirteen British colonies dealt only with the new state governments. In the late 1800s, a number of small, state-administered reservations still remained along the Atlantic Seaboard.

As American settlement expanded westward during the nineteenth century, treaties established borders between the United States and "Indian country," where natives could retain their own lifeways. These borders frequently changed as tribes were relocated. Over time, Washington created a comprehensive reservation policy directed at concentrating Native Americans into restricted areas where they could not threaten settlers and where they could be forced to adopt an agricultural economy. Administered by the Office of Indian Affairs (transferred from the War Department to the newly created Department of the Interior in 1849), this policy was fully realized by the end of the century.

Reservations were headed by an agent who supervised a staff that included clerks, physicians, blacksmiths, farmers, interpreters, teamsters, and teachers, among others. Except for a brief time during the Grant administration, when favored Christian denominations made the selections for many reservations, agents were political appointees serving at the pleasure of the president. Frequently incompetent and often

corrupt, nevertheless, they controlled what could and could not be done on the reservations.

Government policy, supported by influential Eastern reform groups, aimed to transform Native Americans into Christian farmers. To achieve this goal, restrictions were placed on locations where Indians could live and travel, when they could come together for social purposes, and what political autonomy they would retain. Particularly destructive to the integrity of native communities were those policies directed at suppressing native religion, educating children, and dividing tribal landholdings. Indians, the original inhabitants of the country, were to become "Americanized."

Christian missions among the native peoples had existed from the earliest days of European contact. In the late nineteenth century, however, it became possible not only to win converts through word and example, but also to use force to keep natives from worshipping in their own manner. Such sacred ceremonies as the seasonal rituals conducted by the Puebloans and the Sun Dance of the Plains tribes were ridiculed, attacked, and outlawed. New religious expressions, such as the Indian Shaker movement of the Northwest, the Peyote Cult, and the Ghost Dances of 1870 and 1890 were viewed as threats to assimilation. The government used

*Above:* The railroad system, developed from 1826 on, greatly increased the flow of westward migration by Americans. The first transcontinental link was completed in 1869, and by 1883 four routes connected the Atlantic and Pacific coasts. This illustration symbolizes the destruction of the Plains buffalo herds by the advent of the railroad.

legal and, in 1890, military means to prevent their spread. Despite such persecutions, many tribal religions survived into the twentieth century, their adherents passing on the lore and practice of sacred rituals secretly to their young.

At the same time, Indian youth were being taught that to survive and prosper in the America of which they were now part, they must abandon the old tribal ways and embrace the culture of the mainstream society. As one reformer put it in 1886, *"Unless he is taken young and taught to adjust himself to his surroundings* [the Indian] *will always be oppressed, and there will always be trouble. He must be able to work and live as does the civilized white man; this training must be done by the schools East and West, and there is no time to be lost in doing it."* Some native children, particularly in the East, attended public schools with non-native classmates. Most of those who were exposed to the white man's education, however, attended church- or government-run day or boarding schools on the reservations. Toward the end of the century, an increasing number of students were sent to off-reservation boarding schools like the Phoenix School in Arizona or Virginia's Hampton Institute (where Booker T. Washington taught native classes).

In these schools, Native American children were given Anglicized names, required to wear "civilian" clothes, punished for speaking their native languages, and taught such skills as carpentry, masonry, agriculture, and housekeeping. When parents resisted sending their children to school, food rations were withheld, or the children were taken by force.

The most famous of the off-reservation schools was the Carlisle Indian School in Pennsylvania. Founded in 1879 by Captain Richard Pratt, a former army officer, the school offered the usual classes in agriculture, the vocational trades, and home economics. It also achieved a reputation for the caliber of its athletes who, particularly in football, competed successfully against teams from such schools as Harvard and West Point. Regimented like little soldiers, Carlisle students went for years without seeing their parents or other relatives; during summer recess, the children were "put out" to local farms and businesses where, as unpaid laborers, they were further exposed to "civilization."

A disturbingly high number of children sent to Carlisle and other off-reservation schools never returned home at all. The Brule chief Spotted Tail was only one of many Native American parents to receive word that his beloved child had died far from home. Measles, mumps, and other illnesses were responsible for many deaths, but grieving relatives usually blamed simple homesickness for their losses.

Native children did not respond uniformly to their educational experiences. Some pursued their studies with enthusiasm and talent and later received some degree of recognition by non-natives for their achievements. Susan La Flesche, an Omaha, attended Hampton and the Woman's Medical College of Pennsylvania, becoming in 1889 the first Native American

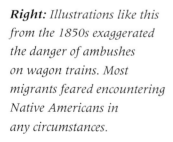

*Right: Illustrations like this from the 1850s exaggerated the danger of ambushes on wagon trains. Most migrants feared encountering Native Americans in any circumstances.*

woman medical doctor in the United States. Her brother Francis became a respected ethnologist with the Smithsonian Institution. Charles Eastman (Dakota) and Carlos Montezuma (Yavapai) also became physicians, while other white-educated natives including Zitkala Sa (Gertrude Bonnin), a Yankton Sioux, and Alexander Posey, a Creek, wrote prose and poetry that was well received by both native and non-native readers. Many within this group, using the English they had been forced to learn in school to communicate across tribal lines, became leaders in the pan-Indian movements that arose in the early twentieth century.

For most Native American students, however, their educational experiences turned out to be irrelevant, even alienating. Skills they had learned were not necessarily needed on the reservations, and their years away from home often made them strangers in their own communities. Sun Elk, a boy from Taos Pueblo, entered Carlisle in 1883 and remained there for seven years. His teachers told him that *"Indian ways were bad. They said we must get civilized."* He and his classmates *"wore white man's clothes and ate white man's food and went to white man's churches and spoke white man's talk. And so after a while, we also began to say Indians were bad.*

*We laughed at our own people and their blankets and cooking pots and sacred societies and dances."* Later, after Sun Elk returned to Taos, several men of the village complained to his father that Sun Elk *"cannot even speak our language and he has a strange smell. He is not one of us."*

Sun Elk was not alone. Throughout the West, a generation of Indians was maturing

*Left: Susette La Flesche, an Omaha activist for Native American rights and the sister of Susan La Flesche, the first Native American woman to qualify as a medical doctor in the United States.*

*Below: Inside a Carlisle School classroom, photographed in 1900.*

who, unable to live their people's traditional life and not fully accepted in white society, questioned the value of their education, a phenomenon that occurred even in such Indian-run schools as the Cherokee Female Seminary. Too frequently, it left them living in an "in-between world," neither Indian nor white. A majority of returning students tried to be intermediaries, helping to create a new reservation culture that included features of both traditional and mainstream American life. Others "returned to the blanket," rejecting all they had been taught. Often they succeeded in living positive lives, passing on to their children what they had learned from their elders. But some became apathetic and withdrawn or slid into alcoholism, a growing problem on reservations during these years. A few acted out their frustrations more violently. Plenty Horses, a Lakota youth who had returned to the Pine Ridge Reservation in South Dakota, found it difficult to prove that he was still an Indian. He arrived home nine days after the massacre at Wounded Knee and shortly thereafter killed a cavalry officer. He said that he was trying to prove the school had not turned him into a white man.

Tribal identity and culture were dependent on the land the people called home. The greatest loss of native lands occurred during the fifty years between 1850 and 1900. The United States acquired title to millions of acres of

Native American lands through treaties until the treaty-making process was unilaterally abandoned by Congress in 1871. Thereafter, so-called agreements with tribes resulted in the loss of more acreage, including the sacred Black Hills of South Dakota. Even reservation land could be cleverly transferred from native to non-native use and ownership.

The U.S. government had experimented with allotment before 1850, but with the passage of the General Allotment (Dawes) Act in 1887 it became entrenched federal policy until disavowed in 1934. (The Five Civilized Tribes, exempted in 1887, had their tribal holdings divided under the terms of the Curtis Act of 1898.) Although certain reservations—including the Iroquois and Navajo—and the lands of Alaska natives were never allotted, most others were eventually surveyed and divided into privately owned parcels. Under the act, each head of an Indian family received 160 acres; all others over the age of eighteen received 80 acres each. After everyone had received an allotment, the surplus tribal land could be sold to non-Indians, the money received being held in trust from the tribe's "benefit." Subsequent legislation even permitted the Secretary of the Interior, under certain circumstances, to sell or lease individual allotments. As a result of this policy, Native Americans collectively lost more than 86 million acres of tribal land.

*Right: The Cherokee Female
Seminary, the first institution
west of the Mississippi for the
education of women and one
of a small number of Indian-
run schools. Originally
founded in 1851, the first
building was destroyed by
fire in 1887; the new
building, pictured here,
was completed in 1888.*

Government policy, with few exceptions, treated Indians as if they were a single, uniform group of people. But Choctaw were different from Klamath, and the Quapaw were strangers to the Apache. During this period, each tribe had its own unique strategies for survival.

## THE GREAT PLAINS

The Great Plains had never witnessed such a sight: In September 1851 nearly 10,000 Lakota, Cheyenne, Arapaho, Crow, Gros Ventre, Assiniboine, Mandan, Arikara, and Hidatsa gathered in a great camp at Fort Laramie, in present-day southeastern Wyoming, to council with representatives of the United States government.

Thousands of emigrants crossing the northern Plains on their way to California or Oregon were disrupting tribal hunting grounds and sometimes introducing infectious diseases among the indigenous populations. Frustrated warriors were attacking or raiding wagon trains with greater frequency. To ensure the safe passage of the settlers, and to end the ongoing warfare and raiding among tribes, the government wanted the tribes to agree to the construction of roads and military posts in their territory and to *"bind themselves to make restitution or satisfaction for any wrongs committed…by any band or individual of their people, on the people of the United States, whilst lawfully residing in or passing through their respective territories."* The treaty concluded at this council, like a similar one with the people of the southern Plains in 1853, set boundaries for each tribe's territory and promised the natives $50,000 per year for ten years, along with *"provisions, merchandise, domestic animals, and agricultural implements."* Oblivious to the actual workings of native political life, the Americans named individual head chiefs for each nation to whom each tribe would "bind" itself and through whom all business with the United States would be conducted.

Congress later reduced the annual payments to $10,000, and some signatory tribes never received the goods that they were promised. Most importantly, despite the good intentions of everyone involved, peace did not come to the northern Plains.

The culture of the Great Plains at mid-century was horse-centered. The arrival of the animals on the Plains during the eighteenth century had affected virtually all the tribes that

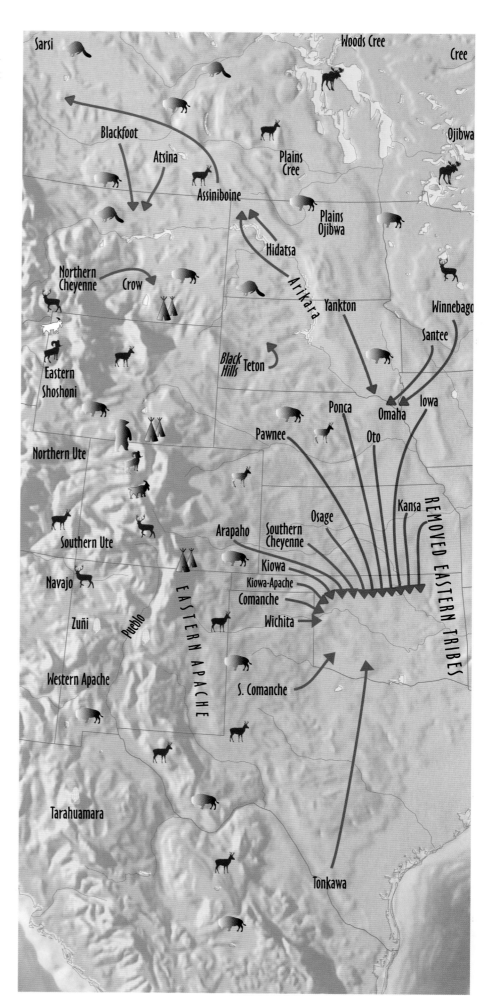

acquired them. Native people became more mobile, able to live on the Plains year-round rather than just seasonally. With horses, Plains people made and moved larger tipis than they could when dogs were their only pack animals. Ponies became status symbols and items of trade within and among tribes. Warriors (usually seeking ponies) were able to raid enemy camps more effectively. Hunting buffalo was easier and less dangerous.

Before the Nez Perce acquired horses in the 1730s, they sustained themselves primarily by fishing for salmon in the Columbia River and its tributaries, hunting elk and bighorn sheep, and gathering wild roots and berries, as described in the Plateau culture region sections of previous chapters. With horses, some Nez Perce bands made regular treks across the Bitterroot Mountains to the northern Plains, hunting buffalo and appropriating some of the traits of the Plains tribes.

*Below:* An Edward Curtis photograph of an Oglala chief, a subtribe of the Lakota or Teton Sioux who now controlled territory from Wyoming and Montana to the Dakotas.

Other native peoples, coming from both east and west, established a more permanent residence on the Plains. When the Cheyenne, an Algonquian people, first encountered Europeans in the late 1600s, they were farmers living in settled villages in present-day Minnesota and Wisconsin. Obtaining horses by the mid-1700s and experiencing increasing attacks by the Dakota Sioux and Ojibwa, they gave up farming, abandoned their villages, migrated westward, and became buffalo hunters. By the mid-nineteenth century, they had divided into two branches. The Northern Cheyenne hunted near the headwaters of the Platte River in present-day Wyoming. The Southern Cheyenne ranged along the Arkansas River in what are now eastern Colorado and western Kansas.

A Shoshonean people who had lived in the mountains of Wyoming and Colorado, the Comanche began moving onto the southern Plains around 1700, as described earlier in this book. Acquiring horses, they soon dominated the Plains from western Texas and eastern New Mexico to southeastern Colorado and southern Kansas, an area that became known as Comancheria. Their warriors, sometimes described as the greatest horsemen the world has ever seen, fought Apache, Pawnee, Kiowa, and other Plains tribes and raided Puebloan and Spanish villages from the upper Rio Grande to deep within Mexico itself. Never subdued by the Spanish, Mexicans, or even the Texans, mounted Comanche offered fierce resistance to the American army after the Civil War.

Of all the native peoples occupying the Plains in the late 1800s, the best known were those collectively called the Sioux. Like the Cheyenne, the Sioux were living in Minnesota in the seventeenth century. Calling themselves the Oceti Sakowin (Seven Council Fires), they consisted of seven divisions speaking three dialects of a common root language. The Mdewakanton, Wahpeton, Wahpekute, and Sisseton divisions were know collectively as the Dakota (or Santee Sioux). They lived in the lake region and based their economy on fishing and harvesting wild rice. The Dakota were still living in Minnesota in 1850, but the other two divisions, pressured by Chippewa (Ojibwa) armed with French guns, had already migrated westward. The Nakota (Yankton and Yanktonai) stopped on the east bank of the upper Missouri River, where they built permanent villages and practiced agriculture. Periodically, they entered the plains on horseback to hunt buffalo. The Lakota (Teton Sioux), the seventh council fire, were the most populous branch and themselves had seven subtribes, including the Oglala, Brule, Miniconjou, and Hunkpapa. Possessing horses by the mid-1700s, they crossed the Missouri and, pushing the Cheyenne, Kiowa, Comanche, and Crow ahead of them, gained control of a large territory that now includes parts of Wyoming, Montana, Nebraska, and the Dakotas.

To contemporary non-natives, as well as to succeeding generations, the nineteenth-century Lakota lifestyle represented the archetype of Plains culture. Nomadic hunters who maintained large herds of ponies, the Lakota depended on the buffalo for survival. *"Every part of this animal is eaten by the Indians except the horns, hoofs, and hair,"* reported the fur trader Edwin Denig. *"The skin is used to make their lodges and clothes, the sinews for bow strings, the horns to contain their powder and the bones wrought into dressing tools, or pounded up and grease extracted."* The hides provided robes, blankets, moccasins, tipi coverings, bullboats, and shields. Horns were transformed into ornaments, spoons, ladles, and club heads. A simple fly swatter was the practical application of the buffalo's tail. Buffalo chips provided fuel; the bladder was used as a storage container; the sinews became thread, bowstrings, and rope; and the hair was used as stuffing.

The buffalo figured prominently in the sacred traditions and rituals of the Lakota. A buffalo skull served as the altar during the Sun Dance, a summer ceremony that the Lakota, with their own variations, shared with some twenty other Plains tribes. One of the seven sacred rituals that the holy White Buffalo Cow Woman had long ago promised would be revealed to them, the Sun Dance was usually initiated by an individual to fulfill a personal vow but performed to receive the Creator's blessing on the whole tribe. Dancers sought that end by having their breasts or backs skewered and tied to a central lodge pole. Then, while dancing and staring at the sun, they tried to break loose. This self-mortification repulsed non-native observers and was a principal reason for the government's ban on the ritual in the 1880s. For the Lakota, however, the three- to four-day ceremony,

*Above: A Plains tipi, easily portable by horses, made from buffalo hide stretched over lodge poles.*

which reunited bands that had scattered for the winter, reaffirmed their identity as a people. Along with vision quests and other sacred practices, the Sun Dance demonstrated the importance of spirituality in Lakota life.

Each of the Plains tribes had its own form of self-government. The political organization of the Oglala may be taken as representative of that of the Teton as a whole. At any given time, the Oglala were organized into at least seven separate bands (*tiyospaye*) composed of ten or more extended families, each of which was led by a headman who retained his position by demonstrating the ability to provide for his camp. Heading each band was a chief known as an *itancan*. The band chief often inherited his position, but could retain it only as long as he could protect and preserve the integrity of the *tiyospaye*. The *itancan* led by commanding respect for his commitment to the virtues most admired by the Lakota: bravery, generosity, fortitude, and wisdom. Band members dissatisfied with his performance were free to join another *tiyospaye*, or to form one of their own. New bands came and went throughout the nineteenth century as the Oglala adapted to new circumstances.

The most respected *itancan* of the oldest *tiyospaye* was called what interpreters often translated as "head chief." The designation conferred no additional authority—and certainly no coercive power—on the individual so named, a fact that was never really grasped by Americans in their dealings with the Oglala. Within his own band, the *itancan* presided over councils attended by other camp leaders but spoke himself rarely and had little or no authority to dictate or enforce decisions. Government was by consensus.

Participating in that consensus, in addition to headmen, were war party leaders, warriors, and holy men. Enforcing the council's decisions were the *wakiconza*, who held authority while the band was in camp, and the *akicita*, who served as messengers and enforced order when the band was on the move. However, consensus was not always achieved. Band chiefs and headmen sometimes could not control the actions of their young men, particularly when it came to war. After the Oglala (and other Lakota) acquired horses and migrated into lands hunted by other tribes, warfare became an especially vital part of their lives. Young men

sought to achieve status within their band through stealing horses, killing or scalping an enemy, or touching an enemy (preferably while still alive) with a coup stick. Exploits that demonstrated bravery, and that could be confirmed by an impartial witness, earned a warrior eagle feathers to add to his headdress. Oglala military societies, including the Kit Foxes, Brave Hearts, and Crow Owners, extended across band lines and accepted only the most promising young men into their ranks. But glory also entailed responsibility. Members of the warrior societies were expected to sponsor giveaways for the needy and host various camp events at their own expense.

Oglala women seldom participated directly in the political or military life of the band, although occasionally an older woman might speak in council, or a young one, like Crazy Horse's sister, might accompany a war party. Nevertheless, women were indispensable within the camp circle. They tanned buffalo hides, set up and dismantled the tipis (which were their property), gathered roots and berries, cooked, cared for the children and the elderly, and crafted items decorated with beads and porcupine quills. They also maintained exclusive societies, among which was the

***Below and opposite:***
*Mounted warfare as depicted by Plains people in ledger books acquired from traders.*

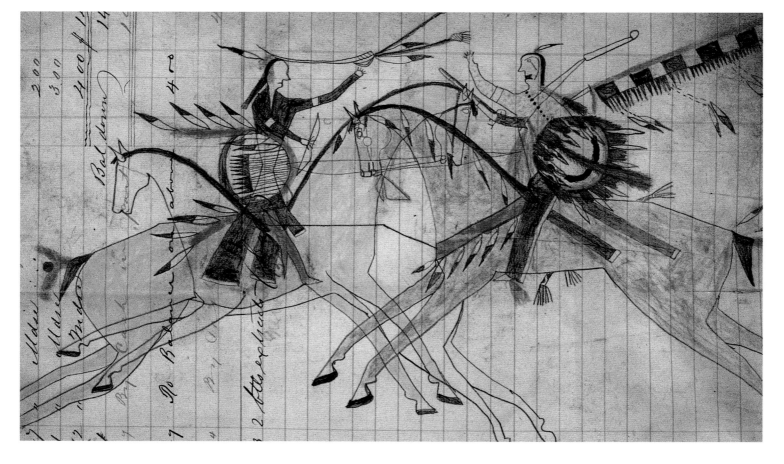

Medicine Society, which prepared war medicine and shields for the young men.

On August 18, 1855, women were going about their tasks in the camps of Oglala, Brule, and Miniconjou who had gathered near Fort Laramie to await the arrival of their yearly annuities. The agent who would distribute them had not yet arrived at the post, and the Lakota were hungry. A lame cow from a passing Mormon wagon train bolted into the Brule camp, where it was killed by a visiting Miniconjou. The Indians feasted. At first, no action was taken when the cow's owner reported the incident at the fort. But then a young lieutenant, John L. Grattan, newly graduated from West Point, persuaded the commander to let him lead a detachment into the camp to capture the offending Miniconjou.

The leader of the camp was Conquering Bear, whom the Americans (under the terms of the 1851 treaty) had designated "head chief" of all the Brule. When negotiations failed and Conquering Bear, who had no authority to do so, failed to turn over the culprit, Grattan ordered his men to fire the two howitzers they had brought with them. Conquering Bear was mortally wounded. Angry Brule warriors quickly retaliated, killing Grattan and the other twenty-nine men with him. The women quickly struck camp and the Brule fled.

Thus began thirty-five years of intermittent warfare between the Sioux and the Americans.

An army expedition in 1856 inflicted heavy losses on the Brule in retaliation for the Grattan "massacre," but the first major war between Americans and Sioux was waged not against the Lakota, but against their eastern relatives, the Dakota. In 1851 the Santee had ceded all their territory except a reservation on the Minnesota River that measured 10 miles wide and 150 miles long. Dependent on their annual treaty annuities, the Dakota obtained other supplies during the year from traders who extended credit. Payoff time for the traders came when the government delivered the Indians' money and goods.

In 1862 the Dakota put off their early summer buffalo hunt to await that distribution. They were still waiting in mid-August. Although foodstuffs were available for distribution, the agent refused to release them until the treaty money also arrived. Hungry Dakota unsuccessfully sought additional credit from the traders in order to purchase food. One of the traders, Andrew Myrick, answered the plea by saying, *"Let them eat grass."*

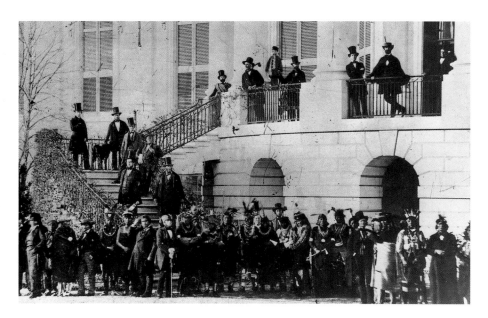

*Above:* A Native American delegation visits the White House to confer with President Andrew Johnson after the Civil War.

When four young Santee, returning from an unsuccessful hunt, stole some eggs from a white farmer and ended up killing two white men and three women, Dakota frustrations turned violent. The four hunters returned to the reservation and confessed their deed. At an all-night council, some tribal leaders spoke for peace, others urged war. The latter argued that the government would punish them anyway and that, with many white men away fighting in the Civil War, it was an opportune time to take up arms against the hated settlers. The session ended with Little Crow, a disgruntled Mdewakanton leader, agreeing to lead warriors against the whites.

The next day, August 18, the Dakota erupted out of their reservation. Before the carnage ended six weeks later, some 800 white men, women, and children had been killed or captured by the Dakota. One of the dead was the trader Myrick, who was found with his mouth stuffed full of grass. The Dakota, too, suffered casualties. At the conclusion of this "uprising" (as the Americans called it), many Dakota were put on trial: 303 were condemned to death. President Lincoln commuted most of those sentences but signed death warrants for thirty-eight Dakota. On December 26, 1862, the condemned were lined up on a specially constructed gallows in Mankato, Minnesota. As they chanted their death songs, a rope was cut that released all thirty-eight trapdoors at once. It was the largest mass execution in United States history. Little Crow escaped the gallows but was shot and killed by a white farmer the following summer. The surviving Dakota were stripped of their Minnesota lands and relocated to a reservation in Nebraska.

The Civil War brought Indian-American fighting of a different kind to the nations in Indian Territory. Soon after hostilities began with the Confederacy, the Union government evacuated all its forts in the Indian Territory, leaving the Five Civilized Tribes without federal protection. Almost surrounded by Confederate states, all five nations signed treaties in 1861 with the secessionist government. The Choctaw and the Chickasaw, who owned many slaves, were the most enthusiastic allies. The action created deep divisions within the other three tribes. Some 5,500 Cherokee, Chickasaw, Choctaw, Creek, and Seminole fought for the Confederacy; another 4,000 fought for the Union. Stand Watie, one of the signatories of the infamous Treaty of New Echota that led to Cherokee removal from the Southeast, attained a general's rank in the Southern army and was the last to surrender a major Confederate force in 1865.

Partisan fighting in Indian Territory especially devastated the lands of the Cherokee and Creek, but all five nations suffered as a consequence of their participation in the sectional conflict. Postwar treaties forced the tribes to emancipate their slaves and to relinquish their western holdings, which were to be set aside as a reservation for other tribes.

Among those other tribes were the Cheyenne and Arapaho. Occupying Colorado by the terms of the Fort Laramie treaty, the two tribes generally provided little trouble for whites, even after the 1859 gold rush brought tens of thousands of miners into the Colorado Rockies. However, a group of militant Cheyenne warriors, organized as the Dog Soldier Society, conducted enough raids and attacks against whites to prompt Governor John Evans and a former Methodist minister, John Chivington, to organize the Third Colorado Cavalry in order to clear all Indians from the territory. Chiefs opposed to the Dog Soldiers—including Black Kettle, a Cheyenne—continued to seek peace even as natives and militia skirmished. Major Edward Wynkoop, commander of Fort Lyon in southeastern Colorado, listened to the peace chiefs' pleas with sympathy, and in the fall of 1864 he persuaded Evans and Chivington to allow the peaceful natives to camp at Sand Creek, 40 miles above his fort. Wynkoop was soon replaced by a less sympathetic commander, who not only withheld rations but also ordered his men to fire on a group of unarmed Arapaho coming to the fort to trade hides for food.

With the militia's term of enlistment about to end, Chivington arrived at Fort Lyon with 750 men on November 28 and rode overnight to Sand Creek from there. Deploying his men and four howitzers around the sleeping camp, Chivington answered three officers who objected to what was planned by saying: *"Damn any man who sympathizes with Indians. I have come to kill Indians, and believe it is right and honorable to use any means under God's heaven to kill Indians."*

And kill he did. Although Black Kettle raised both the flag of the United States and the white flag of truce over his tipi, Chivington's troops opened fire. In the blood bath that followed, 200 Native Americans were killed, most of them women and children. The Arapaho chief White Antelope was among the victims, but Black Kettle escaped. Those who survived the first attack tried to escape on foot. The troops pursued them closely, killing and scalping their victims. Chivington and his volunteers were welcomed as heroes in Denver, but congressional investigation followed and Chivington was forced to resign his command. So infamous was this raid that the name of the creek was later changed to "Big Sandy" to erase its association with the massacre.

Black Kettle and his followers eventually relocated in western Indian Territory. There, in 1868, peacefully encamped on the Washita River, his village was attacked again, this time by the Seventh Cavalry under the command of Lieutenant Colonel George A. Custer. While a military band eerily played "Garryowen," Black Kettle and more than 100 other men, women, and children were shot down. Even the camp's pony herd was slaughtered.

In the decades after the Civil War, Indian-White warfare in the West increased. On the northern Plains, the Lakota wanted to halt travel along the Bozeman Road, a trail that ran through their Powder River hunting grounds from Fort Laramie to the newly developed gold mines in Montana Territory. In June 1866, a group of Lakota warriors, led by Red Cloud of the Oglala's Bad Face band, came to Fort Laramie for talks. While Red Cloud was there,

Colonel Henry Carrington arrived with 700 soldiers under orders to construct four new forts to protect the trail. Red Cloud and the others withdrew angrily from the council.

The subsequent hostilities, often called Red Cloud's War, lasted for two years. Some bands did not take part in the fighting, but there were still enough Lakota warriors to keep the new forts under constant siege. One notable engagement took place on December 21, 1866, when Lakota warriors ambushed and killed a force of 82 soldiers sent to rescue a wood-chopping party outside Fort Phil Kearny, the second—but not the last—time a Teton war party wiped out an entire command. Similar attacks took place in 1867.

At the same time, President Ulysses S. Grant appointed a commission to investigate the hostilities on the Plains, make peace with the hostile natives, and recommend districts into which the native peoples might be segregated. Meeting in 1867 with southern Plains tribes at Medicine Lodge, Kansas, and in 1868 with northern tribes at Fort Laramie, Wyoming, the commission initiated what it considered *"the hitherto untried policy in connection with Indians, of endeavoring to conquer by kindness."* Beginning in April 1868, a number of Lakota chiefs and headmen put their marks to a document pledging that *"from this day forward all war between the parties to this agreement shall forever cease."* Not until November 6, 1868—more than three months after the hated Forts C.F. Smith, Phil Kearny, and Reno had been abandoned and the first two put to the torch by his followers—did Red Cloud affix his mark to the treaty. His war with the whites had ended. He had gained his immediate objective—abandonment of the Bozeman Road. Other Lakota were not so sure their people had achieved a victory. War leaders Crazy Horse of the Oglala and Sitting Bull of the Hunkpapa did not sign the treaty. Rather, they and their followers withdrew into the Powder River country, staying away from the new agencies established by the treaty.

The Fort Laramie Treaty of 1868 created the Great Sioux Reservation in Dakota Territory west of the Missouri River. There, native peoples observed an uneasy truce with government officials and others who were trying to bribe them into "civilization." During the summer of 1874, however, this peaceful

*Above: The negotiations at Fort Laramie, Wyoming, in 1868 created the Great Sioux Reservation in Dakota Territory.*

relationship was threatened when Custer and ten companies of the Seventh Cavalry escorted a team of mineralogists into reservation lands in the Black Hills, an area with many sites that were sacred to the Lakota. When the expedition announced the discovery of gold, miners rushed into the Hills and the military did little to stop them. Commissions were sent from Washington to purchase the Hills, but the Lakota refused to sell. In the winter of 1875–76, when weather conditions made travel impossible, the government ordered all Lakota, including the groups led by Sitting Bull and Crazy Horse, to move onto the reservation or face military action. When the nontreaty Lakota failed to comply, the army prepared a multipronged campaign against them led by Brigadier Generals George Crook and Alfred Terry, the latter of whose command included the entire Seventh Cavalry led by Lieutenant Colonel George Custer.

In June, while the army was moving against them, a large number of Lakota and Cheyenne gathered for the annual Sun Dance. Fulfilling a vow he had made when he felt his people were in danger, Sitting Bull allowed a friend to cut fifty pieces of flesh from his chest and arms. Losing consciousness, Sitting Bull received a vision in which he saw *"many soldiers falling into camp."*

The vision was indeed prophetic. At the same time as the Sun Dance was taking place, Crook,

with approximately 1,000 troops and an additional 300 Crow and Shoshoni scouts, was moving up the valley of the Rosebud River. On June 17, Crazy Horse and a large Lakota war party intercepted Crook's forces and drove them away. With no knowledge of what had happened to Crook, Terry began marching up the Big Horn River, sending Custer ahead on a circular course that would bring him behind the probable location of the Indian camp.

Ever the glory hunter and believing he was about to be nominated as a candidate for the presidency, Custer raced forward, hoping to locate and defeat the "hostiles" without the aid of Terry or Crook. Stumbling upon the vast native encampment along three miles of the Little Big Horn River, Custer deployed his troops in a manner reminiscent of the tactics he had used successfully at the "Battle" of the Washita. This time, however, he faced thousands of seasoned warriors—many better armed than his own 250 green troops—rather than the few hundred old men, women, and children he had attacked with Civil War veterans in the earlier battle. The inevitable result was soon mythologized as "Custer's Last Stand," largely through the writings of his widow, Elizabeth Bacon Custer.

Containing as it does elements of romance, mystery, high tragedy, and even low comedy, it is small wonder that so much analysis has been done and so much written about an event that might otherwise have been a minor footnote to history. Perhaps the true historical significance of the Battle of the Little Big Horn lies in its timing.

The first reports of Custer's death reached the eastern United States on July 4, 1876, at the height of the national Centennial euphoria. Arriving just two weeks after word of Crook's humiliation, the news of Custer's defeat galvanized a public wild with chauvinistic fervor, if ignorant of the facts, to mandate politicians and the military to find a "final solution" to the "Indian Problem"—whatever it took. Much of what would ensue not only for the nations of the northern Plains, but for all Native Americans in the last quarter of the nineteenth century and beyond would result from that public resolve.

For the Lakota and their allies, the Battle of the Little Big Horn was a great victory, but it

the Little Big Horn was a great victory, but it was also their last. From that time until 1877, the army harassed natives across the northern Plains and burned their villages. A particularly ugly incident occurred on November 26, 1876, when troops under Colonel Ranald Mackenzie attacked a Cheyenne village, burning the tipis, slaughtering hundreds of ponies, and leaving the survivors to freeze to death in the −30° cold. Sitting Bull and his followers had fled to Canada after the Custer battle, but Crazy Horse and his Oglala warriors remained in the field throughout the winter. It was not until spring that Crazy Horse finally came into the Red Cloud Agency. Fearful that this *"strange man of the Oglalas"* would stir up further trouble on the reservation, the army eventually ordered his arrest and imprisonment. On September 5, 1877, Crazy Horse was bayoneted and killed at Fort Robinson, Nebraska, while resisting an attempt to jail him.

By then, the Black Hills, which Crazy Horse had fought to keep for his people, were no longer part of the Great Sioux Reservation. In the fall of 1876, a Commission headed by George Manypenny, a former Commissioner of Indian Affairs, came to the agencies to obtain the cession of the Black Hills. Ignoring the provision in the Fort Laramie Treaty of 1868 that required the approval of three-fourths of all adult Lakota males to cede land, the commissioners met instead with the agency chiefs. Subject to martial law, threatened with the possible loss of their rations if they refused to sign, and opposed by the hostiles who were still in the field, the chiefs believed they had no choice but to relinquish the Black Hills.

Later, when dissatisfaction with the terms of the agreement grew, Red Cloud and others claimed that the terms had not been fully explained to them. They may have been right. A note in Lakota records Manypenny's telling the assembled chiefs that the Great Father *"doesn't want the soil, but the gold and other metals that may be in the Black Hills are what he wants. After he has mined all the minerals from them, he will give you back the soil. He wants to lease the land, or soil. This is what he says."* At the time, however, the agency chiefs, including Red Cloud and Spotted Tail, were willing to part with the Black Hills reluctantly in order to make the best of life on the reservation. Nevertheless, the

signing of the agreement was a somber occasion. Fire Thunder put his mark on the paper while blindfolded. Young Man Afraid told the commissioners: *"I give notice it will take me a long time to learn to labor, and I expect the President will feed me for 100 years, and perhaps a great deal longer."* The United States has since acknowledged that the Black Hills were taken illegally, but it has not given them back.

In the 1930s, Black Elk, an Oglala holy man who was a boy at the time of the Battle of the Little Big Horn, recalled that on the reservation his people *"made these little gray houses of logs…and they are square. It is a bad way to live, for there can be no power in a square."* Defeated in war and manipulated in peace, the Lakota—as well as the Cheyenne, Kiowa, Comanche, and other Plains tribes—became dependent on the government as they created a new way of life on their reservations.

Traveling west for the first time in 1834, William Anderson, a young mountain man, recorded in his journal that *"the whole plain, as far as the eye could discern, was covered by one enormous mass of buffalo."* As late as 1870, an estimated 15 million buffalo, divided into northern and southern herds, still ranged the Plains. The southern herd disappeared within a decade, and by the time the Lakota went on their last hunt in 1883, the northern herd, too, was nearly extinct. Hunters in the hide trade, sports-

*Left: Red Cloud, an influential Sioux chief who was a powerful orator and skilled negotiator.*

the extraordinary decline. Indians watched in dismay as the animals upon which their way of life depended were slaughtered. Old Lady Horse, a Kiowa woman, described what happened: *"The white men hired hunters to do nothing but kill the buffalo. Up and down the Plains those men ranged, shooting sometimes as many as a hundred buffalo a day. Behind them came the skinners with their wagons. They piled the hides and bones into the wagons until they were full, and then took their loads to the new railroad stations that were being built, to be shipped east to the market. Sometimes there would be a pile of bones as high as a man, stretching a mile along the railroad track."*

Secretary of the Interior Columbus Delano had a different perspective. *"I would not seriously regret the total disappearance of the buffalo from our western prairies, in its effect upon the Indians,"* he wrote in 1872, *"regarding it rather as a means of hastening their sense of dependence upon the products of the soil and their own labors."* The government believed that the natives, deprived of their most utilized resource and confined on reservations, would turn to agricultural pursuits. Such a complete conversion from a hunting to an agricultural—even a stock-raising—society rarely occurred during this period. Many tribal peoples relied almost totally upon the government for the food they ate and the clothes they wore, even for canvas with which to make their lodge coverings now that buffalo skins were unavailable. When annuity payments were delayed or failed to arrive, Indians suffered, as they also did when corrupt agents and suppliers misappropriated supplies intended for the reservations.

Issue days, when rations were distributed to native families, broke the monotony of reservation life. Coming into the agency from their scattered residences, native peoples had the opportunity to socialize and engage in traditional feasting. On some reservations they even turned the distribution of beef on the hoof into a re-enactment of a buffalo hunt. A visitor to the Standing Rock Sioux Agency in 1881 described such an occasion. As the beef allotted to a band were run out of the chute and into the open, men on horseback *"were turned loose to kill the steers. It was pandemonium; rifles cracked, the bucks yelled and the squaws and children screamed. As fast as a steer was down the squaws were on him with their ripping knives, cutting him open and dragging out the entrails and eating them. They smeared themselves and their children with blood.... This was repeated until the issue was completed."* Following custom, Indians utilized as much of the animals as they could.

Such displays of the persistence of traditional practices were condemned and prevented whenever possible. Even native initiatives that showed a willingness and ability to work within the system were frequently thwarted. By the terms of the Treaty of 1866, the Cherokee had the right to sell farm products, merchandise, and manufactures without paying the excise tax that was levied on such items outside the Nation. E.C. Boudinot opened a factory and began manufacturing and selling chewing tobacco. When non-native competitors complained to their representatives, it was discovered that Congress had subsequently closed this loophole. Challenging the notion that congressional acts could supersede treaty guarantees, Boudinot and the Cherokee—following another tribal tradition—took their case to the Supreme Court. In May 1871 the Court ruled, declaring that treaties with Indians did not have the same status as treaties with foreign nations and could be unilaterally abrogated by Congress.

Despite such setbacks, native peoples—collectively and individually—developed strategies to survive. Many determined that if life were hard for them, it was because they lacked power—not the manipulative powers of political and military strength (which indeed they did lack) but the real power derived from a proper relationship with the sacred. Before the arrival of whites, tribes survived because they

*Below: Arapaho men and women perform the Ghost Dance, depicted by Mary Diven Wright.*

knew how to receive and employ supernatural power. The extension of white control over their lives and the contemporaneous disappearance of the buffalo herds were sometimes interpreted as evidence of a greater power that the whites had received from the Unknown. Others viewed their subjugation as a failure either of properly soliciting sacred power, or of carrying out the responsibilities of received power. The latter conviction became more popular as natives discovered that Christianity had little to do with the secular powers of the whites.

However the obligations of sacred power were exercised, the inability of reservation natives to perform the necessary rituals to secure power was widely believed to constitute the basic reason for their suffering. The unsuccessful attempts by men like Red Cloud and Spotted Tail of the Lakota to alleviate that suffering by working within the white man's institutions demonstrated that they could not expect relief through nonspiritual means. If they were ever to escape suffering and retain their identity, relief would have to come from the only true source: the Creator.

In 1889 word reached the Plains of the Paiute named Wovoka, who lived in Nevada and who had had a powerful vision. Recovering from scarlet fever, Wovoka had taken a journey in which he spoke to God and saw the dead of his tribe living in a land without want. He was told that if his people worked hard, lived in peace with the whites, and dutifully performed a special "dance of goodness," they would be reunited with their friends and relatives from the spirit world. What had been revealed to Wovoka became the doctrine and ceremony of the Ghost Dance, a messianic movement that eventually spread to other tribes, including the Lakota. Drawn from Paiute experience but including elements of Christiantiy and earlier native revivalistic doctrines from the region, Wovoka's message underwent further change as it was incorporated into the different sacred traditions of other tribes.

The Ghost Dance spread rapidly. The Northern Arapaho and the Eastern Shoshoni of Wyoming were the medium through which the news reached eastern tribes. In the fall of 1889, a delegation of Cheyenne and Lakota traveled to Paiute country to hear the message in person. When the Lakota delegates returned to their

*Left: The Sioux warrior Short Bull was instrumental in bringing the Ghost Dance ritual from Nevada to the Plains.*

reservations in March 1890 (the Great Sioux Reservation had been subdivided again in 1889) they began to hold councils. Although agents tried, they could not prevent the spread of Wovoka's doctrine among the Lakota. Despair, intensified by recent reductions in rations, epidemic illness, and the dissatisfaction resulting from the dismemberment of the reservation, increased distrust of whites and created a mood receptive to religious revitalization. Throughout the summer and fall, increasing numbers of Lakota began dancing, adapting the ritual to the requirements of their land, their past religious customs, and their present condition.

At first, Office of Indian Affairs personnel generally saw no danger in the dance, but settlers living off the reservations held different opinions, which they relayed to Washington. Realizing that both the cession of Sioux lands and the concurrent reduction in rations disturbed the natives, they fell back on the familiar idea that the Sioux were about to fight them. It is unlikely, however, that the Lakota as a group ever considered military action as a response to their situation in 1890. Certainly the Ghost Dance was not intended as a masquerade for war. The Ghost Shirts, which became—and remain—associated in non-native minds with a warlike posture, were special garments to be worn for the dance. Their designs were symbolic of the visions received by dancers. Worn by Lakota women and children as well as by men, the shirts were basically ceremonial, although the designs, like those on traditional religious garments, were supposed to offer protection to the wearers. As protective apparel, the shirts were believed to ward off bullets, arrows, or other dangerous weapons. However, the wearing of the Ghost Shirts did not in itself indicate any plan of uprising by the Lakota. Moreover, at no time did the Lakota Ghost Dancers make any threats of violence against whites on or off the reservations. Indeed, except for their usual local travel, dancers did not leave their reservations. The tendency of adherents to withdraw from areas where whites lived on the reservations, and the inclusion of women and children in the dancing camps also support the conclusion that the dance did not camouflage a military action. The ceremony reached its height of acceptance just as winter was approaching. Traditionally, Lakota had not engaged in winter warfare unless it was absolutely necessary. The acceptance of Spring 1891 as the time when the messiah would appear and restore the faithful to a land of plenty made war unnecessary.

The threat of military hostilities originated among the whites. By the fall of 1890, the fear of an outbreak began to affect agents previously unconcerned. On October 9, a new agent, Daniel E. Royer (known to his charges as "Young-Man-Afraid-of-Indians"), arrived at Pine Ridge. Three days later, he reported that the Indian police had lost control of the situation and asked for military assistance. Disaster followed.

Army troops were eventually sent to the reservations, but by then the rumors of military intervention had spread among the dancers. At the request of General Nelson Miles, "Buffalo Bill" Cody (who knew Sitting Bull well) was sent to Standing Rock Agency at the end of November 1890 with orders to try to convince Sitting Bull that any uprising he planned would be futile. The Indian Agent, seeing Cody as infringing on his bailiwick, prevented him from going to Sitting Bull's camp and possibly defusing the situation. When troops arrived at Rosebud Reservation, more than 1,800 Indians of all ages rushed toward Pine Ridge or the Badlands, destroying their own property before leaving. The coming of the army practically ensured armed conflict. The first shot was fired on December 15 on the Grand River, when Sitting Bull, who had been at least a passive supporter of the dance, was killed by native police sent to arrest him.

Groups of Lakota had already congregated in the Badlands of the Pine Ridge Reservation before Sitting Bull's death. Big Foot's band of Miniconjou from the Cheyenne River Reservation had first gone toward its own agency, but, by the last week of December, was on its way to Pine Ridge. The military, possibly fearing hostilities, ordered the arrest of the band. On the afternoon of December 28 it was intercepted by the army near Wounded Knee Creek. Big Foot surrendered to the troops under a white flag of truce. It was agreed that the cavalry would escort the Indians the 20 miles into the Pine Ridge Agency the following morning.

When dawn came, however, the natives found soldiers lined up around the camp, many of them facing each other. The Miniconjou were nervous. An order was given for the Indians to surrender their arms. This frightened the Sioux, for the rifle was a treasured object and security against possible slaughter. Each side was well aware of the other's identity: The Seventh Cavalry, Custer's unit, was facing a "hostile" band of the tribe that had annihilated its forces at the Little Big Horn.

Very few arms were voluntarily presented to the soldiers. The tipis were ransacked in an attempt to locate more arms, an action that bewildered the women and children. At the center of the camp, one searcher attempted to reach under one native's blanket. Accounts differ on the details of what happened next, but all witnesses report that a shot was fired. In a matter of seconds, rifles and a Hotchkiss gun showered bullets into the camp. When silence returned, the ground was littered with the dead. Some of them had fled on foot for several miles before being butchered by the soldiers, who had panicked after the first shot. At least 200 Native Americans, probably more, were killed. Big Foot was one of the first to be slain.

When news of the fighting in South Dakota reached Wovoka, the prophet refused to believe it. His message had been one of peace. Only after many other reports confirmed what had happened did Wovoka accept the fact that his message had been associated with bloodshed. *My father told me the earth was getting old and worn out, and the people getting bad,* he said, *and that I was to renew everything as it used to be, and make it better.*

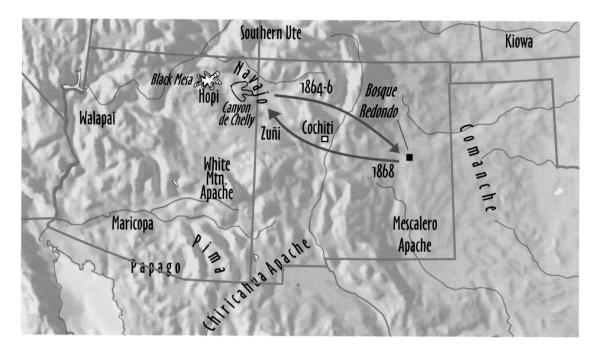

Southern Ute

Kiowa

Black Mesa
Navajo
Hopi
Canyon de Chelly
1864-6
Bosque Redondo
Walapai
Zuñi
Cochiti
1868
Comanche
White Mtn. Apache
Maricopa
Pima
Mescalero Apache
Papago
Chiricahua Apache

*Left:* Under American control, the Navajo were forced into an internment camp at Bosque Redondo, New Mexico. When the government found it could not afford to maintain them, the Navajo were allowed to return to their former lands. The Apache and Ute were also confined to reservations.

The massacre at Wounded Knee was a turning point in the history of tribes on the northern Plains. Among the Five Nations of Indian Territory, the turning point came in 1898 with the passage of the Curtis Act. Exempted from the provisions of the Dawes Act, the Five Civilized Tribes continued to hold their tribal land in common. Realizing its "error," the government sent commissions to the Cherokee, Choctaw, Chickasaw, Creek, and Seminole to negotiate the allotment of their lands. The Dawes Commission failed to achieve its objective, however. With their territory already dramatically reduced as a result of the post-Civil War treaties and the opening of lands to white settlers in the newly created Oklahoma Territory, the Five Nations were reluctant to relinquish anything else to the United States government.

When a negotiated settlement proved unobtainable, Congress took matters into its own hands. Sponsored by Kansas representative Charles Curtis, himself a member of the Kaw tribe and later vice-president of the United States (1929–33), the act of 1898 destroyed the self-government of the Five Nations by abolishing tribal courts and providing the machinery that eventually led to the dissolution of the tribes themselves and the admission of Oklahoma as a state in 1907. The creative experiment of the Indian republics was finally ended. "Indian Country" was destined to have a whole new look and meaning in the twentieth century.

## THE SOUTHWEST

The last half of the nineteenth century saw control of the Southwest shift from Mexico to the United States. Following the Gadsden Purchase of 1853, the continental United States would be complete in its present configuration. Although national governments had changed, the problems experienced by the Spanish and Mexican governments persisted under American control.

During this half century, the Puebloan peoples continued to experience droughts and smallpox epidemics, especially during the 1860s through the 1880s. Although smallpox vaccination had been introduced in 1805 and the periodicity of the disease had lengthened, there were outbreaks throughout the century: one in 1853 at Zuñi and First Mesa, Hopi, and again at Zuñi in 1898. Cochiti Pueblo experienced malaria in 1896. During this period, pueblo population varied from a low of 7,000 in 1850 to 9,026 in 1900. The earlier figure may represent the movement of Hispanicized Puebloans from their pueblos into Spanish towns, thereby further depleting the native population figures.

By 1900 reservations had been created at all the pueblos with an Indian Agent to oversee and address continuing problems. With the Mexican cession, the political status of the Puebloans had changed yet again. Originally wards of the crown under Spanish control, they had later become Mexican citizens. Now under United States administration, they again became wards of the

**Above:** *Hopi women of Oraibi, Arizona, carry water drawn from a government well.*

state, losing many of the rights and privileges that normally accrued to citizenship.

The heritage of slaving raids and reprisals continued for two decades after United States acquisition and kept the territory in turmoil. Pledged to control native raids and protect American and Mexican citizens, the continued raiding created a major crisis for the American military and civilian government.

After a series of raids, reprisals, and ineffective treaties, Governor Calhoun in 1851 again authorized private volunteer companies to campaign against the Navajo and Apache. As under the earlier Mexican policy, payment was to be in captives and any loot taken. By late 1860 groups of New Mexicans, Ute, Puebloans, and friendly Apache were raiding the Navajo and providing a steady stream of servants for New Mexican homes. These campaigns only served to incite the Navajo to further reprisals against both towns and pueblos.

In addition to organized expeditions, slavers, frequently masquerading as merchants to nomadic tribes, entered native territory bartering whiskey and arms for captives from as far away as Mexico and Utah. Having little interest in any peace process, these men helped keep the territory in perpetual warfare.

With the outbreak of the Civil War in April 1861, United States military presence in the territory declined as regular troops were withdrawn and garrisons were abandoned, permitting the Navajo and Mescalero Apache to increase their raiding. Once the Confederate threat to New Mexico had been eliminated, the First and Second Regiments of New Mexico Volunteers were placed under the command of Christopher "Kit" Carson to be used in a campaign to subjugate the Navajo and Apache.

Carson began his campaign initially against the Mescalero Apache using Ute, Zuñi and Hopi scouts. By January 1863, the Mescalero had surrendered and had been placed on a reservation at Bosque Redondo, New Mexico.

Carson then turned his attention to the Navajo. In June 1863, following his scorched earth policy in their homeland, groups of Navajo began surrendering. During their forced march to Bosque Redondo, some 200 died of exposure and exhaustion.

The surrender of the Navajo was seen as the last opportunity to obtain slaves, and companies of irregulars proceeded to capture hundreds of Navajo as they straggled into Fort Wingate to surrender. Due to the expected imminent shortage of new slaves in the marketplace, the pre-Civil War price of $75–$100 per slave now rose to nearly $400 per child.

By May 1864 these independent slaving raids by New Mexicans, Ute, and Puebloans were imperiling the success of the military campaign, but they continued into 1866. Becoming less successful over time, one late campaign, frustrated in its objective, attacked the Hopi town of Oraibi, capturing eleven children who were then sold as Navajo. A Hopi complaint about the abduction led to an official investigation that finally returned the children to their parents.

With the surrender of Manuelito and his band on September 1, 1866, the formal Navajo War was over.

Bosque Redondo was situated on a flat, barren plain and conditions on the reservation for the 12,000 to 15,000 Navajo and Mescalero held there were appalling. Expected to raise some of their own food, poor soil and lack of water led to poor harvests at best and, in 1865, the meager crop was destroyed by insects and storms. Coupled with the lack of government funds, failed harvests soon led to starvation. Pneumonia and measles attacked, further depleting the population.

Compounding this desperate situation, ancient conflicts between the Navajo and the Mescalero prevented their peaceful coexistence on the same reservation. Raids by the Kiowa and the Comanche further exacerbated the already difficult conditions. Finally in desperation, 335 Mescalero fled the reservation in November 1865.

During the Civil War era, Bosque Redondo was the only reservation segregating an important nomadic tribe. Costs ran over budget and the government was unable to support and protect the Native Americans living there. Ultimately, the government was forced to acknowledge that the reservation had been a failure. Recognizing that the Navajo had originally survived in their homeland entirely without government funds, protection, or support, a new treaty was signed in 1868 returning the Navajo to their traditional home.

However, the issue of the return of Navajo captives remained unresolved. At the time of the Civil War, as many as 6,000 native menials may have worked in New Mexican homes. The return of all captives held by each side had been a provision of every Navajo treaty. While the Navajo had complied with these provisions, the New Mexicans rarely had. Consequently, after the latest treaty, the United States government felt compelled to launch an investigation into the fate of these captives. It was

*Below: Navajo women continued to work their fields after they were confined to the tribal reservation.*

found that during the 1860s some 800 baptisms had been recorded in northern New Mexican churches, with an additional 145 in southern Colorado. Of these, 110 were Navajo taken between 1862–64, another 8 were Paiute, and 15 were Apache.

Because the legal position of the menials was not fully covered under the 18th Amendment, Joint Resolution No. 65 was adopted on July 27, 1868, outlawing native slavery and peonage, a traditional Spanish practice virtually equivalent to slavery. It gave the commanding general of the U.S. Army, Lt. General William T. Sherman, the authority to use the most efficient means available to reclaim women and children held in bondage and to return them to the reservation. This resolution met with extreme resistance by New Mexican slaveholders who attempted to evade the loss of their "properties." Nevertheless, Navajo leaders were informed of the military's

intention to implement this law. In addition they were told that, if they wished to pursue their own search, they would be granted leave from the reservation to do so and military funds would be made available to help defray expenses. This opportunity was seized by many, and some Navajo continued their search for lost kin until 1886.

Even so, some 200 children were lost forever to the Navajo Nation. Because many of these children had been taken captive at a very young age, they remembered nothing of their natal parents and culture, and had no desire to return to their people. Baptized and raised in Spanish families, they knew no other language, religion, or culture.

With the onset of the Civil War, relations between the Apache and the settlers of the Arizona Territory deteriorated rapidly. California volunteers, responsible for military operations in Arizona, employed Pima, Papago, and

*Below: This map of the newly created state of Texas was engraved to illustrate* Mitchell's School and Family Geography.

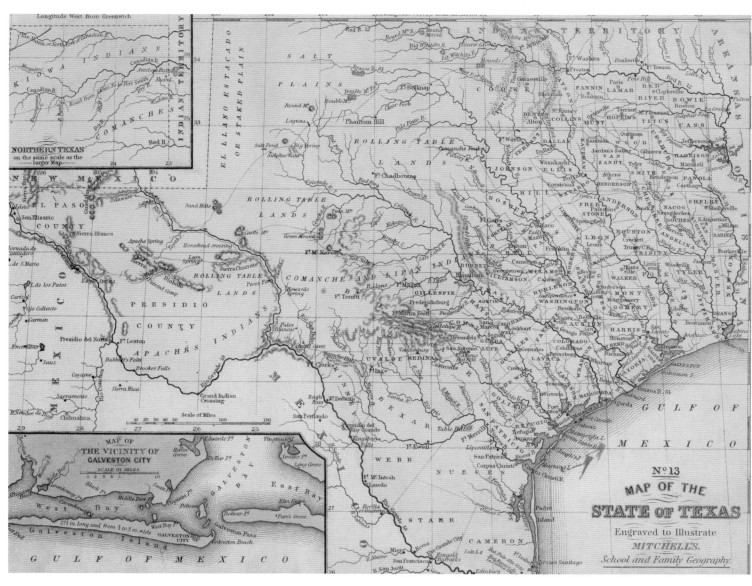

Maricopa auxiliaries along with irregular troops on reprisal raids against the Arizona Apache. After the Civil War, the Pima and Maricopa continued serving the returning regular forces during 1866–67. The Papago and some friendly Apache served through 1866 in a semi-official capacity motivated primarily by scalp bounties.

As a result of these campaigns in Arizona Territory, Chief Miguel surrendered with his White Mountain Apache in 1869, offering his warriors as scouts to campaign against other Apache. The success of this arrangement led to a policy of offering all surrendering warriors employment as scouts. They would later be recognized as having been more instrumental in ending the Indian Wars than the troopers they rode with had been.

In 1871 the citizens of Tucson staged a massacre of surrendered Apache held at Camp Grant, Arizona Territory. While some Anglo-Americans took part, the majority of the participants were Papago, who were apparently even more anxious to take this opportunity for revenge on their Apache neighbors.

When General George Crook took military command of the Arizona Territory in 1871, he initially employed Pima, Papago, and Walapai scouts. However, he soon concluded that Apache hunting Apache produced the best results. Thereafter, he began employing Apache people, first as scouts and later as warriors. So effective were they that the 1872–75 campaigns compelled most Apache bands to surrender and settle on reservations.

During the 1879–80 campaign against the Chiricahua leader, Victorio, White Mountain Apache scouts proved most effective, in addition to some Chiricahua who joined the hunt in an unofficial capacity.

In 1882 General Crook, with permission from Mexico, led his forces across the border to search for the last groups of free Apache. His force consisted of 192 Apache scouts and only one Company (42 men) of the 6th Cavalry. After locating one camp and capturing the women and children, the warriors were forced to surrender. Geronimo, beginning a pattern he was to follow in the coming years, surrendered at a later date, only to escape from his captors. In May 1885, 140 Chiricahua including Geronimo and 35 warriors plus eight boys of fighting age, fled the reservation back into Mexico. Of the eighty warriors remaining on the reservation, fifty

*Above:* A Mohave village on the Colorado River, from a contemporary engraving made for the Railway Survey of 1855 from Mississippi to the Pacific by the U.S. War Department.

**Right:** *A studio portrait (1886) of the Chiracahua Apache warrior Goyathlay, known as Geronimo, after his thirty-year resistance to the government ended in surrender.*

immediately signed up as scouts to aid in the recapture of the escapees. Another military expedition followed the fleeing Apache into Mexico. After this group was forced to surrender, Geronimo again broke away and escaped back into the mountains.

Military anger over this event led to the replacement of General Crook with General Nelson Miles. Miles, assuming the reservation Chiricahua were aiding the escapees, ordered the arrest of all the reservation Chiricahua including former scouts and promptly shipped them all to Florida. An expedition was then launched to bring in Geronimo. His final surrender on September 4, 1886, brought to a close the Indian Wars in the Southwest. He and his small band were shipped to Florida to join the other Chiricahua prisoners. Later, the tribe was shipped to Mt. Vernon Barracks in Alabama, where a quarter of them died from tuberculosis and other diseases.

In 1894 the Chiricahua were sent to Fort Sill, Oklahoma, where most of the men (including Geronimo) enlisted as scouts. As a former leader, he held the rank of sergeant with the official authority to keep order until his death in 1909. In 1912 the Chiricahua were given the choice of either remaining in Oklahoma or removing to the Mescalero Reservation in New Mexico. Most chose to return to New Mexico.

Those San Carlos and Fort Apache Reservation scouts who had originally surrendered in the 1870s continued in their capacity as scouts, a job that eventually evolved into a tribal police force.

The Indian Scouts were a component of the U.S. Army into the twentieth century, seeing their last serious deployment with General Pershing in his campaign against Pancho Villa in 1916. As the twentieth century proceeded, the army perceived less need for their talents and the last scouts were pensioned off in 1943.

As the foregoing paragraphs show, native auxiliaries were widely used in many military and civilian expeditions, both official and unofficial. As independent nations, they frequently regarded other native nations as enemies and willingly attacked them. Even bands perceived by Anglo-Americans as members of the same group were willing to fight each other, like the White Mountain against the Chiricahua Apache. Only in the next century would native peoples begin to form a national identity that would cut across band and tribal lines.

With the influx of immigrants, miners, lumbermen, and ranchers into the Southwest, land had become an increasingly important issue in the last half of the nineteenth century. Coupled with the perception that natives no longer needed all of their traditional homelands, tribal land cessions became a standard part of the reservation process. As a result, the Navajo lost land between 1850 and 1870, and the Apache during 1870–1890. At mid-century the Ute were in the White River region of Colorado, but by 1880 were forced into ceding this area and resettling on smaller parcels in Colorado and Utah. In addition, Comanche, Walapai, Papago, Pima, and Maricopa ceded lands as they settled into reservation life. In the twentieth century many of these tribes would file legal land claims for the lost territories in an effort to reclaim them.

The close of the nineteenth century saw the last of the Indian Wars in the Southwest and all of the tribes finally confined to reservations. An assimilationist policy adopted by the national government, with the support of missionaries and humanitarians, would create projects, education, and aid programs to this end. Efforts to promote individualism and a new identity were promulgated in an effort to break tribal ties and weaken traditional leadership.

The twentieth century would usher in new forms of interaction between the United States government and the native nations. The venue for these contests would change from the battlefields of previous centuries to modern courts of law, but the issues would remain those of land, water, religion, and cultural identity.

## THE PLATEAU

By the mid-nineteenth century the peoples of the Plateau were experiencing pressures similar to those faced by the Plains nations. The Nez Perce, like the Lakota, had been arguing with the United States for years about land rights. And as with the Lakota, there were "Treaty" and "non-Treaty" Nez Perce. Heinmot Tooyalakekt, better known as Chief Joseph, was a leader among the non-Treaty Nez Perce.

In 1855 some Nez Perce chiefs signed a treaty with the United States, ceding some of their lands to white settlers and establishing a large Nez Perce reservation at Lapwai in present-day Idaho. Joseph's father, Wellamotkin, was one of those who had signed the treaty, but he and his band of about 200 Nez Perce did not move to Lapwai. Instead, they remained on their traditional lands in the fertile Wallowa valley in present-day Oregon, tending their herds of Appaloosa horses. In 1860 white miners found gold on the Lapwai Reservation and began crowding into Nez Perce country. In 1863 white officials invited the Nez Perce to a new treaty council and asked them to cede more of their territory, including the Wallowa valley, to the whites. A few Nez Perce signed the new treaty, but Wellamotkin and the majority refused. Joseph later explained: *"My father was the first to see through the schemes of the white men, and he wanted his tribe to be careful about trading with them."* Wellamotkin died in 1871.

In 1875, when a presidential edict opened the Wallowa to white settlers, Joseph and his brother Ollokot protested that the valley belonged to their people. In late 1876 a commission of five men, including the one-armed General Oliver Otis Howard, was appointed to settle the matter. The commission ruled that the Wallowa Nez Perce would have to move to the Lapwai Reservation by the following April.

Joseph and Toohoolhoolzote, another Nez Perce leader, protested that their people needed more time to move their families and horses to Lapwai. General Howard responded by throwing Toohoolhoolzote in jail. In order to obtain his release, Joseph reluctantly agreed to Howard's demands. It was spring, however, and the Snake River, which lay between the Wallowa valley and the Lapwai Reservation, was in flood. The Nez Perce managed to cross the Snake without loss of human life, but hundreds of brood mares and their colts were drowned. Other horses were stolen by whites who harassed them as they withdrew. Tensions were high and before they reached Lapwai, three Nez Perce youths killed four white men. After the first killings, other Nez Perce killed fourteen or fifteen more whites.

When he received the news of the killings, General Howard sent a detachment of the First Cavalry to round up the "hostiles" and force them onto the reservation. Fearing another Little Big Horn, he also called for reinforcements, and troops were sent to him from as far away as Alaska and Georgia. Some of Howard's troops attacked the "friendly" village of Chief Looking Glass on the Lapwai Reservation. This caused Looking Glass and his band to join the hostiles. Other troops attacked the hostile camp and in the ensuing battle, thirty-four cavalrymen lost their lives. There were no Native American casualties from this battle, but the Nez Perce War had begun.

The "hostiles" consisted of about 200 warriors and approximately 550 women, older men, and children. With a herd of around 2,000 horses, they retreated into the Salmon River wilderness in present-day Idaho with Howard

*Left: The revered Chief Joseph of the Nez Perce almost succeeded in removing his tribe to Canada before he was intercepted by government troops in 1877.*

and 400 cavalrymen in hot pursuit. The Nez Perce knew the terrain and Howard's troops did not, so the natives managed to keep ahead of their pursuers. There were several skirmishes between the two groups in the course of what became a 1,300–mile exodus across the rivers and mountains of present-day Idaho, Wyoming, and Montana. Throughout their retreat, the Nez Perce behaved in what white observers considered a remarkably "civilized" manner. Joseph was credited by the whites with being the master strategist of both the retreat and the several battles between the Nez Perce and Howard's troops. In fact, however, the Nez Perce made all their decisions in council, and although Joseph spoke at council meetings, so did Ollokot, Toohoolhoolzote, Looking Glass, and other leaders. These leaders together decided to try to move their people to Canada, where they believed they could live in peace. "Grandmother Victoria" seemed preferable to "Uncle Sam."

Howard had the advantage of telegraph communications, and he was reinforced with fresh troops at several points along the way. The Nez Perce had not expected this. For them, all wars were local and all pursuers eventually became discouraged and gave up. As their own casualties mounted and Howard relentlessly pressed them onward, they began to lose heart.

On September 30, 1877, the Nez Perce were stopped by an early snowstorm in the Bear Paw Mountains of northern Montana, a mere thirty miles from the Canadian border. The combined forces of General Howard and General Nelson Miles caught up with them. These forces succeeded in driving off most of the natives' horse herd and in killing several Nez Perce leaders. Many women and children ran off into the snow and died of exposure. Joseph had little choice but to surrender, which he did on the morning of October 5th. His surrender speech was recorded by Howard's adjutant:

*"I am tired of fighting. Our chiefs are killed [and]...the old men are all dead....The little children are freezing to death. My people, some of them, have run away to the hills, and have no blankets, no food. No one knows where they are—perhaps freezing to death. I want to have time to look for my children and see how many I can find. Maybe I shall find them among the dead. Hear me, my chiefs. I am tired. My heart is sick and sad. From where the sun now stands, I will fight no more forever."*

Howard and Miles promised to send the Nez Perce back to Lapwai, but instead the U.S. government sent them to Indian Territory in present-day Oklahoma. In 1885 many of the Nez Perce were allowed to return to Oregon and others, including Joseph, to the Colville Reservation in present-day Washington. They were never allowed to return to the Wallowa valley, however.

In the southwestern Plateau, where the Basin, Northwest, and California culture areas blend, the Oregon Trail became a conduit for both gold-seekers and emigrants in 1848. Some native peoples preyed upon the emigrants and some Forty-niners abused the natives, but retribution too often fell upon the blameless, and the endless cycle of "justified" retaliation was soon begun.

Around 1853, Pit River Indians killed some emigrants near what is now Alturas, California, and a responding posse killed several Modoc by mistake. Living along Tule Lake and Lost River on the California-Oregon border, the Modoc, who had been friendly to whites, were outraged. The nearby Combutwaush (Rock Indians) held council with them on how to react, agreeing to attack. Only Kie-in-to-poses, the fourteen-year-old son of the Modoc chief, seeing the futility in that, argued for peace. When his people were chased into hiding after ambushing a wagon train, his wisdom became clear.

In 1856, Ben Wright led 100 Rogue River "volunteers" on an "Indian hunt" east of the Cascade Mountains, wantonly killing Modoc, Klamath, and Paiute. Using the pretext of a peace treaty, he lured the hiding Modoc into an ambush. Only five native survived, Wright shooting the chief himself. Succeeding his father, Kie-in-to-poses (later called Captain Jack) could never forget Wright's treachery.

Under a real peace treaty in 1864, Captain Jack agreed to move onto the Klamath Reservation in Oregon. Outnumbered by the Klamath and living in their territory, the Modoc were taunted daily despite treaty promises that they would be protected from such harassment. The Indian Agent threatened to kill Captain Jack for reporting Klamath thefts from his people, and dismissed his plea for a separate reservation.

Fed up, Captain Jack led his band back to Lost River in 1870. They lived in peace with the settlers there until late 1872 when, based on false charges by one settler, troops were sent to bring them back. Forewarned by Jack's cousin, Winema, the wife of a white trader, the Modoc promised local settlers they would not be harmed if they stayed at home when the soldiers came. The whites agreed.

Breaking their pledge, the settlers crept up on the Modoc camp during the night. When the soldiers came in the morning, Jack agreed to return peaceably, but their commander, Major Jackson, insisted they disarm. As Wright had attacked when they were disarmed, the natives were tense when a lieutenant tried, at gun-point, to take a pistol from a Modoc. Both weapons discharged and the troops opened fire as the Modoc retrieved their weapons. The Modoc War had begun.

When the soldiers retreated, the settlers fired, killing an old woman and a baby before three of their own died. The Modoc killed fifteen more male settlers that night, but no women or children. The soldiers returned to the camp the next day to find only an old, blind woman, unable even to walk. They burned her alive.

The Modoc retreated to the "Stronghold," a natural fortress where the south shore of Tule Lake then met the jagged terrain of the Lava Beds. The Army found them in January, but their initial attack, aided by volunteers and Klamath, was a dismal failure.

In February, Winema brought friendly whites to the Stronghold to set up a meeting with a Peace Commission. Jack agreed, meeting with General E.R.S. Canby, Colonel A B. Meacham, and Reverend Dr. Thomas, in March.

Wright's specter looming over him, Canby moved 1,000 troops plus artillery near the Stronghold. When Winema brought word that Canby wanted to meet at a place halfway between the Stronghold and the army camp on the soutwest shore of the lake, Captain Jack reminded her of Wright, but attended the meeting. Canby demanded total surrender, offering nothing in return. Believing that Canby was stalling while more troops were brought up and that war was inevitable, the Modoc insisted that Jack kill Canby at their next meeting. Winema warned the Peace Commissioners, but Canby ignored her. Refusing again to give the Modoc anything, he and two others were shot.

The army opened fire three days later, and after three more days of infantry and artillery attacks, the Modoc evacuated the Stronghold by night, unnoticed by the army. The next day, the infantry charged again only to find that, with the exception of four invalids (whom they killed), the enemy had vanished.

Between late April and early May, three units were sent into the Lava Beds, each taking far more casualties than they inflicted. After

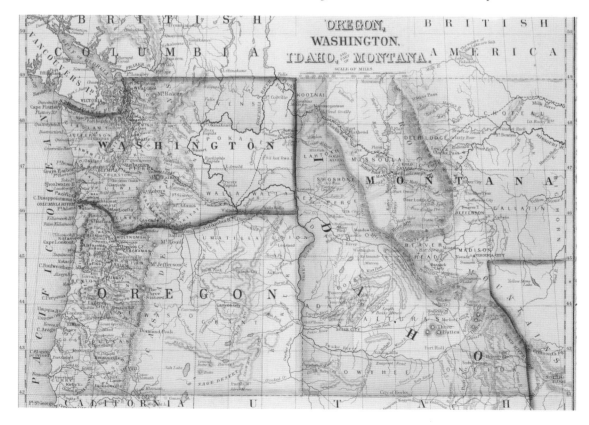

*Left: A late nineteenth-century map of the Pacific Northwest and adjacent states bordering on Canada, which is identified as "British America."*

the third battle, a dispute caused the Modoc to split into two groups. Soon after, four Modoc defected, offering to hunt down their own people in exchange for their lives. Within weeks, almost all of the warring Modoc had been captured. Captain Jack and three of his followers were hung on October 3, 1873. Two others were imprisoned and the remainder sent to the Quapaw Agency in Indian Territory.

### CALIFORNIA

The lives of California Indians were forever changed by two events in early 1848. By the Treaty of Guadalupe-Hidalgo, ratified by the U.S. Senate on May 30, 1848, the United States acquired the province of California from Mexico, a transfer of jurisdiction that would have lasting significance for its native residents. Of more immediate, and devastating, consequence, however, was the discovery on January 24 of gold on the American River. Near a Maidu village called Coloma, the first nuggets were found: When announced to the world, this would set off a frantic rush to the area by gold seekers from the United States, Australia, and South America.

James Marshall, who was in charge of building a sawmill there for Sutter's Fort, forty miles to the southwest, claimed credit for the discovery, but the precious metal may actually have been first found by one of the many native workers at the site. In any case, the Maidu and other tribes from the foothills soon became miners themselves. Many of them had previously worked on *ranchos*; now they panned for gold. Some worked for Marshall or for one of the many other mining companies that sprang up after the discovery. Still others worked for themselves. Among the native miners were members of tribes from elsewhere on the Pacific coast and from as far away as Kansas. Some of the latter, along with the native "Argonauts," died during the trip from an outbreak of cholera that spread across the country in 1849.

Adept at mining, the Indians were often cheated by whites when they purchased goods from traders. The acquisition of trade goods, rarely obtained during the Spanish or Mexican periods, alarmed conservative natives, who feared—correctly—that their people would soon become dependent on them. Equally disturbing was the establishment of mining towns that attracted entire families to their environs. Yet, while some Native Americans resisted the influx of the early gold seekers, Indian-White violence was only sporadic during the early days of the Gold Rush.

That changed as manual extraction of gold from alluvial deposits (panning and rocking) was replaced by more efficient industrial mining techniques including hydraulic (washing gold-bearing sand banks into sluices using high-pressure hoses) and hard-rock mining. Native methods of mining had become obsolete, and native miners (who included women) were unwelcome in the fields. At the same time, attitudes toward natives changed. Although by terms of the Compromise of 1850 California was admitted to the Union as a free state, its early statutes allowed for the indenture or virtual enslavement of Indians and also made their testimony inadmissible in court. Between 1850 and 1863 some 10,000 California natives were forced into de facto slavery in the United States and Mexico. An 1854 article in a California newspaper reported: *"Abducting Indian children has become quite a common practice. Nearly all of the children belonging to some of the Indian tribes in the northern part of the state have been stolen. They are taken to the southern part of the state and there sold."* In the mining camps, where the ratio

**Below:** *The California Gold Rush was catastrophic for the West Coast tribes, who had no legal protection against forced labor in the mines under the terms that admitted the state to the Union in 1850.*

of men to women was often ten to one, native women were frequently raped. In his autobiography, General George Crook remembered that when he was a young lieutenant serving near the mining camp of Yreka in northern California: *"It was of no unfrequent occurrence for an Indian to be shot down in cold blood, or a squaw to be raped by some brute. Such a thing as a white man being punished for outraging an Indian was unheard of."*

Two groups on the western slopes of the Sierra Nevada, the Miwok and the Yokut, fought back in what became known as the Mariposa Indian War. In 1850 Miwok and Yokut warriors began to attack prospectors and isolated trading posts in their region. The owner of several of the trading posts responded by organizing the Mariposa Volunteer Battalion and pursuing the Native Americans. There were several skirmishes, but as whites continued to pour into the area, the natives gave up fighting.

On several occasions military or vigilante groups massacred large groups of native peoples. In 1850, for example, more than 100 Pomo men, women, and children were slaughtered on an island in Clear Lake in northern California. According to William Benson, a Pomo born in 1862, the murder of two white men by Pomo natives triggered the massacre.

Benson reported that the two whites had enslaved a group of Pomo and were abusing them. The Pomo were starving. Fathers and mothers who withheld their daughters from the two whites were whipped. Other Pomo were whipped for minor offenses. Some of the Pomo men were working for the whites as herdsmen but were given only four cups of boiled grain per day for their labor and had to share this meager food with their families. The herders attempted secretly to kill a cow but botched the attempt and lost a horse. Fearing punishment, they killed their two white bosses. They then stole several horses and cows, and with their families hid on the island in Clear Lake.

Two or three weeks later, the U.S. Army found their camp on the island. In Benson's account: *"The Indians wanted to surrender. But the soldiers did not give them time. The soldiers went in the camp and shot them down as if they were dogs. Some of them escaped by going down a little creek leading to the river. And some of them hid in the brush. And those who hid in the brush most of them were killed. And those who hid in the water was overlooked. They killed mostly women and children."*

The victims of two additional massacres were the Yahi of northeastern California. In 1865 settlers slaughtered most of the inhabitants of a Yahi village on Mill Creek. In 1868 settlers killed thirty-eight more Yahi found hiding in a cave. The last surviving Yaki, Ishi, died in 1916, having spent the last years of his life demonstrating his native crafts.

In treaties that were signed in 1851 and 1852, California natives gave up 75 million acres of land, retaining only 8.5 million acres. Congress, however, never ratified those treaties, but passed laws in 1852 and 1853 depriving the natives of rights to all the land. In 1860, Congress did establish four small reservations capable of supporting only small populations in California, and, toward the end of the century, 117 additional tiny reservations, sometimes called *rancherias*, were established in that state by the U.S. government.

Because of the Gold Rush of 1849, traffic increased dramatically on the several trails leading into California. One major route was the Southern Overland Trail, also known as the Butterfield Stage Route. The trail ran through Mohave and Yuma country on both sides of the Colorado River. For a time the Yuma provided a ferry service across the Colorado River, but they were angered when a group of whites established a competitive service. Both the Yuma and the Mohave began harassing travelers on the Butterfield Route. In 1850 the establishment of Fort Yuma on the California side of the river temporarily quieted the situation, until the Yuma attacked the fort and caused the military to abandon it for a year. When the fort was later regarrisoned, 150 Yuma were taken prisoner and the resistance was abandoned.

## THE GREAT BASIN

In the harsh desert environment of the Great Basin, native peoples dug for camas and other roots, which prompted the dismissive name "diggers" used by some Euroamericans. They also ate nuts, fruits, seeds, rodents, reptiles, and insects. When Americans began invading the Great Basin, they disrupted these traditional food supplies. All four of the major tribes of the Great Basin cultural area—the Bannock, Paiute, Shoshoni, and Ute—fought against settlers dur-

**Right:** *Sarah Winnemucca was a prominent spokeswoman for the Paiute people after they were settled on barren reservations.*

ing the second half of the nineteenth century.

The first significant group of settlers to arrive in present-day Utah were the Mormons. In 1847 Brigham Young, a prophet of the Church of Jesus Christ of Latter-Day Saints, led a group of Mormons to the Great Salt Lake, which no other settlers seemed to want. The Territory of Utah was organized in 1850 and Young was appointed its first governor. The Mormons tried unsuccessfully to convert their new neighbors.

The Great Basin slave trade continued to plague the Mormons into the second half of the nineteenth century, but Brigham Young resolved to abolish it in their territory in 1851. All slave traders apprehended in the Mormon area would be fined and have their horses confiscated before being expelled from the territory.

Unwilling to travel outside Utah to sell their slaves, the Ute continued to intimidate Mormons into buying Paiute children by using the same ploy they had used the first time. To relieve the mental anguish caused by violating Mormon religious doctrine, the Utah Legislature passed a unique law on January 5, 1852. Proposed by Brigham Young, the statute declared that natives could lawfully be "purchased into freedom," but not into slavery or servitude.

The New Mexican slave traders continuing to operate in Utah despite the 1851 decree, a Utah territorial militia was organized on April 23, 1853. Charged with seeking out and seizing any slavers in the territory, the militia was also responsible for warning outlying settlements of itinerant merchants in the area and generally keeping the peace.

Walkara, angered by these attempts to restrict his profitable slaving operations, used an argument and resulting fight over a trading transaction as a pretext for opening hostilities. The Ute raids on Mormon settlements during the summer and fall of 1853 became known as the Walker War.

Rejecting retaliatory raids as probably leading to prolonged, escalating warfare, the Mormons resorted to improving their defenses. Smaller settlements were abandoned while larger ones were fortified. Salt Lake City was enclosed in a palisade six miles long.

Thwarted by these tactics, the Ute proposed a peace council in November 1853. Walkara and Young finally agreed upon peace terms at a meeting on May 9, 1854, ending the

Walker War. Even so, the traffic in Paiute children did not cease immediately, but conditions were evolving which would eventually put an end to it.

In 1854 an epidemic of measles decimated Walkara's followers, and Walkara died of pneumonia on January 25, 1855. Arrapeen, his brother, assumed leadership of the diminished group but was unable to recoup its former power or prestige. Before the end of the century, the once-feared Ute would be confined to reservations.

The southern Paiute continued to harass wagon trains, stage coaches, and Pony Express riders on the Central Overland Trail to California. Hostilities between whites and the Paiute reached a climax in May 1860 when whites at a Pony Express station near Pyramid Lake kidnapped and raped two Paiute women. Paiute warriors burned the station, killed five whites, and rescued the women. Soon afterward, Major William Ormsby organized a force of 105 volunteers to deal with the Paiute. The Paiute chief Numaga and his warriors ambushed the volunteers on the banks of the Truckee River, killing Ormsby and more than forty of his men.

One month later a larger volunteer force defeated the Paiute at Pinnacle Mountain. The U.S. Army established Fort Churchill near Carson City and put a stop to most Paiute raiding. In March 1861 Congress created the Territory of Nevada.

North of the Paiute country the Shoshoni were disrupting the growing traffic along the Oregon Trail. In 1862 California officials sent Colonel Patrick Connor and the Third California Infantry to pacify them. Connor established Fort Douglas in the Wasatch Mountains overlooking Salt Lake City. In January 1863 he and his troops attacked the camp of Chief Bear Hunter on the Bear River. The camp was well barricaded in a steep walled ravine, but Connor's forces pounded it with artillery, killing more than 250 Shoshoni and capturing another 150. Afterward the Shoshoni signed a treaty, agreeing not to interfere with traffic on the trails or with the construction of a railroad through their lands. Promontory Point, Utah, where the Union Pacific and Central Pacific Railroads came together in 1869, was in Shoshoni country.

Another Paiute war broke out in 1867. After its conclusion most of the Paiute were settled on reservations, where they frequently suffered for want of food and other supplies. Sarah Winnemucca, a Paiute woman, reported in 1883 on reservation life and complained that the government never sent enough supplies. She remembered one shipment from which *"a family numbering eight persons got two blankets, three shirts, no dress-goods. Some got a fishhook and line; some got one and a half yards of flannel, blue and red; the largest issue was to families that camped together, numbering twenty-three persons: four blankets, three pieces of red flannel, and some of blue, three shirts, three hooks and lines, two kettles. It was the saddest affair I ever saw."*

Sarah Winnemucca also complained that some Indian agents cheated her people. She remembered one who had *"his own method of making my people divide the produce. If they raise five sacks of grain, they give one sack for the Big Father in Washington; if they have only three sacks, they still have to send one. Every fourth load of hay goes to the Big Father at Washington, yet he does not give my people the seed."*

The Paiute, too, were relocated to reservations far from the watered oases they had traditionally inhabited. Late-nineteenth century anthropologists who studied them in their new locations as they struggled to eke out a living drew inaccurate conclusions about their native culture and lifeways. In turn, that misunderstanding colored interpretation of the Great Basin's archaeological record until the 1960s when a new generation of scholars began to question the "wisdom" of the past.

In recent years it has been recognized the Paiute were not merely a people endlessly in search of food and water. Rather, they had learned to make highly intelligent use of the available resources in the Great Basin's delicate ecosystem. It was, in fact, the introduction of livestock into the Great Basin which destroyed that ecosystem and brought them to the condition in which anthropologists found them.

Some native Basin peoples worked for the U.S. Army or for volunteer militia as scouts against other natives. The Ute helped Kit Carson in his 1864 campaign against the Navajo. In 1876 the Wind River Shoshoni helped General Crook against the Sioux at the Battle of the Rosebud. In 1877 the Bannock scouted for General Howard in the Nez Perce War.

In 1878 Chief Buffalo Horn and other Bannock who had scouted for General Howard instigated what became known as the Bannock War. In 1863 the Bannock had been assigned to a reservation at Fort Hall. They were always short of food on the reservation, however, and left it periodically to hunt buffalo or to harvest camas roots. The chief cause of their 1878 war was the destruction of the camas prairies by the settlers' hogs. The war began when two Bannock warriors, one of whom was the son of Chief Buffalo Horn, shot and wounded two white cattlemen who were trespassing on reservation land.

Buffalo Horn and a group of warriors then left the reservation and plundered a wagon train for ammunition and supplies. Chief Egan of the Northern Paiute left the Malheur Reservation in Oregon and joined the hostile Bannock. In June 1878 Chief Buffalo Horn was killed in a skirmish with volunteer militiamen. When the military encountered the

Indians near Pendleton, Oregon, the native peoples were forced to retreat and scatter. Chief Egan and his Paiute took refuge on the nearby Umatilla Reservation, but the Umatilla killed him and several of his warriors. After the death of Chief Egan, the remaining hostiles lost heart and dispersed. General George Crook commented later, saying: *"The encroachments upon the camas prairies was the cause of the trouble....This root is their main source of food supply. I do not wonder...that when these Indians see their wives and children starving, and their last source of supplies cut off, they go to war. And then we are sent out to kill them."*

In 1879 other troops were sent to deal with the Ute in northwestern Colorado. In 1876, when Colorado became a state, whites had tried to expel the Ute from their reservation on the White River. The first governor of Colorado was elected on a "Utes Must Go" platform. The Ute were skilled horsemen and were willing to raise cattle, but did not farm. Their agent Nathan Meeker insisted they take up farming, and when the Ute resisted, Meeker called for federal troops. Major T.T. Thornburg and 140 soldiers were sent from Fort Steele, Wyoming, to deal with the situation. The Ute ambushed them at Milk Creek, killing Thornburg and keeping his men pinned down for a week. Meanwhile, other Ute killed Meeker and nine other whites and took five hostages. Additional troops came to the rescue of both the hostages and Thornburg's men. In 1880, the Ute were pressured into leaving their White River territory and resettling on the Uintah Reservation in eastern Utah.

Meanwhile the Shoshoni on the Wind River Reservation in Wyoming had mounting grievances. They had accepted a number of Arapaho refugees on the reservation. The U.S. Cavalry had driven the Arapaho out of their own Powder River country to punish them for having taken part in the Battles of the Rosebud and the Little Big Horn. The Shoshoni regarded the Arapaho as their temporary guests, but the U.S. government decided that the Arapaho should remain at Wind River permanently. Despite this decision, the government refused to increase its allocations for the reservation. In 1891 Chief Washakie of the Shoshoni protested: *"At the time the Arapaho came to this Reservation, we did not tell them they could come here and stay nor did we give them any land. They*

*and the Sioux had been fighting the soldiers and got whipped; they came up here and we have allowed them to live here since, thinking they would not hurt the land by living on it, we do not think that this would give them any right to the land."*

## THE NORTHWEST

Some Northwestern peoples initially encountered Europeans during an earlier period than did many nations of the North American interior, but people of European ancestry did not settle in significant numbers in their region until the middle of the nineteenth century. The settlement of Victoria, for example, was established in 1843 on Kwakiutl and Nootka land on Vancouver Island. The settlement of Seattle was established in 1852 on Duwamish land on Puget Sound. In British Columbia, Canadians of European ancestry had begun to outnumber the native people of the province by 1880.

In 1855 the Duwamish were relocated from their traditional lands to a reservation at Suquamish on the other side of Puget Sound. Before moving to the reservation, the Duwamish Chief Seattle (or Seathl), for whom the fledgling settlement at Seattle had been named, addressed a farewell speech to the governor of Washington Territory. Chief Seattle told the governor that: *"Every part of the soil is sacred in the estimation of my people. Every hillside, every valley, every plain and grove, has been hallowed by some sad or happy event in days long vanished. Even the rocks, which seem to be dumb and dead as they swelter in the sun along the silent shore, thrill with memories of stirring events connected with the lives of my people, and the very dust on which you now stand responds more lovingly to their footsteps than to yours, because it is rich with the blood of our ancestors and our bare feet are conscious of the sympathetic touch."*

Agreements between the United States and Great Britain and Russia opened the way for European settlements in the Northwest. In 1846 the United States and Great Britain signed a treaty ending their joint occupation of Oregon and establishing the 49th parallel as the boundary between the United States and British North America. In 1848 the U.S. Territory of Oregon was formally organized. Five years later it was divided into the two territories of Washington and Oregon. Oregon achieved statehood in 1859, and Washington followed in 1889. In 1867 the United States purchased Alaska and the Aleutian Islands from Russia.

Also in 1867, British North America became the Dominion of Canada. In 1871 British Columbia joined the Dominion as its sixth province. British Columbia was outside the treaty system whereby native peoples in other parts of Canada ceded their lands to the British Crown, but by 1876 eighty-two small native reservations had been established in the western province British Columbia.

There were several gold rushes to the Northwest during the second half of the nineteenth century, all of which had an impact on the native peoples of the region. Between 1850–53 there was a small gold rush to the Queen Charlotte Islands that disturbed the Haida. In 1857 a larger gold rush to the Thompson and Fraser Rivers brought 25,000 gold seekers into Salish country. The prospectors built roads, disrupted the Salish hunting and fishing economy, stole supplies from Salish villages, and even looted graves. Salish warriors under Chief Spintlum killed two miners in what became known, perhaps melodramatically, as the "Fraser River War." Another small gold rush to the Stikine River in 1862 led to an outbreak of smallpox among the Tsimshian, which then spread to other tribes all along the coast.

A smallpox outbreak in British Colombia in 1862–63 killed more than 20,000, nearly 60 percent of the native population. An infected person who had arrived in Victoria by ship soon spread the disease to a nearby encampment of native traders. Rather than quarantine the camp, city officials evicted the Tsimshian, Kwakiutl, Haida, and Tlingit residents, who then carried the epidemic to their home communities.

Several factors heavily influenced mortality rates during this outbreak. A vaccination program in the 1830s protected the older Tlingit and some Kwakiutl, while many Tsimshian had just been immunized during the Stikine River outbreak. Other members of those tribes had developed immunity by surviving a smallpox epidemic twenty-four years earlier.

The Haida, in contrast, having been neither inoculated nor exposed to smallpox for about ninety years, fared far worse. The Hudson's Bay Company census for 1839–42 put the number of Haida at more than 8,400, a level which

remained fairly constant for the next twenty years, but the 1882–84 census counted less than 1,600, a decline of over 80 percent. Their populations severely reduced, many Haida villages were abandoned and, by the early twentieth century, only four would remain.

The largest gold rush of the period, the rush to the Klondike in 1896–99, brought more than 100,000 prospectors into Alaska, northwestern British Columbia, and the Yukon. Many of these prospectors poured into the gold fields by way of the Pacific coastal region inhabited by the Tlingit. Traditionally the Tlingit had controlled not only the coast, but also the main routes into the interior across the Chilkoot, Chilkat, and Taku passes. At the start of the gold rush, however, twenty prospectors fired a few rounds from a machine gun and forced the Tlingit to open the Chilkoot pass. Thereafter, as prospectors streamed across the Chilkoot, Tlingit went with them as packers and load carriers. Some Tlingit earned as much as $100 a day carrying loads.

As the nineteenth century progressed, the Northwestern peoples found it increasingly difficult to maintain their traditional lifeways. Prospectors destroyed traplines and fishing weirs and killed or drove away many of the local game animals. The growth of settlements and the building of roads also made hunting more difficult. When natives were settled onto reservations, they often lost their freedom to hunt elsewhere. Officials encouraged many tribal groups to turn to agriculture, but in the rain forests and the climatic conditions of British

*Left: An elder of the Northwestern Nakoaktok tribe paints ceremonial designs on a hat woven of reeds.*

*Right:* The Northwestern tribes evolved an elaborate culture based on hierarchical kinship groups identified with totem animals, as depicted in carved masks, poles, dugouts, and other artefacts.

Columbia and Alaska, agriculture was often not a viable alternative. Many people found low-paying jobs within the developing wage economy instead. They worked as wage laborers in the fisheries and canneries, and the lumber and mining camps. Others simply turned to alcohol.

Because of the near-extinction of the sea otter earlier in the nineteenth century, the adaptable Haida of the Queen Charlotte Islands turned from trading in sea otter pelts to trading in potatoes. Enterprising Haida artisans also discovered new uses for the unique variety of siltstone found only on their islands and carved it into bowls, pipes, miniature totem poles, and other objects for trading.

During the second half of the nineteenth century, the traditional arts and crafts of the Northwest Coast became increasingly commercialized as more tourists visited the area and international museums scrambled to fill their exhibition halls. At the same time, Christian missionaries in Canada worked tirelessly to outlaw the making and displaying of totem poles and ceremonial masks, condemning them as symbols of a pagan belief system.

Missionaries also played an instrumental role in the 1884 decision of the Canadian government to ban the potlatch ceremony. For one, William Duncan, an Anglican missionary who had helped the Tsimshian build a fish cannery at Metlakatla, argued that the ritual was barbaric.

From the Nootka word *"patshatl"*—giving—the potlatch was deeply rooted in native tradition as a kind of wealth-sharing, but these status-generating giveaways had grown steadily in scale and frequency as a result of the increasing amounts of goods being amassed from trade with outsiders. Moreover, the potlatch had become a substitute for intergroup warfare, which the American and Canadian governments suppressed.

As such, the potlatch evolved from giving away property to destroying it, with the person who could destroy the most being the victor. It was this aspect which government officials saw as undermining their efforts to encourage private ownership and a capitalist economy among the native peoples.

Despite the ban, some continued to stage potlatches secretly. In 1896 a Kwakiutl told an anthropologist: *"We do not want anybody here who will interfere with our customs....It is a strict law that bids us dance. It is a strict law that bids us distribute our property among our friends and neighbors. It is a good law. Let the white man observe his law, we shall observe ours."*

### THE ARCTIC

During the second half of the nineteenth century the peoples of the Arctic came increasingly into contact with fur traders, whalers, and missionaries. One consequence of these contacts was that the Inuit and other Arctic peoples were ravaged by disease. Another consequence of the increased trade was that goods including guns, knives, kettles, nails, twine, and cloth became more readily available to them. As with the native peoples of other regions, these goods would erode tribal traditions and cause changes that were not foreseen.

In 1840 the Hudson's Bay Company established the Peel River Post, the first of several trading posts in the western Arctic. Company officials bought furs from the natives of the Peel River area in exchange for guns, tea, and other commodities. Other posts built soon after Peel River included Fort Selkirk, at the confluence of the Pelly and Yukon Rivers, and Fort Yukon at the confluence of the Porcupine and the Yukon Rivers in present-day Alaska. In 1860 Fort Anderson was established near the Anderson River for the express purpose of trading with the Inuit.

Fort Anderson was closed in 1865, however, when an epidemic of scarlet fever broke out there, killing three-quarters of the people who lived along the Anderson River. Scarlet fever also struck the Kutchin in the area around Fort Yukon. In 1866 influenza killed more than 1,000 people near Fort Simpson on the Mackenzie River. It also killed some 30 percent of the Inuit on Victoria Island. In 1876 an epidemic of whooping cough broke out in Labrador.

Britain transferred jurisdiction over the High Arctic to Canada in 1880, thus adding many Inuit to Canada's administrative responsibilities. By this time, because of the increased exploitation of Arctic wildlife, subsistence for some Inuit groups was becoming increasingly uncertain. In two consecutive hard winters in the late 1880s, many Inuit died of starvation. In 1900 measles struck in the MacKenzie River region. By then the Inuit population along the Mackenzie River had fallen to around 400, approximately one-fifth of their former number.

Meanwhile, commercial whaling had become an important industry in the Arctic. Whaling ships had been working the eastern Arctic since mid-century, basing their operations at Pond Inlet, Cumberland Sound, and Roes Welcome Sound. The whalers, desiring fresh meat, employed Inuit as hunters. They also employed them as crew members and harpooners. By 1900 epidemic diseases had reduced the Inuit

population of the eastern Arctic by about one-third. And in the areas where the whalers were most active, the caribou, musk ox, and walrus had been hunted almost out of existence.

In 1888 the first two whaling ships wintered at Herschel Island in the Beaufort Sea. Thereafter the island became the wintering place for the western Arctic whaling fleet. In its heyday more than 1,000 whaling ships wintered at Herschel Island, and it soon became infamous for lawlessness, alcohol abuse, and violence. Epidemic diseases quickly broke out among the Inuit of the region. Game animals in the area thinned out significantly. When the whaling industry collapsed around 1900, the Inuit found it impossible to return to their former lifeways.

Missionaries tried to assist the Inuit by providing educational and health services, but they also brought irreversible change into their lives. Aside from unwittingly introducing diseases, they also campaigned against polygamy. The Anglicans established missions at Fort Yukon in Alaska and on Herschel Island. The Oblate Fathers and the Grey Nuns brought the Catholic faith to the Mackenzie River and the Northwest Territories. The German Protestant Moravians had established a series of missions

*Left:* This nineteenth-century drawing by an Inuit artist shows the graphic skill that made such artefacts prized by traders and collectors.

along the Labrador coast, and by 1860 most of the Labrador Inuit belonged to the Moravian church. At each of their missions the Moravians operated a trading store. They sold guns and twine and encouraged the Inuit to develop the new industries of basket weaving and ivory carving. The Newfoundland cod-fishing fleet began to call at Labrador ports every summer.

### THE SUBARCTIC

For the peoples of the Subarctic culture region, 1867 was a watershed year: The United States purchased Alaska from Russia, and British North America became the Dominion of Canada. Alaska was administered by the U.S. War Department until 1884, when Congress organized an Alaskan territorial government. The Dominion of Canada consisted initially of only the four confederated provinces of Ontario, Quebec, Nova Scotia, and New Brunswick. It operated under its own constitution, but maintained strong ties to the British Crown. The indigenous peoples, according to Canada's 1867 constitution, were wards of the Dominion.

Disease still haunted the Subartic natives after 1850. Among the eastern Dene tribes, an epidemic of scarlet fever raged from 1862 through 1865 with another outbreak in 1897. During the 1880s, diphtheria swept among the tribes.

*Below: Wild rice harvested from canoes was a staple for peoples of the Great Lakes region and western Canada.*

The new Canadian government had two policy objectives for its native peoples. The first was to assimilate them as quickly as possible into the mainstream of Canadian society. The second was to extinguish peacefully their titles to their lands. The Canadian government wished to avoid the costly wars the United States had fought and was fighting with its native peoples. Excepting the case of the second Riel Rebellion of 1885, it succeeded in this objective.

There was a first Riel Rebellion as well as a second, but the first was largely bloodless. It broke out in 1869, two years after the confederation of the Dominion of Canada. Louis Riel, the leader of the rebellion, was one of some 9,800 Métis living at that time near the Red River in present-day Manitoba. Riel, who had some college education, believed that the Métis constituted a "New Nation," neither native nor white but having the strengths of both.

Riel and other Métis became alarmed when large numbers of settlers from Ontario began moving westward after confederation in 1867 into the Red River region, which the Métis, Ojibwa, and Cree considered their own. The Métis were also alarmed when the Hudson's Bay Company agreed to transfer administrative control of the vast northwestern territory known as Rupert's Land to Canada. From 1670 until 1870 the Hudson's Bay Company held official charter to a land greater than the size of Canada itself.

In November 1869 Riel and some five hundred Métis occupied Fort Garry near Winnipeg. They declared their independence from Canada, and formed a provisional government with Riel as president. Riel issued a List of Rights and a statement proclaiming that: *"a people, when it has no Government, is free to adopt one form of Government in preference to another, to give or to refuse allegiance to that which is proposed."*

Prime Minister John Macdonald sent a military expedition to Winnipeg in 1870. He also met with members of Riel's provisional government and confirmed most of Riel's List of Rights. Riel himself went into hiding. Parliament hastily enacted legislation which established Manitoba as the fifth province of the Dominion of Canada. The Canadian government then began negotiating with the Ojibwa and Cree for title to their Manitoba lands. As planned, the Hudson's Bay Company transferred Rupert's Land to Canada.

*Left: An Ojibwa wigwam of ash bark, photographed by a nineteenth-century ethnologist.*

The Cree and Ojibwa asked that two-thirds of Manitoba be reserved to them. The government made the counter-offer of one hundred and sixty acres of land and a fifteen-dollar annuity for each family of five. The government also warned that if the natives refused these terms they were likely to lose both their land and any further chance for compensation. In 1871, feeling they had little choice, the Cree and Ojibwa signed Treaties One and Two.

Within the next fifty years the Canadian government entered into nine more treaties with different groups of Indians. In each of these, known as the numbered treaties, the native peoples exchanged their lands for reservations, annuity payments, and services. Treaty Three was signed in 1873. Together, Treaties One, Two, and Three gave the Canadian government title to most of Manitoba, paved the way for white settlement there, and justified the 1870 legislation which had made Manitoba a province.

Treaty Three was the first of the numbered treaties specifically to provide for the Métis, and the Métis played an active role in the negotiations that preceded its signing. In the course of these negotiations, Ojibwa chief Mawedopenais asked that the treaty include: *"those children that we call the Half-breed—those that have been born of our women of Indian blood. We wish that they should be counted with us, and have their share of what you have promised."* Alexander Morris, the Canadian government's chief representative, replied that the Métis would have a choice. Any of them wishing to be counted as whites would be eligible to receive land grants like other home-steaders. Any of them wishing to be counted as Indians would receive the same land allotments and annuity payments as other Indians.

In 1871 British Columbia became the sixth province of the Dominion of Canada. In 1873, the same year that Treaty Three was signed, Prince Edward Island became Canada's seventh province and the North-West Mounted Police was created to maintain law and order in its western territories. The "Mounties" were specifically charged with suppressing the sale of alcohol to natives and with protecting them from unlawful exploitation by whites.

Treaties Four, Five, and Six were signed with different groups of natives in 1874, 1875, and 1876 respectively. In Treaty Six, Cree and Blackfoot negotiators won the provisions that rations would be given them in time of famine and that a "medicine chest" would be maintained for them. They wanted the first of these provisions because, with the disappearance of the buffalo, it was becoming increasingly difficult for the Blackfoot and other buffalo-hunting tribes to survive. They wanted the second because the 1869–70 smallpox epidemic had killed more than 2,000 Blackfoot and the Cree. The "medicine chest" provision eventually provided the legal basis for the free health care now enjoyed by all Canadian natives.

In Treaty Seven, signed in 1877, the Blackfoot ceded 50,000 acres in present-day southern Alberta to their "Great Mother" Queen Victoria. Treaty Seven also cleared the way for the construction of the Canadian Pacific Railroad. The Blackfoot chief Crowfoot (or Chapo-Meixco)

*Above: A Cree hunter sounds the call that will attract a moose within range of his weapons.*

*Below: Prospectors on the Chilkoot pass during the Klondike Gold Rush.*

was one of those who signed Treaty Seven. Several years later he met with Louis Riel in Montana. Riel hoped to persuade the Blackfoot to join the Métis in new actions against Canada. Crowfoot told him that: *"One must consider what benefit is ever gained from war. The buffalo have gone from the plains; the fault is partly ours, but more the fault of white men far south where they are killed in thousands for their skins, and not for food. The food*

*we eat now the White Mother gives us. Without it we starve. There is nothing to be gained by the war you suggest."*

After Manitoba became a province, some 1.4 million acres of land were set aside there for the Métis. By 1882, however, only 600,000 acres had been distributed to them. Many Métis had moved westward from Manitoba into present-day Saskatchewan. During the 1870s some of them, including a hunter named Gabriel Dumont, did a brisk business in buffalo robes. Louis Riel moved to Montana and taught school there. By the 1880s, however, the buffalo trade had withered and the partially completed Canadian Pacific Railroad was bringing increasing numbers of white settlers into Saskatchewan.

In 1884 Gabriel Dumont invited Louis Riel to return to Canada and lead the Métis in a new campaign for land rights. Riel accepted the invitation. Soon afterward, he sent a petition to Ottawa, listing the grievances of both the Métis and the natives. He pointed out that because of both crop failures and administrative mismanagement, many Indian groups were starving on their new reservations.

Meanwhile, he sent Métis envoys to several influential chiefs and attempted to enlist them in his cause. Most of the Blackfoot rejected Riel's overtures, but several Cree and Assiniboine chiefs agreed to side with him. Two of the Cree chiefs who did so were Pitikwahanapiwiyin (Poundmaker) and Mistahimaskwa (Big Bear). Both had taken part in the negotiations that had led to Treaty Six in 1876. Poundmaker signed the treaty. Big Bear initially refused to do so, but eventually agreed to sign in 1882 in order to obtain government rations for his people.

By March 1885 Riel had established a new provisional government at Qu'Appelle in present-day Saskatchewan. He directed the Métis in a campaign of sabotage that included occupying government property and cutting telegraph wires. On March 26 Gabriel Dumont and a group of Métis ambushed a Mounted Police force at Duck Lake, north of Saskatoon, and killed twelve Mounties. Poundmaker and his people left their reservation and headed toward Saskatoon. Big Bear and his people attacked and looted a Hudson's Bay Company trading post at Frog Lake, near the present border between Alberta and Saskatchewan, killing the Indian Agent and eight other whites.

By early April three separate military units under the respective commands of General Frederick Middleton, Colonel William Otter, and General Thomas Strange were marching into the troubled area. Gabriel Dumont and his Métis force ambushed General Middleton at Fish Creek. Colonel Otter and his forces attacked Poundmaker's camp at Cut Knife Hill but the Cree stood them off. Eventually, General Middleton defeated a force of 350 Métis at Batoche. Riel, Poundmaker, and Big Bear surrendered. The government had spent $5 million suppressing the rebellion.

Riel was convicted of treason and was hanged on November 16, 1885. Eight natives were hanged the following day. Gabriel Dumont and many other Métis fled to Montana. Poundmaker and Big Bear were each sentenced to three years in prison, where both languished and died before completing their terms. Other Cree who had participated in the rebellion lost their annuities for a five-year period.

Throughout Canada the First Nations were subjected to oppressive administrative procedures following the rebellion of 1885. They were already barred from purchasing alcohol. They were now also barred from leaving their reservations without written permission. A nervous Parliament enacted legislation aimed at suppressing their cultural traditions. In 1895 the Blackfoot and other tribes were barred from performing their Sun Dance ceremonials.

Meanwhile, the railroad reached Calgary in present-day Alberta in 1883 and Edmonton in 1891, bringing more non-natives into the Canadian West. The Sarsi signed Treaty Seven and were settled on a reservation near Calgary in 1880. The Chipewyan signed Treaties Six and Seven and were settled on several reservations throughout northern Alberta and Saskatchewan. In 1890–91 a geological survey estimated that rich resources of tar, natural gas, bitumen, oil, and pitch were to be found in the Athabasca River basin. In 1895 the North West Mounted Police established their first permanent post in the Yukon.

In 1884, when the U.S. Congress established a territorial government for Alaska, there were few non-natives in the territory. Beginning in 1896, however, when gold was discovered in

the Klondike, more than one hundred thousand fortune seekers of many nationalities, but primarily from the United States, rushed into Alaska and the Yukon. Tent-cities mushroomed, both in the gold fields and along the main routes to the gold fields. Almost overnight the population of Edmonton in present-day Alberta had increased fivefold. By 1898 the population of Dawson City in the Yukon had reached 18,000.

Three of the four people who first discovered gold on a tributary of the Klondike River were Tagish, and the fourth, George Washington Carmack, was married to an Indian. Carmack, his wife Kate, and her two brothers, Skookum Jim and Tagish Charlie, were fishing for salmon and doing a little prospecting when they found gold on what became known as Bonanza Creek. On

*Above: Edward S. Curtis photographed this Chipewyan tipi in a camp surrounded by aspens.*

August 17, 1896 they staked the claim that triggered the gold rush. Carmack, his wife, and her brothers became rich. Carmack left Kate for another woman, but Kate created a stir in Seattle when she and her brothers stood on a hotel balcony throwing bank notes and gold nuggets to passers-by on the street below. Eventually, Kate, Jim, and Charlie returned to their homeland in the Yukon.

For most of the Tagish people and for other native peoples in Alaska and the Yukon, the gold rush was both a blessing and a curse. It briefly created jobs for native men as dog-sledders or load carriers, as deckhands on river boats, and as hunters and guides. It created jobs for native women as cooks and laundry workers. Some of the prospectors, however, were rough men who abused the native men and women. They also exploited the fish and game resources, disrupted the traditional hunting economy, and brought epidemic diseases.

The Yukon had been established as a district of Canada in 1895 and became a territory three years later. Several tribal bands in the Yukon, northeastern British Columbia, and present-day northern Alberta and northwestern Saskatchewan agitated for a treaty that would protect their hunting and fishing rights and safeguard them from famine. The Ottawa entered into negotiations with the Cree, Beaver, Chipewyan, and Etchareottine peoples for 324,900 square miles of their land, and in 1899 Treaty Eight was signed.

## THE SOUTHEAST AND NORTHEAST

In 1889 citizens of Groton, Connecticut, and invited guests gathered on Mystic Hill to dedicate *"a bronze statue, of heroic size, of Captain John Mason"* who in May 1637 had led the surprise attack on the Pequot fort in which hundreds of men, women, and children had perished. The statue stood near where the massacre had taken place. When the Connecticut General Assembly authorized the statue there were discussions about having it represent both the Indian and English people. But this was a time when Americans everywhere were celebrating the conquest of the West, and those wishing to memorialize Mason as a hero and the massacre as a grand victory foreshadowing that "manifest destiny" won the day. There were no Pequot present at the dedication to tell their side of the story.

In an era when the native population as a whole was declining and indigenous lifeways were exhibited in museums and at world fairs as historical curiosities, rather than vigorous living traditions, it was easy for Americans to accept the notion that natives were vanishing, particularly in the East, where, collectively and individually, they lived on the margins of American society. Writers of the town and county histories that were so popular at the close of the century almost invariably included a paragraph or more about the "last" member of the local tribe. So entrenched was the idea that Vermont (which always reported the fewest Native Americans in the national census) lacked contemporary tribal residents that a myth developed: The Abenaki had not even lived there when white settlers first entered the region. The loss of tribal languages and customs, as well as intermarriage with other ethnic groups, also made Eastern natives "invisible" to their neighbors. "Real" Indians—Sioux, Cheyenne, Pawnee—were to be found in traveling Wild West shows, not on the streets of New York or the potato fields of Maine.

Although centuries of acculturation had transformed the tribal communities of the East, time had not destroyed them. From Maine to Louisiana and from Wisconsin to Florida, Indians insisted on being Indians. This was nowhere more true than in the Southeast, where large-scale removals, the Civil War, and institutionalized racial segregation threatened tribal integrity.

The last Indian war east of the Mississippi was fought against the Florida Seminole from 1855 to 1858. As in the earlier wars, the Seminole fought vigorously. In early 1858 Secretary of War Jefferson Davis admitted that they *"had baffled the energetic efforts of our army to effect their subjugation and removal."* As an alternative, a delegation of Seminole from Indian Territory was sent into the Everglades to entice Chief Billy Bowlegs and his followers to emigrate. Offering sums of money ranging from $100 for each woman and child to $6,000 for Bowlegs himself, the effort was partially successful. Fewer than 200 natives went west; another 300 withdrew deep into the peninsula's interior swamps, where extended families established camps.

For two decades the Seminole led virtually isolated lives. By the 1880s, however, as white settlement came closer to their refuge, contact between the communities became more frequent. Seminoles exchanged plumes, pelts, and alligator hides—all in demand by the international fashion industry—for guns, ammunition, canned foods, coffee, sewing machines, and other goods they could not manufacture themselves. But, in a replay of what had happened on the Plains, professional hunters soon took control of the market, destroying the Seminole's economic independence by the early twentieth century. While the Seminole economy was collapsing, that of white Floridians was entering a boom that would continue until the Great Depression. As new towns sprang up in southern Florida, the Seminole, who held no title to the land they occupied, were dispossessed and became wanderers. In the 1890s the federal government began purchasing tracts of land to be held in trust for the Seminole, but it was not until this century that such reservations were occupied.

Because of their isolation, the Seminole avoided involvement in the Civil War. Other Southern Indians, however, took up arms in that conflict. The Catawba from South Carolina and Choctaw from Mississippi enlisted as soldiers in the Confederate army, and approximately 400 Eastern Cherokee made up part of a unit known as Thomas's Legion. While the latter were fighting in Virginia in 1864, their families back in the mountains of western North Carolina were "in a starving condition" brought on by forced requisition of foodstuffs for Confederate troops, devastating frosts, and outbreaks of outlawry and pillaging by desperate mountain people. Cherokee soldiers learned that some of their friends and relatives were attempting to survive by eating bark and weeds. These homefront sufferings foreshadowed the "troubled times" Eastern Cherokee would face after the war: tribal factionalism and a smallpox epidemic that killed about 125 people.

Not all Southern Indians who fought in the Civil War wore gray uniforms. Pamunkey natives—descendants of one of the chiefdoms headed by Powhatan in the seventeenth century—served as river pilots, land guides, and spies for Union forces in Virginia. To the south, in North Carolina, the natives known today as the Lumbee (but in the late nineteenth century as the Croatan Indians of Robeson County) waged guerilla warfare on behalf of the Union.

Lumbee origins are obscure. When white settlers first encountered them in the early eighteenth century, they were speaking an Elizabethan English and displaying no characteristic cultural traits. Tradition links them to

*Left: By 1850 only a few remnants of the native peoples remained in the Southeast.*

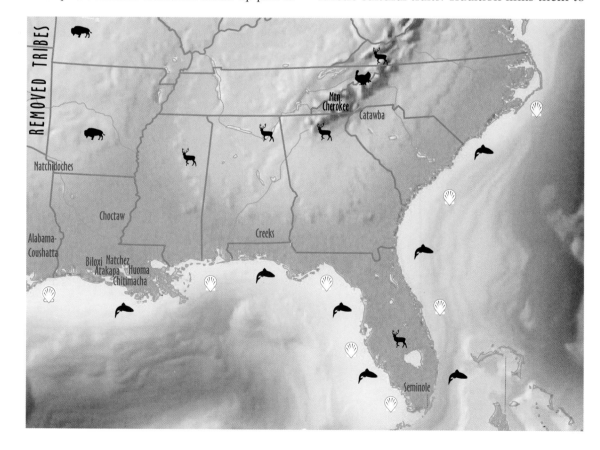

the lost colonists of Roanoke Island, but it is also possible that they are descended from coastal tribal peoples who banded together after their tribes were decimated by war and disease. The Lumbee enjoyed the privileges of North Carolina citizenship until 1835 when, in the wake of Nat Turner's slave rebellion in nearby Virginia, a new constitution was drawn up with provisions intended to exert greater control over the state's non-white population. "Persons of color" could not vote, serve on juries, testify against whites, learn to read and write, or bear arms. The Lumbee were not specifically named in the new constitution, but subsequent court decisions applied its provisions to them as well as to free blacks.

Excluded from Confederate service because they were not white, the Lumbee were drawn into the conflict in 1862 after a yellow fever epidemic hit the region. Facing a shortage of free white workers and unwilling to antagonize planters by conscripting slaves, authorities began drafting Lumbee men to construct forts along the lower Cape Fear River. To avoid forced labor, many men hid in the swamps, where they met up with Union soldiers who had escaped from a nearby Confederate prison. This contact engendered sympathy for the Union cause.

With Lumbee men hiding rather than farming, hardship soon befell the women and children left behind. Despite the economic impact of the naval blockade, planters were still widely perceived as prosperous at this time. Resentment toward the planters grew and soon became violent. In 1864 teenager Henry B. Lowry and two brothers stole some hogs from a planter and brought them to their father's home. When conscription officers came to the house, the brothers ambushed them and fled to the swamps, where Lowry organized the Lumbee into a band that fought a guerilla war against the Confederacy until 1865. Contrary to their expectations, the end of the war left the Lumbee no better off than they had been at its start. The Republican Party, which the Lumbee supported, gave them no help, and the band continued its raids against the prosperous landowners. When Conservative Democrats regained control of the state government, they branded the Lowry band as outlaws.

In the late 1860s and early 1870s, Henry B. Lowry achieved legendary status, an Indian Robin Hood who robbed from the rich and gave to the poor. But, after raiding a store in Lumberton in February 1872, Lowry disappeared forever. The Lumbee who remained in

*Right:* By the end of the nineteenth century, Native Americans were being romanticized for advertising purposes, as seen in these cards for Telonette Cigars. The "cigar store Indian" became a feature of nostalgic Americana.

*Left:* The "Americanization"
of a Navajo at the Carlisle
Indian School is exemplified
by these "before and after"
pictures of the young
Tom Torlino, taken two
years apart.

Robeson County soon found themselves part of a society based on institutionalized racial segregation. Separate schools were established for them, and in 1887 the state legislature established the Croatan Normal School near Pembroke to train Lumbee teachers. When the state failed to appropriate funds for a school building, the Lumbee constructed a two-story structure themselves. The school prospered and later became known as Pembroke State University, now a part of the University of North Carolina. Like the Nanticoke of Delaware, who as a non-white minority in a segregated state fought to have their children attend all-Indian rather than black schools, the Lumbee turned segregation to their own uses and began cultivating a strong native consciousness that served them well in the next century.

The Lumbee were only one, albeit the largest, group of people of at least partial native descent who lived in self-contained enclaves scattered throughout the South and Middle Atlantic states. Shunned, ridiculed, and discriminated against, they held no reservation land, spoke no tribal language, and followed no distinctively traditional customs but steadfastly insisted on their Indianness. Generally impoverished, they supported themselves by farming, or by working as miners, teamsters, lumbermen, or other semi-skilled laborers.

Communities of non-reservation natives also existed north of the Mason-Dixon Line. Living both in isolated rural communities and in cities and towns, they, too, struggled to maintain tribal identities after centuries of acculturation. Some, like the Western Abenaki in and around Swanton, Vermont, minimized their native background in dealings with their white neighbors. Among themselves, however, the Abenaki continued to preserve what they could of their heritage, in part by retaining close ties with their relatives on the Okanak Reserve in Quebec. In addition to maintaining such traditional pursuits as hunting and fishing, the Abenaki sustained themselves as farmers and workers on the railroad that ran through Vermont to Canada.

Along with the Penobscot and Passamaquoddy people in Maine, the Wampanoag on Cape Cod and Martha's Vineyard, and the Schaghticoke and Mohegan in Connecticut, the Vermont Abenaki discovered they could earn extra money by providing services and craft items to tourists. Until mass-produced replicas took their place, ash-splint baskets provided steady (if limited) income. While most New England natives who engaged in this activity traveled to summer resorts in the White Mountains or along the coast, a few, such as Solomon Attaquin, a Mashpee Wampanoag, opened their own establishments. In Maine, the Penobscot guides Joseph Polis and Joseph Attean gained considerable reputations by introducing Henry David Thoreau and lesser-known visitors to the northeastern wilderness. Elsewhere in that vast forest, Penobscot and Passamaquoddy men felled trees on lands that had passed from their hands to those of large logging companies. In Aroostook County, local Micmac (Mi'kmaq) and their relatives from

sale of Native American land to non-natives. The legislation had a particularly disastrous effect upon the Wampanoag of Cape Cod. Since 1834, when the Indian District of Mashpee was established, they had governed themselves with little outside control. After the passage of the Indian Enfranchisement Act, however, the district was abolished and the town of Mashpee incorporated. In 1878 all the common land, except that used for hay and meadow, was sold at public auction. Few Wampanoag could afford to buy any of the land, and most of the 2,536 acres went to whites, who from then on exerted a growing influence over town—and, therefore, Indian—affairs.

The Connecticut General Assembly also made it easier to alienate tribal land. An 1854 law, ironically called "The Preservation of Indians, And the Preservation of Their Property," called for court-appointed tribal overseers to protect native lands from being sold unless it could be shown that such transfers would benefit a private owner without hurting the tribe. Another law passed the next year was less subtle. Under its terms, more than 600 acres of Mashantucket Pequot land was sold at public auction without the tribe's consent. The Pequot were left with about 180 acres.

The Pequot were not the only Connecticut tribe to lose their land. By an act of 1860 the Connecticut legislature also extended state control over the land, and thus the lives, of the

New Brunswick worked as wage laborers in the potato fields.

The New England natives had no formal relationship with the federal government. They were entirely at the mercy of state governments. In Maine, the legislature set aside some funds for native use when it leased or (illegally) sold tribal lands. The state-appointed Indian Agent, not the Indians themselves, determined how the money would be spent. In Massachusetts, the legislature passed a law in 1869 conferring state citizenship upon resident Indians, thereby removing restrictions on the

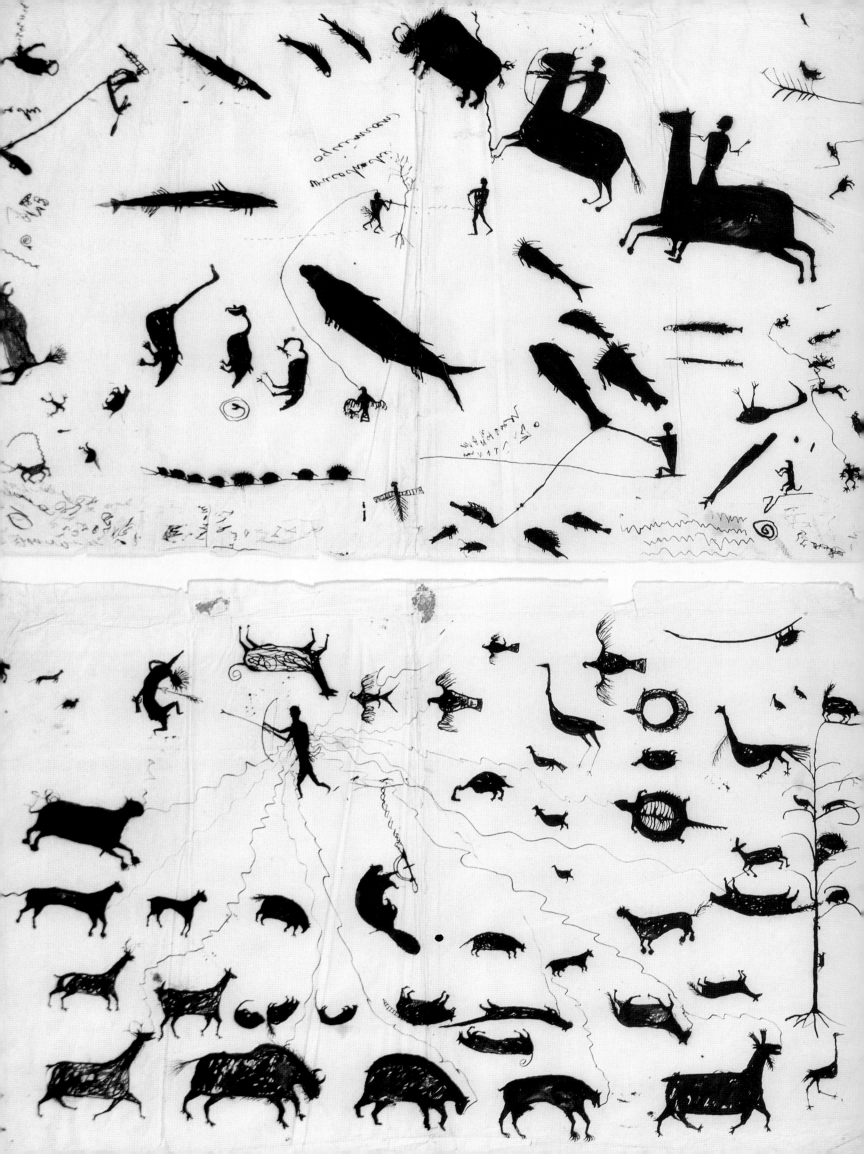

Mohegan. A redistribution of the tribe's common lands among the reservation's approximately 85 residents was intended to accelerate the assimilation of the Mohegan into white society. What it did in actuality was to give the tribe's overseers greater power to manage the land and financial affairs of the Mohegan. Reacting to these tighter state controls, the tribe petitioned the legislature in 1872 to free them from the guardianship of the state. The request was granted, and all tribal properties, except their church and burial grounds, were removed from reservation status. As citizens of the state, the Mohegan now had to pay taxes on their land.

West of New England, in New York State, were some of the reservations of the tribes that made up the historic Iroquois Confederacy. Over the course of the nineteenth century, they clung to some time-honored traditions while simultaneously adopting values and customs of the dominant white society. While traditionalists preserved the ceremonial structure of the Great League, individual tribes felt free to organize themselves by other standards. In 1848 the Seneca living on the Cattaraugus and Allegany Reservations, dissatisfied with the way in which the chiefs distributed annual annuity payments from the United States, staged a quiet revolution. They overthrew the hereditary chiefs and established an elective system of government under a written constitution. The Tonawanda Seneca did not participate in this revolution, however, preferring to maintain their traditional government with chiefs appointed by clan mothers.

In the far west of the Northeast culture area, remnants of the once powerful Stockbridge Mahican and Munsee Delaware shared a small reservation in northern Wisconsin. Dissatisfied with both their isolation from possible employment and their barren farmland, half of their members had moved off the reservation by 1861. When smallpox broke out among them in 1865, many more left, spreading the disease to the nearby Menominee.

During the Civil War, the Union army welcomed native soldiers into its ranks. Although some natives, notably the Mohegan, protested attempts to draft them into service, many others, including Ottawa and Pequot, enlisted, primarily for economic reasons. A total of 162 Iroquois soldiers and sailors served the Union,

the most notable of whom was Ely S. Parker, a Tonawanda Seneca. Trained in law and engineering, Parker attained the rank of brevet brigadier general and served as Ulysses S. Grant's military secretary. In 1865, at Appomattox Court House, Parker transcribed the terms of surrender accepted by Robert E. Lee. When Grant became president, Parker served briefly as Commissioner of Indian Affairs, the first Native American to hold that position.

Parker's success in the white world was unique, but other Iroquois were making their own adaptations to white society. In 1855, 4,149 Iroquois were living in New York State; by 1890 that number had increased to 5,239. A special United States Census in 1892 compiled extensive statistics designed to show the Indians' progress in assimilation. The report revealed that most Iroquois could speak English and were financially comfortable. Farmers, basket makers, and common laborers were the most usual occupations, but there were also twelve musicians, thirty-two carpenters, and nine medical doctors.

Thirteen Iroquois were listed as being employed in show business. By the last decades of the nineteenth century, performing before white audiences had become one of the means of economic survival for many Native Americans. Recruited by the likes of P.T. Barnum and William F. ("Buffalo Bill") Cody—as well as by lesser impresarios and government agencies—natives danced, sang, recited, and re-enacted "historic" events and traditional ways of life for audiences in theaters, arenas, and museums throughout North America and Europe. While the Penobscot, Creek, and Mohawk were among the Eastern tribes represented in the entertainment business, the most popular performers were from the recently conquered Plains and Southwestern tribes. Crowds flocked to see Sitting Bull, the "Slayer of Custer," when he toured with Cody during the year 1885, and eager autograph seekers besieged Geronimo at his numerous public appearances.

Since the beginning of the Republic, native delegations had visited the capital to meet with government officials and receive medals from the Great Father. Touring Wild West shows introduced an even larger number of native peoples to the urban centers of the East. Some tribesmen, like Sitting Bull, found the poverty they encountered incomprehensible among a people who claimed to represent a civilization superior to theirs. Others were intrigued by the life of the cities and sometimes took up permanent residence in them.

Most were only temporary visitors, but while in the East they created distinct native communities. One such community existed in New Haven, Connecticut, during the last years of the century. The Kickapoo Indian Medicine Company, headquartered there, was one of the most popular road shows of its kind. Some of the Indians the company recruited—mostly Sioux—stayed in New Haven only briefly before going on tour. Others settled down in the city, employed in the manufacture of the potion that was to cure all ills. One section of the huge factory, known as the Principal

Wigwam, was *"occupied with tents erected and equipped exactly as though they formed a settlement on the plains. The clothing and food supplies of the band are scattered about with that unstudied elegance of disorder which…forms a great attraction to the free and easy red and pale faces, constituting the grandest charm of life away from the trammels of civilization."*

In New Haven, where the first reservation had been established in 1638, "real" Indians were not the ordinary-looking descendants of local tribes, but dressed-up performers from the West acting in stage productions complete with pinto ponies and feathered headdresses. Soon, natives from Virginia to Massachusetts would don the apparel of Plains peoples when they made public appearances. Only by so doing could they be sure that they would be identified as Native Americans.

*Left:* This poignant photograph of a Lakota woman and child against a backdrop of Plains pictographs was taken in 1891.

# Forgotten People

The turn of the century marked a nadir for many Native Americans. The massacres and most of the killings had ended only recently. Native Americans had already been stripped of most of their lands. They had been deprived of their freedom and had lost much of their culture and traditional ways of life. Within the United States in 1900, only some 250,000 Indians remained—probably an "all-time" low—confined on 171 reservations and other restricted areas in twenty-one states and territories. Questions lingered over the legality of the many reservations that had been established by executive order rather than by an act of Congress. The native population of Canada stood at approximately 50,000 at this time.

Despite the recommendations of such influential men as Army General Philip Sheridan and future president Theodore Roosevelt, it was clear that the governments of the United States and Canada would not attempt to exterminate all Native Americans. Still, with the exception of conditions for some Inuit and Subarctic tribes and other widely scattered groups, poverty and dependence had replaced the free life, health was generally poor, traditional culture was under attack, and native peoples were continuing to lose their remaining lands at an alarming rate.

While it is easy to see the period as uniformly dismal, few aspects of native history and culture have ever been consistent. At this time some groups were beginning—in some cases, continuing—to take legal and other actions to halt abuses and to force the governments of the United States and Canada to respect treaty rights. These activities increased in scope and intensity in the early decades of the twentieth century. There were also signs of regrouping and incipient cultural revivals. Literacy among

Indians made great gains during the period, increasing from about half to about three-quarters of all adults. In general, however, for most Native Americans the early years of the new century were a bleak continuation of the old.

In Canada, as well, the early twentieth century was only too much like the nineteenth. Treaty-making, suspended for more than twenty years during the Métis struggles, resumed under pressure of the 1899 Yukon gold rush with the conclusion of Treaty Eight. Treaties Nine and Ten were signed in 1905 and 1906, respectively. Together, these three treaties covered the surrender by various tribes—including the Cree, Ojibwa, and Chipewyan—of more than 937,500 square miles of land in the Far North. The final "numbered treaty" was Treaty Eleven, in which the Canadian government acquired approximately 625,000 square miles of oil-rich Slave, Dogrib, Hare, and Loucheux (Kutchin) land. When the First Nations (as Canadian bands are called) began the process of seeking land-claim settlements, the Canadian government in 1927 amended the Indian Act to state that no group among the First Nations could raise money—without which appeals were impossible—related to land-claim appeals without the written permission of the Superintendent General. Needless to say, such permission was not always forthcoming.

The period was disastrous for at least one Inuit group, the Inuvialuit of western Canada. The arrival every winter after 1888 of the mostly American Arctic whaling fleet transformed Inuvialuit territory into a wide-open frontier district. While trade was initially profitable to both groups, Inuit culture and health soon declined precipitously. Some officials and missionaries thought that territorial status for the Yukon and

*Opposite: Government rations are distributed on the Pine Ridge Reservation in South Dakota, according to treaty provisions.*

the arrival of the Northwest Mounted Police (renamed the Royal Canadian Mounted Police in 1920) would arrest the decline, but they were mistaken. By 1920 virtually all of the Inuvialuit had been wiped out. Today's population of "Inuvialuit" are not descended from the original people, but from migrants who came to the region after about 1920.

In 1900 the tribes in the western United States were still dealing with the ramifications of the General Allotment (Dawes) Act of 1887. This act provided the mechanism by which American authorities sought to dissolve the tribes and to break up the reservation system by conferring individual land ownership on Indians through allotment. Although the act itself did not allot any land and some tribes were able to negotiate terms more favorable than the government might have intended, within four or five decades of its enactment, the process of allotment and the sale of "surplus" lands resulted in the loss of nearly two-thirds of the lands remaining in Native American hands at the close of the nineteenth century.

In the Great Basin, for example, local pressure was intense to abolish reservations and to allot all native land without any restriction as to how it could be alienated. Two reservations, Malheur (in Oregon) and Lemhi (in Idaho), were, in fact, abolished altogether. Local agents often circumvented the restrictions on land sale, ostensibly in the best interests of "their" Indians. With the encouragement of activists like the Northern Paiute Sarah Winnemucca, who believed that natives needed to own farmland in order to rise to the level of the majority, Native Americans were indeed given land allotments, but they were the poorest lands, in parcels too small to support them.

At the same time, non-reservation Great Basin Indians were being concentrated into tiny "camps" or "colonies." With little employment and no territory adequate to support their traditional subsistence economy, they soon began to resemble the typical rural poor. Most of the few jobs that existed were in the mining industry. When mining collapsed in the 1920s and 1930s, the high poverty levels that prevailed in most of the camps became desperate.

Because they had been left especially destitute by their centuries-old experience with non-natives, the peoples of California were perhaps more vulnerable to abuses under the allotment system and concurrent policies. The Indian Service excluded all non-reservation natives, of whom there were many, from health care and other government services; this policy ultimately resulted in state and local aid being denied to their people as well. Hunger and extreme poverty were the rule among the surviving California Indians. Shamed, finally, into taking some action, Congress agreed in 1906 to study the condition of California's landless natives and soon appropriated funds for their welfare. Nevertheless, Native American access to health care improved only marginally, because the government remained insistent that landless native peoples, who numbered perhaps one-third of all those in California, were not covered by federal programs.

The issue of land, then, was at the root of the miserable living conditions of most native Californians. Pressured by both native and non-native groups, Congress enacted a series of laws designed to provide some land to these people. Unfortunately, these efforts fell short for a number of reasons. First, most of the funds were appropriated to expand existing reservations. This had the effect of encouraging more Native Americans to leave their traditional locations to move to "foreign" reservations. Some did move, but others remained "home" and landless. Furthermore, most existing reservations comprised mainly substandard land. The government refused to release to the natives some of the millions of acres of valuable land—often located in or near their aboriginal territories—to which they were entitled by law. Many reservations did not provide access to adequate water supplies, a problem aggravated by overcrowding, and which considerable government expenditure did little to alleviate.

With some partial exceptions, as among the Puebloans, native self-government had been eviscerated by the early twentieth century. The Office of Indian Affairs dominated native political life. Decisions governing most tribal activities were made in Washington, D.C., and carried out locally by such government officials as Indian Service superintendents and their agents. The powers of the agents were extensive. They controlled the distribution of food and agricultural tools, and they had authority over the native police. Most of these agents were corrupt to a greater or lesser degree. Few of them regarded their charges with care or respect. At best, the agents hoped that the native peoples might some day be assimilated into the majority culture and learn to live by its tenets.

With limited accountability, and certainly none toward those whose lives they ruled, the superintendents made a wide range of decisions for the tribes. They decided which social and religious activities would be permitted and whether or not to lease native land—and on what terms—to non-native interests. The superintendents were also the arbiters of criminal justice, responsible for defining offenses and appropriate punishments. Traditional tribal councils were either banned or rendered powerless. This situation aggravated growing factionalism within many tribes, in which "traditionalists" were pitted against "progressives" or "assimilationists." Denied the right to make decisions about the lives of their own people, formerly vigorous local leadership declined into powerlessness, dependence, and apathy. It may be fairly questioned to what extent both government paternalism and the Dawes Act were designed to keep native communities divided and thus politically powerless. Whether intended or not, they certainly had the effect of exacerbating tensions and legal conflicts among those whom they were ostensibly helping.

As culpable as Indian Office personnel were in encouraging factionalism, many of the divisions in tribal life predated the activities of the Indian Office and, in some cases, the very existence of the United States. Among the Hopi, for example, complicated conflicts between "progressives" and "traditionalists" dated from at least as early as the seventeenth century and the self-destruction of one of their own villages (Awatovi) in around 1700. In the early part of the twentieth century, with Hopi self-government still relatively strong, Hopi life was again riven by internal disagreements. When a "conservative" leader invited sympathizers to settle in the major village of Oraibi, the "progressives" engaged them in battle and forced them out. At that point, all "traditionalists" left Oraibi to found a new village. Within four years, the tribe had been effectively divided.

Among the Zuñi, as well, religious and civil conflict increased in the early twentieth century as the tribal council, itself a creation of the Spanish period, became increasingly powerful. In 1916 an agent sympathetic to one side forced the sharply divided council to provide land for the construction of a new Catholic mission. The tribal divisions over this issue—"progressive" and Protestant, "traditionalist" and Catholic—soon hardened into factions. Eventually the two factions evolved into political "parties" when the Zuñi reorganized in the 1930s under the IRA, as described below.

The corruption and incompetence of Indian Office personnel and the effects of fragmentation and dependence did not escape the notice of certain government officials. In a well-meaning but futile effort to correct the situation, a bill was introduced in Congress in 1912 giving Native Americans a say in the nomination and retention of their superintendents. Although the bill avoided the issue of allowing any effective self-government, it did mark a radical departure from the past in that it specifically, if tentatively, acknowledged the ultimately essential role of natives' participation in their own governmental affairs. The bill was defeated, as was a similar one submitted in 1916.

In the early twentieth century, a series of laws and court decisions further institutionalized the power of the government over native life. The Curtis Act of 1898 had provided for the allotment of land owned by the so-called Five Civilized Tribes—Creek, Cherokee, Choctaw, Chickasaw, and Seminole—living in the "permanent" Indian Territory (Oklahoma). These tribes, and a few others, had been specifically exempted from the Dawes Act. Ultimately, they lost their land completely, their reservations redefined as "historic areas." The Curtis Act also mandated abolition of their tribal governments. Although the law was never enacted formally, each tribe having reached separate agreements with the federal government, its provisions were realized in all cases, and the United States began appointing the principal chiefs of the tribes. This process is instructive because it demonstrates both the agency of the tribes as well as the ultimate futility of resisting government plans to strip Indians of their land.

In *Lone Wolf v. Hitchcock* (1903), the Supreme Court ruled on a key provision of the Dawes Act. Lone Wolf, a Kiowa, challenged the right of the government to declare certain Indian land "surplus" and then sell it to non-natives. The Court upheld the provision, ruling that the government, acting in its role as guardian of the tribes, did not need the permission of the groups involved to carry out these activities. Part of the significance of this decision was the acknowledgment that the government could break treaties unilaterally. Needless to say, *Lone Wolf v. Hitchcock* was a major blow to tribes seeking to retain their land as tribal property.

Finally, Commissioner of Indian Affairs Francis Leupp, himself a former Dawes Act "reformer," lobbied successfully for passage of the Burke Act of 1906, which gutted even the flimsy protection offered against abuse of the new allotment policy. In terms specifically designed to thwart the widespread practice of swindling Native Americans out of their lands, the Dawes Act contained language that made it difficult for Indians to sell or otherwise part with their allotments. In 1902 Congress had already weakened the protection by allowing the sale of inherited land. The Burke Act provided for further removal of restrictions on land sales. Government officials could now declare individual natives "competent" to manage their allotments. In these cases, Native Americans received "patent-in-fee," or title to their land in fee simple. They were then responsible for all taxes, and all restrictions on sale were removed.

U.S. citizenship, dictated from above with no input from the individuals involved, was conferred together with competency status. In Canada at that time, despite the fact that hardly any First Nations opted for assimilation and citizenship, the government automatically conferred such status on any native who had obtained a university degree. With the removal of restrictions, land swindling and desperation land sales became more common. Transfers of allotments to non-natives soared: Tens of millions of acres of fee-simple land had been sold by the early 1930s. Not surprisingly, natives also lost a considerable amount of land through non-payment of taxes.

By 1900 Native Americans had lost almost half—approximately 60 million acres—of the tribal land they had controlled only thirteen years earlier. Much of what remained was interspersed or "checkerboarded" with non-native land, thus rendering it unfit for large-scale, land-intensive tribal enterprises. Nor was land loss the only, or perhaps even the major, problem faced in the early twentieth century. Poverty was endemic. Its obvious causes included the forced abandonment of subsistence economies, in which most Indians had always had more or less enough to eat. The buffalo, upon which the Plains peoples had depended, had been hunted to virtual extinction. Other key wildlife resources—fish and game species and various food plants—had also become rare, or had disappeared entirely. In any case, many natives had long since become dependent on foods and goods of non-native origin and manufacture.

Less easily understood is the extent to which many Indians tried to adapt to the newly imposed living conditions but were denied the chance to succeed. This occurred in various ways in different areas. For instance, despite their often fierce resistance, many formerly nomadic peoples were officially encouraged to become farmers. This was, in fact, the economic rationale for the allotment system. Yet its supposed beneficiaries were almost always left without the necessary resources. Either their land was unsuited for farming, or they could not obtain the necessary capital, or they had no access to markets. These factors, in various degrees and combinations, made success unlikely or impossible. Other farmers could obtain capital by mortgaging their land; Native Americans were prohibited by law from doing so. They did have access to government loans for up to six hundred dollars, but these funds were usually insufficient to allow them to compete successfully against non-native farmers.

In some cases, including the "Five Civilized Tribes" of Oklahoma, the successful practice of communal agriculture was disrupted by the imposition of individualized farming. In the Southwest, a region where natives had farmed successfully for centuries, policies that ultimately destroyed their agriculture arose from government hostility toward their culture, an obsession with individual rather than communal economic activity, and, possibly, a desire on the part of the authorities to prevent natives from competing successfully with non-natives. Where flood irrigation had once worked well for such tribes as the Zuñi, the government now built dams to provide irrigation to individual farms. The unforeseen consequences of silt accumulation behind the dams and soil erosion, however, soon made farming impossible, and most native farmers were left worse off than they had been before the expensive dams were built.

Similar problems prevented the success of ranching enterprises. While mandating this economic activity (often because policies forcing Indians into farming had already failed) the government continued to break up native land holdings, thus making it less likely that ranching could succeed. Neither farming nor ranching were possible in the arid West on land parcels of the size allocated to individuals. Superintendents and Indian agents resolutely insisted that tribal land, which might have been used to augment allotments and thus expand the land available for grazing, be leased to non-natives. For example, the Superintendent of the San Carlos Apache made the decision—without consulting the Apache, of course—to lease prime grazing land to non-natives. This decision was unwise for several reasons, and even the proceeds from the leasing, held in trust by the U.S. government, were denied to the tribe.

Government officials also determined that cattle ranching would be a good activity for some Dakota (Sioux) tribes. Dakota cattle herds did indeed increase dramatically in the early years of the twentieth century. Under pressure to lease their lands to non-natives, however, many natives sold their herds in the late 1910s. By 1920 the Dakota had effectively become landlords without cattle. When cattle prices fell in the 1920s, the lessees defaulted. To make up for the loss of income, natives were encouraged to sell their allotments. By 1930 Dakota who only a generation before had owned both land and cattle were left with neither, just as the Great Depression began.

Nor were these the only problems that hampered economic activity during these years. Among Native Americans who controlled mineral resources, mining was one of the most divisive issues. Mining could generate needed jobs and money, but its opponents argued that job creation for natives had traditionally been limited and did not in any case offset the costs of pollution, ill health, and environmental destruction, all of which touched the heart of native religious convictions.

Oil was discovered in the late nineteenth century on the Osage Reservation and on other native land in Oklahoma. It brought fantastic wealth to the Osage during the 1920s, but with it came widespread cheating and corruption, violence, debauchery, and a legacy of divisiveness. Nevertheless, the Osage actually did receive significant financial benefit from their oil resources, which made their case atypical of native experiences with the exploitation of natural, and especially mineral, resources in the early and middle twentieth century. Far more often, government officials acting as trustees negotiated leases and other contracts with non-native companies. These contracts enriched the companies, but often left little more than an enduring legacy of serious health and environmental problems. Timber resources in the far West brought limited prosperity to such tribes as the Karok, Yurok, and Klamath, but clear-cutting, erosion, and the general loss of forest habitats by government mismanagement severely limited the possibilities of sustainable economic benefit to the tribes.

Furthermore, even where natural resources remained that would have sustained their former subsistence economies, natives often were denied access to the hunting and gathering grounds and the lakes, rivers, and beaches where they were to be found. In the Northwest and parts of the Plateau, fishing disputes flared shortly after Washington became a state in 1889. Although the terms of various treaties preserved the rights of local tribes to fish at their "usual and accustomed places," non-native commercial fishing and canning companies soon began to crowd them out. The government yielded to pressure from commercial interests and from sporting interests as well, severely limiting native access to off-reservation hunting and fishing. The construction of dams also denied the native peoples access to resources. These developments were very hard on those whose lifeblood, for millennia, had been salmon and other fish.

The federal government, charged under its treaty trust obligations to protect the rights of native peoples, seemed unable or unwilling to act. In 1905 the first Native American fishing rights case presented to the U.S. Supreme Court involved a Plateau tribe, the Yakima. The court upheld the tribe's treaty rights, but also affirmed the right of the state to regulate their fisheries in ways that remained unspecified. The ruling was unsatisfactory and ambiguous, and throughout the early twentieth century natives in the Northwest and Plateau regions continued to be harassed for exercising their fishing and hunting rights. Locally, they were often arrested and physically intimidated, and state courts ruled against them continually. In the early twentieth century, Canadian officials banned traditional fishing equipment and even destroyed the salmon weirs of the Carriers, a Subarctic Athabaskan tribe in British Columbia.

Officials also often regarded native lands as good places to undertake reclamation projects, most of which proved detrimental to the communities concerned, but advantageous—at least in the short term—to non-natives. The 1905 Derby (Truckee) Dam is an excellent example. Leading to decades of expensive litigation, its construction destroyed a thriving fishery that had sustained the Pyramid Lake Paiute for thousands of years. Nevada lawmakers, representing constituents who were unhappy with competition from successful natives, had already restricted the Paiute fishery severely in the previous century, banning their fishing equipment and forbidding them to transport fish during certain key months.

Although Congress had both the authority and the obligation to protect tribal land, it generally bowed to political pressure from the Western states and failed to do so. Even when the tribes did win legal victories like the 1908 Winters decision, an important ruling in support of native water rights, the federal government echoed President Andrew Jackson's refusal to honor the 1832 Supreme Court decision prohibiting the Cherokee removal and continued to allow the states to appropriate and divert native water resources. At the end of the 1930s, for instance, when the City of Los Angeles had acquired most of the Owens valley, its diversion of the valley's water resources ended almost all local farming and ranching there. The residents of California's El Capitan Reservation suffered a similar situation when their water resources were appropriated outright for public use. Illegal diversions of native water were tolerated and even encouraged. In one California case, the government rewarded a non-native who had diverted Indian water to irrigate his own land by purchasing his project. The federal government refused to exercise its trust responsibilities to provide legal help to Native American victims of countless other violations of their water rights.

To complete this picture of Native America in the early twentieth century, we must now turn to social issues. This period saw, for example, the culmination of the practice of forcing native children to attend boarding schools whose mission was to eradicate their "Indianness." By 1900, 10,000 native children were enrolled in twenty-five off-reservation government boarding schools. They were also enrolled in such private institutions as the Carlisle Indian Industrial School in Pennsylvania. Thousands more were educated in various government and religious institutions, mostly on the reservations. Government schools began to appear in Alaska during this period as well. So great was the impetus to manage native affairs without consulting them or obtaining their consent that even successful Indian-managed schools were dismantled. In Oklahoma, for example, despite bitter resistance by the Choctaw and Cherokee, native-run schools

were dissolved and replaced by new and far less effective institutions managed by the government.

In Canada, approximately 15 percent of school-age native children were enrolled in industrial, boarding, or day schools in 1900. These were usually under the control of missionary groups. The distribution of schools varied widely across the nation. The official compulsory education laws of 1894 had been largely ignored, and little real effort was made to enroll all native children in schools before 1920, the year of compulsory enfranchisement. In 1930 only 3 percent of native students progressed beyond the sixth grade, and many of these were in their middle to late teens.

The native response to boarding schools was mixed, ranging from apathetic to openly hostile. Intense resentment was generated by the fact that force, extending even to kidnapping and withholding of food rations, was often used to compel school attendance. The academic facilities of native schools in both the United States and Canada were often inadequate and in need of repair. Native children were often forced to perform exhausting manual labor to help maintain the schools, while non-native school employees managed to hold outside jobs. The children also suffered from severe health problems aggravated by overcrowding and poor sanitation.

Children were regularly beaten or otherwise humiliated for speaking their native language or engaging in "Indian behavior." Furthermore, the curricula of such schools were generally based either on standard Christian teachings, or on such secular topics as Christopher Columbus, the Pilgrims, and the Boston Tea Party. These topics were ill designed to capture and hold the interest of young Native American students. Despite these somber realities, the widespread enrollment of native children in schools was achieved, and some did benefit from the "white man's education," finding both intellectual challenge and even spiritual engagement in the studies offered.

Some of these schools provided students with the opportunity to work outside the school for non-native families and businesses. These initiatives exposed many Native American students to exploitation, but they often provided real opportunities to earn money and to acquire skills, which worked to the satisfaction of students and employers alike.

Despite the accomplishment of the mass enrollment of native children and such initiatives as work programs, the government- and church-sponsored boarding institutions and reservation schools generally failed to provide appropriate and effective vocational or academic training to their students. Too often, these schools were little more than agencies of cultural repression and forced assimilation. Such vocational skills as were taught merely prepared the native children for menial jobs that were generally unavailable to them on or off the reservation. The values and reference systems of the prevailing culture had no lasting meaning to the students, and few of them assimilated their lessons.

Although death rates from diseases during the early twentieth century did not approach those of the initial contact period, when they had reached levels of 90 percent or more in some areas, Indian health was generally very poor during this period. The incidence of tuberculosis had become epidemic among natives, who also suffered widely from influenza, trachoma, smallpox, and venereal and other diseases, and from high rates of infant mortality, malnutrition, and alcoholism. Health care was generally more available than it had been toward the end of the nineteenth century, but poor facilities, lack of transportation, inadequate supplies, and native resistance to alien medical practices severely limited the effectiveness of that care.

The federal government did not begin to offer dental services until 1913, when it authorized a handful of itinerant dentists to visit reservation communities. Around this time, the government also responded to epidemic diseases among the natives, setting up medical education programs and establishing numerous tuberculosis sanitoria. After the passage in 1921 of the Snyder Act, which assigned the federal government the overall responsibility for providing routine health care, the federal Indian Medical Service was reorganized and strengthened. The budget for the Indian Health Services rose from $40,000 in 1911 to $1.5 million in 1930. Despite these important efforts, the state of Indian health remained bleak. The good intentions of some government officials did not outweigh the general lack of will to respond adequately to the challenge of improving native health.

Finally, we must look at tribal communities themselves in the early twentieth century. As usual, generalizations can be dangerous. These communities differed in important ways. However, it is possible to perceive certain facts or patterns common to the various regions. The remnants of the Eastern tribes were in some ways further along the road to recovery from the devastation caused by the loss of their traditional ways of life. Groups like the Mohawk in the Northeast and the Seminole in Florida had been able to adjust to their new situations and to preserve many of their traditions. The Seminole, of course, were never entirely conquered. The Mohawk, while divided by the border of the United States and Canada (which they considered artificial), as well as by various political issues, had been adapting to significant cultural changes since at least the seventeenth century. Both tribes had sufficient land, as well as strong social and political structures that made it possible for them to maintain some traditional activities.

Some Eastern tribes were not as fortunate. Even those groups with land found it difficult to maintain a positive identity in the face of economic hardship, political powerlessness, and social discrimination. Many tribes had been left with no land at all. In various degrees, their peoples had been absorbed into mainstream society. The "Five Civilized Tribes," which, until the early twentieth century, had retained much of their land and their political structures in Oklahoma, lost both along with important social institutions.

It was in the western United States that more recent social dislocations produced crises of social cohesion within many tribes. Customs and institutions that had held them together for centuries had been devastated by the end of the nineteenth century. What did it mean to be Cheyenne, Mohave, or Puyallup in the early twentieth century? The lifeways of the Great Plains peoples had revolved around the buffalo, but now the buffalo were gone. Life in the river valleys of the Southwest had revolved around an annual growing cycle, but now water had been diverted for use by non-natives, and the land was no longer productive. In the Northwest, life had revolved primarily around fishing, but the salmon catch was no longer sufficient to feed the people. With the destruction of subsistence economies came the decline of traditional religion and the unraveling of clan and other social bonds. Thus the weakening of social cohesion—of group identity, or the bonds that keep people united and strong—was another characteristic of early twentieth-century Native American life.

One social institution—religion—both reflected the breakdown of the traditional order and provided a way for people to reorient themselves within their own heritage while easing the transition to modern life. New or redefined native religions manifested a trend toward pan-Indianism throughout the United States. Pan-Indianism had deep roots. The Iroquois League, the All-Indian Pueblo Council, and the Pontiac Alliance were all examples of intertribal cooperation. We have seen in the last chapter how contact among tribes increased during the late nineteenth century, finding expression most notably through the various Ghost Dances of the Basin and Plains tribes. In the Pacific Northwest and throughout northern California, the Indian Shaker Church became popular in the 1920s. This religion, like the Ghost Dance, contains elements of both traditional regional and Christian religious practice whereby methods of faith healing freely incorporate shamanistic elements and are used against allegations of witchcraft.

The Peyote religion emerged during the 1880s and blossomed in the early twentieth century. A non-addictive psychotropic plant, peyote had been used by healers in Mexico for at least 10,000 years. It first reached the Indian Territory of Oklahoma in the late nineteenth century. Native travelers brought peyote to the United States, probably from Rio Grande natives via tribes of eastern New Mexico and southern Texas, such as the Mescalero and Lipan Apache and the Caddo. The peyote ceremony, as it was developed in Oklahoma, is a blend of elements from ancient Mexico and modern Christianity. The Peyote religion quickly spread from Oklahoma throughout the Plains and into the Great Basin and beyond. It was rejected, at least initially, in much of the Southwest.

Consistent with its past rejection of Native American religious beliefs and practices, the non-native power structure—particularly the Bureau of Indian Affairs and the Christian churches—vigorously opposed the ceremonial use of peyote.

By 1918, however, even some members of Congress were persuaded to accept its value. Peyotists did not drink or gamble, but rather advocated responsibility, tribal unity, and family cooperation. The Peyote religion helped many natives to center themselves and to forge links between their traditions and the tug of non-native society during a period of cultural drift and difficulty. After the defeat of federal legislation to outlaw the use of peyote, Oklahoma peyotists—in an action that reflected the new "respectability" of peyote ceremonialism among non-natives—incorporated in 1918 as the Native American Church.

Native American political activity increased in some areas during the early years of the twentieth century. These activities were related to the reform energies of the period after World War I, but grew mainly out of local situations and grassroots activism. In the Pacific Northwest and Plateau regions, for instance, tribes engaged in political action to counter threats to their fisheries. They also fought to obtain recognition and reservation land for a number of tribes that had been left landless by the treaties of the previous century. The Tillamook and Clatsop won important land-claims cases around 1910, ushering in a long period of legal activity.

After the United States entered World War I, at least 10,000 natives joined the armed forces. Given the treatment that they had received, and the fact that many of their parents had fought against the United States, this is a surprisingly large number. It is also notable because many of these soldiers were volunteers. Perhaps half of all Native Americans in the United States were not citizens and were therefore ineligible for the draft. In addition to those volunteering for active service, another 10,000 native men and women worked with the Red Cross during the war, and countless others invested their extremely limited funds, purchasing 25 million dollars' worth of war bonds. These contributions led Congress, in 1924, to grant citizenship to all Indians living in the United States.

Of course, not all Native Americans supported the war, or tribal involvement in it. In 1917, for example, the Upper Creek in Oklahoma joined a coalition of Indians, African Americans, and poor whites to oppose the war and to urge that federal funds be redirected to improve the lives of the rural poor. Participation in the war was equally controversial among the members of the Society of American Indians, a national educational organization founded in Ohio in 1911. Although the society, with a single voice, opposed plans to organize native soldiers in segregated units, the war divided the group into "traditionalist" and "progressive" factions. The traditionalists opposed participation in the war, arguing that natives, especially as non-citizens, owed nothing to the government of the United States. The progressives saw participation in the war as an opportunity to advance their goals of assimilation and citizenship.

World War I proved to be a mixed experience for Native Americans. Among some groups, such as the Lakota, participation in the war was a way to revive warrior traditions; returning veterans were honored with traditional ceremonies and prizes. The war offered many people an escape from the isolation of reservation life and an opportunity to meet and talk with members of other tribes and regions. They shared their experiences and formed new alliances, setting the stage for increased pan-Indian political activism after the war. Important groups such as the American Association on Indian Affairs (later the Association on American Indian Affairs), the All-Indian Pueblo Council, the Grand Council Fire of American Indians, the American Indian Defense Association (AIDA), and the Mission Indian Federation formed or re-formed during the postwar period and were active in the policy debates of the time. On the other hand, many Native Americans were killed in the war. The funding of their social services was cut in budget-tightening measures taken during and after the war. The acquisition of U.S. citizenship, widely seen as a "reward" for wartime service, also came to be viewed in a critical light by many people in the years that followed.

Canada's first intertribal organizations were also created during the postwar period. In 1916 several bands from British Columbia formed the Allied Tribes of British Columbia, primarily to work on land-claims issues. A Canadian Mohawk veteran formed the League of Indians in 1919. This group called for natives to be enfranchised while maintaining their special legal status: Many official suffrage plans linked the acquisition of citizenship to the elimination of special status. The League of Indians also advocated greater control over tribal funds and property. But the group proved to be ineffective, and significant pan-Indian activity in Canada was delayed until the 1960s.

In many instances, economic considerations that had little or nothing to do with reform motivated intensified political activity. Before the twentieth century, the Navajo had remained organized primarily by band. Until 1904, when they created local business councils—their first and most important community-level political bodies—the Navajo had developed little true tribal consciousness. In 1915 the Bureau of Indian Affairs divided the Navajo Reservation into six districts, each governed by a non-native superintendent. Oil was discovered on the reservation in 1921. The government insisted on the formation of a central body with the authority to negotiate oil leases. A Navajo business council was organized and began to meet in 1922. In 1923 the Secretary of the Interior appointed a non-native commissioner and a tribal council. That same year Henry Chee Dodge—who had assumed the position of head chief after the death of the warrior Manuelito—became the first tribal chair. The council's first order of business was to approve a BIA-written resolution granting the appointed commissioner the right to sign oil and gas leases on behalf of the tribe.

Contrary to the intentions of the BIA that had created it, however, the Navajo Tribal Council soon began to assert real authority. Although the decision to drill for oil was essentially made in Washington, the council—in a move designed to strengthen local self-government—chose to allocate oil income by jurisdiction rather than on a per capita basis. It also condemned the government's plan to use tribal funds for the construction of a bridge outside the reservation. In the 1920s, in the face of opposition from the Secretary of the Interior, the council pressed for passage of a bill granting the tribe royalties on certain subsurface mining operations. The bill was signed into law in 1927 as the Indian Oil Act.

Little such political activity developed in the Far North, where Inuit groups were struggling after being hit hard by the collapse of the fur market and the influenza epidemic of 1918. In order to demonstrate Canadian "ownership" of the land, the Northwest Mounted Police established a presence in the Far North in the early twentieth century and continued there for many years as the sole representative of official Canada. While the fur market remained prosperous in the first two decades of the twentieth century, traditional systems of exchange were replaced by the use of currency. The collapse of the fur market in the 1920s left native groups ill prepared to provide for themselves. Nor was the Canadian government ready to help, having left the administration of the Far North in police hands. Starvation, alcoholism, and cultural conflict were among the serious problems that resulted in violence and death for many natives during these chaotic years.

Meanwhile, life in the region was changing rapidly. As late as the 1930s, most medical facilities and schools in the Far North were operated under the auspices of missions. Steamships had penetrated into the major river systems as early as 1900. Natives began acquiring outboard motors in the 1920s, and air transportation arrived at the same time. The relatively dramatic increase in non-native economic activity led to the sharp decline of game stocks upon which the indigenous peoples had depended for the necessities of their traditional lifeways. Relief efforts were left in the questionable hands of local traders. The Canadian government did establish some game and trapping regulations and set aside two huge game preserves in 1923, but until the 1950s—unlike other non-native powers in the Far North, such as the United States and Greenland—it failed to address the many problems of its aboriginal residents there.

Reformers in the United States grew stronger in the 1920s, their influence enhanced to some extent by widespread recognition of the wartime sacrifice and loyalty of Native Americans. Neo-reform groups included the American Indian Defense Association, the Indian Rights Association, and the General Federation of Women's Clubs. Reformers criticized policymakers on the grounds that the latter did not respect the basic humanity of the native peoples and the value of their traditions. They pointed to the appalling health conditions among native peoples and their continuing loss of land as evidence of egregious violations of the government's legally mandated trust responsibilities and of the failure of U.S. Indian policies to protect the interests of Native Americans.

The fact that Indians were no longer perceived as an internal threat was certainly an important factor contributing to stronger neo-reformist sentiments among non-natives, who no longer felt menaced by Native Americans and looked upon them somewhat nostalgically. The glorification of Indians only made their conquest by non-natives seem to have been more valorous and justified. There would have been no honor in having vanquished unworthy enemies and no reason to have persecuted nonthreatening peoples so relentlessly. The victors could now afford to relax their hostility and extend some compassion to their once-proud foes. People began to take an interest in Indian cultures and to understand the value of their preservation. Furthermore, a new scientific ethos emerged that maintained the proper way to study alien cultures was on their own terms, not according to the norms of the investigators. Finally, the horror of World War I had dealt a serious blow to the concept of America as an evangelical Protestant nation, and the growth of science and technology encouraged a growing secularism that eroded old notions that progress was inextricably based on religion. In this context, there was more room for new approaches to Native Americans.

Alaska natives also formed a significant intertribal organization during this period. The Alaska Native Brotherhood (ANB) did not have its origins in the burst of pan-Indian activity in the wake of World War I, but rather began in 1912 as a self-help group with ties to the Presbyterian Church. A companion group, the Alaska Native Sisterhood (ANS), was founded three years later. Strongest by far among the Tlingit and Haida in southeast Alaska, the ANB's relatively conservative agenda initially stressed citizenship for natives through political action. The organization also led boycotts against businesses that discriminated blatantly against native peoples.

In 1915 the Alaska territorial legislature passed a law permitting Native Americans to become citizens under highly restrictive conditions. Although few among them qualified for citizenship under this law, seven years later a judicial decision awarded suffrage to all Alaskan natives. Several Tlingit were subsequently elected to the legislature. In the 1940s the ANB began fighting for the abolition of fish traps, which were causing the rapid decline of fish stocks and made it impossible to compete against the non-natives who used them. The traps were abolished in 1959. In a case with national implications, the ANB also succeeded in filing and ultimately winning a land claim on behalf of the Tlingit and the Haida.

Political activism in California on behalf of Native Americans began in the early years of the twentieth century, when such groups as the Sequoya League and the Northern California Indian Association were formed, primarily comprised of non-native membership. These groups actively assisted dispossessed and homeless Indians. By the 1920s, intertribal groups including both the Society of Northern California Indians and the Mission Indian Federation had become prominent. The MIF was galvanized by a government crackdown on internal dissent and went on to oppose allotment of reservation lands and to promote the participation of women in tribal councils. Eventually, this group appointed its own reservation officials to counter those of the BIA and became active in the land-claims process.

Other intertribal reform groups, including the California Indian Brotherhood, which was organized in 1926, worked on such issues as creating better and more accessible educational opportunities, securing small farms for California natives, and establishing the rights of tribes to sue the government over the many unratified treaties that were causing so much difficulty among Native American communities. The activities of reform groups in California brought sufficient pressure on the state assembly to pass the Jurisdictional Act of 1928, which empowered the state to bring suit against the federal government on behalf of Indians living within its borders. The passage of this act resulted ultimately in the award of small cash payments to many of California's native peoples.

One corollary of the new mood for reform was the recognition that the practice of removing federal restrictions on the sale of Indian allotments aggravated the development of native poverty by leaving them without land and a means of self-support. This policy was formally ended in 1920. Throughout the following decade, federal officials continued to oversee tribal land losses, but further loss of land was restrained significantly. The pace of dividing remaining tribal lands into individual allotments was also checked. Still, although many Native Americans lived in regions where farming and ranching were the primary economic activity, few became effective farmers or ranchers. The pursuit of these activities became increasingly difficult for the same reasons that had applied in the past: Indians could not raise sufficient capital to compete in the marketplace; individual allotments were too small to permit effective farming or ranching; and government personnel constantly encouraged Native Americans to sell or lease their holdings to non-natives.

The impetus toward reform also grew out of such governmental actions as the efforts to regulate the use of peyote and alcohol among natives, the suppression of their languages and cultural practices, and the consequences of a number of Supreme Court cases. Such decisions as *Lone Wolf v. Hitchcock* upheld government power over native rights, but in *United States v. Sandoval* (1913), while denying Puebloans the right to dispose of their own land, the court acknowledged a federal responsibility to protect their rights just as, in theory, it protected the rights of other tribes. This decision threw into doubt the legality of non-native titles to land sold by the Pueblo or appropriated by non-natives. The disputed land comprised roughly 10 percent of Pueblo territory, much of which was well irrigated and thus particularly valuable. Following the announcement of the Sandoval decision, tensions immediately increased between Puebloans and claimants of the disputed lands.

In an effort to resolve the title issue, New Mexico Senator Holm Bursum, at the request of Albert Fall, the new head of the Department of the Interior, introduced a bill in 1921 designed to recognize most non-native land titles. Its provisions called for recognizing the legal rights of good-faith purchasers as well as trespassers on native land: More than 60,000 acres were at stake. Furthermore, claims involving native water rights were to be placed under the jurisdiction of hostile state courts. A coalition of neo-reformists, joined by New Mexico artists and intellectuals, mobilized to fight the bill. As a step toward mobilizing their own resources, the Puebloans themselves convened the All-Indian Pueblo Council for the first time in almost 300 years. They also sent a delegation to Washington to lobby against the bill.

In the end, the political pressure proved too much for the anti-Indian coalition: The bill was tabled and ultimately replaced in 1924 by the successful Pueblo Lands Act. This law provided monetary compensation in lieu of title to most non-native owners of disputed land. All compensation was to be paid by the federal government in recognition of the fact that its negligence was responsible for the loss of native land. The U.S. was also to compensate the Pueblo peoples for lost land and water rights.

Although the Bursum Bill was defeated, and the battle for Pueblo lands had been resolved in their favor, battle lines had been drawn clearly. Secretary Fall pushed for legislation calling for the effective removal of all tribes from federal responsibility. He was opposed by reformers who were enraged by the ruthless measures proposed by the government. As it happened, the very able General Federation of Women's Clubs had recruited a teacher from San Francisco State College named John Collier to help in the fight against the Bursum Bill. Collier quickly organized the American Indian Defense Association. Ten years later, he was named Commissioner of Indian Affairs.

With the defeat of the Bursum Bill (and the indictment and resignation of Secretary Fall), a "Committee of One Hundred" was appointed to make recommendations for future Indian policy. Not surprisingly, the committee consisted principally of non-natives, including celebrities, politicians, and anthropologists. But a number of prominent native spokesmen, including Henry Roe Cloud, Charles Eastman, and Arthur C. Parker, the latter of whom became presiding officer, were also appointed. The committee called for higher standards of native education with less emphasis on boarding schools, the extension of federal financial assistance for supplemental educational and vocational programs of study, and an end to native exclusion from public schools. The committee recommended an assault on the poor health and sanitary conditions then prevalent on reservations. It also urged a resolution of tribal land claims. These measures all reflected the continuing desire to dissolve native nations altogether and to complete assimilation. While the government did act on a number of these proposals, it also continued to promote crudely colonialist measures that served only to fuel the fires of reform. One such measure was the proposal advanced in 1926 to ban traditional native marriages and divorces and replace them with a system of registration and licenses, granted and supervised under the sole authority of the government-designated superintendents.

Reform took a different direction in Canada, where the government moved to assert greater control over certain tribes. At the Six Nations (Iroquois) Reserve, for example, the government capitalized on deep intertribal divisions to strip official powers of self-government from the people of the reserve. The "Upper Tribes" (Mohawk, Oneida, and Tuscarora) were more favorably disposed to Christianity and assimilation than were the "Lower Tribes" (Onondaga, Seneca, and Cayuga). In the early twentieth century, the "Upper Tribes" organized the Indian Rights Association, or Dehorners, a movement to reform what they saw as the archaic practices of traditional tribal government, particularly the ancient hereditary system of selecting leaders. The reformers steadily pressed the federal government to impose an electoral system.

World War I also marked a watershed in the intertribal struggles among the First Nations of Canada. Although Canadian Indians volunteered in greater numbers than might have been expected proportionate to their population, the official position of the traditional council at the Six Nations Reserve was that, as the government of a sovereign nation, it could not support the war effort unless asked to do so by the king of England himself. Tensions escalated after the end of the war. The chiefs ceased to co-operate with local administrative officials, in part out of fear that renewed pressures by government officials to make farmers of their people would ultimately be destructive. A younger group of more militant chiefs finally assumed power in the early 1920s. The council's position regarding sovereignty remained firm, and the Dehorners continued to press for government intervention. Authorities in Ottawa unilaterally reversed themselves and in 1924 ordered an (all-male) election. This action officially ended the centuries-old authority of the Iroquois Confederation, although, like so many other banned activities, the traditional council continued to meet secretly and would reassert its authority in the decades to come.

The reform movement in the United States in the 1920s differed in at least one important respect from that of the late nineteenth century. Where the earlier reformers had operated from the fundamental assumption that the acquisition of private property would be the salvation of the Indian, the later reformers focused on the problems of daily life within the native communities and tried to alleviate them. Beginning in the late 1910s, these reformers undertook a number of studies. Among their last and most important reports was *The Problem of Indian Administration*, called the Meriam Report, which was issued in 1928.

The Meriam Report clearly condemned virtually every aspect of Indian policy over the previous fifty years. Native schools had completely failed to prepare children to participate in any meaningful way in the mainstream of American life. The schools had played a role in the destruction of the old culture, but they had provided nothing substantial in its place, a situation that encouraged a state of dependence. Native Americans had lost more than 90 million acres of land during the period; most of the approximately 48 million acres that remained in their hands was unproductive. Landlessness was also a major problem. Nearly half of those who lived on reservations divided into individual allotments owned no land at all. As the authors of the Meriam Report viewed the situation, the attempts to resolve the "Indian problem" had been a complete failure. Policies that had been conceived to transform the native peoples into individual property owners and assimilated citizens—education, land allotments, and others—had been destructive of their culture and society and had driven most into a state of poverty, economic dependence, and social alienation.

The Meriam Report did not reject assimilation as an ultimate goal, although it proposed (in condescending terms) toleration of a reasonably healthy native society "in the presence of…civilization." In fact, the report did not advocate a change in the basic structure of the management of Indian affairs, only a shift in focus from an apparent obsession with private property to concentration on education and increased funding for efficiently run programs. Perhaps its greatest importance lay in its assertion that Native Americans could succeed through their own intelligence and resources and that controls and policies imposed from above—all subject to approval by the Secretary of the Interior—were ultimately counterproductive.

The Meriam Report and other reports on irrigation, justice, and farming and ranching provided policymakers with a wealth of new information about native communities and the record of past federal policies. Following the publication of these studies, members of Congress visited reservations personally and conducted their own hearings on related affairs. Although disinclined to accept the idea that Native Americans could best control their own affairs through direct self-government, the legislators were generally shocked at the degree to which they lacked political representation. By the early 1930s, a clear consensus had emerged for a radical reform of the way the United States conducted its relations with its native population.

The election in 1932 of Franklin Delano Roosevelt to the presidency set the stage for what became known as the "Indian New Deal." In 1933 Roosevelt appointed John Collier, perhaps the most visible pro-Indian reformer of the period, to the post of Commissioner of Indian Affairs. His superior, and the man who recommended him for the job, was Secretary of the Interior Harold Ickes, himself a well-known reformer and a member of the AIDA. Collier immediately used his power to issue a number of orders implementing his vision of reform. He moved, for instance, to guarantee respect for native religion and cultural traditions; one manifestation of this was his refusal to force native children in government schools to attend Christian religious services. He also canceled a great portion of the Indian debt owed to the federal government.

Collier succeeded in persuading Congress to carry out additional reforms. He oversaw the augmentation of monetary compensation to the Puebloans under the 1924 Pueblo Lands Act. The Indian Arts and Crafts Act of 1935 encouraged the marketing and production of Indian crafts, both as a way to help Native Americans economically and as an acknowledgement of their positive contribution to American culture. Collier was also responsible for passage of the landmark Johnson-O'Malley (JOM) Act of 1934, which gave the federal government authority to contract with states for educational, medical, agricultural, and social welfare services for Native Americans. A subsequent amendment to the act (1936) allowed other entities including the tribes themselves to contract directly with the government. Problems inherent in the act and in its administration included its focus on reservation (as opposed to non-reservation) Indians, limitations on parental contributions and responsibility, and a complicated funding formula that allowed some of the states to benefit far more than others.

On balance, however, the Johnson-O'Malley Act was constructive and important legislation that facilitated entry into public schools for many native children and provided a mechanism by which numerous supplemental and enrichment programs were put into effect. Received at first without enthusiasm by the native community, the program won support and influence as parents were given a greater voice. Over time, the act stimulated a powerful tribal interest in education. Interestingly, even as native support increased, the Bureau of Indian Affairs itself remained unenthusiastic, funding Johnson-O'Malley programs at relatively low levels and trying without success to eliminate them altogether in 1986.

The main component of the "Indian New Deal" was the (Wheeler-Howard) Indian Reorganization Act (IRA) of 1934. This was the most important Native American legislation of the twentieth century. It is no surprise that it was controversial. In almost a mirror image of the great New Deal debate—did Roosevelt save or destroy American capitalism?—many people praised the IRA for ending land allotment and heralding an era of native self-government, while its critics damned it for co-opting that very self-government and forcing the tribes to remake themselves in the image of the cultural majority.

Collier's initial plan was grandiose. Most remarkably, he proposed the creation of new authorities and structures to facilitate tribal self-government. These included the right to levy taxes and the creation of tribal courts with jurisdiction over tribal laws. He also called upon Congress to demonstrate officially its respect for the value of native culture, in part through the funding of educational programs in this area. A third component of the bill halted the process of land allotment and returned available "surplus" land to Native American ownership. Other land-related provisions called upon the government to fund the reacquisition of tribal land and to restrict grazing and forestry activities on it. Finally, Collier hoped to persuade Congress to create a special court system with procedures strongly influenced by "Indian tradition" that would have initial jurisdiction over those who organized under the provisions of the IRA.

Congress accepted some of these proposals and rejected others. The final version of the IRA halted land allotment and provided procedures for the establishment of tribal constitutions and corporations. The bill had a provision that allowed tribes to accept or reject the IRA as it applied to them. The act also created a revolving loan fund and a significant educational loan program, and it granted preference for BIA employment to Native Americans. Finally, in one of its most controversial provisions, the bill called for various conservation measures, including a dramatic stock-reduction program. The native peoples of Oklahoma and native Alaskans were excluded from some of the bill's provisions, although these restrictions were subsequently reduced in part. Furthermore, while the plan to return unallotted surpluses to the tribal governments survived initial Congressional scrutiny, it was ultimately removed as a result of pressure from Plains tribes who feared the loss of their individual allotments.

For the first time, the tribes could decide for themselves whether to accept or to reject important federal legislation that applied directly to them. However, the power to make this decision was not as broad as it appeared, because the government exerted multiple pressures designed to influence voting in favor of the proposal. Since Collier knew that many traditional Indians would not vote in any election called by the government of the United States, he fashioned the law so that IRA provisions would automatically take effect unless tribes voted *against* them. Thus the deck was clearly stacked in favor of acceptance, especially given the fact that democratic government was still a new and not entirely welcome practice for many Native Americans. Although only some 39 percent of all those eligible voted for the IRA—the rest voted "No" or abstained—more than two-thirds of the 258 tribal entities that voted on the act agreed to reorganize. Ninety-two tribal entities wrote new constitutions, and seventy-two others created charters of incorporation.

Implementation of the process was extremely complicated. Among the Western Shoshoni, for example, there was a group that advocated a number of such political goals as the return of unoccupied lands. However, from the government's point of view, these Native Americans, who included the traditional Shoshoni chief Muchach Temoke, were not a recognizable tribal entity, since they were scattered on different reservations, or, more commonly, lived on no reservation at all. Few of them had an opportunity to vote on acceptance or rejection of the IRA. Some Western Shoshoni did propose to create a council called the Te-Moak Western Shoshoni, but the government in Washington rejected the proposed constitution on the grounds that the geographically dispersed Western Shoshoni did not constitute a legitimate tribe.

A compromise was eventually achieved with the creation of a Te-Moak Bands Tribe, which some communities joined, as well as a Western Shoshoni council. The council existed only on paper, however, the various colonies and reservations having declined to re-form as separate tribes, as mandated by the BIA. Instead, a "traditional council" convened periodically by the traditional leadership continued to link the various Western Shoshoni communities, but was prohibited from exercising specific political responsibilities.

It is important to note that, even with the creation of new tribal governments, the IRA actually increased the level of government supervision over tribes. The authority of BIA superintendents remained strong, and corruption still made daily life even more miserable than it might otherwise have been for many. Partly because of government heavy-handedness in influencing the referenda, the new councils and business committees, while achieving some economic, political, and social successes, were often resisted by more traditional members. This antipathy continued to fester for decades.

Though the enactment of the IRA introduced many important reforms, the "Indian New Deal" extended even further. Through various New Deal programs, Collier found ways to advance native interests, to affirm their cultures, and to strengthen tribal identity: Reservation infrastructures were improved and new facilities were constructed; more than one million acres were added to tribal lands; emergency employment funds were channeled to reservation natives; and federal sponsorship was provided for their arts and crafts programs, making it easier for schools to teach native customs and traditions as part of their curricula.

Reform groups were also active in Canada during the 1930s. Métis living on the Great Plains, for instance, had been pressing for the resolution of land claims at least since their rebellion in the 1880s. Denied access to capital, and victimized by counterproductive government land policies, between 12,000 and 75,000 Métis were largely landless and destitute in the 1920s. A Royal commission was established in 1934 to investigate the situation and to make recommendations to remedy it. Responding to the commission's report, the government agreed to create farm colonies on good land with access to water, and to open individual trapping areas in the North. Both of these could be enlarged and were to be administered solely by the government. Unlike most legislation before or since, the original Métis Population Betterment Act of 1938 was put together in close consultation with the Métis themselves.

Like all government and most non-government programs, the IRA and associated reforms achieved mixed results. The land reforms were generally successful. Simply ending the policy of land allotment was a major step forward. Allotment had been disastrous for Native Americans, and its termination marked a real beginning of tribal rebirth. By 1950 tribal land had increased by millions of acres. After 1950, however, the tribes lost to government appropriation more than three times the acreage they had gained under IRA land-acquisition programs. Collier encountered significant resistance from native peoples themselves, both from those who favored the eradication of distinct native cultures and full integration into mainstream society and from those who objected strenuously to various programs like those requiring stock reductions.

Of all the IRA programs, stock reductions were certainly the most controversial. This policy cost Collier the support of the Navajo people and contributed to the derailment of Navajo self-government in the 1930s as well. In 1933 the Navajo already had an effective tribal government, and their authorities had begun to deal with erosion and overgrazing, which they had recognized as problems since the end of the nineteenth century. The first voluntary stock-reduction program went into effect in 1926. Sheep, goats, and horses, however, were an important source of wealth to the Navajo. Furthermore, sheep were used for various ceremonial purposes. As much as they may have agreed that overgrazing was a problem, the Navajo were loathe to part with their animals.

The government stepped in and enforced a stock-reduction program on its own terms. In theory, the Navajo were to be compensated by receiving more land, water, schools, and jobs, but Collier was unable to compel Congress to honor many of these promises. Since the government could not afford to ship the livestock to market, the animals were simply shot and left to rot. The tribal government, in an effort to carve out a moderate position, supported stock reduction while attempting to mitigate its effects, but their position was seen by many Navajo as treasonous. Many stock owners simply refused to co-operate with the programs. Navajo anger at this program led directly to their rejection of the IRA. Meanwhile, and perhaps in retaliation, the government unilaterally reorganized the tribal government. The livestock of other Southwestern tribes, including the White Mountain Apache, Tohono O'Odham (Papago), and Hopi, was also reduced.

IRA critics grew in number and strength as the 1930s drew to a close. These critics included not only conservative non-natives but various disaffected natives. Within the native community, the assimilationist American Indian Federation (AIF), a group consisting mainly of Oklahoma tribes, led the anti-IRA campaign. The AIF flirted with and was partly used by such extreme right-wing groups as the American Nazi Party. By around 1940, having failed to achieve its goals of abolishing the BIA, the AIF splintered and lost any effectiveness it may have had. However, one of its key ideas—termination—was, in fact, attempted in the 1950s, with predictably disastrous consequences for the tribes it affected.

By the beginning of World War II, Collier's conservative opponents had gained (or regained) political power and New Deal reform had effectively ended. Collier remained commissioner until 1945. In the context of overall U.S. Indian policy, the

"Indian New Deal" may be seen as a forward-looking and successful set of policies. With its focus on tribal councils, it laid the groundwork for the official acceptance a generation later of Indian self-determination. Moreover, it helped Native Americans to retain and even increase the tribal land so crucial to their identity and to their plans for economic development. Many tribal economies improved as well, some, such as those based on livestock, quite dramatically. Alaska fishing co-operatives and co-operative businesses in other states were established as a result of hard work by tribes who were given access to federal loans.

Conversely, the period may also be seen as the consolidation or institutionalization of a decision-making structure imposed from without, a structure antithetical to native traditions and prone to be supportive of government objectives. In fact, many tribes possessed effective governing structures long before the IRA and had no use for the new tribal councils. The IRA also forced many groups to become "tribes" in the political sense when they had never been specifically tribal in the past. Far from making tribes economically self-sufficient, IRA policies can also be seen as having bound them closer to exploitation by corporations and to have led directly to future economic abuses and political confrontations.

As was the case for so many others in the United States, World War II marked a turning point for Native Americans. For the first time, reservation natives were exposed on a relatively large scale—perhaps as many as 100,000 people—to the world at large, including both native peoples from outside (or other parts of) their communities and non-natives. Elders wondered uneasily how the war would change the men and women who left the reservations by the tens of thousands to work in war industries, not to mention how it would change those who had left to enlist in the armed services. Indeed, World War II caused many of the soldiers to question their identity as Native Americans, often for the first time. Their answers would reshape themselves and the world of their people.

Indian reservations have changed in important ways since the prewar era. It is difficult today to appreciate the extent to which Native Americans were virtual prisoners on their reservations until World War II. Before the war, some children had left the reservations to attend boarding schools, but most returned to live out their lives at home. Even the exodus of men who had left the reservation to serve in World War I had occurred on a much smaller scale. Apart from the experience of war, three different experiences influenced Indian combatants in World War II: exposure to the world at large, contact with non-natives, and contact with other Native Americans.

Within the insular world of the reservation, people might live their entire lives without meeting, much less talking with, a non-native. Natives and non-natives were suddenly thrust into intimate contact in the armed services. Unlike African American soldiers, Native Americans did not serve in segregated units.

Interracial contact bred suspicion, but also provided opportunities for respect and understanding. Regardless of their rank, natives were invariably called "chief" by their non-native peers, a word intended and taken as a slur. After all, some of the parents and grandparents of these soldiers had faced each other as enemies on other battlefields, and in racially intolerant America Indians were generally held in low regard by non-natives.

As happens in times of war, however, barriers weakened with proximity, and in their place grew a measure of interracial awareness and even respect. Native Americans were considered good soldiers, good people to be around in a difficult situation. This attitude may have arisen from stereotypes of them as warriors, but, in fact, many did come from cultures with important warrior traditions and sought to distinguish themselves in that very way. It was also true that even people without such a tradition volunteered for service in great numbers in order to demonstrate both bravery and loyalty.

One U.S. Marine in particular—Ira Hayes, a Pima from Arizona—for better and for worse gained a place as both an American hero and an American icon. In February 1945, he landed on Iwo Jima and took part in the attack on Mount Suribachi. An Associated Press photographer captured the feat of six Americans raising the flag under heavy fire. Hayes was one of those soldiers. The photograph became one of the most famous of all wartime images. While all of the soldiers received national attention, Hayes was singled out because he was an Indian. For many Americans the photograph was a powerful image of reconciliation and of absolution for the Indian wars. The image served as a symbol of unity in the face of a common enemy. Many natives saw Hayes as a genuine hero and as a symbol of success in the non-native world. Hayes tried for years to live up to this uninvited celebrity. Feeling deeply unworthy, however, and faced upon his return with having to readjust to anti-Indian prejudice and economic discrimination, he died in 1955 of alcoholism and exposure. He was buried with full military honors at Arlington National Cemetery.

There were many other Native American heroes as well. Among them were the so-called Code Talkers, a special communications unit composed mainly of Navajo. This group worked behind enemy lines using a code based on the Navajo language that the Japanese were never able to decipher. The Code Talkers—approximately 400 of them—reported on troop movements and other enemy activities and helped to coordinate U.S. military actions. They played a key role in the Pacific theater, winning high praise for their deeds. The actions of these U.S. Marines, and those of countless other Native American soldiers, demonstrated that they could perform their military duties as well as anyone in the armed forces.

Many native peoples who had been largely unaware of life outside the reservations found travel to other parts of the country and abroad to be both frightening and liberating. Just to see other parts of the world and to talk to people with experiences vastly different from their own was revealing. Soldiers and defense-industry workers also enjoyed steady incomes, something few reservation Indians could claim. An income meant consumer goods, the ability to send money back home, and a taste of the "white man's world." Furthermore, the easing of interracial suspicion and hostility worked both ways. Many natives who had rejected non-native society began to re-evaluate their ideas. They began urging friends and relatives back home to prepare for life outside the reservation. Thousands were already prepared: They married non-natives and declined to return to reservation life after the war. Among those who did return home, many men (the mainly female group of defense workers was ineligible) took advantage of the GI Bill to obtain higher education. Veterans soon assumed many positions of leadership within their communities.

The picture of Native American experience in World War II as one of liberation from reservation life, while true to a considerable degree, is incomplete and one-sided. For one thing, it was reservation life, or, more precisely, their tribal identity that gave many soldiers and workers the courage and determination to succeed in the radically different wartime activities. Native American servicemen and defense workers encountered many problems as well. Both faced severe discrimination. Pay increases and promotions came less often than they did to non-natives. As mentioned, racial slurs were a way of life. Furthermore, although native men and women learned valuable skills during the war, many returned to reservations where those skills were not in demand. Of those who did not return, some were able to find work in cities (many with the help of education acquired through the GI Bill), but, as tens of thousands of Native Americans were soon to discover, urban life came with its own set of problems, among them feelings of alienation, dislocation, and depression.

These were not the only problems that were faced by Native Americans during the war. Despite the reforms of the previous decade, the federal government found reasons to appropriate even more native land, this time in the name of the war effort. Internment camps were located on land belonging to the Colorado River tribes. The government also took part of the Passamaquoddy Reservation for use as a POW camp and later sold the land to non-natives. In Alaska, where the Cold War was to affect the lives of many native peoples, the Unangan (an Aleut people) were evacuated from their villages following Japanese attacks on the Aleutian Islands. Placed in internment camps for the duration of the war, the Unangan suffered from disease and many died. When the survivors were allowed to return to their villages after the war, they found their homes vandalized or destroyed by members of the U.S. military. For many Unangan, there was nothing left. Their population declined precipitously, and their culture has yet to recover fully.

The wartime experiences of Canadian natives, both at home and abroad, were equally profound. The Alaska Highway was built in the early 1940s, opening up the region on an even larger scale than had the gold rush two generations earlier. Along with the highway came branch roads, airstrips, and various government installations. Whole towns sprang up almost overnight, with their attendant economies, job opportunities, and temptations. The influx of non-natives and the expansion of a cash economy were both helpful and unsettling. Traditional practices of sharing broke down, while increasing social stratification created new or heightened existing conflicts. Some native men volunteered for the war and returned with experiences similar to their brothers in the United States; some saw the injustice of their situation and for the first time vowed to fight it; others were more determined than ever to assimilate if possible. The construction of the Distant Early Warning (DEW) Line, a Cold War development, would soon bring to the region an even greater non-native presence. By the end of World War II most of the Far North had been permanently removed from the fur-trade era and pushed into the modern world.

Just as it did for many non-natives, the crucible of war brought natives from different backgrounds and regions together and provided the context for camaraderie and enduring friendships. Comparing notes with others who shared many of their experiences, Native Americans were able to assess their situations, both as individuals and as members of tribes and a race. Intertribal suspicions and rivalries going far back in time were dissected and broken down, some for the first time. In the course of countless discussions about native history, ideas, beliefs, identity, and their roles in contemporary society, many Native Americans developed the foundation for the pan-Indian political, social, and cultural activities that were to mark the postwar period. When they returned home, many native veterans maintained and expanded their contacts with other natives. Many acquired automobiles for the first time and used them to travel to meetings within their own communities or elsewhere.

One tangible result of these expanding contacts was the founding in 1944 of the National Congress of American Indians (NCAI). The NCAI was the first organization created by native peoples of many tribes (more than fifty at the outset) to work on issues of national import in the United States. This was a significant development: A new generation, educated and grounded in World War II experiences, determined to function independently and to cease relying on well-meaning, non-native organizations. Activists, lobbyists, and organizers, the members of the NCAI were grounded as well in the Indian New Deal. The group's constitution and bylaws were deeply influenced by those of the IRA tribal councils, and among its initial leaders were native bureaucrats and government officials, including organizers D'Arcy McNickle and Vine Deloria, Jr., and the first president, Napoleon Johnson.

Reflecting its liberal origins, the NCAI advocated two primary goals: preservation of cultures and the extension of full civil rights to Indians. These two goals were not necessarily incompatible, although the group's critics consistently failed to understand how they could coexist. For instance, the NCAI supported the creation of the Indian Claims Commission (see below), but it did so out of a desire to champion Native American treaty rights and sovereignty. Another of the group's initial projects was to obtain state voting rights for natives in Arizona and New Mexico. Throughout its early years it worked effectively with the power structure in Washington, generally supporting mainstream, integrationist legislation, and built a reputation as the leading Indian organization.

Meanwhile, the government began the postwar period with an Indian policy far removed from that of the previous decade. That is, while the ultimate goal—assimilation—remained largely unchanged, the methods were radically different. In place of a New Deal affirmation of government responsibility and respect for Indian culture, legislators called not only for an abdication of government treaty responsibilities, but for the elimination of the tribes themselves. This new set of policies became known as termination. It was implemented fully for only a handful of tribes, but in these cases the tribes were almost destroyed. It would take another swing of the pendulum, this time in the 1960s, to reverse this disastrous course.

The idea and practice of termination had always been present in intercultural relations. Even before there was an official government policy, or a federal government for that matter, non-natives did everything in their power to remove native peoples from their lands. Non-natives had negotiated with the natives when useful, and had made treaties with them when necessary, but they had also broken the treaties regularly. In the twentieth century alone, official Indian policy began with Dawes Era "reformers" pushing for total assimilation and the abolition of the Office of Indian Affairs. Soon, however, policies were applied to foster tighter and more restrictive government control. By the 1920s, and especially with the Indian New Deal, the emphasis was again on safeguarding tribal interests and respect for native culture.

Republicans regained control of Congress in the postwar era and took the White House again in 1952. The country was preparing to enter a period of conformity, political conservatism, reaction, and strict anti-communism. Indians, with their focus on communal land ownership, their desire for sovereignty, and their "difference" from "mainstream" Americans at least appeared to challenge the climate of the time. As "nations within," to use the title of a book by Vine Deloria, Jr., natives were at best viewed suspiciously by politicians intolerant of dissent and pluralism. Furthermore, unlike other federal agencies, the BIA did not have the support of a well-developed or powerful constituency that could protect it from efforts to undo its work. Republicans couched their termination plans in the language of conservative ideology: They were going to "free" native peoples from the stifling effects of "big government."

Other social factors made themselves felt as well. Many Indians newly returned from the war, and anxious to join the consumer culture, supported the general idea of termination. There was pressure as well from the private sector which, riding the wave of economic recovery, was anxious to exploit native lands for their own gain. Finally, some misguided liberals supported the policy as a civil-rights issue, viewing termination as an opportunity to "integrate" Native Americans into American society. In 1949 a special commission formally recommended the abolition of all federal Indian programs.

The opening salvo was the creation in 1946 of the Indian Claims Commission (ICC). While some native supporters saw the new claims court as a vehicle for their people to receive justice after years of land theft, its true purpose was to resolve land titles once and for all so the government could proceed with termination. Almost 400 treaties had been concluded between the United States and native nations from 1783 to 1871, when the United States effectively ceased making such agreements. In that time, the tribes had ceded roughly two billion acres of land, for which they had generally been paid, if at all, an unconscionably low price. Beginning in 1881, when the Choctaw gained formal standing in the Court of Claims, many tribes had sued the government for the return of land, or for monetary compensation, or for both. By the 1940s, the courts were clogged with such cases. The Indian Claims Commission acted as a court to hear them.

Originally intended to sit for only ten years, the ICC heard almost 300 claims (it dismissed around 200 others) and awarded approximately one billion dollars before disbanding in 1978. By that time, termination had come and gone. The tribes faced countless obstacles on their way to successful resolution of an ICC claim: For instance, they had to establish the standing as well as the basis of the claim—which may have had its origins centuries before—and to provide documentation for it. They had to acquire the proper government records, pay extensive legal and other professional fees, settle any outstanding relevant issues with nearby tribes, await government accounting, surveying, and other such determinations, and overcome a pervasive anti-Indian bias on the part of the commission.

Although many tribes pressed for the return of land rather than compensation, they invariably received money. The few cases of tribes that reacquired appropriated land, such as Taos Pueblo's Blue Lake, were not achieved before the ICC, but rather through the courts or by acts of Congress. Furthermore, awards were made on the basis of the land's worth at the time of its loss, not on the basis of its current valuation. This policy cost tribes tens of millions of dollars. Nevertheless, the funds received were almost always much needed and were generally put to good use. Furthermore, the claims process served as an important vehicle for native legal training and practice. By the end of the decade, Native Americans felt themselves under assault from both the federal government and the generally conservative mood within the United States.

# A Time of Remembrance, A Time of Action

The decade of the 1950s saw the last major victories for the hard-core assimilationists as well as for those non-natives who coveted Indian land. In the following two decades, events occurred that even the next hard swing to the right—the Reagan Interior Department under James Watt ("Indian reservations prove the failure of socialism")—could not erase. Already, however, in the midst of termination, natives joined by non-native social and political activists were marshaling their energies for the titanic struggles of the 1960s and 1970s.

Thanks mainly to improvements in health care and nutrition and a consequently higher birth rate, the Native American population in the United States had increased from about 237,000 in 1900 to 358,000 at mid-century. In Canada, for similar reasons, Indian and Inuit populations that had declined from an estimated 200,000 at the onset of European contact have recovered during the second half of the twentieth century. Some 27,000 Inuit inhabit the Far North at this writing, while those legally defined as status-Indians—some 542 bands—occupy more than 2,250 reserves.

Many native Canadians enlisted in the armed services in World War II. Unlike the Indians of the United States, however, they were not confronted with the issue of termination when they returned. In the period immediately following the war, Indian policy in Canada centered on a major revision of the Indian Act. The Canadian government adopted the fresh approach of consulting its native population, and by 1951 the revised act had been made law. Its provisions set forth fundamental changes in policy. The ministerial role in determining tribal policies was greatly reduced, although a veto power was retained, and opportunities for tribal self-government were expanded significantly.

In more specific terms, bands were permitted to incorporate as municipalities and to determine their own by-laws. Native men and women could cast secret ballots for the election of tribal officers. Within two years more than 250 bands had held or scheduled elections. They obtained new authority over their own funds, including the right to draw on them to finance the legal costs of land-claims litigation. The bands were also granted more authority to manage their reserve lands. Laws banning native cultural practices such as the potlatch and certain dances were repealed; compulsory enfranchisement was ended; and restrictions on political organizing were relaxed. Natives were also integrated into provincial programs, particularly those relating to education and child welfare. It is important to note, however, that the 1951 revisions stopped well short of permitting full self-government, a goal of most, if not all, Canadian First Nations. Furthermore, the Inuit were specifically excluded from the Indian Act at this time.

Indian policy took a different direction in the United States. In 1947 Congress was presented with a plan that would terminate federal responsibility for all tribes. Three of the plan's main points were: Tribes would be removed from federal responsibility in a multi-tiered process

*Opposite: An Inuit child carries a dogsled pup on a ramble through her family's summer camp.*

applied according to the readiness of given tribes for termination; termination should be subject to both tribal and state consent; and new tribal assets would remain tax-free for a number of years in order to spare the tribes undue financial stress. These recommendations, which emphasized self-government and minimized risk, offered a plausible formula for success.

However, with the land-claims process underway and the election of a Republican president in 1952, Congressional leaders were impatient, so much so that for the first time in history the House and Senate Indian Affairs Subcommittees sat in joint session to avoid subsequent conferences where bills might be amended or delayed. The legislators simply ignored the recommendations of earlier studies and advanced to their main Indian-affairs objective: the removal of as many tribes as possible, as fast as possible, from federal responsibility through the unilateral abrogation of treaties. The process was overseen by Commissioner of Indian Affairs Dillon Myer, who had recently been in charge of Japanese internment camps.

Public Law 280, passed in 1953, gave the states complete jurisdiction over reservations in California, Minnesota, Nebraska, Oregon, and Wisconsin. The law also authorized any other state to assume such powers without native consent. House Concurrent Resolution 108, also passed in 1953, was a policy statement that set forth the objectives of eliminating the BIA and terminating separate native status. In an early incarnation of 1990s-style "devolution," states were given primary responsibility—but not the funds to pay for it—for native education and other aspects of native life. Laws were also amended to make it easier to sell or lease native land to non-natives, although at least nominal consent was required in this process. Another strategy proposed to advance the program of termination was a government project to offer strong incentives to reservation Indians to leave their land and relocate to cities.

By 1954 Congress had passed six termination proposals. The first natives to be terminated were Southern Paiute bands from Utah. They agreed to termination in exchange for federal recognition of tribal marriages, but the final bill spoke only of the removal of federal services. The Paiute bands were far from ready to survive on their own. The new private trustee proved more restrictive than had the federal government, and they now had no recourse to federal agencies. By 1962 Congress had terminated 109 tribes and bands, about 3 percent of all federally recognized tribal entities. Ninety percent of these were small communities in California and western Oregon.

Many members of the remaining tribes, such as Oklahoma's Ottawa, Peoria, and Wyandotte, supported termination. The Alabama-Coushatta of Texas were told that the government would no longer permit timber harvesting on their lands if the tribe did not agree to termination. Without consulting state authorities, much less obtaining their agreement, Congress passed a bill terminating the tribe and making it a ward of Texas. Mere chance, or the intercession of powerful politicians and interest

groups, spared other tribes this kind of treatment. A group of North Dakota Ojibwa was slated for mass removal to a city until the state notified the federal government that it had no intention to fund such services as health care or education for the tribe.

The policy of termination has become synonymous with two tribes in particular: the Klamath of Oregon and the Menominee of Wisconsin. Some Klamath actually supported termination. The tribe was already relatively well assimilated; all of its members spoke English, and its tribal council long predated the IRA. Members were already receiving significant private incomes from shares of revenues generated by leasing timber rights to non-native companies. After 1945 a group of tribal politicians, most of whom were living off the reservation, vigorously promoted terminating the Klamath. They were willing to exchange native lands, which had long been coveted by non-natives, for the extra money they would receive when the reservation was liquidated. This faction was strongly encouraged by the federal government, which withheld a $2.6 million land-claims award until the more traditionalist leaders on the reservation, who opposed termination vigorously, yielded to the demands of the tribal politicians who were determined to liquidate reservation land.

Congress passed the Klamath Termination Act in 1954. The law terminated federal trusteeship and offered tribal members two choices: They could separate from the tribe and receive an individual share of tribal assets, or they could remain with the tribe and place their share of unsold tribal assets into a government trust. Subsequent amendments to the law permitted private buyers to purchase the tribe's timber tracts if they would manage them on a sustainable basis (the original bill had called for clear-cutting the forests). Other parts of the former reservation would be converted into a national forest and wildlife refuge. In 1958, 77 percent of the Klamath voted to withdraw from the tribe. Each received an individual payment of $43,000, the payments financed by the sale of most of their former reservation.

Ironically, but not surprisingly given the history of government policy, the terminated Klamath did not achieve self-sufficiency. The government found only 15 percent of the Klamath "competent" to manage their own affairs; these few remained on the remnants of their former reservation alongside newly arrived non-natives. As with the Southern Paiute, far from achieving control over their own resources, the majority of the Klamath simply moved from federal to private trusteeship. Their affairs were placed under the management of the U.S. National Bank. In 1974, when the remaining members also withdrew from the tribe, the rest of the reservation was sold. In 1986 the Klamath became federally recognized again.

The Menominee entered the termination period as one of the most self-sufficient tribes in the United States. Their thriving lumber industry and paper mill generated many jobs. The tribe had also accumulated millions of dollars in cash reserves. This was in part the result of compensation paid to them after a government decision to authorize the clear-cutting of reservation timber lands, thus depriving the Menominee of future income that would have been available to them had the forest been managed on a sustainable-yield basis. Seeking to block the tribe from spending the money that had been awarded to them as compensation, the senator who chaired the House and Senate Indian Affairs Joint Subcommittee misled tribal representatives, declaring that they would have to accept termination in exchange for release of the funds. Only 8 percent of the tribe agreed, but this was enough for Congress.

According to the termination plan, the Menominee formed a corporation to operate and manage the paper mill. Each tribal member was given a bond and 100 shares of stock. The tribe also assumed responsibility for funding the social-service programs previously paid for by the federal government. Within a few years after the Menominee Termination Act was signed in 1954, termination-related expenses had drained nearly all of the tribe's cash reserves. Financial crisis forced the closing of the tribal hospital. Infant mortality and the number of tuberculosis cases rose sharply. Shares in the corporation soon passed out of native hands as tribal members used them as loan collateral. Termination also harmed the quality of tribal leadership. As intratribal tensions increased, many of the better educated younger generation, anxious about the future, left the reservation, depriving the Menominee of needed leaders.

When the tribe's termination officially took effect in 1961, the former reservation became a new county in Wisconsin. Social and economic indicators immediately rated the county's living standard among the lowest in the state. The county's tax base could not begin to pay for needed government services, nor could the corporation raise enough money to qualify for federal grants. Confronting imminent collapse, the corporation bowed to the inevitable and began selling off prime waterfront lots to non-natives for development. This action not only fragmented the remaining land of the Menominee, but also raised the possibility that non-natives who were establishing residence in increasing numbers would soon control the county politically.

As a component of the program of termination, Congress in 1956 passed Public Law 959, the "Relocation Act." This law provided funds to underwrite the expenses of natives willing to relocate to a number of "approved" urban centers. The law also provided additional funds for job training. Within two years, 1957–59, approximately 35,000 Native Americans left their reservations. Of course, not all of these people moved because of this government program: Urbanization was a national phenomenon at the time. Government support merely encouraged the moving trend among native peoples and served as another way to undermine the health and vitality of reservations. Furthermore, in order to pay for this program, the government cut back sharply on spending for non-terminated tribes. Social indicators on the reservations soon revealed increased health problems, reduced educational services, rising unemployment, and a decline in per capita income.

One of the ultimate paradoxes of termination was that, while many natives longed for self-government and self-sufficiency, most were far from being able to realize these goals in the 1950s. Although they did indeed wish to be free from government control, at the same time, by virtue of the treaties signed by the United States and all that the Indian groups had given up, they had both a legal and a moral claim to governmental assistance. The tribes reserved the right to surrender their claims to that assistance, if at all, when and how they themselves determined. During the 1950s, tribes were faced with the very real prospect of having this support withdrawn. Although those directly affected by termination were relatively few in number, their fate—the loss of tribal identity, the loss of land, sharply worsening health conditions, fewer educational opportunities, growing hunger, despair, and hopelessness—frightened tribes throughout the nation.

By the late 1950s, the policy of termination was under serious general attack. Some tribes, such as the Blackfoot of Montana and the Oglala Lakota, physically resisted termination by occupying tribal buildings, harassing BIA personnel, and other such methods. These actions gravely disturbed the Commissioner of Indian Affairs. In its own manifestation of the politically repressive mood of the 1950s, the bureau proposed and almost obtained a law that would have permitted the summary arrest without warrant of natives who violated BIA regulations.

The growing organized opposition was led by the National Congress of American Indians (NCAI) and the Association of American Indian Affairs (AAIA). Socially aware church groups began to question the morality of termination. State and local government officials began to realize that the benefits of taxing native land did not outweigh the costs of providing services that had formerly been the responsibility of the federal government. When Republicans lost their legislative majorities, even members of Congress decried the policy as inimical to native rights. By 1958, official enthusiasm for the policy began to wane, although it would not be reversed completely until 1970.

In the meantime, native society had entered a period of fundamental change, due more to its internal dynamics than to the pressures brought to bear by the policy of termination. In addition to native opposition to termination, many factors—urbanization, increased mobility, the spirit of pan-Indian cooperation, a growing freedom of movement among non-natives, increased levels of education among many Native Americans in part as a result of the GI Bill, the inspiration of the civil-rights movement, as well as the general influence of the nascent American youth culture—had combined by the early 1960s to lead to an era of Native American political activism.

All such movements may be traced, conveniently if somewhat simplistically, to a single defining event. For the new generation of Native American activists, this pivotal event was the week-long American Indian Chicago Conference (AICC), held at the University of Chicago in June 1961. Preceded by a number of regional conferences, the AICC was attended by nearly 500 Native Americans from ninety different communities, with scholars and government officials also in attendance. Anthropologist Sol Tax and his assistant Nancy Lurie organized the meeting as part of a project to update the 1928 Meriam Report. One of Tax's most important contributions to the project was his insistence that Native Americans should have a central role in the analysis and production of any comprehensive report to be issued about the state of Native America.

Having obtained an initial foundation grant to fund the project, Tax turned to the National Congress of American Indians (NCAI) for additional support. This organization, still attempting to battle termination as well as a number of water projects that threatened native lands, gladly lent its assistance with the stipulation that all tribes, including those who were not officially recognized, be allowed to participate in the planned conference. This condition turned out to be fruitful and even visionary, because the involvement of unrecognized natives, formerly excluded from most such conferences, gave to many among them the support and encouragement that they needed to begin the process of seeking federal recognition for their communities.

And it was not only unrecognized natives who were inspired toward a greater degree of activism. By the end of the conference, its participants had drafted a *Declaration of Indian Purpose*. Among other items, this policy statement called for the end of termination, more economic development, more programs for education, better health care, protection of Indian water rights, and the abolition of several BIA area offices. The declaration also called upon the president to reconsider plans to build the Kinzua Dam, a project (ultimately carried out) that threatened to flood 9,000 acres of Seneca land at tremendous cost to the integrity of tribal land and culture. In August 1962, thirty-two delegates from the AICC met with President John F. Kennedy, Vice-President Lyndon B. Johnson, and other federal officials to present the declaration in person and to discuss federal Indian policy.

At the same time that delegates to the AICC were formulating their ideas, a group of uninvited guests arrived to work on an agenda of their own. This gathering of young, mainly college-educated, Native Americans was united by the idea that they should govern their own affairs by right of their existence as sovereign nations. Not only were they were able to insert these ideas into the *Declaration of Indian Purpose*, but the themes of sovereignty and self-government resting on the pillar of traditional native values was the principle upon which they formed a new organization. The National Indian Youth Council (NIYC), founded in Gallup, New Mexico, in August 1961, became the second national Indian organization in the United States.

The NCAI achieved an enhanced stature at the AICC and received the blessing of tribal elders present at that meeting. Focusing on the perceived need for young Native Americans to set the agenda and help define native issues in the coming years, the pan-Indian NCAI committed itself to providing leadership

to achieve this. Mel Thom, Clyde Warrior, and Shirley Hill Witt were among those who led the NCAI in its early days. The group soon became involved in the controversies of the period, among the most prominent of which was the issue of fishing rights in the Northwest. Taking its cue in part from the civil-rights movement, NCAI tactics included highly visible protests and civil disobedience as well as voter-registration drives and lobbying efforts before the United Nations. Although it never lost its primary focus on Indian issues, the NCAI quickly made common cause with the civil-rights movement, participating in "freedom rides," marches, and other movement activities.

The controversy over fishing rights in the Northwest and Columbia River Plateau dated from the original treaties with local tribes, which were concluded in 1855. Among other guarantees, natives were accorded the right to take fish from their "usual and accustomed places." We have seen in the last chapter how conflict between natives and non-natives over fishing had begun almost immediately and had developed into a critical problem. The fact that fishing remained an activity important to the subsistence of many native peoples underscored the seriousness of the situation. By the 1960s, however, decades of protest to state officials had achieved nothing.

In western Washington in 1964 the NCAI helped organize "fish-ins," highly visible actions in which natives fished in violation of local and state ordinances but in keeping with their treaty rights. The first fish-in took place along the Quillayute River in March of that year. When officials arrived to arrest the NCAI volunteers, local fishermen quickly replaced them. Unable to arrest hundreds of people for fishing, the state authorities retreated. Soon thousands of natives throughout the region adopted these tactics to build support and publicize their plight.

When the NCAI called a meeting in the Puget Sound area, representatives of fifty-six native nations from across the country attended to demonstrate their support. Non-native organizations and celebrities also publicly supported the efforts of the NCAI. The nations revived ancient first-salmon ceremonies to ground themselves in their own traditions and to derive strength from them. Despite increasingly violent attempts by non-native fishing interests to suppress the protests, the fish-ins continued throughout the decade, ending only in 1974 with a decisive court victory in favor of the natives.

Another shift in the political winds produced the election of a Democrat to the presidency in 1960. After the assassination in 1963 of President John F. Kennedy, his successor, former Vice-President Lyndon Johnson, inaugurated the "War on Poverty" that made infusions of federal funding available to a wide range of social programs. For many Native Americans who were suffering disproportionately from poverty, this initiative was good news. Indeed, despite the general economic boom of the 1950s, the situation of Native Americans had deteriorated. In the west, tribal land had become so divided by inheritance that ranching was no longer a possible subsistence activity. Farming also declined, with native farmers lacking skills and strangled for credit. Leasing provided a meager income for some, but fragmented land that might otherwise have been used to sustain subsistence economies or for more effective income-producing activities. Government controls and paternalistic policies largely prevented tribal governments from pursuing plans for economic development, and many tribal governments were wholly preoccupied with their efforts to block termination.

One of the cornerstones of the War on Poverty was the 1964 Economic Opportunity Act, under which the new Office of Economic Opportunity (OEO) was organized. With funding provided by the OEO, Community Action Agencies (CAA) led innovative local anti-poverty campaigns. The genius of the program, for Native Americans, was that it empowered tribes to act as CAAs. This was something for which the tribes had been waiting a long time: the possibility of taking local initiatives within the supportive context of legitimate government responsibility. The OEO soon oversaw the creation of programs for tribal employment and development, and the introduction of health and educational programs, including Head Start, Youth Development, and Home Enrichment. Other federal organizations including the Economic Development Administration (EDA) and the newly created Department of Housing and Urban Development (HUD) soon entered the picture and began funding tribal programs as well.

The new laws enabled tribes to bypass the traditional bureaucracy and instead to apply directly for program grants without having to go through the BIA. Native groups also formed such regional entities as the Eight Northern Indian Pueblos Council to plan, co-ordinate, and administer various local programs. With direct responsibility for administering their own programs and overseeing their own payrolls, Native Americans gained invaluable experience as planners and managers. Furthermore, the War on Indian Poverty did achieve significant success. Housing improved dramatically on many reservations, as did overall health and educational achievement.

Robert Bennett, an Oneida, became Commissioner of Indian Affairs in 1968. Bennett supported the OEO development efforts and vowed to bring the tribes into full partnership with the federal government in the making of policy. In an important 1968 speech on Native Americans, President Lyndon B. Johnson announced the creation of a new, well-funded, White House-based National Council on Indian Opportunity that was designed to work with the tribes to advance their economic development. Ironically and unfortunately, however, Native Americans themselves, still anxious and distrustful after the shock of the termination era, sometimes blocked this kind of effort, fearing that signs of independence would encourage the federal government to cast them adrift again. This attitude led to the cancellation of at least one important federal development program.

Legal gains accompanied economic progress in the 1960s. In 1968, after consideration and promptings from such groups as the NCAI, Congress passed the Indian Civil Rights Act. Designed to protect individual rights against actions by tribal governments, it also formally ended termination as a federal policy. Like the Bill of Rights, upon which it was based, the ICRA attempted to strike a balance between individuals and the government, or the tribal governments. It guaranteed equal protection under and due process of the law, as well as the right to counsel. Enforcement was limited to the right of habeas corpus in federal courts, and state jurisdiction over reservations was curtailed. Furthermore, tribes could not detain an individual for longer than six months nor impose a fine greater than $500 (both limits were increased in 1986). Unlike the Bill of Rights, the ICRA made allowances for certain unique aspects of tribal identity, like the existence at some pueblos of a "state" religion.

One unintended result of the Indian Civil Rights Act was the initiation of lawsuits against tribes. Prior to 1968 tribes had seldom been sued, largely because they were immune from suit under federal common law. The act contained no waiver of immunity. However, a non-native almost immediately sued the Navajo Tribal Council. In upholding his suit, a federal court reasoned that Congress had implicitly intended to override tribal sovereign immunity by creating a new federal civil right. Soon, tribes were literally inundated with lawsuits covering a broad range of issues. Courts consistently ruled that the tribes could be sued under the Civil Rights Act until a landmark Supreme Court decision in 1978 affirmed tribal immunity.

While appearing to strengthen native self-government, the Indian Civil Rights Act also had the effect of binding reservations even closer to federal institutions. Moreover, it bestowed upon the tribal court system an inordinate amount of power that in most cases was wholly alien to traditional native practices. In place of the informal traditional network of native customs and interpersonal relationships, the ICRA transformed the Indian court system into the ultimate arbiter between the individual and "the tribe." By removing itself from such traditional practices of reconciliation as the use of the sacred pipe, this judicial structure, at least in the eyes of some, even further weakened tribal governments and left them open to charges that they were merely tools of "colonialism."

Politics was not the only arena of dramatic change for Native Americans in the 1960s. The general cultural exuberance and the growth of ethnic pride that was manifested during the decade affected Native Americans in many ways. For generations, even centuries, prejudice and oppression had forced many Native Americans to reject or at least question the validity of their heritage. The government practice of forcing children to attend boarding schools disrupted the intergenerational transmission of cultural knowledge and skills. Beginning in the 1960s, a start was made toward reversing this process. Political activism was only one area that reflected a new pride in being an Indian.

Throughout the decade and beyond, Native Americans took decisive steps to halt and then reverse the slow destruction of their cultures. These trends were reflected in the popular culture of film and literature, working both to dissolve persistent stereotypes and to assert authentic native cultures.

The quality and degree of innovation in Native American arts have always ebbed and flowed, depending on the traditions and internal dynamics of the tribes themselves. The Navajo, now widely known for their silver jewelry, did not learn to work in this medium until the mid-nineteenth century. Many groups attained a cultural apogée in the late eighteenth and early nineteenth centuries. Native painters in the Southwest received critical attention after World War I, and a group of Kiowa artists introduced an exciting new style in the 1930s. Beginning at least as early as the 1931 Exposition of Indian Tribal Arts, and certainly reflected in the postwar appeal of so-called primitive and folk art, museums and scholars alike began to take an active interest in the aesthetics of native cultures. The creation of valuable artworks in many media increased and helped to stimulate demand.

Many forms of native art received attention during the postwar period, from basketry and pottery to wood carving and weaving. Many of the old artisans were still alive and were eager to teach a newly inspired younger generation; the young artists both absorbed and consciously departed from older traditions. Moreover, an increase in federal funding, coupled with a new power to shape budgets according to their own priorities, made it possible for native groups to support the arts as a means of enhancing ethnic pride and tribal identity. Programs of instruction in the traditional arts were soon established in schools and in other settings. The Institute of American Indian Arts, a government school in New Mexico, became a magnet for talented artists with a particular interest in contemporary themes. This phase of the native art revival peaked in the 1960s and 1970s. As a reflection of these activities, and with the purpose of encouraging them, the Institute of American Indian and Alaska Native Culture and Arts was formed in 1962 to promote the development and appreciation of Native American artistic traditions.

Indians, or pseudo-Indians, have had a presence in American film for nearly as long as the medium has existed. The images of Indians in films—savage, cunning, bloodthirsty, and exotic—were lifted directly from those found in the dime novels of the nineteenth century. As early as 1911, Native Americans launched official protests against the film industry's inaccurate depiction of their peoples. Few filmmakers even employed natives to play their roles; those who did were almost always producers of documentaries that reflected popular stereotypes of the Indian in the framework of documented "reality." Beginning in the 1940s, the Hollywood film industry churned out Westerns that with few exceptions portrayed natives in the most simplistic terms. Millions of radio, then television, audiences became acquainted with Native Americans through the character of Tonto ("fool" in Spanish), the stoic sidekick of the (very) white Lone Ranger.

Hollywood conservatism responded slowly to the pressures of the new awareness and activism of the 1960s. Plots began to include more complex and multi-dimensional Indian characters, and films began to examine native cultures more closely. Native actors appeared more and more often. Locations became more authentic as well. Documentaries on native tribes and nations proliferated. After the mid-1960s, as literacy increased and groups acquired the funds and marketing skills to target increasingly specific audiences, Native American periodical publishing took off. The forces of Indian nationalism and cultural awareness gave rise to a number of native publications, among them the Mohawk Nation's *Akwesasne Notes*.

Similarly, a new generation of native writers came of age during the 1960s and 1970s. Such Native Americans as N. Scott Momaday, Louise Erdrich, Paula Gunn Allen, Leslie Marmon Silko, and James Welch brought contemporary perspectives to a long and distinguished tradition of Indian literature. The texts of these and other writers formed the focus of many Native American Studies programs that began to spring up at universities across the United States.

Before examining the Red Power movement, the renewed phase of Native American political activism of the late 1960s and the 1970s, a look at the postwar transformation of native life in Canada is in order. In the wake of World War II, native life in the Far North changed in many ways. The Distant Early Warning (DEW) line, the Mid-Canada line, and other Cold War military installations brought roads, airlines, and non-native populations and commerce into regions that had been exclusively native. Other industries like mining and oil exploration also became established. Many natives left their traditional territories during this period, abandoning or curtailing subsistence activities in favor of life in the new towns and villages. Great dams were constructed, bringing employment and dependable water supplies, but destroying important hunting grounds and undermining subsistence economies.

At the same time, the federal and provincial governments of Canada began to play a much more active role in the lives of the Inuit and the natives of the Far North. Although they were little consulted about this change, natives who could no longer hunt, trap, or fish were of necessity drawn to the support of government payments and food allowances. For many native peoples of the Far North, educational opportunities increased, health care became dramatically more accessible, and income began to rise. Many natives acquired such modern conveniences as radios, televisions, and telephones during this period. Of course, these changes were not uniform throughout the North: The end of wartime employment and a delay in government assistance caused some communities to remain mired in abject poverty for years. In order to alleviate some of the worst conditions, the Canadian government forcibly relocated some native people to areas where there were greater opportunities either for employment or for subsistence activities.

The Canadian government also sponsored programs designed to encourage native peoples to adopt alternative ways of making a living. Farming, gardening, and animal husbandry were urged. Canneries were opened to package seal, whale, and fish meat. Ships and canoes were built for export. Most of these programs ultimately failed. Others, such as the establishment of wildlife preserves and cross-breeding yak and cattle, were designed to help some people to continue traditional subsistence activities, albeit in a modified form. One idea that did catch on, and in fact became very important to local economies, was the co-operative movement. Built on native traditions of sharing and a decentralized economy, co-ops dealing in everything from food and clothing to construction and crafts have helped many natives gain valuable experience in business and the modern economy. Beginning in the mid-1960s, co-ops began to join one another to increase buying and marketing power.

As the Inuit adopted new ways of life, traditional structures began to break down. This process had serious health and social consequences. Less exercise and a diet with more fats and sugars led to diabetes, gum infections, obesity, and other health problems. Rates of venereal disease and substance abuse skyrocketed, as did the incidence of prostitution and suicide. Involuntary relocations meant leaving a homeland to live among people with different customs and languages. Parents, torn from secure cultural moorings, deprived of the opportunity to hunt, fish, or trap, and forced to grapple with a non-traditional economic and social system, faced any number of personal crises. Their children, attracted to cultural trends originating in the south, were troubled by feelings of being caught between native and non-native worlds, unable to belong truly to either.

Meanwhile, the postwar revision of the Indian Act did little to stem the marginalization of Canada's native population. A 1966 report on the situation advocated several changes in policy, including the abandonment of coercive assimilation, as well as the cancellation of the veto powers held by non-native authorities over the decisions of native self-government. It also called for education in native languages and local civic instruction in models of self-government. In response, and with an eye also to the growing demands for self-determination of natives in the United States, the government in Ottawa proposed sweeping changes in its administration of native affairs in 1969.

The Canadian "White Paper" was couched in the same language as the termination policy of the United States in the 1950s. The government proposed to eliminate the legal distinction between native and non-native Canadians, to repeal the Indian Act, and to phase out all federal Indian Affairs departments. Like termination, treaties were to be unilaterally abrogated and Indians and Inuit were to be "set free." An advisory Indian Claims Commission was to be created, although the government explicitly stated its rejection of the concept of native rights. This bold new policy was proposed without any real effort having been made to consult the natives.

When they were finally asked to comment on the subject, Canada's natives, to the shock of policymakers, flatly rejected the move. Moreover, they did so with near unanimity. Unilateral abrogation of treaties, they stated, was simply not possible. Furthermore, natives retained rights that derived from their status as indigenous peoples, These included rights to land that they had never ceded and treaty rights. The blizzard of condemnation, led by the National Indian Brotherhood (formed in 1970) and other native groups, soon forced the government to reconsider. Ottawa declared that it would not compel natives to accept the policies, and in March 1971 it formally withdrew the White Paper.

Canada's withdrawal of the White Paper was a clear acknowledgement that termination policies and major policy changes made unilaterally were no more acceptable in Canada than they were in the United States. By the late 1960s, the postwar rise of pan-Indian associations, higher levels of education, the solidarity of growing numbers of urban natives, the civil-rights movement, the youth movement, the anti-war movement, technological change, and the growing militancy of certain sectors of American society had combined to produce Red Power, a movement that asserted native pride and native rights. The movement was a remarkable concentration of energy drawn from Native Americans all over the country who, far from having "vanished," were in reality poised on the brink of a renaissance based on their identity as Indians.

Insofar as leadership can be established, the National Indian Youth Council (NIYC) was at least initially in the forefront of the Red Power movement. From its founding in 1961, the NIYC vowed never to "sell out" to the non-native power structure. The NIYC continued to articulate its positions on issues and led the 1964 "fish-ins" in Washington State. By 1968 other groups had risen to power within the movement, notably the American Indian Movement (AIM), which was founded in 1968. In 1969 a group of between eighty and one hundred people calling themselves Indians of All Tribes (IAT) occupied the former federal prison on Alcatraz Island in San Francisco Bay and held it from November 20, 1969, until June 11, 1971.

The IAT action was inspired by the 1964 occupation of Alcatraz by a group of Lakota who had claimed the island under the 1868 Fort Laramie Treaty. As many as 300 IAT members, led by a Mohawk student named Richard Oakes, occupied Alcatraz and remained there for a year and a half. During the course of the occupation, the group called upon natives to reclaim control of their own destinies through intertribal co-operation. Toward this end, it called for a pan-American tribal conference on the island. Worn down by the passage of time and an eventual government shutdown of water and electricity, the last fifteen members were compelled to leave after having obtained an agreement (later broken) from the government to establish a native school and cultural center on the island. The occupation focused worldwide attention on the Red Power movement and generated widespread support for many of its goals.

The American Indian Movement was certainly the best known Native American advocacy group of the period. Its founding members included Dennis Banks, Mary Jane Wilson, and George Mitchell, all Anishinabe (Ojibwa). Employing the methods of the Black Panther Party from which it derived inspiration, AIM initially planned to establish a presence in Minneapolis in order to stem the systematic harassment by police of the city's native population. Having achieved success with this project, and recognition through the IAT occupation of Alcatraz Island, AIM launched a recruitment campaign. Chapters were established in cities across the country. Other important leaders who joined the organization at this time included Russell Means, an Oglala Lakota, and John Trudell, a Santee Dakota.

In the early 1970s, Means led the group in a series of high-profile actions designed to focus public attention on native issues. AIM staged a "counter-celebration" on Mount Rushmore in 1971 and seized the *Mayflower* on Thanksgiving of that year. In 1972 AIM pressured Nebraska authorities to bring charges against the murderers of an Indian man (the accused later became the first non-natives in that state ever sentenced to prison for killing an Indian). Later that year, shortly before the presidential elections, AIM led approximately 2,000 natives and supporters on the "Trail of Broken Treaties," a cross-country caravan to Washington, D.C., whose purpose was to meet with government officials to discuss their grievances. When the meetings failed to materialize, some 400 AIM members took over the BIA headquarters. They held it for six days, until the Nixon administration publicly agreed to respond to each of the group's grievances. The occupiers departed BIA headquarters with confidential files documenting government collusion with energy firms at the expense of various tribes.

The action soon shifted to South Dakota. Against a backdrop of systematic anti-Indian prejudice and abuse reminiscent of the Nebraska case, a white man was charged with manslaughter for stabbing a Native American to death. AIM demanded that the charge be upgraded to murder. When local authorities refused, a fight broke out at the county courthouse. Several AIM activists were charged with serious crimes and ultimately sent to prison. The white killer never saw the inside of a jail.

Also in South Dakota, traditionalists at the Pine Ridge Reservation requested help from AIM to defend themselves against the gangster tactics of Dick Wilson, who had been elected tribal chair in 1972. Wilson had established a reign of terror on the reservation. His followers beat and murdered the residents with impunity. Traditionalists and those who objected to Wilson's tactics were the primary victims. Wilson's power rested not only on his willingness to use force and intimidation; he also received direct support from the government of the United States under the infamous COINTELPRO operation to neutralize internal dissent. Possibly because Wilson supported a government bid to retain illegally a large section of the Pine Ridge Reservation, federal officials backed him with money and trained his thugs with federal SWAT teams.

Tribal members unsuccessfully sought the intervention of the Justice Department to halt the pattern of violence. When tribal members initiated impeachment proceedings against Wilson, the BIA appointed Wilson to oversee the process. Not surprisingly, he defeated the motion to impeach, and immediately banned all further meetings of his opponents. It was at this point that his opponents requested the help of AIM. Refused a meeting with Wilson, AIM decided to hold a rally at Wounded Knee, the site of the 1890 massacre by the U.S. Army of approximately 300 Oglala, mainly women and children.

When they awoke on February 28, 1973, AIM members and their supporters discovered that Wilson's men had erected a series of roadblocks to prevent them from leaving the hamlet. Tribal police and Wilson's gang were soon joined by hundreds of heavily armed U.S. Marshals, called in to contain some 200 "dangerous" AIM activists. The "occupiers" armed themselves with weapons from a nearby trading post and began constructing bunkers and made preparations to defend themselves. Meanwhile, a group of AIM members who had gone to Rapid City to coordinate media attention for the planned rally found themselves with quite a different project on their hands. Americans from all walks of life, horrified by the images of anti-personnel weaponry used in the Vietnam War being used to threaten Native Americans at home—and at Wounded Knee, no less—rallied behind AIM. Supporters stole through police lines to deliver supplies to the defenders. Newspaper editorials thundered against government repression and excess.

For its part, the government launched an FBI investigation of AIM sympathizers and arrested hundreds for attempting to assist the people barricaded at Wounded Knee. The siege lasted for seventy-one days. Federal officials killed two AIM members and wounded fifteen others in the course of firing more than a half-million rounds of ammunition into Wounded Knee during the siege. One U.S. Marshal was also hurt.

On March 11, the government agreed to let the defenders leave. Much to the surprise of government officials, however, traditionalist Native Americans poured into the hamlet and, under the media spotlight, proclaimed the existence of the Independent Oglala Nation (ION). Now a party to the negotiations, the ION, along with AIM, met with government officials to discuss an end to the standoff. On May 3 the government agreed to various demands and indicated willingness to discuss the implementation of the Fort Laramie Treaty of 1868. The siege formally ended on May 8, 1973.

Despite the enormity of the event, results were inconclusive and unsatisfactory on both sides. The government spent millions of dollars arresting hundreds and prosecuting scores of people, but obtained only a handful of convictions for relatively minor crimes. It did succeed in delivering a blow to AIM, however, by saddling the organization with huge legal bills and tying up its leaders for years in court proceedings. As for the natives of the Pine Ridge Reservation, Wilson continued as tribal chair and repression at Pine Ridge, if anything, intensified. Although scores of people identified with AIM were killed, the FBI failed to solve even one such murder. The government never sat down to discuss the Fort Laramie Treaty and honored none of the commitments it had made during the negotiations.

It was in this context that a firefight erupted on June 26, 1975, between AIM members and federal officials near the village of Oglala, South Dakota. Two FBI agents and one AIM member were killed. After surviving AIM members escaped, the FBI launched the biggest manhunt in its history and eventually indicted four men for the murders. One was released due to insufficient evidence and two others were acquitted at trial, a jury ruling that they had fired in self-defense. The judge presiding over the trial of Leonard Peltier, the fourth man, would not permit a plea of self-defense. Peltier was convicted and sentenced to two consecutive life terms in prison, despite the fact that the only eyewitness recanted her testimony and even prosecutors dismissed her evidence as worthless. Since the conviction of Peltier, a number of U.S. judges as well as legal experts and human rights activists from around the world have called for his release. Peltier remains incarcerated, perceived by many as a political prisoner and a poignant symbol of Native American resistance to repression.

The decade of the 1970s also saw a number of landmark legal settlements related to Indian affairs. Shortly after the United States purchased Alaska from Russia in 1867, the federal government asserted its right to pass legislation affecting the vast territory's native population, which numbered some 30,000 at the time. Alaska's importance to the United States grew during World War II, especially after the Japanese invasion of the Aleutian Islands. Soon after the war, the territory's mineral wealth became increasingly apparent. Without consulting its native peoples, and with only minimal participation by them, Alaska was admitted into the Union as the 49th state in 1959. According to the Statehood Act, the United States was permitted to claim millions of acres of "vacant" land, while at the same time it was enjoined from acquiring title to native land.

Alaska's natives quickly responded to the effects of U.S. control. Twelve regional associations formed to meet the challenges posed by the loss of land as well as by proposed nuclear development and dam construction. This decentralized regional approach failed to deal effectively with federal plans for a general claims settlement, however, and in 1966 the Alaska Federation of Natives (AFN) was created as a statewide association to work more effectively to resolve land-claims disputes. The government, for its part, wanted to resolve the issue so construction could begin on the proposed trans-Alaska oil pipeline. All sides reached agreement in 1971.

The Alaska Native Claims Settlement Act (ANCSA) attempted to resolve all issues related to the extremely complex question of land claims. It funneled all settlement monies (almost one billion dollars) and title to almost forty-four million acres of land

through new private native corporations. The ANCSA called for the creation of hundreds of village corporations and twelve regional corporations. Aboriginal claims to the approximately 375 million acres of land were extinguished, paving the way for private land acquisition and development and for other projects including the establishment of national parks and wildlife preserves. Energy companies were poised to reap extremely high profits from resource exploitation; the state also benefited enormously from such activity.

A number of problems with the 1971 agreement have emerged in recent decades. Many of the problems stem from the host of administrative and legal issues surrounding it. One issue involved the date after which corporate shares could be sold on the open market. Like the sale of allotments, the sale of corporate shares rendered Native Americans vulnerable to the loss of their land and, ultimately, their money as well. In addition to these difficulties, natives born after December 8, 1971, were not permitted to own stock. A series of amendments to the original act addressed these last two problems.

Finally, the Alaska Native Claims Settlement Act did not provide adequately for native peoples to carry on with subsistence activities. This last issue is an ongoing legal quagmire, pitting tribal governments against those who oppose land-use regulations. The state of Alaska has generally opposed any strengthening of tribal governments. Even the AFN is deeply divided over the issue, a situation which has resulted in the creation of the Alaska Inter-Tribal Alliance (1992) by natives seeking a more partisan advocate. Even beyond this action, Alaskan natives began to act firmly and independently on their own behalf. They established tribal courts, consulted with international organizations, and resisted outside interference.

At the other end of the continent, tribes in Maine reached an accord with the federal government in 1980. The two largest tribes, the Penobscot and Passamaquoddy, had become increasingly active politically in the postwar period. Neither was federally recognized at the time. The Penobscot, having received the right to vote in state elections in 1954, re-formed as the Penobscot Nation and began pressing for improved state services. In the 1960s the Passamaquoddy sprang into action when they learned that the state had sold or leased roughly 6,000 acres of their land. Their struggle culminated in a 1972 lawsuit against the state. The courts ultimately ruled in *Passamaquoddy v. Morton*, to which the Penobscot were also party, that the tribes were entitled to a federal trust relationship. The ruling also implied that the tribes might have valid claims to approximately two-thirds of the state of Maine.

The tribes welcomed and the state feared the implications of this ruling. As a result, both eventually signed the Maine Indian Claims Settlement Act (MICSA). In exchange for dropping their claim to most of the state, each tribe received more than $13 million and an additional $26.5 million was allocated for the purchase of some 150,000 acres of land. Both of the tribes won federal recognition as tribal entities and state recognition as municipalities, each retaining certain internal legal rights. The tribes have the right to enact their own game laws as long as they conform to state regulations. The Houlton Band of Maliseet also became a party to MICSA. Under the Aroostook Band of Micmacs Settlement Act, passed in 1991, the Aroostook Micmac achieved equal status with the other Maine tribes under MICSA.

Legal disputes over fishing rights in the Northwest and Plateau were also resolved in the 1970s. As described above, fishing rights had been a contentious issue in these regions for a century. The fish-ins of the 1960s and subsequent lawsuits culminated in a historic decision in 1974. Federal district court Judge George Boldt ruled that the tribes were entitled to as much as a 50 percent share of all harvestable fish. The U.S. Supreme Court affirmed this ruling in 1979. Furthermore, the courts agreed with local natives that treaty rights permitted them some exemptions from state and local fish and game regulations. While the backlash that ensued included increased violence and anti-native activity on the part of non-native officials, these decisions effectively signaled the end of the fishing wars in the region. Fishing regained its key role in the cultural identity of riverine tribes of Oregon and Washington, and tribes began opening fish hatcheries and playing an important role in managing the fisheries there.

The case of the Black Hills of South Dakota was, and remains, far more complex and difficult. The Black Hills are a region which the Lakota Dakota (a Sioux people) regard as sacred. In the mid-nineteenth century, natives of the northern Plains successfully forced the United States to sue for peace. The result of those peace negotiations, and the document upon which all contemporary tribal claims to the region rest, was the Fort Laramie Treaty of 1868. Among its many provisions was one that bound the United States to prevent anyone except persons on official Native American business from entering the region that included the Black Hills. Whether the government ever had any intention of honoring the treaty is debatable, but the fact remains that when gold was discovered in the Black Hills, almost immediately after the treaty was signed, miners and other non-natives swarmed into the area and the U.S. military did nothing to stop them. The government quickly proposed to purchase the Black Hills. Although the signatures of three-fourths of native adult males were required to approve the sale, and only a small fraction of such signatures had been collected, the treaty was enacted by Congress. Under the terms of the Black Hills Act of 1877, Congress appropriated 7.7 million acres of the most important of all Lakota land.

No avenue for legal redress existed until natives were allowed to bring suit in the 1920s. A long series of legal battles followed their initial lawsuit. In 1974 the Indian Claims Commission ruled that federal appropriation of the Black Hills was illegal, because the natives had never been compensated for the land. It established an award of roughly $102.5 million, including interest. The government appealed this decision successfully. However,

the court had also ruled under another section of the ICC Act that the Black Hills had been taken unfairly and dishonorably. The government did not appeal this part of the ruling. Awards under this section of the Act were not subject to interest payments. The commission therefore awarded the natives $17.5 million as compensation for the Black Hills. Before any action could be taken on this award, Congress in 1978 removed the basis of the government's successful appeal of the original ICC decision. Upon reconsideration, the ICC re-established its original award of payment plus interest. A United States appeal of this decision to the Supreme Court failed.

At this point, the tribes could have taken their monetary award, but they had never sought financial compensation in the matter. All eight signatories to the Fort Laramie Treaty of 1868 had formally declined to accept any compensation for the Black Hills. The natives had never surrendered the Black Hills and they wanted them back. Only Congress had the power to restore land to tribes. In 1985 the Sioux Nation Black Hills Act, calling for financial compensation and the return of land, was introduced. The South Dakota congressional delegation, among others, has steadfastly opposed it. The act remains in limbo, while the monetary award remains in the United States Treasury gathering additional interest.

In addition to various important land settlements of the 1970s, government policy began to reflect the influence of a generation of Native American activists as well as the changing national conscience. Termination, formally rejected in the late 1960s, was replaced by policies favoring self-determination. In fact, the federal government began reversing some of the damage caused by termination. In 1973 President Richard Nixon signed the Menominee Restoration Act, restoring federal recognition to the tribe and returning nearly all of its former reservation in Wisconsin. In the 1970s and 1980s, federal recognition was restored to many other tribes, although many of them did not recover all of the land and the rights whose loss they had suffered during the termination period. The Klamath, again recognized in 1986, have yet to recover anything close to resembling their former tribal identity and resources.

Federal programs were expanded and became more responsive in the process. Agencies overseeing various programs established "Indian desks" to act as liaisons with tribes and to oversee contracts, thus facilitating contacts between the tribes and the federal government. The Departments of Commerce; Education; Health, Education and Welfare (HEW, now the Department of Health and Human Services); and Housing and Urban Development (HUD), among other departments and agencies of the federal government, strengthened the process and increased the availability of direct tribal grant-in-aid programs. Later in the decade, a Congressional committee proposed to strengthen tribal governments by permanently integrating them into the system of federal domestic assistance. They also recommended that Congress move to extend federal recognition to the numerous tribes and groups that lacked it. Congress responded to this recommendation by creating the Federal Acknowledgement Project.

New programs were developed as well. Beginning in 1967, the government began taking a fresh look at native education, relieved for the first time of a missionary or assimilationist bias. The "Kennedy Report" was initiated by a Senate committee chaired by Robert Kennedy and, after his death, by his brother Edward Kennedy and Walter Mondale. Like many before it, this report condemned the state of native education. Unlike its predecessors, however, it was used along with contributions from the native community—in this case, a new organization called the National Indian Education Association (NIEA)—to serve as the basis of new federal legislation. The result of these efforts was the Indian Education Act (IEA) of 1972, now known as Title V.

The IEA focused on four major areas of policy change for Native American education in the United States. The act provided funding guarantees for schools enrolling Native Americans, especially those controlled by natives. It mandated direct grants to tribes and native organizations, making it more likely that the particular educational needs of native students would be met. It funded adult-education and job-training programs. Finally, the IEA created various administrative entities designed to provide formal channels for ongoing consultation with natives respecting federal education policy. This last section produced contention, as the new National Advisory Council on Indian Education turned out to be too politically charged to be very effective. Funding of the various IEA programs grew markedly through the 1970s, declined during most of the 1980s, and recovered to a degree in the 1990s.

The landmark 1975 Indian Self-Determination and Education Assistance Act (ISDEAA) was another important step on the path toward native self-determination. Formally renouncing the tradition of federal control of Indian policy, the act proposed to designate natives as the principal architects of programs designed to assist them. In fact, the act's net effect was to shift the administration of programs rather than the development of policy toward native groups. Title I of the Act allowed—in fact, encouraged—the tribes to subcontract a wide range of federal services. Title II aimed to increase parental involvement in schools served by Johnson-O'Malley programs. It also provided funding for the education of certain classes of native children.

Both the IEA and ISDEAA are widely considered to have helped raise Native American achievement in schools and increase the number of native professionals. The availability of federal funds, coupled with strong parental involvement, the development of appropriate curricula that included recognition and affirmation of tribal culture and identity, and a sharp increase in educational opportunities for the very young as well as adults all contributed to educational advances. By 1980 native groups had taken advantage of the new laws to subcontract approximately $200 million in services.

On the other hand, these programs were hampered somewhat by a lack of centralized responsibility for Native American education, as well as the tendency of native administrators to focus on the annual funding cycle rather than on education itself. Furthermore, as bureaucracies are difficult to change, many people noted resistance and even obstruction on the part of the BIA in yielding some of its authority to the tribes. The tribes themselves were also plagued by a lack of skills both to administer the various programs and to complete the mountains of associated paperwork. Finally, the entire scenario was played out against the backdrop of the continuing psychological consequences of termination, including an inability on the part of many tribes to accept full responsibility for many of the programs over which they now could exercise control. In short, the essential paradox remained: How to balance the need for an ongoing federal presence against the desire for full native self-determination?

Both Congress and the tribes moved haltingly to resolve this dilemma in the decades that followed ISDEAA. The Indian Health Care Improvement Act of 1976 encouraged ISDEAA-style Native American involvement in the area of health care. The Indian Child Welfare Act of 1978 renounced the long-standing policy of removing native children from their families and placing them in non-native, assimilationist environments, establishing procedures for placing adoptive or foster native children in native homes. In the same year, Congress passed the American Indian Religious Freedom Act (AIRFA). Designed to ensure a climate within which native religion would be protected, the act lacked provisions for its enforcement and, in any case, was repeatedly undercut by Supreme Court rulings limiting native religious practice and expression.

Seeking to bolster the position of Native Americans in the wake of recent protests and violence, in 1977 the American Indian Policy Review Commission (AIPRC) submitted a report with more than 200 policy recommendations. The commission, many of whose members were Native Americans, used the word "sovereign" to describe tribes while at the same time asserting federal responsibility for overall Indian policy. Its 206 recommendations, most of which simply called for more federal spending along familiar lines, stood in stark contrast to the "Twenty Points" developed by participants in the "Trail of Broken Treaties" protest of 1972. These points focused on existing treaties and called for the restoration and revitalization of the treaty process, speaking from the perspective of natives within a tribal context and indicating practical and ultimately less expensive methods for natives to recreate functioning tribal societies.

In the legal realm, the U.S. government also sent mixed signals concerning tribal sovereignty. In the 1978 case of *U.S. v. Wheeler*, the Supreme Court conceded that the tribes enjoy a measure of sovereignty, albeit subject to the will of Congress, which could formally withdraw it. In 1978, as well, the Court ruled in *Oliphant v. Suquamish Indian Tribe* that tribes do not have jurisdiction over non-natives on tribal land. Three years later, it broadened this exclusion to include members of other tribes. Moreover, despite the existence of the AIRFA, the Court ruled in 1988 and again in 1990 that natives could not practice aspects of their religion that violated state laws and, furthermore, that they had no legal recourse against such prohibitions.

Meanwhile, some of the more activist Indian leaders continued to take matters into their own hands. True to its promise, AIM brought its case against the United States to the world stage in the mid-1970s. Under the leadership of the Cherokee Jimmie Durham, AIM's International Indian Treaty Council (IITC) reached out to indigenous people throughout the Americas. In 1977, before the United Nations Economic and Social Council in Geneva, Switzerland, the group arranged a hearing concerning the relationship between America's native groups and the non-native nations within which they were living. Many elders testified at this hearing. The Council responded by creating a Working Group on Indigenous Populations. The IITC itself was accorded with formal NGO (Non-Governmental Organization) status, the first native group to achieve such designation in U.N. history. Buoyed by the results of this initiative, tribal elders continued to appear before U.N. commissions concerned with various aspects of oppression and cultural preservation.

AIM continued to function despite the persecution of its leadership. In 1978 Dennis Banks organized the "Longest Walk," a cross-country series of rallies and workshops in the style of the 1972 Trail of Broken Treaties. The group was also active at the local level, perhaps especially in South Dakota where it has helped focus attention on the Black Hills, both in terms of tribal claims and of environmental threats to the region. Other AIM groups have organized projects as diverse as providing security to thousands of Diné threatened with forced relocation to creating alternatives to the Columbus Quincentennary.

Slow, unsteady movement toward native sovereignty continued into the 1980s. Tribes continued to take advantage of government grants-in-aid, administering their own programs without BIA oversight. In 1983 President Ronald Reagan underscored the new "government-to-government" relationship between the tribes and federal, state, and local governments by placing the management of executive Indian Affairs programs under the auspices of the Office of Intergovernmental Affairs. As constituencies for various federal tribal programs became established, they not only received regular funding, but also exerted increasing influence on Congressional policy makers. However, tribal programs had generally failed to improve the dismal socioeconomic status of Native Americans. President Reagan's sharp cuts in domestic spending underscored the extent of native vulnerability and dependence upon the federal government.

Intertribal cooperation, having grown so strong in mid-century, remains an important force in Native American society. We have seen how tribes have come together to work on native concerns within the framework of the United Nations. The NCAI today represents the interests of more than 150 tribes. There are many other national organizations, as well as regional groups, such as USET (United South and Eastern Tribes, Inc.), the Great Lakes Inter-Tribal Council, the Intertribal Council of California, and the Nevada Inter-Tribal Association, that help amplify the voice and promote the agendas of individual tribes, nations, and groups. Such special interest groups as the Indian Law Resource Center, the National American Indian Court Judges Association, the Columbia River Inter-Tribal Fish Commission, the Council of Energy Resource Tribes (CERT), and the National Indian Council on Aging serve as planning and policymaking bodies that represent native interests in various aspects of American life.

Many contemporary Native Americans point with pride to efforts to reacquire and rebuild their own cultures. Severely interrupted when an entire generation was lost to boarding schools and forced assimilation, the transmission of cultural knowledge and skills from elders to their grandchildren has been re-established as young Native Americans rediscover pride in their heritage. Legal gains have led in some cases to corresponding cultural awakenings, as when renewed First Salmon ceremonies grew out of revitalized native fisheries in the Northwest and Plateau regions. In a twist on this theme, the Samish of the Pacific Northwest defiantly chose to celebrate the rejection of their demand for federal recognition with the construction of a huge sculpture of a mythological figure that they dedicated with a traditional potlatch ceremony.

Other tribes have also transformed disappointments and challenges into opportunities for rediscovering or reinventing their cultural traditions. The Mashpee of Massachusetts transformed a centuries-long legal battle into an opportunity to redefine and renew their culture. The Cumash in California, faced with the threat of environmental degradation from oil drilling, drew upon ancient traditions as they mobilized to defend their land. In the Far North, Inuit groups have maintained important aspects of their culture as they have moved from subsistence hunting to other economic activities. Many native peoples have preserved the vitality of their traditions through art. Some groups have even exploited access to cable television to revive and perpetuate dances and ceremonies. Contemporary Native American history is filled with similar examples.

Tribal or intertribal powwows also provide wonderful forums for individuals and groups to display aspects of contemporary native culture. While many powwows, or gatherings, are open to the public, many are also held for the exclusive benefit and participation of Native Americans. Some festivities require weeks or even months for the preparation of songs, dances, and costumes. Most powwows are held at a set time of year. For many tribal peoples, they are important occasions for the celebration of their identity and culture.

Once primarily a practice of the Plains peoples, powwows became a more general practice after World War II. Today they are held in large cities as well as on reservations. Some are even held in Europe. Powwow dancing, singing, and costuming combines traditional styles with regional and more contemporary variations. In recent years dance contests have become widely popular. Prizes given in recognition of the contributions or achievements of others are often a feature of powwows. They provide opportunities to socialize, affirm native identity, eat frybread and other traditional foods, and play traditional games.

Like many aspects of culture, art reflects ancient technological and aesthetic traditions and owes much—in some cases, everything—to contemporary innovation. In general, textile art has had a long and distinguished tradition among Native Americans, particularly in the twentieth century in the Southwest and Northwest Coast. In the Northwest, the revival of the potlatch ceremony and the general resurgence of Native American pride led directly to artistic revivals as well. The Totem Heritage Center in Ketchikan and the Institute of Alaska Native Arts have served as focal points for modern artistic production. Important local textiles include Salish woven goods and Tlingit robes. Because of the hiatus in the intergenerational transfer of knowledge and skills, the fine art of rug and blanket weaving among the Navajo had almost died out before it was revived in recent years. Some Navajo woven textiles now sell for tens of thousands of dollars. Sewing and embroidery, particularly of traditional clothing, are important textile arts among the natives of the Rio Grande pueblos.

Native peoples of the Great Basin, as well as the Hopi, Tohono O'odham, Yokut, Miwok, Pomo, and Cherokee, continue to make outstanding baskets both for functional use and for the tourist market. Hopi, Zuñi, and Navajo craftsmen and -women are well known for their outstanding silver and turquoise jewelry; Alaskan natives and indigenous peoples from other groups, including the Inuit and Haida, also produce fine work. Native painters are displayed both in traditional trading posts and in galleries. One particularly interesting contemporary development is the extent to which artistic creation has elevated the status of some women artists relative to that of men. Furthermore, traditional gender barriers are dissolving; men are now found weaving and making pottery and beadwork, while women enjoy success as jewelers and sculptors.

Closely associated with art—in many cases, inseparable from it—are religion and spirituality. Important aspects of religious knowledge and practice were lost when such ceremonies as the potlatch and Sun Dance were banned, or when elders died before they were able to pass along vital, usually oral, traditions. Nevertheless, the religious practices of many groups remained vital and essentially uninterrupted, while other groups have readopted, revitalized, and recreated older ceremonies and beliefs.

"Traditional" native religion is something of a misnomer. There are elements of contemporary religious practice that undoubtedly predate contact with non-natives. On the other hand, "traditional" religions such as the Native American Church, the Iroquoian Longhouse religion, and Pueblo belief practice contain some elements of Christianity. These are long enough established

and sufficiently identified as Indian that many natives regard them as "traditional." Furthermore, among some Iroquois, Lakota, Anishinabe, Creek, and other tribes, traditional religious practice is often linked with a less assimilationist, more militant political agenda. Despite the general movement toward self-determination, many continued to be persecuted for (as in the case of the Native American Church) or otherwise discouraged from (by prison restrictions, the theft of ceremonial paraphernalia, and the desecration of sacred sites) practicing their religion.

A majority of Native Americans consider themselves to be Christians. Some among these also maintain native ceremonies and beliefs, allowing both traditions to coexist in their lives and sometimes combining them in innovative ways. One phenomenon that many people regard as highly ironic, not to mention offensive, is the movement on the part of non-natives to imitate presumed or ersatz native religious practice as part of a general "New Age" spirituality. There is debate within the Native American community as to the advisability of opening their ceremonialism and spirituality to non-natives, but, in general, most people remain highly skeptical of the motives and sincerity of non-native practitioners.

Despite—or, in some cases, because of—decades of government programs intended to improve their economic conditions, Native Americans remain one of the poorest, if not the poorest, single groups in North America. Some tribes have been able to exploit such natural resources as coal, uranium, timber, and marine life. Some have managed to attract or create businesses on the reservations. During the 1980s, many tribes established gaming operations. These remain controversial for a number of reasons, but there is no doubt that they tend to provide a reliable source of income. Despite this economic activity, the situation remains bleak for many Native Americans. The unemployment rate on many reservations is often several times the national rate and sometimes reaches 50 to 80 percent. In 1990 the average income of Indian families was approximately half that of white families, while per capita annual incomes remained below $10,000.

Other social and economic indicators are equally discouraging. Accidents, often involving firearms, are by far the leading cause of death among native adults, killing at a rate more than three times higher than that of all other races combined. Three times as many natives—approximately one-third in all—as non-natives die before the age of forty-five. Suicide and homicide rates are equally high. Alcohol abuse remains a serious problem among many tribal groups. Substandard or otherwise inadequate housing remains an ongoing problem for many Native Americans. Educational levels remain relatively low, although the advent of tribal scholarship funds, federal assistance, and such institutions as Navajo and Sinte Gleska Community Colleges, as well as tribally controlled educational programs, have encouraged native children to finish school and to acquire some form of higher education.

## BIBLIOGRAPHY

Allen, Paula G. *The Sacred Hoop: Recovering the Feminine in American Indian Traditions.* Boston: Beacon Press, 1986.

Axtell, James. *Beyond 1492: Encounters in Colonial North America.* N.Y.: Oxford Univ. Press, 1992.

Bailey, L.R. *Indian Slave Trade in the Southwest.* N.Y.: Tower Publications, 1966.

Balikci, Asen. *The Netsilik Eskimo.* Garden City, N.Y.: Natural History Press, 1970.

Balthazar, Richard. *Remember Native America! The Earthworks of Ancient America.* Santa Fe: Five Flower Press, 1992.

Bancroft, Hubert H. *The Works of Hubert Howe Bancroft,* vol. I, *The Native Races: Wild Tribes.* San Francisco: A.L. Bancroft, 1883.

Barber, John W. *History and Antiquities of New England, New York and New Jersey.* Hartford: Parsons Press, 1842.

Beck, Warren A., and Ynez D. Haase. *Historical Atlas of New Mexico.* Norman, Okla.: Univ. of Oklahoma Press, 1969.

Bordewich, Fergus M. *Killing the White Man's Indian: Reinventing Native Americans at the End of the Twentieth Century.* N.Y.: Doubleday, 1996.

Bowers, Alfred W. *Hidatsa Social & Ceremonial Organization.* Lincoln, Neb.: Univ. of Nebraska Press, 1963.

Brandon, William. *The American Heritage Book of Indians.* N.Y.: American Heritage, 1982.

Brennan, Louis A. *American Dawn: A New Model of American Prehistory.* N.Y.: Macmillan, 1970.

Brown, Dee. *Bury My Heart at Wounded Knee: An Indian History of the American West.* N.Y.: Holt, Rinehart & Winston, 1970.

Burt, Jesse, and Robert B. Ferguson. *Indians of the Southeast: Then and Now.* Nashville, Tenn.: Abingdon Press, 1973.

Calloway, Colin G. *Crown and Calumet: British-Indian Relations 1783–1815.* Norman, Okla.: Univ. of Oklahoma Press, 1987.

Cave, Alfred E. *The Pequot War.* Amherst, Mass.: Univ. of Massachusetts Press, 1996.

Cooley, D.N. *Report of the Commissioner of Indian Affairs for the Year 1865.* Wash., D.C.: Government Printing Office, 1865.

Crosby, Alfred W., Jr. *The Columbian Exchange: Biological and Cultural Consequences of 1492.* Westport, Conn.: Greenwood Press, 1972.

Crowell, Aron, and William W. Fitzhugh. *Cross Roads of Continents: Cultures of Siberia and Alaska.* Washington, D.C.: Smithsonian Institution Press, 1988.

Cutter, Donald C. *The Journey of Coronado, 1540–1542.* Golden, Colo.: Fulcrum Publishing, 1990.

Deloria, Vine, Jr. *Custer Died For Your Sins: An Indian Manifesto.* N.Y.: Avon Books, 1969.

Denig, Edwin T. *Five Indian Tribes of the Upper Missouri.* Norman, Okla.: Univ. of Oklahoma Press, 1961.

Dickason, Olive P. *Canada's First Nations: A History of Founding Peoples from Earliest Times.* Norman, Okla.: Univ. of Oklahoma, 1992.

Dix, Byron E., and James W. Mavor. *Manitou: The Sacred Landscape of New England's Native Civilizations.* Rochester, Vt.: Inner Traditions Intnl., 1989.

Dole, William P. *Report of the Commissioner of Indian Affairs Accompanying the Annual Report of the Secretary of the Interior for the Year 1861.* Wash., D.C.: Government Printing Office, 1861.

Donaldson, Thomas. *The George Catlin Indian Gallery in the National Museum (Smithsonian Institution) with Memoir and Statistics,* in *The Annual Report to the Board of Regents of the Smithsonian Institution to July 1885, Part II.* Wash., D.C.: Govn't Printing Office, 1886.

Drake, Samuel G. *The Book of the Indians to the Year 1841.* Boston: Antiquarian Bookstore, 1841.

Drimmer, Frederick, ed. *Captured By The Indians: 15 Firsthand Accounts, 1750–1870.* N.Y.: Dover Publications, 1985.

Drucker, Philip. *Indians of the Northwest Coast.* Garden City, N.Y.: Natural History Press, 1963.

Ducheneaux, Karen, and Kirke Kickingbird. *One Hundred Million Acres.* N.Y.: Macmillan, 1973.

Dunlay, Thomas W. *Wolves for the Blue Soldiers: Indian Scouts and Auxilliaries with the United States Army, 1860–90.* Lincoln: University of Nebraska Press, 1982.

Eaton, Bob. *Algonkian: Lifestyle of the New England Indians.* Amherst, Mass.: One Reed, 1998.

Ehle, John. *Trail of Tears: The Rise and Fall of the Cherokee Nation.* N.Y.: Doubleday, 1988.

Fagan, Brian M. *The Great Journey: The Peopling of Ancient America.* London: Thames & Hudson, 1987.

Fehrenbach, T.R. *Fire and Blood: A Bold and Definitive Modern Chronicle of Mexico.* N.Y.: Collier Books, 1973.

Fenton, William N. *The Great Law and the Longhouse: A Political History of the Iroquois Confederacy.* Norman, Okla.: Univ. of Oklahoma Press, 1998.

Ferguson, T.J., and E. Richard Hart. *A Zuñi Atlas.* Norman, Okla.: Univ. of Oklahoma Press, 1985.

Fite, Emerson D., and Archibald Freeman, eds. *A Book of Old Maps Delineating American History From the Earliest Days Down to the Close of the Revolutionary War.* N.Y.: Dover Publications, 1969.

Fitting, James E. *The Archaeology of Michigan: A Guide to the Prehistory of the Great Lakes Region.* Garden City, N.Y.: Natural History Press, 1970.

Fitzhugh, William W., ed. *Cultures in Contact.* Wash., D.C.: Smithsonian Institution Press, 1985.

Foreman, Grant. *The Five Civilized Tribes.* Norman, Okla.: Univ. of Oklahoma Press, 1982.

Fowler, Don D., ed. *In A Sacred Manner We Live: Photographs of the North American Indian by Edward S. Curtis.* Barre, Mass.: Barre Publishers, 1972.

Francis, Lee. *Native Time: A Historical Time Line of Native America.* N.Y.: St. Martin's Press, 1996.

Fritz, Dr. Henry E. *The Movement for Indian Assimilation, 1860–1890.* Univ. of Pennsylvania Press, 1963.

Garretson, Martin S. *The American Bison.* N.Y.: New York Zoological Society, 1938.

Gattuso, John, ed. *A Circle of Nations: Voices and Visions of American Indians.* Hillsboro, Oreg.: Beyond Words, 1993.

Gentilcore, R. Louis, ed. *Historical Atlas of Canada,* vol. 2, *The Land Transformed, 1800–1891.* Univ. of Toronto Press, 1993.

Giddings, J. Louis. *Ancient Men of the Arctic.* N.Y.: Alfred A. Knopf, 1967.

Goetzmann, William H., and Glyndwr Williams. *The Atlas of North American Exploration.* Englewood Cliffs, N.J.: Prentice Hall, 1992.

Goss, John. *The Mapping of North America: Three Centuries of Map-making 1500–1860.* Secaucus, N.J.: Wellfleet Press, 1990.

Graymont, Barbara. *The Iroquois in the American Revolution.* Syracuse, N.Y.: Syracuse Univ. Press, 1972.

Grinnell, George B. *The Cheyenne Indians: Their History and Ways of Life,* vols. I & II. Lincoln, Neb.: Univ. of Nebraska Press, 1992.

Gutiérez, Ramón A. *When Jesus Came, the Corn Mothers Went Away: Marriage, Sexuality and Power in New Mexico, 1500–1846.* Stanford, Calif.: Stanford Univ. Press, 1991.

Hall, Charles F. *Arctic Researches and Life Among the Esquimaux.* N.Y.: Harper & Brothers, 1865.

Harjo, Lisa D, and Karen D. Harvey. *Indian Country: A History of Native People in America.* Golden, Colo.: North American Press, 1994.

Harris, R. Cole, ed. *Historical Atlas of Canada,* vol. I, *From the Beginning to 1800.* Univ. of Toronto Press, 1987.

Hauptman, Laurence M. *Between Two Fires: American Indians in the Civil War,* N.Y.: Free Press, 1995.

Hazen-Hammond, Susan. *Timelines of Native American History.* N.Y.: Berkeley Publishing Group, 1997.

Hill, Richard W., and Tom Hill, Sr., eds. *Creation's Journey: Native American Identity and Belief.* Wash., D.C.: Smithsonian Institution Press, 1994.

Hodge, Frederick W., ed. *Handbook of American Indians North of Mexico,* 2 vols. N.Y.: Pageant Books, 1959.

Horan, James D. *The McKenney-Hall Portrait Gallery of American Indians.* N.Y.: Crown Publishing, 1972.

Howard, David A. *Conquistador in Chains: Cabeza de Vaca and the Indians of the Americas.* Tuscaloosa, Ala.: Univ. of Alabama, 1997.

Howe, Henry. *Historical Collections of the Great West,* 2 vols. N.Y.: Henry Howe, 1856.

Hoxie, Frederick E., ed. *Encyclopedia of North American Indians.* Boston: Houghton Mifflin, 1996.

Hudson, Charles. *Knights of Spain, Warriors of the Sun.* Athens, Ga.: Univ. of Georgia Press, 1997.

Hungry Wolf, Adolf and Beverly. *Shadows of the Buffalo: A Family Odyssey Among the Indians.* N.Y.: William Morrow, 1983.

Jackson, Helen H. *Century of Dishonor (1880).* Minn.: Ross & Haines, 1964.

Jaimes, M. Annette. *The State of Native America: Genocide, Colonization, and Resistance.* Boston: South End Press, 1992.

Jennings, Francis. *Empire of Fortune: Crowns, Colonies & Tribes in the Seven Years' War in America.* N.Y.: W.W. Norton, 1988.

———. *Behind the Trail of Broken Treaties: An Indian Declaration of Independence.* N.Y.: Delacorte Press, 1974.

Jennings, Jesse D., and Robert F. Spencer et al., *The Native Americans: Ethnology and Backgrounds of North American Indians,* 2nd ed. N.Y.: Harper & Row, 1977.

Josephy, Alvin M., Jr. *Now That The Buffalo's Gone: A Study of Today's American Indians.* N.Y.: Alfred A. Knopf, 1982.

———. *500 Nations: An Illustrated History of North American Indians.* N.Y.: Alfred A. Knopf, 1994.

———. *America in 1492: The World of the Indian Peoples Before the Arrival of Columbus.* N.Y.: Alfred A. Knopf, 1992.

———. *The Indian Heritage of America*. Boston: Houghton Mifflin, 1991.

Kehoe, Alice B. *North American Indians: A Comprehensive Account*. Englewood Cliffs, N.J.: Prentice-Hall, 1992.

Kennedy, Roger. *Hidden Cities: The Discovery and Loss of Ancient North American Civilizations*. N.Y.: Viking Penguin, 1996.

Kessell, John L. *Kiva, Cross and Crown: The Pecos Indians and New Mexico 1540–1840*. Albuquerque: Univ. of New Mexico Press, 1987.

Kroeber, A.L. *Handbook of the Indians of California*. N.Y.: Dover Publications, 1976.

LaFarge, Oliver. *A Pictorial History of the American Indian*. N.Y.: Crown, 1956.

Lazarus, Edward. *Black Hills White Justice: The Sioux Nation Versus the United States, 1775 to the Present*. N.Y.: HarperCollins, 1991.

Leon-Portilla, Miguel, ed. *The Broken Spears: The Aztec Account of the Conquest of Mexico*. Boston: Beacon Press, 1992.

Lepore, Jill. *The Name of War: King Philip's War and the Origins of American Identity*. N.Y.: Alfred A. Knopf, 1998.

Liberty, Margot, and Raymond W. Wood, eds. *Anthropology on the Great Plains*. Lincoln, Neb.: Univ. of Nebraska Press, 1980.

Lorant, Stefan, ed. *The New World: The First Pictures of America*. N.Y.: Duell, Sloan & Pearce, 1965.

Lowie, Robert H. *Indians of the Plains*. Garden City, N.Y.: Natural History Press, 1954.

Lyons, Oren, et al. *Exiled In the Land of the Free: Democracy, Indian Nations, and The U.S. Constitution*. Santa Fe: Clear Light Publishers, 1992.

MacLeish, William H. *The Day Before America: Changing the Nature of a Continent*. Boston: Houghton Mifflin, 1994.

Malinowski, Sharon, ed. *Notable Native Americans*, Detroit: Gale Research, 1995.

Mander, Jerry. *In the Absence of the Sacred: The Failure of Technology and the Survival of the Indian Nations*. San Francisco: Sierra Club Books, 1991.

Margolis, Carolyn, and Herman J. Viola. *Seeds of Change: A Quincentennial Commemoration*. Wash., D.C.: Smithsonian Institution Press, 1991.

Marks, Richard L. *Cortes: The Great Adventurer and the Fate of Aztec Mexico*, N.Y.: Alfred A. Knopf, 1993.

Matthiessen, Peter. *In the Spirit of Crazy Horse*. N.Y.: Viking Press, 1983.

Mayhall, Mildred P. *The Kiowas*. Norman, Okla.: Univ. of Oklahoma Press, 1962.

Meinig, D.W. *The Shaping of America: A Geographical Perspective on 500 Years of History*, 3 vols. New Haven: Yale Univ. Press, 1986.

Meyer, Roy W. *History of the Santee Sioux: United States Indian Policy on Trial*. Lincoln, Neb.: Univ. of Nebraska Press, 1980.

Morgan, Ted. *Wilderness at Dawn: The Settling of the North American Continent*. N.Y.: Simon & Schuster, 1993.

Nabokov, Peter, ed. *Native American Testimony: A Chronicle of Indian-White Relations from Prophecy to the Present, 1492–1992*. N.Y.: Viking Penguin, 1991.

Newman, Peter C. *Caesars of the Wilderness: Company of Adventurers*, vol. II. N.Y.: Viking, 1987.

———. *Empire of the Bay: An Illustrated History of the Hudson's Bay Company*, N.Y.: Viking Studio Books, 1989.

Nielson, Marianne O., and Robert A. Silverman. *Native Americans, Crime, and Justice*. N.Y.: HarperCollins, 1996.

Oswalt, Wendell H. *Eskimos and Explorers*. Novato, Calif.: Chandler & Sharp, 1979.

Pertula, Timothy K. "French and Spanish Colonial Trade Policies and the Fur Trade among the Caddoan Indians of the Trans-Mississippian South," in *The Fur Trade Revisited: Selected Papers of the Sixth North American Fur Trade Conference, Mackinac Island, Michigan, 1991*. East Lansing: Michigan State Univ. Press, 1994.

Ray, Arthur J. *Indians in the Fur Trade: Their Roles as Trappers, Hunters, and Middlemen in the Lands Southwest of Hudson Bay, 1660–1870*. Univ. of Toronto Press, 1974.

Riddle, Jeff C. *The Indian History of the Modoc War*. Eugene, Oreg.: Urion Press, 1974.

Roberts, David. *Once They Moved Like The Wind: Cochise, Geronimo, and the Apache Wars*. N.Y.: Simon & Schuster, 1993.

Robinson, Charles T. *Native New England: The Long Journey*, No. Attleborough, Mass.: Covered Bridge Press, 1996.

Rogin, Michael P. *Fathers & Children: Andrew Jackson and the Subjugation of the American Indian*. N.Y.: Alfred A. Knopf, 1975.

Rountree, Helen C. *Pocahontas's People: The Powhatan Indians of Virgina Through Four Centuries*. Norman, Okla.: Univ. of Oklahoma Press, 1990.

Royce, Charles C. "Indian Land Cessions in the United States," in *The 18th Annual Report of the Bureau of American Ethnology, 1896–97, part 2*. Wash., D.C.: Government Printing Office, 1899.

Russell, Howard S. *Indian New England Before the Mayflower*. Hanover, N.H.: Univ. of New England Press, 1980.

Salisbury, Neal. *Manitou and Providence: Indians, Europeans, and the Making of New England, 1500–1643*. N.Y.: Oxford Univ. Press, 1982.

Salmoral, Manuel L. *America 1492: Portrait of a Continent 500 Years Ago*. N.Y.: Facts on File, 1990.

Sauer, Carl O. *Sixteenth Century North America: The Land and the People as Seen by the Europeans*. Berkeley: Univ. of California Press, 1971.

Schoolcraft, Henry R. *History of the Indian Tribes of the United States*. N.Y.: J.B. Lippincott, 1857.

Schultz, Duane. *Month of the Freezing Moon: The Sand Creek Massacre, November 1864*. N.Y.: St. Martin's Press, 1990.

Slotkin, Richard. *Regeneration Through Violence: The Mythology of the American Frontier*. Middletown, Conn.: Wesleyan Univ. Press, 1973.

Spier, Leslie. *Yuman Tribes of the Gila River*. N.Y.: Dover Publications, 1978.

Stoutenburgh, John, Jr. *Dictionary of the American Indian*. N.Y.: Philosophical Library, 1950.

Swanton, John R. *The Indian Tribes of North America*. Wash., D.C.: Smithsonian Institution Press, 1968.

Terrell, John U. *American Indian Almanac*. N.Y.: Barnes & Noble Books, 1998.

Thomas, David Hurst. *Exploring Ancient Native America: An Archaeological Guide*. N.Y.: Macmillan, 1994.

Thomson, Don W. *Men and Meridians: The History of Surveying and Mapping in Canada*. N.Y.: Crown, 1990.

Thornton, Russell. *American Indian Holocaust and Survival: A Population History Since 1492*. Norman, Okla.: Univ. of Oklahoma Press, 1987.

Tillett, Leslie, ed. *Wind on the Buffalo Grass: The Indians' Own Account of the Battle at the Little Big Horn River & the Death of Their life on the Plains*. N.Y.: Thomas Y. Crowell, 1976.

Todorov, Tzvetan. *The Conquest of America: The Question of the Other*. N.Y.: Harper Perennial, 1984.

Turner, Frederick. *Beyond Geography: The Western Spirit Against the Wilderness*. Rutgers, N.J.: Rutgers Univ. Press, 1983.

Ubelaker, Douglas H., and John V. Verano, eds. *Disease and Demography in the Americas*. Wash., D.C.: Smithsonian Institution Press, 1992

Underhill, Ruth M. *Red Man's America*. Chicago: Univ. of Chicago Press, 1971.

Van Doren, Charles, and Wayne Moquin, eds. *Great Documents in American Indian History*. N.Y.: Praeger Publishers, 1973.

Van Doren, Mark, ed. *The Travels of William Bartram*, N.Y.: Macy-Masius Publishers, 1928.

Van Every, Dale. *Disinherited: The Lost Birthright of the American Indian*. N.Y.: William Morrow, 1966.

Veniaminov, Ivan. *Notes on the Islands of the Unalashka District*, trans. by Lydia T. Black and R.H. Geoghegan. Kingston, Ont.: Limestone Press, 1984.

Verrill, A. Hyatt. *The Real Americans*. N.Y.: G.P. Putnam's Sons, 1954.

Viereck, Philip, ed. *The New Land*, N.Y.: John Day, 1967.

Viola, Herman J. *After Columbus: The Smithsonian Chronicle of the North American Indian*, Wash., D.C.: Smithsonian Books, 1990.

———. *Diplomats in Buckskins: A History of Indian Delegations in Washington City*. Wash., D.C.: Smithsonian Institution Press, 1981.

Waldman, Carl. *Atlas of the North American Indian*. N.Y.: Facts on File, 1985.

———. *Encyclopedia of Native American Tribes*. N.Y.: Facts on File, 1988.

Warhus, Mark. *Another America: Native American Maps and the History of Our Land*. N.Y.: St. Martin's Press, 1997.

Washburn, Wilcomb E. *The Indian In America*. N.Y.: Harper & Row, 1975.

Weatherford, Jack. *Indian Givers: How The Indians of the Americas Transformed the World*. N.Y.: Crown, 1988.

———. *Native Roots: How The Indians Enriched America*. N.Y.: Crown, 1991.

White, Henry. *The Early History of New England: Illustrated by Numerous Interesting Incidents*, 7th ed. Concord, N.H.: I.S. Boyd, 1842.

Wilbur, C. Keith. *The New England Indians*. Old Saybrook, Conn.: Globe Pequot Press, 1996.

———. *The Woodland Indians*. Old Saybrook, Conn.: Globe Pequot Press, 1995.

Williams, Jeanne. *Trails of Tears: American Indians Driven From Their Lands*. Dallas: Hendrick-Long, 1992.

Zolbrod, Paul G. *Dine bahane: The Navajo Creation Story*. Albuquerque: Univ. of New Mexico Press, 1984.

## ACKNOWLEDGEMENTS

The publisher would like to thank the following individuals for their assistance in the preparation of this book: the contributors, editors, cartographer, and consultants listed on the copyright page; Frank Oppel, for inspiring this project and for access to his antique map and print collection; Margit Kaye, curator of the Yale University Map Collection, for advice and assistance on period map research; Joseph Szaszfai, for specialized map photography; Charles J. Ziga, art director; Wendy Ciaccia Eurell, graphic designer; Christopher Berlingo, cartographic artist; and Lisa Langone Desautels, indexer. Grateful acknowledgement is also made to the individuals and institutions listed below for permission to reproduce the photographs on the following pages: © **Glenn O. Myers:** 15 (both), 24b, 80–1b, 84–5t, 107; © **Lorraine B. Myers:** 14t, 24t, 33, 88, 89, 106t, 130; © **Jay Olstad:** 232b; © **Jeanne Walker Rorex:** 126; © **Charles J. Ziga, from the Collection of Glenn and Lorraine Myers:** 13, 20t, 25t & r, 60b, 61b; © **Charles J. Ziga:** 20b; **Collection of Frank Oppel:** 190, 211, 215; **Collection of Glenn and Lorraine Myers:** 16b, 17b 26, 29t, 35, 37b, 46, 49, 52, 53b, 54, 58b, 59t, 62, 63 (both), 67t, 70, 71, 72 (all), 76t, 77b, 78b, 82, 90, 97, 99b, 101, 105, 111, 113, 123, 175 (both), 178b, 223, 224, 225, 230 (both); **Corbis-Bettmann:** 17t, 22b, 37t, 57, 77t, 153, 163, 183b, 191, 192, 202, 203, 204, 208, 232t; **CorelDraw:** 61t; **Cumberland County Historical Society,** Carlisle, Penn.: 231 (both); **Field Museum of Chicago:** 95; **Iowa State Historical Society:** 233; **Maps by Glenn O. Myers:** 10, 28, 36b, 40t, 44, 48, 56, 60t, 73, 81r, 85b, 96, 107, 117, 127, 131, 142, 152, 165, 168, 176, 179, 180t, 181, 184b, 188, 195, 207, 229; **National Archives of Canada:** 93t, 141, 226 (both), 252; **The National Archives (USA):** 174, 205; **The National Archives, Public Record Office, Kew (UK):** 74–5, 99t, 146–7, 172; **Nebraska State Historical Society:** 193t, 235; **Nevada State Museum:** 218; **Planet Art:** 12, 14b, 16t, 25b, 45t, 53t, 55, 109, 115; **Prints and Photographs Division, Library of Congress:** 18, 19, 22t, 30, 34, 38, 39, 40b, 42, 45b, 47, 50–1, 58t, 59b, 66, 67b, 76b, 78t, 79, 83, 86, 87, 91, 92, 93b, 94, 100, 104, 106b, 116, 118, 132, 144 (both), 145, 150b, 159, 164, 170, 193b, 196, 197, 200, 212, 213, 216, 221, 227; **Saraband Image Library:** 21 (both), 27 (both), 29b, 31, 32, 36t, 41; **South Dakota State Historical Society:** 236; **UPI/Corbis-Bettmann:** 209; **USMA Library, West Point, NY:** 198–9 (Collection of John Gregory Bourke); **Western History Collections, University of Oklahoma Library:** 194; **The Yale University Map Collection, photograph © Joseph Szaszfai:** 2, 64–5, 68–9, 98, 102–3, 110, 114, 120–1, 124–5, 128, 129 (both), 134, 135, 137, 138, 139, 140, 149, 150–1, 154–5, 156, 158, 160–1, 162, 167, 169, 171, 173, 177, 178t, 180b, 182, 183t, 184t, 185, 186–7, 190, 210, 215.